EMILE COHL, CARICATURE, AND FILM

Frontispiece. Emile Cohl, ca. 1895.

EMILE COHL, CARICATURE, AND FILM

DONALD CRAFTON

PRINCETON UNIVERSITY PRESS

LIBRARY OF CONGRESS CATALOGING-IN-PUBLICATION DATA

Crafton, Donald.

Emile Cohl, caricature, and film / Donald Crafton.

p. cm.

Filmography: p.

Bibliography. p.

Includes index.

ISBN 0-691-05581-5 (alk. paper)

1. Cohl, Emile, 1857-1938.   2. Animators—France—Biography.

3. Cartoonists—France—Biography.   I. Title.

NC1766.F82C6433   1990

741.5'092—dc20   89-31015

Publication of this book has been aided by a grant from the
Paul Mellon Fund of Princeton University Press

This book has been composed in Linotron Caledonia

Clothbound editions of Princeton University Press books are printed on acid-free paper,
binding materials are chosen for strength and durability.
Paperbacks, although satisfactory for personal collections, are not usually suitable
for library rebinding

Printed in the United States of America by
Princeton University Press,
Princeton, New Jersey

To Marilyn

CONTENTS

X ■ ILLUSTRATIONS

38. Portrait of André Gill at Charenton, January 26, 1883.
39. André Gill: "Nouveaux Croquis" (three portraits of Emile Cohl), *La Nouvelle Lune*, March 4, 1883.
40. Charles Studio: Photograph of Cohl and Gill.
41. André Gill (or Emile Cohl): "En attendant," *La Nouvelle Lune*, December 15, 1883.
42. Albert Robida: "A l'exposition des oeuvres d'André Gill," *La Caricature*, December 29, 1883.
43. Uzès (A. Lemot): Portrait of Emile Cohl, *Le Courrier Français*, September 12, 1885.
44. "André Gill," *La Nouvelle Lune*, May 15–31, 1885.
45. Self-photograph, 1885.
46. Photograph of Edouard Norès, 1885.
47. Photograph of Jean Moréas.
48. Photograph of Emile Goudeau.
49. Photograph of Paul Verlaine.
• 50. Photograph of "Léon Cladel."
51. "Edouard Philippe," *La Nouvelle Lune*, February 12, 1881.
52. Adrien Marie: "Souvenirs du bal des Incohérents," *Le Monde Illustré*, April 17, 1886.
53. Carte d'exposant, Incoherent Exhibition, 1886.
54. Anon.: Portrait of Emile Cohl, *Catalogue de l'exposition*, 1886.
55. "L'Enterrement de l'Incohérence," *La Nouvelle Lune*, March 13, 1887.
56. Jules Chéret: Cover for *Catalogue illustré de l'exposition des arts incohérents*, 1889.
57. "Francisque Sarcey," *Catalogue illustré de l'exposition des arts incohérents*, 1889.
58. "Quelques Envois au Salon (Section de sculptures)," *Le Charivari*, April 26, 1886.
59. "La Poésie en 1886," *Le Charivari*, June 17, 1886.
60. Moloch (B. Colomb): "Au bal costumé," *La Chronique Parisienne*, January 23, 1887 (detail).
61. "Grande Revue des peintres passée par Gustave Boulanger," *La Caricature*, May 21, 1887.
62. "Félicien Champsaur," *Les Hommes d'Aujourd'hui* no. 327.
63. "Albert Robida," *Les Hommes d'Aujourd'hui*, March 27, 1897.
64. "De Toulouse-Lautrec," *Les Hommes d'Aujourd'hui* no. 460, 1898.
65. a) Uzès (A. Lemot): "Emile Cohl," *Les Hommes d'Aujourd'hui* no. 288, 1886.
b) Uzès (A. Lemot): Original drawing for above.
66. *Les Chambres Comiques*, October 26, 1886.
67. *Les Chambres Comiques*, November 16, 1886.
68. *Les Chambres Comiques*, January 11, 1887.
69. *Les Chambres Comiques*, October 12, 1886.
70. Illustration for Jules Lermina, *L'Auberge des adrets*, 1887.
71. Portraits of Jules Lermina and Cohl from *L'Auberge des adrets*, 1887.
72. Cover for Félix Galipaux, *Encore des Galipettes*, 1889.
73. Illustration for Coquelin cadet, *Pirouettes*, 1888.
74. "Les Deux Salons," from Jules Oudot, *Chansons fin de siècle*, 1891.
75. "Edouard Drumont règlant la question du Panama," *La Libre Parole Illustré*, September 25, 1897.
76. View from the studio on Lisle Street, London, 1895.
77. "Partage de la galette des rois . . . du cycle," *Le Vélo Illustré*, ca. 1900.
78. "Le Meilleur Moyen pour prendre beaucoup de poissons," *Le Grand Illustré*, 1906.

X ■ ILLUSTRATIONS

38. Portrait of André Gill at Charenton, January 26, 1883.
39. André Gill: "Nouveaux Croquis" (three portraits of Emile Cohl), *La Nouvelle Lune*, March 4, 1883.
40. Charles Studio: Photograph of Cohl and Gill.
41. André Gill (or Emile Cohl): "En attendant," *La Nouvelle Lune*, December 15, 1883.
42. Albert Robida: "A l'exposition des oeuvres d'André Gill," *La Caricature*, December 29, 1883.
43. Uzès (A. Lemot): Portrait of Emile Cohl, *Le Courrier Français*, September 12, 1885.
44. "André Gill," *La Nouvelle Lune*, May 15–31, 1885.
45. Self-photograph, 1885.
46. Photograph of Edouard Norès, 1885.
47. Photograph of Jean Moréas.
48. Photograph of Emile Goudeau.
49. Photograph of Paul Verlaine.
•50. Photograph of "Léon Cladel."
51. "Edouard Philippe," *La Nouvelle Lune*, February 12, 1881.
52. Adrien Marie: "Souvenirs du bal des Incohérents," *Le Monde Illustré*, April 17, 1886.
53. Carte d'exposant, Incoherent Exhibition, 1886.
54. Anon.: Portrait of Emile Cohl, *Catalogue de l'exposition*, 1886.
55. "L'Enterrement de l'Incohérence," *La Nouvelle Lune*, March 13, 1887.
56. Jules Chéret: Cover for *Catalogue illustré de l'exposition des arts incohérents*, 1889.
57. "Francisque Sarcey," *Catalogue illustré de l'exposition des arts incohérents*, 1889.
58. "Quelques Envois au Salon (Section de sculptures)," *Le Charivari*, April 26, 1886.
59. "La Poésie en 1886," *Le Charivari*, June 17, 1886.
60. Moloch (B. Colomb): "Au bal costumé," *La Chronique Parisienne*, January 23, 1887 (detail).
61. "Grande Revue des peintres passée par Gustave Boulanger," *La Caricature*, May 21, 1887.
62. "Félicien Champsaur," *Les Hommes d'Aujourd'hui* no. 327.
63. "Albert Robida," *Les Hommes d'Aujourd'hui*, March 27, 1897.
64. "De Toulouse-Lautrec," *Les Hommes d'Aujourd'hui* no. 460, 1898.
65. a) Uzès (A. Lemot): "Emile Cohl," *Les Hommes d'Aujourd'hui* no. 288, 1886.
    b) Uzès (A. Lemot): Original drawing for above.
66. *Les Chambres Comiques*, October 26, 1886.
67. *Les Chambres Comiques*, November 16, 1886.
68. *Les Chambres Comiques*, January 11, 1887.
69. *Les Chambres Comiques*, October 12, 1886.
70. Illustration for Jules Lermina, *L'Auberge des adrets*, 1887.
71. Portraits of Jules Lermina and Cohl from *L'Auberge des adrets*, 1887.
72. Cover for Félix Galipaux, *Encore des Galipettes*, 1889.
73. Illustration for Coquelin cadet, *Pirouettes*, 1888.
74. "Les Deux Salons," from Jules Oudot, *Chansons fin de siècle*, 1891.
75. "Edouard Drumont règlant la question du Panama," *La Libre Parole Illustré*, September 25, 1897.
76. View from the studio on Lisle Street, London, 1895.
77. "Partage de la galette des rois . . . du cycle," *Le Vélo Illustré*, ca. 1900.
78. "Le Meilleur Moyen pour prendre beaucoup de poissons," *Le Grand Illustré*, 1906.

CHARTS AND DIAGRAMS

PHOTOGRAPHIC SOURCES

PERMISSION to reprint photographs is gratefully acknowledged to:

The Courtet-Cohl family (figs. 53, 65b, 76, 77, 78, 118, 119, 122, 123, 124, 127, 147, 154, 155, 158, 159, 165, 166, 173, 174, 175, 184, 197, 201, 202, 210, 211, 212a, 215, 278);

La Gazette des Beaux-Arts (1, 32);

Raymond Maillet (196, 207, 209, 214);

The British Museum (82, 85, 87, 88, 89, 91, 95, 96, 97, 105, 106, 108, 112, 113, 115, 126, 129, 148, 221, 229);

The British Film Institute, National Film Archive (138, 153, 160, 259);

Cinémathèque Gaumont-Actualités (140, 141, 156, 162, 163, 258, 266, 288, 292, 309, 312, 314, 315, 316);

Library of Congress (267);

George Eastman House (151, 263);

Cinémathèque Française (167, 307, 308);

Centre Culturel Américain (317);

Centre National de la Cinématographie, Service des Archives du Film (168, 169, 170, 171, 189, 199, 200, 208, 282);

New York Public Library (177, 178, 179, 180, 182);

The Museum of Modern Art (181, 275, 313);

Wisconsin Center for Film and Theater Research (152, 183, 185, 187, 188, 206, 237, 256, 318);

Bibliothèque Nationale (all remaining photos).

PREFACE AND ACKNOWLEDGMENTS

ON SATURDAY mornings when our children turn on the television to watch the networks' two or three hours of cartoons, or when they (or we) pick up the comic section in the next day's paper, it is not likely to occur to us that these entertainments have a history. Since the chronological development of cartoons and comics and the causes and ramifications of that development have seldom been the subject of academic discourse—if we bother to think about it at all—it is easy to jump to the conclusion that these trifling, even juvenile, distractions and their histories are not worth studying. Yet, like all institutions, these media are the products (and not necessarily the end products) of many years of constant industrial and social forces. Visual humor is deeply embedded in the thicket of chronological, social, textual, artistic, psychological, ideological and technological tangles that make up the unexplored underbrush of modern culture.

This study seeks to trace one somewhat gnarled strand of this cultural network, typified in the life and work of the French artist Emile Cohl, who lived from 1857 to 1938. He was an innovative contributor to one institution—popular graphic humor—at a critical moment in its history when it changed from traditional caricature to narrativized visual exposition. He was also a progenitor of another institution—the animated film.

In some ways this book is a conventional biography; it attempts to assimilate all the retrievable pertinent facts about the artist's life into a chronicle and to set them within the context of his times. With Emile Cohl we are more fortunate than the academic protagonist of Robertson Davies's novel *Leaven of Malice*, who is faced with writing the biography of the obscure playwright Charles Heavysege. "I'll make it appear that little Heavysege hopped right into the middle of a very interesting time, which is a lie, but absolutely vital to any scholarly biography."[1] Not only was Cohl born into Paris, "the capital of the nineteenth century," but he was an active participant in its popular culture and was in turn an influence on his milieu. His life was amazingly varied, tinged with politics, art, invention, romance, duels, mirth, and tragedy—the stuff that biographers and authors of made-for-TV-movie scripts yearn for. Davies's would-be biographer continues, "What happened between 1816 and 1853, when Heavysege came to Canada, I don't know, but I'll fake up something." Again, we are lucky. Unlike Davies's fictional biographer, we do not have to fake up a record. Finding our way is facilitated by Cohl's own notes and clipping files, corroborated by the paper trail made possible by the rise of trade journalism in the early twentieth century and the guidance provided by Cohl's extant films. These provide the armature for his life story. Still there are gaps, but the portrait that emerges is that of a complicated, gentle but stubborn individualist pursuing whatever fanciful turn his fertile imagination took.

I have also tried to avoid the traditional role of the biographer who defends the subject as a Great Man; Cohl's works, though sometimes masterful contributions to film history, are not necessarily Masterpieces. Rather than insist on the artist's singularity, I have chosen to monitor more closely than usual the context of his various productions, pointing out how he was in sync with other artists and filmmakers of his time. Thus speculations concerning Cohl's social and intellectual milieu are augmented by analyses of popular graphics drawn by others who may or may not have influenced him, but whose works are part of his background, and by a discussion of the early film industry in France and the United States.

Since Cohl was prolific in popular graphic humor and cinema, the reader necessarily will learn about both domains as they were during the period between the mid-1880s and World War I. Therefore this can be regarded, using Robert C. Allen's useful phrase, as a study in media interaction, with Emile Cohl as the link between media.

It was Cohl's lot in life (shared by many at the turn of the twentieth century) to be directly affected by the dynamic technological changes that transformed virtually every Western urban environment at the time. Mass culture, then as now, was especially sensitive to the influence of new communications technologies. First lithographic, then photoengraved printing processes increased the manufacturing capacity for producing drawings. Rail lines and highways, and improved vehicles to ply them, made possible distribution on a national—even international—scale. New cameras, projectors, and emulsions made moving pictures possible, while receptive mass audiences for new media made them economically rewarding for entrepreneurs (though not necessarily for their workers). Cohl was deeply committed to the technologies of printing and cinema and attempted to adapt his own work habits and interests to them in a way that would satisfy his *bricoleur* instincts (his insatiable drive to tinker) while gaining a livelihood. He was one of the heretofore unsung pioneers of the comic strip. And he became the father of the animated cartoon, an epithet conferred upon him late in life by his appreciative professional colleagues, which he quickly appended to his developing biographical legend.

While Emile Cohl was exploring and contributing to these new technologies, to some extent he was also becoming their victim. The comic strip, which would eventually make the old style of caricature commercially obsolete, would become dominant in the United States rather than France. Films would quickly become studio-made mass-produced commodities, subordinating the role of the individual creator. The time of the lone genius gave way to the era of the assembly-line system.

Writing just after the animator's death in 1938, Jean Renoir remarked, "At first the Mélièses, the Cohls, then the Max Linders, the Rigadins, and the Joë Hammans occupied the screens of the whole world, from Siberia to Colorado, by way of Andalusia. Since then, dishonest industrialists have sold out the French cinema—piecemeal, wholesale and retail—to their rich foreign competitors."[2] Renoir's nostalgic looking back to a golden age of prewar cinema was jaundiced by his pessimistic view of a national industry in disarray in the late 1930s, as he was about to embark on *Rules of the Game*. But in fact the industry of Cohl's epoch was every bit as insecure as later, although the specific threats were different. Competition was ruthless among domestic producers attempting to regulate the market to serve their own interests while resisting the invasion of foreign imports. The business in Cohl's time was also undergoing a change in artistic and economic conception (the two always being related) on the part of producers and audiences—a new orientation that was as cataclysmic as the coming of sound would be around 1930, or the failure of the great French studios in the late thirties.

Although it is commonplace to conceive of everything before 1915 as "early" or "primitive" cinema, without national distinction, the various film industries developed distinctive forms of production and exhibition in each country. Unlike the earliest dominant American viewing apparatus, Edison's Kinetoscope, which linked film conceptually to the peep show and its aim of attracting droves of individual spectators, French cinema from the start was an outgrowth of a much stronger tradition of audience-oriented projected spectacle. Furthermore, unlike the heterogeneous American market, French cinema was always aimed at a middle-class audience. The "lower class" depiction of early French cinema was generally a distortion, first by uplifters, then later by populist and socialist commentators. But French producers made their fortunes exploiting the crowds of families that flocked to the traveling fairs and carnivals sponsored by provincial church parishes and by filling the leisure hours of urban bourgeois families. Unlike the United States, France experienced no great waves of immigrants at the turn of the century (at least none that film producers wished to entertain), and the domestic audience for film throughout Cohl's period was much more homogeneous than in America.

Cohl's films illustrate the industry's desire to annex as much of this expanding middle-class market as possible. His producers' encouragement, or at least tolerance, of Cohl's experiments in animation reflects a desire to sustain the interest of an implied audience of literate bourgeois spectators. The market was not just theatergoers but also family consumers of mass-circulation humor magazines. From the producers' viewpoint, the value of Cohl's roots in caricature was obvious; the intertextuality of popular graphic humor and film was not fortuitous but rather the result of calculated experimentation. In the end, however, Cohl's work inevitably will be seen as unique, not fitting comfortably into any preexisting genre or within one model of reception such as "primitive" or "institutional." While this does give Cohl considerable authorial status for us retrospective historians, for him at the time, practically speaking, his position of marginality in the industry made it difficult to maintain employment. And eventually it led to his involuntary withdrawal from animation practice.

Chapters One and Two recount the particular biographical details of Cohl's early life and formative years as a caricaturist when he worked with André Gill and then developed his own idiosyncratic style. The chief intellectual influences on his art as he grew into a kind of boulevard-culture jack-of-all-trades are discussed. Chapters Three, Four, and Five reconstruct Cohl's first film work, his position within a major French growth industry, and the influence of his work on the new art of the animated film.

In Chapter Six we see how Cohl attempted to create and bolster his own legend as his career ended and his life approached its tragic finale. His promotional efforts indirectly provided some of the earliest cogent writing on the techniques and generic definitions of animation. Chapters Seven and Eight are more theoretically oriented speculations on the aesthetic roots of Cohl's art and its intertextual fabric.

ONE wonders how scholars in Emile Cohl's day, armed only with a Waterman pen and a ream of foolscap, published anything at all. My work of tracing Cohl's life and career was aided by numerous highly technological aids yet still took a long time to complete. It would never have reached this state were it not for the experts and the artist's surviving relatives who assisted me. Most of the gathering of data was done in Paris with the warmth, generosity, and cooperation of Emile Cohl's daughter-in-law, Mme. André Courtet-Cohl, and his grandchildren, Pierre and Suzanne Courtet-Cohl. They gave me access to Cohl's papers and will find many of their family mementos reproduced in my illustrations. Michel Legros, Cohl's great-grandson, also provided me with valuable information.

At Gaumont, Messrs. Loubeau and Petiot allowed me to look through the old records of their company and gave me permission to use the corporate archive in Joinville-le-Pont, La Cinémathèque Gaumont-Actualités. At that time Mlle. Mathieu reigned as directrice, ably accompanied by her little white poodle. She allowed me to examine all the films that remain that were made by Cohl for Gaumont. I viewed these in the form of duplicate camera negatives that ran on a specially converted Steenbeck table equipped with a video system for reversing the polarity of the image, changing negative to positive. Later Laure Forestier of Gaumont struck new positives from these when they generously assisted me in the various retrospectives of Cohl's work in which I have participated. The quality of these new 35mm prints is astonishing. They capture the brilliance and clarity of Cohl's films as they appeared to audiences before World War I.

I owe a special and heartfelt debt to Jacques Deslandes, historian of the French cinema, who befriended me, loaned me rare original documents from his extensive collection, and pored over my catalogue in its earliest form. Frantz and Nicole Schmitt screened many films for me at the Archives du Film in Bois d'Arcy and provided me with important documentation. Raymond Maillet, director of the Association Française du Cinéma d'Animation gave me free access to his files.

My research began at the Cinémathèque Française during a low ebb in that institution's history. While I was attempting to work there, I resented Henri Langlois's apparent lack of interest and assistance. But since his death, and the publication of biographies of Langlois by Richard Roud and by Georges Patrick Langlois and Glenn Myrent, I have grown to appreciate Langlois's difficulties at the time I met him.

I will always be grateful to Lotte Eisner, who at last provided my "open sesame" to the Cinémathèque's treasures, and to Marie Epstein. Retrospectively I am also glad to have had the opportunity for many interesting discussions with Mary Meerson.

I benefited from the encouragement of Jean Adhémar (Bibliothèque Nationale), Mme. Charron (Cinémathèque Pathé-Journal), Charles Ford, A. Haigron (Société d'encouragement pour l'industrie nationale), M. d'Aubarède (Concours Lépine), the librarians of the Bibliothèque de l'Arsenal and the Bibliothèque de l'IDHEC.

Geneviève Acker, director of the Commission Franco-Américaine, my Fulbright-Hays sponsor in France, facilitated my research and my life in many ways. Maurice Delavier contributed, during our long and pleasant conversations, more toward my education than any landlord is required to do.

Others who helped as much as they could include Jeremy Boulton, Jacques Ledoux, Jan de Vaal, Torsten Jungstedt, and Colette Borde.

For their guidance, sharing of information, loans of prints, and/or general enthusiasm, I am grateful to Anne Carré, Jon Gartenberg, Charles Silver, Ron Magliozzi, Ted Perry, Paul Spehr, Patrick Sheehan, Patrick Loughney, Barbara Humphrys, Emily Seeger, Anthony Slide, Harvey Deneroff, Mike Barrier, Louise Beaudet, David Shepard, David R. Smith, Marshall Deutelbaum, and Jan-Christopher Horak.

John Canemaker, historian and animator, has been an intelligent and sympathetic critic of my work since its inception. I am lucky to have his expertise available.

Eileen Bowser, of the Museum of Modern Art, frequently offered her advice and generously loaned prints to me. I am grateful for her constant encouragement and kindness.

Kristin Thompson, Richard Abel, Alan Williams, Robert Herbert, and Jean Gaudon carefully read the manuscript and made many suggestions—filmographic, bibliographic, stylistic, and linguistic—which I have incorporated as fully as possible. My dissertation adviser, Anne Hanson, helped to transform my data into prose. I appreciate the effort and advice expended on my behalf by Standish Lawder and David Cast. Dudley Andrew has always inspired me as a professor and as a friend.

Linda Henzl contributed many services and her considerable erudition in Amcan literature. Peter Schofer assisted with poetry translations. Robert Goldstein offered valuable advice. Barbara Adams and Nancy Walchli stood by me like guardian angels during the years this was in the works. Doug Riblet and Mary Carbine assisted in preparing the manuscript.

I am very grateful to the Swann Foundation for Caricature and Cartoon, Henry J. Goldschmidt, president, for continuing support of this project and for my first book on animation.

The dedication of this book to Marilyn Crafton is not just a sentimental gesture but a sign of her real contribution during the decade of support, research and writing that the book has entailed.

Madison, Wisconsin
April 26, 1988

PART ONE

The "Caricaturiste"

Va, frère, va, camarade,
Fais le diable, bats l'estrade
Dans ton rêve et sur Paris,
Et par le monde, et sois l'âme
Vile, haute, noble, infâme
De nos innocents esprits!

Grandis, car c'est la coutume,
Cube ta riche amertume,
Exagère ta gaieté
Caricature, auréole,
La grimace et le symbole
De notre simplicité

Paul Verlaine, from
"Pierrot Gamin," ca.1886

A Caricaturist's Life

EMILE COHL claimed to be the oldest Parisian. That impulse by itself indicates something about the person, his perception of his place in a particular culture, and his desire to let others know of it. To substantiate his claim he produced a meticulously researched genealogy showing that, since 1292, his family had been living in the vicinity of what eventually became the Bourse neighborhood.[1] There were some lacunae in the older branches of the family, but the post-revolutionary descendants were easily traced as far back as his paternal grandfather, Jean Eustache François Courtet (1795–1875), and his grandmother, Rosalie Elisabèthe Clotilde Aubert (1798–1830). Their son, Elie Courtet, was born in 1821 and married Emilie Laure Coulon in 1853. Four years later their only child was born on January 4, 1857, and was christened Emile Eugène Jean Louis Courtet. Later he called himself Emile Cohl, and he would grow up to be one of the best-known Parisian caricaturists of his day, one of the pioneers of the comic strip, and, even later in life, the creator of the animated cartoon film. At the time of his birth, the family lived at 20, rue Cadet in the ninth arrondissement (not far from the present site of the Folies-Bergères).

Emile Courtet's birthplace would have telegraphed essential information to his fellow Parisians in the nineteenth century. As inhabitants of the Faubourg Montmartre, his family would have been categorized as bourgeois with upwardly mobile aspirations. Elie Courtet, a stereotypical *faubourien*, was a salesman representing his great-uncle Alexandre Aubert's rubber-manufacturing plant in Grenelle. Mme. Courtet supplemented the family income as a linen seamstress. Their fortunes were linked, as were those of many others in the Industrial Revolution, to the fortunes of the plant and the fluctuating economy in general. Courtet's rising and falling resources necessitated many moves, first to rue Lamartine, then back to rue Cadet in 1859.[2]

As a baby, Emile was frail and overprotected by his mother. He suffered occasional convulsions and carried a permanent scar from an injury he received during one of them. Later in life, when he set down notes for an autobiography, his earliest memories were vivid images: the swallows departing in autumn, a horse pawing in the courtyard, soldiers marching down boulevard Poissonnière. He recalled attacking his mother's sewing table with a toy saw and could remember his older cousin dressed up as Pierrot. Once someone gave him some paints.

I see myself sitting in a chair before a table, having before me a box of colors and a big glass of water and smearing drawings (?). I must have been desperate because I see vague forms agitating all around me.

He was first sent to school about 1861. There a magician with shiny copper instruments fascinated him on the first day, but the party ended and "I began my battle with the alphabet." At year's end there was a class play:

It was in a little theater inside the elementary school in the rue de la Tour d'Auvergne. We were all over the stage and in the bleachers. The set represented a forest, or at least some foliage. At one point I started to cry. Everyone came at me: "What's the matter?" I peed, and continued to cry. There was wild laughter everywhere. It was the only time I ever provoked laughter in a theater. . . . Let's go on.

There were few recollections of his father, except for his Garde Nationale uniform, rifle, and bright buttons. But he had warm memories of his mother. Unfortunately she had never recovered from a fall during her pregnancy, and her condition grew worse. His worried father sent Emile to stay with his maternal grandmother Coulon in Montreuil-sous-Bois, then still a village outside Paris. He had become excessively shy and was teased at school. Once he was punished for falling into the public drinking fountain and again for pinching brussels sprouts belonging to the village constable.

Mme. Courtet died in 1863. Emile's father entrusted the six-year-old to the Parrotte family, tie manufacturers in Les Lilas (Romainville). Their next-door neighbor in this area, near what is now the nineteenth arrondissement, was Paul-Charles de Kock (1794–1871), the author of spicy romantic novels whom the neighbors regarded as a cranky old man, but who would reward Emile's stories of the day at school with two sous and laugh when addressed as "Monsieur Poil de Coq" (Mr. Rooster-Hair). Once he intervened on behalf of the young pupil when he was unjustly punished by a teacher "with a quick hand." De Kock was frequently the butt of caricaturists—Nadar was the most famous—and one naturally wonders whether the youthful Emile was exposed to any of these drawings.

In 1864 Courtet enrolled his son at the Ecole professionnelle de Pantin, a boarding school more commonly called the Institut Vaudron after its director. At first he was placed in the lower division because of his inability to perform during the initial examination, but soon it was realized that he was simply too timid and frightened, and by the third day he had moved up to the first division. Two days later there was another triumph when it was time for drawing lessons:

They set before me a model taken from the notebooks of Monzocq (all the schoolchildren of my day will recognize it). It was a picture of a thatched roof and I sketched it in five secs flat, before the master returned. "He draws! Go get M. Vaudron." He arrived a few minutes later. "What, what, he knows how to draw?" You could say that

I was a phenomenon. "Yes, and he can read and count. . . ." "And can he do fractions?" That doused it. "No, Monsieur, not yet." And I put my head down on my desk.

Despite his ignorance of fractions, he was promoted, and the teacher, Vaudron's alcoholic son, let him draw in class as much as he wished.

Emile Courtet's early education at père Vaudron's, which apparently left him to his own devices, helped to channel his compulsive doodling into natural drawing talent. He had even more time to practice in 1865 when he was confined to his father's apartment (now on rue d'Enghien) with a serious cold. Drawing was his only distraction until the housekeeper gave him all the beautiful stamps from the letters of her relatives in Martinique. Little did she know that she was kindling a stamp-collecting passion that would burn all his life. His father encouraged this new interest by contributing stamps from the daily business mail and taking him to visit Arthur Maury's stamp shop, one of the largest, in the heart of Paris's stamp-trading district, across from the Théâtre Français.[3]

Cured and returned to school in Pantin, he was allowed to draw caricatures on the walls, a large map of France, and some pictures of locomotives. He easily became first in school in drawing and in 1869 earned the duty of teaching the "dolors of the alphabet" to younger children.

In 1870, still at Vaudron's, there were two candidates for the honor of singing the *Marseillaise* at the August awards ceremony. Emile won. (The loser, Lédart, later became the director of the Théâtre de Montmartre.) However, the declaration of war against Prussia dispersed the class, and the ceremony never took place. This time M. Courtet sent his son to live with the family of a cousin who owned a greengrocery on the avenue des Ternes.

He returned to live with his father after the fall of the Second Empire on September 4, 1870. One immediate result of the social turmoil following the war was brought home when Uncle Alexandre Aubert was forced to give up his interest in the rubber-manufacturing plant, leaving an uncertain future facing Elie Courtet and his young family.

CARICATURE: THE IMAGE OF OPPOSITION

The economic and political upheaval that formed the backdrop of Emile Courtet's youth coincided with the rise of what Richard Terdiman, in his account of journalism in the nineteenth century, has called "newspaper culture."[4] Emile's was in fact the second generation to grow up in the age of lithography—the process that enabled images drawn by the artist's own hand to be reproduced and disseminated by the hundreds or thousands only a few hours after being sketched on the printing stone. While the process had its utilitarian and decorative uses, it also made possible the spread of overtly oppositional political imagery to an extent that would have been inconceivable in the previous century. It was Emile Courtet's fortune to grow up in the midst of an eruption of satirical cartooning. While important in its own right—Cohl would have warranted a biography as a caricaturist even had he not found the cinema—his involvement with caricature, with its connotations of marginality, will become especially pertinent during his later career in film.

As soon as he could afford it, Elie Courtet enrolled Emile in another school, the Ecole Turgot. There the boy quickly excelled in drawing, but he was still too distracted by events in the streets to be interested in anything else. During the Siege he picked up his allotted piece of horse meat and straw bread. His father could not stand the meat, so he gave his share to Emile and instead ate the bread, which had to be soaked in oil, rubbed with garlic, and fried to make it palatable. With no heat, Emile suffered frequently from colds and chilblains. When he was well, he played with his friends in the streets and watched the soldiers at the barricades. Once he saw Rochefort make an inspection of the lines while he was headquartered on rue Cadet. According to a biographical sketch written in 1886, it was during the Commune (March–May 1871) that he was first exposed to political caricatures.

> On March 17, the stripes of the Commune officers and the parades of soldiers held a disturbing fascination for him and distracted him from his school work. He took advantage of these troubled times when the teachers had other cats to skin besides their undisciplined pupils. Like a real Paris urchin, he spent his days hanging out in the streets, stopping for a long time in front of the bookstore windows where so many infantile caricatures were shown off during these feverish days.[5]

He was becoming aware, through these anarchic drawings, of an aspect of the visual environment that had been increasingly evident since the first third of the century. Two factors in particular stimulated his interest in the art of caricature.

The first was his physical proximity to rue du Croissant, the "Fleet Street of caricature."[6] The editorial offices of most of the satirical publications were centered around this narrow street, just across boulevard Poissonnière from the Courtets' Faubourg Montmartre. The electric atmosphere of the street on Saturdays when the latest issues of *Le Charivari*, *L'Eclipse*, and *Le Journal Amusant* were hawked was captured in a print by Régamey (fig. 1).

The second factor was the sheer quantity of caricatural images that covered the walls and saturated the streets and cafés in defiance of all attempts at control. Many commentators, such as Duranty, mentioned "the innumerable comic papers that abounded in Paris during this epoch."[7] Throughout most of the Second Empire Napoleon III had attempted to suppress all political caricature by enforcing strict censorship. When he was overthrown in 1870, the streets erupted with blistering posters and broadsheets

1. Félix Régamey: "La Rue du Croissant," 1868.

pillorying the regime. During the Franco-Prussian War, the Siege, and peaking during the Commune, there was an enormous outpouring of vicious and hateful imagery directed toward various rapidly changing enemies.[8] These were not the established illustrated papers, all of which had ceased publication during the turmoil, but crudely printed *feuilles volantes*. These broadsheets, literally "flying leaves," were often illustrated by anonymous hacks who wished to communicate their inflammatory messages directly to the public.[9] Albums of anti-Commune caricatures circulated freely and replaced the bitter anti-Prussian broadsheets.[10] It was this type of imagery that first caught the eye of the street urchin Emile Courtet.

After the boy finished his schoolwork at the Ecole Turgot, presumably around 1872, his father obtained a three-year apprenticeship for him with a jeweler. Emile tried to relieve the monotony of the job by joining a magician's act, but, according to an account apparently written by Cohl himself in 1890, "He only dreamed of drawing, or rather, of caricature, and sketched everything he saw."[11] He continued to caricature passionately after he had finished the dull apprenticeship and enlisted for voluntary service with a Cherbourg regiment.

Then the philatelist Maury hired him to work in his shop and design his albums, a sideline that would continue until 1889 when they argued over wages.[12] His father still hoped that his son would seek a commercial career and found him a fifty-franc-a-month position with a maritime insurance broker. But this, too, was intolerable.

All of a sudden, one fine day, abandoning his appointments, our caricaturist made a clean break with his papa and declared that henceforth he would live off his pencil—an ultimatum that immediately introduced him to *la vache enragée*.[13]

The final phrase was slang for going hungry. But as Jerrold Seigel has noted, the term was also a contemporary euphemism that indicated to readers that Emile Cohl was venturing into the realm of Bohemia.[14]

The aspiring caricaturist was somehow able to obtain a letter of recommendation from Etienne Carjat, an important photographer who was best known for his portraits of the actor Frédérick Lemaître. But he was also a painter and a caricaturist. Carjat referred him to his close friend and former collaborator, André Gill, the best-known caricaturist of the day. Cohl's biographers, writing as "Pierre et Paul," described this momentous day in his life with florid and fanciful prose:

> On a beautiful morning in the month of October 1878—it begins like a novel by Montepin—a solid young blond man strode feverishly up and down the sidewalk of rue d'Enfer, since changed by an administrative pun into Denfert-Rochereau, finally stopping at number 89. The traces of violent interior emotions could be read on his juvenile face upon which long practice at living had not yet imposed the impenetrable mask of impavidity. And under the rule of this emotion that he was trying in vain to master, a little quiver agitated the upper lip of our hero, imprinting an undulating motion to his fine blond moustache, the points of which fluttered, musketeer fashion, while his right hand nervously crumpled the letter that was concealed in the pocket of his jacket.
>
> After a long hesitation which had already been preceded by two or three attempts, the young man plucked up his courage, lifted the heavy door knocker and let it fall back with a dull thud.
>
> "Enter!" responded a heavy voice from inside, which, far from reassuring our timid visitor, made him tremble all the more.
>
> However, in spite of the shivering that this imperative injunction had induced, he resolutely pushed open the door. He found himself at the foot of a steep staircase whose steps, quickly skipped, led to the half-opened door of a big room cluttered with easels on which were displayed canvases containing rough outlines. A drawing board hung from the ceiling and at it sat a man, a kind of Hercules in shirt sleeves, before a table overloaded with scraps and sketches. He was drawing and from time to time he would wipe the point of his pen on his fingertips which he would then run through his leonine hair, the jet black ink mixing with a few streaks of silver, then he would throw his mane back with a brisk movement of his head.
>
> This Hercules was André Gill.[15]

The young man displayed some natural talent and was admitted into the Gill atelier. Although the details of Gill's working habits are unknown, it seems certain that the large number of "pupils" who frequented the studio actually worked as Gill's assistants. Life there was a swirl of activity and excitement punctuated by the famous caricaturist's soirées. Emile Courtet was absorbed into the circle, and most of his new acquaintances remained personal friends until their deaths. There was dramatist François Coppée, the actors Daubray and Gil-Naza (David-Antoine Chapoulade), Constant Coquelin cadet and âiné (junior and senior). The poet-politician Gustave Rivet recited there. Sculptor Jean Chapuy, musician Olivier Metra, and painter H. C. Delpy joined some of the best-known caricaturists, including Sapeck (Marie-Félicien Bataille), Paul Hellé, Adolphe Willette, and Georges Lorin. Ernest d'Hervilly, Cattelain ("engraver, furniture mover and pianist"), and the *café-concert* proprietor Théodore Bullier also attended.[16]

The central attraction was, of course, André Gill (born Louis-Alexandre Gosset de Guines). At this time, in 1878, he was the preeminent caricaturist of France, owing largely to his daring attacks in the illustrated press against the Second Empire, openly defying the censors and earning a reputation for personally revitalizing the underground art of political caricature.

The days of relatively free political expression enjoyed by Daumier's generation from 1830 to 1835 had vanished by 1859, when Gill's first drawing appeared in *Le Journal Amusant*. Hired in 1865 by the courageous publisher François Polo to illustrate his new satirical journal *La Lune*, Gill was frequently the target of attempts by Emperor Napoleon III to suppress political caricature. In spite of this, the paper had a circulation of 500,000 by 1867. Gill constantly tested the limits of a censorship apparatus that forbade not only unauthorized representations of the government but allegorical content as well. "The Masked Wrestlers" of November 3, 1867, was taken to be an antipapist statement, although it showed only two wrestlers, one wearing a red mask, the other in black. It was enough, in December when the case was tried before a magistrate, to send Polo to jail with a stiff fine and meant the end of *La Lune*. Meanwhile, the provocative skirmishes continued. On November 17, 1867, Gill attacked the emperor directly with his "Authentic Portrait of Rocambole." He gave the dandyish fictional character the unmistakable features of Napoleon III. The suppression of *La Lune* became a cause célèbre that contributed further to the swaying of public opinion against the Second Empire.[17]

Eight days after the last *La Lune*, Polo started a new paper to replace it and petulantly called it *L'Eclipse*. In the issue of August 9, 1868, he published Gill's "Monsieur X...?," a drawing of a melon with a slice removed. The features of a magistrate could be recognized among the bumps on its surface. When the issue was restrained from circulation, Gill was charged with obscenity instead of the expected grounds of unauthorized political caricature. The charge mystified everyone (and still does). Gill was livid and wrote in a front-page letter to the editor of *Le Temps*, "My drawings have often had a mischievous intention, but never an obscene intention. . . . If *L'Eclipse* must be prosecuted, let it be for the intentions that it has, not for those attributed to it."[18] We presume that the government felt that it could argue a case for the "slice" in the drawing as a vaginal image. But the ploy backfired. Hawkers scalped the issue in the streets and a boisterous trial ensued that received extensive press coverage. The obscenity charge was dropped after Gill effectively argued that obscenity was in the eye of the beholder, but the paper was fined nevertheless. Once again, the empire was held up to public ridicule. Although seizures of *L'Eclipse* continued routinely, the growing weakness of the government allowed less stringent enforcement of the censorship laws. Eventually *Le Journal Amusant, Le Petit Journal pour Rire, La Vie Parisienne*, and *Le Charivari* all became bolder. Gill was generally credited with the new freedom of expression, and his name was familiar to those Parisians of Republican sentiment who browsed through the journals in the streets and cafés.

During the Franco-Prussian War of 1870–1871, Gill ceased drawing in order to join the defense against the Prussian Siege.[19] On April 17, 1871, he was elected to the Commune-endorsed Fédération des Artistes de Paris, chaired by Gustave Courbet, and was assigned the duty of protecting and organizing the Luxembourg Museum. One month later he was named its "provisional administrator."[20] After the bloody suppression of the Commune, Gill narrowly avoided the condemnation meted out to Courbet and others associated with it.

L'Eclipse resumed in June 1871. With the return of peace, the satiric press, despite censorship, continued the expansion that had begun in the final months of the Second Empire. Among the many new political papers was *La Lune Rousse*, founded by Gill in December 1876, in which some of his best work appeared. When Emile Courtet met him in 1878, Gill had become an almost legendary figure. Although not well known today outside of France, to his contemporaries and to later historians he was the heritor of Daumier's talent and social position of a generation earlier. Other artists respected Gill for his politics, his courage, and his art. When Camille Pissarro, for example, painted his *Portrait of Paul Cézanne*, he pictured his friend haloed by a little caricature of Courbet and a drawing by Gill from *L'Eclipse* (fig. 2).[21]

Gill's career is exemplary of the practice of "symbolic resistance," as discussed by Terdiman.[22] Like Daumier before him, Gill was profoundly committed to caricature as oppositional, not just to specific individuals but to what they stood for—the domination of society by conformist bourgeois values. Caricature then was primarily an ideological weapon, not merely a vehicle for the artist's style or wit. As Terdiman argues, "The nineteenth century is no doubt the counter-discourse's classic moment. The open and virulent anger felt by the antibourgeois for the bourgeois can rarely have been more evident or more focused."[23] Yet at the time when Cohl was entering the studio, the opposition was beginning to lose its unified front. The old issues were becoming blurred, and former enemies (such as Patrice de MacMahon, forced to resign as president of France in 1879) were not as menacing. Gill was frequently depressed and nearly penniless. *La Lune Rousse* went out of business in December 1879.[24]

Cohl's first works may be seen as typical of the period—transitional, moving away from the ferocity of old-style Republicanism (which he could not have known except

2. André Gill: "La Délivrance," *L'Eclipse*, August 4, 1874.

vicariously) and toward an increasing awareness of style and composition. At a time when Gill felt abandoned by his old friends, he became strongly attached to his new generation of admirers, of whom Cohl was by far the most ardent. It was around 1879 that the apprentice caricaturist adopted his foreign-sounding pseudonym. Why he chose "Cohl" has never been explained. Perhaps it had something to do with the pigment kohl, but more likely it was a pun that signaled his intention to stick to his master like glue ("colle").[25]

Not surprisingly, Cohl's first caricatures were closely patterned on Gill's style. Since the 1860s, Gill had mastered the *portrait-charge*, the practice of drawing a large caricatural head on a squat comic torso.[26] But he had transformed the stiff, repetitious forms of many of his predecessors into a highly refined mode of representation marked by individuality, life, and motion (fig. 3). Cohl learned his techniques firsthand in the atelier, where he was probably assigned the completion of the backgrounds and other finishing touches before the drawings were rushed off to the engraver Lefman. Some of the drawings signed by Gill may have been executed entirely by Uzès (A. Lemot), Georges Lorin, Bataille, or Cohl.

An 1881 caricature of statesman Léon Gambetta by Cohl shows that he was not

3. André Gill: "Bonjour! — Bonsoir!" *La Lune Rousse*, December 24, 1876.

extraordinarily precocious, but that Gill's lessons were learned well (fig. 4). The large head sits upon the stocky, disproportionately small body, modeled by quick cross-hatching strokes. The figure fits neatly into the space on the page, and the composition is enclosed by a rectangular frame. But Cohl's drawing lacks the balance and discipline visible in Gill's best work. There is a tendency toward clutter in the composition, and Gill's linear clarity is missing. Nevertheless, Cohl's caricature projects a strong sense of Gambetta's personality. Casting him as the proprietor of a boutique was ingenious and, on the whole, the drawing compares favorably with those by other artists of Gill's "school," such as Pépin (Edouard Guillaumin) or Alfred Le Petit.

Despite Gill's strong influence, Cohl began to show certain maverick tendencies that identified his personal style even in his earliest works. His figures often overstepped the boundaries of their frame, or the hair or a limb would extend past the margin. Usually this was done to introduce the idea of a figure in motion (fig. 5). Another unusual characteristic was that, more than any other caricaturist, Cohl was attracted to the puppet stage for inspiration. Occasionally, as in "Les Poupées de l'infante" (The Infante's Dolls, fig. 6), the *guignol* iconography is explicit. In other works, such as "Serment aujourd'hui, serrement demain" (Oath Today, Handshake Tomorrow, fig. 7), it is implicit in the doll-like figures, especially the sergeant.

4. Emile Cohl: "Grand Bazar génois,"
La Nouvelle Lune, June 5, 1881. (Hereinafter works
for whom no other artist is cited are by
Emile Cohl.)

5. "Le Baron de San Malato contre Edouard
Philippe," *La Nouvelle Lune*, March 6, 1881.

6. "Les Poupées de l'infante," *La Nouvelle Lune*,
May 8, 1881.

7. "Serment aujourd'hui, serrement demain,"
La Nouvelle Lune, January 16, 1881.

At first it seemed as though Cohl were trying to fill up the simplified backgrounds that had marked the best of Gill's work. "Souffle toujours" (Keep Blowing, fig. 8) has a bold black-and-white patterned background made from the arrangement of lanterns. "Que d'or! Que d'or! Que d'or!" (Gold! Gold! Gold!, fig. 9) also shows his readiness to fill backgrounds with decorative detail. He later reversed this tendency by eliminating the background altogether, as well as the "frame" (figs. 10–11). This style typifies some of Cohl's best graphic work, but ironically some of his least inspired in terms of wittiness of characterization.

Cohl was attempting to introduce some of his own innovations in the *portrait-charge* as defined by Gill. There are spontaneous and subtle humorous touches that one finds infrequently in the older caricaturist's more careful, restrained work. Once Cohl represented Gambetta by drawing only his famous silhouette and a beckoning hand (fig. 12). Little touches such as the faces on the fencing masks in "Le Baron de San Malato contre Edouard Philippe" (fig. 5) and the diva's caricature in the profile of the Gymnase Theater in "M. René Langlois" (fig. 13) add to the ingenuity of the drawings, though possibly distracting from the overall compositional impact.

There was also a marked propensity for grotesque physical distortion—over and above that to be found in other caricature of the time. Elongated noses were a favorite joke (fig. 14), and there were several distorted balloon-men (fig. 15).

8. "Souffle toujours," *La Nouvelle Lune*, July 24, 1881.

9. "Que d'or! Que d'or! Que d'or!" *La Nouvelle Lune*, September 3, 1882.

10. "Rentrée du grand Jules," *La Nouvelle Lune*, February 25, 1883.

11. "Les Auteurs de Vièrge," *La Nouvelle Lune*, May 31, 1884.

12. "Actualité," *La Nouvelle Lune*, August 15, 1880.

13. "M. René Langlois," *La Nouvelle Lune*, April 17, 1881.

14. "Vêtement de saison," *La Nouvelle Lune*, August 28, 1881.

15. "Vue du Ministère Duclerc, de la lune," *La Nouvelle Lune*, August 20, 1882.

Cohl's most unusual experiments were some full-page facial portraits in which the heads were so large that they swelled over the margins of the folio-sized pages (figs. 16–17). The portrait of "Plon-Plon" transforms the subject's chin into buttocks and his shoulders into a chamber pot. The portrait of Gill's friend Clovis Hugues is especially effective because the open mouth and speech balloon suggest the Marseillais's garlic-laden breath. His pockmarks give the viewer the impression of uncomfortable proximity to the huge face.

Cohl's group caricatures show the same innovative approach. Instead of arranging the staff of *L'Indépendant* in a procession—standard since Nadar's *Panthéon*—he pictured them as five puppets on a stage against a backdrop emblazoned with sketches of the other contributors (fig. 18). "La Rédaction du *Tam-Tam*" (Staff of the *Tam-Tam*, fig. 19) caricatures some of the staff as puppets and others as childish sketches. In "Tapons dans le tas" (fig. 20) at a carnival boutique a hand offers the reader a ball to throw at the "dolls" representing journalists or papers. Cohl's most ambitious group caricature was "Le Ciel et l'enfer en 1881" (Heaven and Hell in 1881, fig. 21), in which he assigned over fifty political figures to heaven (presided over by Jules Grévy) or to hell (ruled over by the devil Henri de Rochefort). The two-page supplement to *La Nouvelle Lune* was intended to be sold separately for ten centimes.

In only a few years Cohl had become part of the "counter-discourse" of caricatural representation. His contributions to these Republican periodicals indicate that he

16. "Les Prétendants du carnaval," *La Nouvelle Lune*, January 28, 1883.

17

18

19

17. "Le Député de la bouillabaisse," *La Nouvelle Lune*, March 5, 1882.

18. "L'Indépendant," *La Nouvelle Lune*, January 20, 1880.

19. "La Rédaction du *Tam-Tam*," *La Nouvelle Lune*, May 29, 1881.

20. "Tapons dans le tas," *La Nouvelle Lune*, January 8, 1882.

21. "Le Ciel et l'enfer en 1881," *La Nouvelle Lune*, December 22, 1881.

shared Gill's political orientation, but Cohl's drawings also reveal individualistic tendencies in his work that testify to his maturing creative independence and his interest in form and style above ideology. More pragmatically, they also reflect the fact that Gill, whose health was failing and whose commitment to the "cause" was being strained, even questioned by former colleagues, was no longer Cohl's exclusive artistic influence.

THE HYDROPATHES

It was through Gill's circle that Emile Cohl was introduced to the band of Bohemian literary and theatrical personalities known as the Hydropathes. While the group formerly has been regarded as little more than a footnote to literary history, for Cohl, and his graphic and cinematic work, they were crucially important. They provided a network of friends and acquaintances that would endure throughout his lifetime, and their ideas about art and the individual's relation to society would inform his later work.

The Hydropathes had their first meeting in October 1878, just as Cohl was presenting himself to Gill. Their roots grew from the old Cénacle des Vivants, a group comprised mainly of Gill followers who had met at the Bal Bullier and at a café called the

Sherry-Cobbler. The favorite spots for the younger Hydropathes were the Café de l'Avenir on the Place St. Michel and the Café Voltaire, near the Odéon Theater. The guiding spirit of the group was Emile Goudeau, described by André Salmon as "awesomely moustached and the terror of the literary banquets because he obstinately declaimed one or another of his masterpieces until dessert."[27] The new group quickly grew from just a few friends to over three hundred devotees. One of them, Jules Lévy, described their soirées:

Contrary to belief, many of the participants drank very little at the Hydropathe soirées. One steeped oneself in poetry, music and total art. What unforgettable evenings!

From nine to midnight, poets and singers followed one another. It was not mutual admiration though. Quite frankly for each of these performers it was a curative of art, gaiety and wit. One felt better when one left, thanks to the beauty of the sovereign mistress [i.e. Art] to whom one had submitted for the preceding three hours.[28]

Although the meetings took place in the Latin Quarter, the group was not dominated by students. It was what we would now call young professional types—bureaucrats and functionaries in their twenties—who seem to have been attracted. Anyone who performed or who regularly attended had the right to call himself a Hydropathe. According to Goudeau, this audience was intentionally courted as a market for the performers' publications.[29] Most frequently recitals were given by François Coppée, Monselet, Paul Arène, and by Gill, who read from his poem *La Muse à Bibi* in his rich theatrical voice.[30] Félix Galipaux recalled that "André Gill, the master caricaturist, would sit among us and bring his enthusiastic disciple, Emile Coll [*sic*]."[31] The shy Cohl never performed on the stage, but his contribution was nevertheless important because on October 28, 1879, he became the editor of their publication, *L'Hydropathe*. Paul Vivien and Georges Lorin had brought out the first issue on January 22 of that year.[32]

Cohl came to the periodical from the staff of *Le Carillon*, which had rivaled *La Lune Rousse* in its fervent Republicanism. A front-page drawing by Cohl, for example, had shown considerable daring when it cast MacMahon as a fake blind beggar with the punning placard "Aveugle par Ac-Sedan" (untranslatable pun on "Accidentally Blind" and "Sedan," fig. 22). In 1873, MacMahon had imposed severe penalties for caricaturing him and, after the election of Jules Grévy as president of France in January 1879, censorship continued to intensify. The publisher of *Le Carillon* and its regular artist were on trial for unauthorized political caricatures. Ten days after Cohl's drawing, they were each sentenced to ten days in prison and fined 100 francs. Cohl publicly hoped that they would appeal their conviction.[33]

Cohl and Paul Vivien launched a series of portraits in *L'Hydropathe* called "La Presse satirique," which they intended to publish as an album. In each installment an editor or contributor to the satiric press was caricatured by Cohl and described in a prose portrait by Vivien (fig. 23).

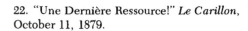

22

23

22. "Une Dernière Ressource!" *Le Carillon*,
October 11, 1879.

23. "Alfred Delilia," *L'Hydropathe*,
October 28, 1879.

24. Cabriol (Georges Lorin): "L'Hydropathe
Emile Cohl," *L'Hydropathe*, April 5, 1880.

24

L'HYDROPATHE EMILE COHL

Each week *L'Hydropathe* also featured a brick-red caricature of a member of the group drawn by Lorin, who signed himself "Cabriol." On April 5, 1880, Emile Cohl was the Hydropathe-of-the-week (fig. 24). Lorin's portrait shows a hirsute young man aggressively striding over two fallen silhouettes (perhaps the jeweler and the broker to whom he had been apprenticed). His "star," André Gill, is guiding him. Lorin provided another portrait of the young artist in the form of a sonnet:

EMILE COHL

Blême, blond, doux, cependant	Pale, blond, gentle but
Avec ardeur, il s'apprête	passionately, he taught himself
A glisser comme une arête,	to slide his dark aspiring
En travers d'un coup de dent.	pencil like a fish bone
Ténébreux de prétendant,	through a bite.
son crayon. . . . Maint interprète	. . . Many interpreters
De l'art, assez souvent prête	of art rather often attribute
Sa souplesse à quelque ardent	his versatility to some ardent
Amateur de boucherie.	lover of butchery.
Mieux je crois, vaudrait qu'on rie:	It would be better, I think, if one were to laugh:
Ainsi pense en sa bonté,	so speaks his kindness,
Ayant pour patriotisme	having for patriotism
Ce qu'on nomme: Humanité,	that which is called: Humanity,
Mon collègue en binettisme.	My colleague in cartooning.

CABRIOL.

A biographical note by Vivien reveals that Cohl was even trying his hand at some paintings.

At the same time he is indulging in painting, somewhat realist in style, and he is so timid that he has not dared bring one picture to the Salon. Every year he puts off "until next year." Let us hope, however, that he will make up his mind. We are certain that his work will be noticed.[34]

Vivien concluded with a prediction: "Our friend is a valiant young artist. The future belongs to him."

Who were the Hydropathes? The demography of the group was outlined by Goudeau:

At first the Hydropathes were an inextricable jumble of diverse and contrary tendencies: think of a bouillabaisse. There were young political men who dreamed of transforming the meetings into a cabal, modernist poets who couldn't stand the romantics, amateurs who took a chance on a brisk song or an ultra-spicy monologue, young actors and students from the Conservatory who had just auditioned for a recital of Théramène, as well as others more talented and better brought up, who gave us *La Bénédiction* by Coppée or *The Blacksmiths' Strike*, some mad ones who mistook the meeting for a café-concert and demanded some cancan music, while others, pontificating with authority, did not for a moment understand that one should be able to laugh. There were rabble-rousers up to their tomfoolery next to catholic elegiacs offering hymns to the Virgin. Naturally there were law, medical and pharmacy students, as well as students from the Beaux-Arts and from the Conservatory. There were ministry and city employees, engineers and concièrges' sons. There were also a few simple drunks who had come to make a row. It was like a miniature Chamber of Deputies: ideal and real diversity rubbed against each other in this microcosm.[35]

Despite the variety of their occupations, the Hydropathes were more or less united in their love of poetry. The majority of the older participants had been associated with the Vivants: Gill, Paul Arène, Félicien Champsaur, Jean Richepin, Gustave Rivet, and Maurice Rollinat.

There were also the remnants of Verlaine's Parnassians: François Coppée, the vagabond mystic Germain Nouveau, Léon Valade, and Emile Blémont (founder of *La Renaissance Littéraire et Artistique* and publisher of Rimbaud, Mallarmé, and Cros).

The "modernists" Goudeau referred to were the future Symbolists, Decadents, and Hirsutes. The critic Gustave Kahn attended the get-togethers, where he first met Jules Laforgue. He also met Jean Moréas, who had just arrived in Paris and was making himself known in literary circles. There were the dandies Laurent Tailhade, Ernest Raynaud, Joseph Gayda, and Fernand Icres.

From the theatrical world Coquelin cadet, Ernest Grénet-Dancourt, Paul Mounet, and Félix Galipaux dropped by for impromptu monologues. Sarah Bernhardt was caricatured on a *Hydropathe* cover by Lorin, but her membership was purely honorary.[36]

The painters Jules Bastien-Lepage and Luigi Loir (with whom Gill had studied at the Ecole des Beaux-Arts) were regulars. Besides the caricaturists Cohl and Lorin, there were Sapeck, Willette, and Henri Somm. The prolific writer Alphonse Allais was a member, as were Carjat and the remarkable Charles Cros, who regaled the group with his bizarre pseudoscientific stories.[37]

This hodgepodge of bohemian *littérateurs*, some well known and others distinctly marginal types, constituted the first important influence on Cohl's intellectual development. Through them he was injected into the mainstream of "modern" ideas while they were still in their exciting embryonic form. (Verlaine's proclamation of the *poètes maudits* did not take place until 1883, and Moréas did not publish his Symbolist manifesto until 1886.) In the pages of *L'Hydropathe*, at the recitals, during the innumerable arguments in the cafés and studios, Cohl must have become aware of the leading controversies of his day over Naturalism, Impressionism, and the nascent aesthetics of Symbolism.

In 1880 there was a schism in the group, and Goudeau's faction moved to the Right Bank. Their publication was renamed *Tout-Paris* and advertised "drawings by Alfred Le Petit, Demarre, Cabriol, Sapeck, Emile Cohl, etc." Cohl contributed sketches of Coquelin cadet and André Gill, who was shown leaving his Commune job at the Lux-

25. "Démissionnariat d'un an," *Tout-Paris*, June 13, 1880.

26. "Gill et le Luxembourg," *Tout-Paris*, June 26, 1880.

embourg (figs. 25, 26). Most of the members gradually drifted to other attractions on the Butte Montmartre, including André Gill, who became associated with a club originally called the Cabaret des Assassins. Gill painted a sign depicting a jumping rabbit, which made a visual pun on the artist's prominent signature (*agile* = A. Gill), and the bohemian patrons began calling the establishment the Lapin A. Gill.[38] In 1886 it was renamed the Lapin Agile and would become a favorite hangout of Picasso and other Montmartre inhabitants in the early twentieth century.

Most of the former Hydropathes became regulars at the larger Cabaret du Chat Noir, which the ex-members Rodolphe Salis and Jules Jouy opened in December 1881.[39] Cohl went to the Chat Noir only rarely, owing in part to his opinion of the club as Gill's competitor and also due to some personal differences with Jouy.

La Nouvelle Lune AND OTHER PERIODICALS

Even before the last issue of *L'Hydropathe*, Cohl's signature was appearing in other Parisian papers. The next five years (1880–1885) would be his most prolific period as a caricaturist. He was experiencing many changes in his personal life. His father had died in 1879 without becoming reconciled to his son's apparent profligacy, but because he was the sole survivor, Emile inherited a modest legacy that enabled him to marry a nineteen-year-old woman, Marie-Louise Servat, on November 12, 1881.

This period was also marked by his increasing devotion to André Gill, caring for him during the course of the older caricaturist's degenerative illness. Cohl also was becoming known in his own right, at first through the pages of a new illustrated paper, *La Nouvelle Lune*.

The four-page weekly was founded by S. Heymann in February 1880 as the continuation of *La Lune* and *L'Eclipse*. Obviously there were close ties with Gill and his circle. Testing the waters of censorship after MacMahon's resignation, the tenor of the paper was anticlerical and liberal. In April 1880, for example, it dared to print *Le Procureur*, a mock trade paper for pimps that perfectly illustrates the outlandish Hydropathe sensibility that Goudeau had called *fumisterie*.

Cohl's earliest contribution was a theatrical rubric signed "Emilio," but soon his first anticlerical drawings appeared: "Comment on fait les jésuites" (How They Make Jesuits, May 2, 1880, fig. 111) and "Diplôme de parfait jésuite" (Diploma of a Perfect Jesuit, May 13, 1880).

Not surprisingly, the journal was soon in trouble with the censors. Drawings had to be approved by an office in the Ministry of the Interior before publication, although written material was generally exempt from censorship.[40] The Cohl drawing of August 22, 1880, "Les Prix de *La Nouvelle Lune*" (fig. 27), was printed partially censored.

27. "Les Prix de *la Nouvelle Lune*," *La Nouvelle Lune*, August 22, 1880.

Originally one of the five panels showed Admiral Amédée Ribourt with a megaphone and paper boat. In its place Cohl issued a printed statement against the censor (known as "Dame Anastasie"):

THE PRIZE FOR INNOCENCE that we, in our generosity, awarded to the overly celebrated Cherbourg admiral, did not receive the assent of our old ANASTASIE: The minister wants hands off his men.—Amen

The situation grew worse. On September 5 another Cohl drawing was rejected, but the editors published its complete description:

Another drawing refused today. Nevertheless. It showed us the gentle Marcerou, Marcerou the lamb, so mischievously unveiled by *L'Intransigeant*, seated with the famous cane in his hand in the witness chair, transformed for him into a chamber pot, waiting for the hearing. Below, this caption: "He'll finally fall in." After going in vain six times to the censor, on the seventh they told our Cohl to put his drawings back in their boxes and gave him threatening looks. Cohl, who is timid, stammered a few objections, rightly pointing out that the censor is authorizing pornographic slop in a pile of disgusting papers, but forbidding political drawings which are scarcely dangerous, but nothing came of it. They showed him the door.[41]

Despite its problems with Dame Anastasie, which diminished after the Press Freedom Law of July 29, 1881, *La Nouvelle Lune* quickly became an important Paris paper, and Emile Cohl was clearly its driving force. He published his own poetry, theater and book reviews, and anecdotes about contemporary Parisians. Many former Hydropathes were represented. In 1880 twenty-five of Cohl's full-page drawings were published. He illustrated the paper almost single-handedly in 1881, with forty-one drawings, and in 1882, with thirty-five. He became editor-in-chief on November 30, 1883. This promotion relieved him of most of his drawing duties, so he could tend to Gill. Accordingly his share decreased to thirteen caricatures in 1883 and twenty in 1884.

He was one of the most illustrious members of the staff and widely appreciated as a practical joker. "Dr. Cohl," for example, once gave a strange presentation:

The illustrious doctor and artist E. Cohl presented a remarkable study of heart anesthesia that he produced in five young ladies simply by making them frequent the promenade of the Folies-Bergères for a month.

Their viscera had become so completely desensitized that they experienced not the slightest palpitation at the reading of a burning sonnet declaimed by the great seducer Deltombe, of the Variétés [Theater].

At this, Professor Bighorns threw himself at Cohl's feet and begged him to apply this process to his wife who is so sensitive that she swoons at the sight of a casket and

experiences fevers of such intensity that all the firemen on the rue de l'Ancienne-
Comédie cannot put them out. . . .

Meanwhile, Cohl, who, thanks to his steam reading machine was able to skim the
complete Medical Encyclopedia, showed Bighorns a treatise on the experiments of
Dr. Val Vigor, which demonstrated that in a case of hysteria like this, heart anesthesia can only be produced by a *lover*.

"So?" said Bighorns.

"So, put the case to your cousin."

It only took Bighorns fifteen minutes to reach him, thanks to Edison's Pun-o-
phone.[42]

Who was the author, "Dr. Asinus"? Perhaps he was Edouard Norès, Cohl's friend
and fellow practical joker on the staff, or humorist Alphonse Allais. Perhaps Charles
Cros was responsible for this piece, with its pseudoscientific jargon and bizarre steam
reading machine. Or Cohl may have written it himself.

Another sign of Cohl's becoming known in Parisian circles was his initiation into the
overly popular custom of dueling. He fought Jules Jouy at the Swiss border on December 12, 1880, "following a violent discussion provoked by purely artistic motives."[43]
Jouy, the poet and songwriter who with Salis would open the Chat Noir a year later,
was typically eccentric. He wrote a song every day, loved to attend capital punish-
ments, and still had time to invent gadgets.[44] The artistic motives probably involved
some sort of slur against Gill, with whom Jouy once had been close. Cohl touched
Jouy's wrist on the first pass, but, since it did not draw blood, the fight continued. Then
Jouy put Cohl *hors de combat* with a minor wound on the shoulder. It would not be his
last duel.

Cohl's interests extended to areas other than caricature. In January 1881, for exam-
ple, *La Nouvelle Lune* reported that he was designing the costumes for Tillier's operetta
La Calza at the Fantaisies-Parisiennes. Soon Cohl was collaborating with Norès and
Arthur Cahen on his own play, *Plus de têtes chauves!* (No More Bald Heads!), which
opened on June 13, 1881.[45] The title is from an advertising slogan that appeared in *La
Nouvelle Lune* and other papers for Eau Malleron, a patent-medicine hair restorer.

The plot is complicated and full of witty innuendo. Eléanore laments that her father,
the eccentric inventor Valcomblé, spends more time on his work than in trying to
arrange a match for her. The doctor insists that any fiancé must be bald and therefore
eligible for his experiments. This disqualifies her ardent lover, Raoul, who has a magnificent mane. Rather than follow the doctor's advice to come back in thirty years,
Raoul instead returns disguised as an American Indian. The doctor takes him into his
service upon learning about his talent as a scalpist. Valcomblé tries to get a bald member of the Academy of Science interested in Eléanore by giving him a free treatment of
"Eau d'Hirsus." Raoul chases the academician away, then returns dressed in his regular

clothes but wearing a bald wig and claiming to have been scalped in the stairway. M. Valcomblé gladly gives the "bald" Raoul his daughter's hand.

"Sélénio" reviewed the farce in *La Nouvelle Lune*:

> Our cartoonist E. Cohl, with the aid of two accomplices, perpetrated an insanity that, every night at the Fantaisies-Parisiennes, gives the spectators great misfortune in their entrails.
>
> The title of this continual belly laugh stimulant: *Plus de têtes chauves!*
>
> I protest!
>
> If this scheme were successful, what would become of the ancient and powerful Society of Pate Advertisers, founded by our late lamented Simon who was the first to notice the abundance of plucked scalps in the orchestra seats. He had the magnificent idea of figuring how many millions of francs of rental income could be generated by pasting ads for toilet waters and American suspenders on these naked domes.[46]

The comedy was given thirteen performances, a rather mediocre run.[47]

The next year Cohl, Norès, and Cahen presented another one-act play, *Auteur par amour* (Made an Author by Love).[48] This was the story of Rita, a singer in a *café-concert*, who aspired to be a legitimate actress. She despises her suitor Gontran because he cannot offer her glory—only money. The chambermaid advises Gontran to disguise himself as a secret admirer. Rita receives him and listens to the play he is writing for her. But she discovers the hoax when a carte de visite falls from his pocket. Nevertheless she likes the play: "Write it and I'm yours!" Gontran says the story of the play will be the story of their love and they send for the mayor to marry them.

Cohl's next collaboration with Norès was not on a play, but on the *Lutèce* affair in 1884. In *La Nouvelle Lune* of May 31 and June 15 a writer named "J. Paralès" protested an attack on him by the Symbolist-Decadent periodical *Lutèce*. It had been founded in April 1883 by Léo Trézenick (Léon Epinette) as a review for young Left Bank poets. Cohl was listed as a collaborator, with Verlaine, Tailhade, et al., and he was hired to photograph the editors.[49] On June 30 *La Nouvelle Lune* printed a solemn obituary for Paralès, citing an overdose of sausage as the cause of death. It stated that Paralès and the editor of *Lutèce* had dueled. Cohl and Norès had acted as seconds. The weapons chosen were the "metric sausage of Nancy" and mustard. The unfortunate Paralès had suffocated after eating the sixth meter.[50]

Although it was such antics at *La Nouvelle Lune* that put Cohl into the limelight in the early 1880s, he contributed to other periodicals as well. He served on the staff of *Le Tam-Tam*, published by Alfred Le Petit (fig. 19). His friend Sélénio paid him another backhanded compliment about this association: "No surprise that the *Tam-Tam* is puffing itself up so much about its success."[51]

There were other minor contributions to *L'Esprit Gaulois*, *La Chronique Parisienne*, and *Le Charivari*—still the most prestigious of the satirical papers.[52] In 1885 he con-

28. "Progrès!" *L'Auberge des Adrets*, December 26, 1885.

29. "Ah quel nez!!!" *Le Bon Bock*,
April 18, 1885.

tributed drawings to two unusual publications, *L'Auberge des Adrets* and *Le Bon Bock*. The former revived the characters Robert Macaire and Bertrand from vaudeville, the bourgeois comic theater. Cohl's versions were derived from the archetypal character created by Daumier (after the actor Lemaître) in *Le Charivari* (fig. 28). The spirit of the paper was left-wing and anticapitalist. *Le Bon Bock (Echo des Brasseries Françaises)* was another publication with an ax to grind. Its goal was "to combat the invasion of German beer by encouraging the consumption of French beers." It was also the literary organ of the Société du Bon Bock, founded by Emile Bellot, the engraver made famous by Edouard Manet's portrait exhibited in the Salon of 1873. A small reproduction of the painting was part of the masthead of the paper. Cohl participated in Bellot's banquets[53] and drew a strange picture of a venomous German brasserie proprietor being choked by a little Frenchman (fig. 29). The magazine lasted only six months.

THE INCOHERENTS

With the breakup and dispersion of the Hydropathes, several smaller sects were formed. Cohl became involved with a group that was even more eccentric. Very little is known about the Incoherents,[54] but the evidence that we have indicates that he was one of the prime movers in the formation of the group.

The publisher Jules Lévy coined the phrase *les arts incohérents* as an antagonistic foil to the everyday expression *les arts décoratifs*. He succinctly expressed the philosophical basis of the group: "Gaiety is properly French, so let's be French."[55] Accordingly, he invited his friends to make some "incoherent" works of art to exhibit in his office in 1882. Cohl's "Lunes politiques et incohérentes" (Political and Incoherent Moons, fig. 30) was probably included in this first exhibition.

The joke caught on, so Lévy organized a month-long exhibition in September 1883 at the Vivienne Gallery, which was open to the public. It was advertised as "an exhibition of drawings by people who do not know how to draw." According to the published "rules," all works submitted would be shown except those considered obscene or serious. Cohl documented some of the entries in a cover for *Le Charivari* (fig. 31). In

30. "Lunes politiques et incohérentes," *Le Charivari*, October 25, 1883.

31. "Un Voyage chez les Incohérents,"
Le Charivari, October 25, 1883.

addition to his own "Portrait garanti ressemblant" (Portrait—Resemblance Guaranteed), there were strange drawings by Mesplès, Paul Bilhaud, Banès, and Langlois. Coquelin cadet's "Souvenir d'Etretat" captured the spirit of the show; his parody of Monet's 1883 Impressionist seascapes was nothing more than a horizontal squiggle. The success of the exhibition surprised everyone; 6,700 francs were raised from paid admissions and donated to public assistance.

In 1884 the group met regularly and was photographed on a May outing (fig. 32).[56] (In the photograph Lévy is the one crowned with a horn; Cohl is at the upper right, thumbing his nose.) Their fall show was eagerly awaited. To advertise it, Cohl again drew covers for *La Nouvelle Lune* (November 1, 1884) and *Le Charivari* (fig. 33). A typical exhibit was the travesty of John Singer Sargent's "Madame X" in the tradition of Salon caricatures by Cham (Amédée de Noé) and Bertall (Charles-Albert d'Arnoux). Cohl's entries included "La Salle Graffard," a parody of a painting by his friend Jean Béraud; "La Nuit de noces du brave charbonnier (Grande composition tragico-comique)" (The Coal Man's Wedding Night); and "Le Pauvre Pêcheur dans l'embarras" (The Poor Fisherman Having a Lot of Trouble), a satire of Puvis de Chavanne's "Pauvre Pêcheur," which had been shown at the Salon of 1881 (figs. 34, 35). The entrants were given mock Salon catalogue entries. Cohl's described him as "Caricaturist, amazing—

32. An Incoherent outing in 1884.

33. "Chez les Incohérents," *Le Charivari*, October 30, 1884.

ÉMILE COHL

LA SALLE GRAFFARD

34. "La Salle Graffard," *Catalogue illustré de l'exposition des arts incohérents*, 1884.

35. "Le Pauvre Pêcheur dans l'embarras," *Catalogue illustré de l'exposition des arts incohérents*, 1884.

when he blows his nose. Lives in the main section of Père-Lachaise [cemetery], third tomb on the right as you enter."[57]

La Nouvelle Lune praised Cohl's work in tongue-in-cheek Baudelairian terms:

The most fantastic canvases, the most bizarre still lifes, the zaniest puns, you'll find them all assembled and catalogued here. For his part, our collaborator Em. Cohl exposed masterpieces of humor and gaiety capable of eradicating the strongest *spleen*.[58]

The 1884 show was popular enough to contribute 9,000 francs to the Society for Public Education. A cartoon by Albert Robida captured the Dionysian public image of the group (fig. 36). It also reported the Incoherent invasion of the Ecole des Beaux-Arts.

36. Albert Robida: "Réveillon des artistes incohérents," *La Caricature*, December 27, 1884.

On March 11, 1885, a masked ball was held instead of an annual exhibition. Cohl attended dressed as an artichoke. By now the Incoherents were known to all fun-loving Parisians, as evidenced when *Le Courrier Français* devoted its entire issue of March 12 to the group. One page was filled by the startling drawing "Jules Lévy, Father of the Incoherents, Incoherently drawn by Emile Cohl" (fig. 37). Lévy's laughing face is surrounded by an aura of black-and-white rays through which a headless jester can be discerned with some difficulty. Over Cohl's backward signature at the bottom is Lévy's motto: "Frères, il nous faut rire" (Brothers, We Must Laugh). In the text, Lévy protested that his disciples were not the anarchists that academic painter Jean-Léon Gérôme had accused them of being, "but a new force, a complement and a supplement to the rules of art."[59]

Cohl's involvement with the Incoherents did not end in 1885. But increasingly his worries about André Gill were impinging on his other activities. Now his friend and master was suffering and near death in the notorious asylum of Charenton.

37. "Jules Lévy, le père des Incohérents, dessiné incohérentement par Emile Cohl," *Le Courrier Français*, March 12, 1885.

The Death of André Gill

On October 6, 1881, the editors of *La Nouvelle Lune* announced that Gill would begin contributing regularly to the paper. But only two weeks later they said that he had been hurt in an accident and could send no more drawings. The "accident" was a mental breakdown that Gill had suffered while traveling in Belgium.[60] He had been arrested and returned to Charenton for treatment for hallucinations.

Cohl's despair was evident when he reported the shocking event:

Only the memory of what used to be André Gill remains to us. When we would walk in the studio, the boss (as we liked to call him) would have a big smile for us and would regale us with real friendship. He took care of us, was interested in our little struggles, amazed at our progress, gave his precious advice with admirable patience. Ah! Especially those of us who lived next to him, in the community of our thoughts, we know what a loss to art it is with his disappearance.

He is mad. Poor and great artist, in you we see disappear more than a master, more than a friend: we lose a brother, a good and gentle older brother.[61]

Cohl was shocked and infuriated when, in the journal *Réveil*, Gill's former Communard stalwart and founder of *Le Temps*, Jules Vallès, wrote two articles that linked Gill's madness with what he perceived as Gill's political wavering.[62]

As Gill languished, Cohl proposed a subscription and organized a benefit performance at the Bouffes-Parisiens to provide him with a private room.[63] But as suddenly as it came, his "madness" unexpectedly went into remission and he was released on January 28, 1882.

Gill now devoted his time to painting and completed an ambitious entry for the Salon of 1882, "Le Fou" (The Madman),[64] for which his friend the actor Gil-Naza posed. He had played the insane Coupeau in the stage version of *L'Assomoir*. Gill based the picture on actual conditions at Charenton. But the public gave the painting a blasé reception, in part because the picture was badly hung, in part because of the unpleasant subject.

On May 9 Gill relapsed into confusion and wandered about the countryside for four days, terrifying the farmers of Bergères before he was arrested and permanently recommitted to the asylum of Saint-Maurice in Charenton.[65]

The next disaster happened in January 1883. The administration of Charenton obtained an order permitting them to seize Gill's property to settle their bill, and they hastily arranged a sale at the Hôtel des Ventes for January 17.[66] Prominent journalist Jules Claretie was appalled by the lack of justice and mercy shown the former enemy of the government, and by the fact that even Gill's most personal mementos were auctioned off:

They sold everything: drawings, pictures, sketches, ceramics, photographs with autographs, notebooks. It was all dumped in a macabre pile. At the madman's auction, one could feel the cruelty and misery.

Poor Gill! He is still alive, stirring—maybe he'll be back to normal tomorrow—but he has nothing left in the world, not a brush, not a palette, not a chair, not a volume of verse, nothing, not even the memory he possessed. And the glimmer of his brilliant past, extinguished.[67]

La Nouvelle Lune, on January 14, had urged its readers to attend the sale. Those sympathetic to Gill were angered by the callousness of the auctioneers, the lack of a catalogue, and the unannounced early start. Paul Eudel reported:

This auction, badly planned, was carried out to the end with an irritating carelessness. The felt hats, berets and old red wigs were disturbed; the sympathetic group yelled, whistled, stomped.

The whole room was riled up.[68]

After all the commotion, when the proceeds were counted, the sale brought only 10,320 francs.[69] About a week later Cohl sketched a portrait of Gill at Charenton, who appears oblivious to what had happened (fig. 38).

In February Cohl devoted his time to nursing the caricaturist, visiting him daily and neglecting his duties on *La Nouvelle Lune*. He sent in three portraits by Gill which he claimed demonstrated the artist's mental progress (fig. 39). Cohl also edited some memoirs and essays that were published as *Vingt années de Paris* in the hope of raising funds. In the preface Alphonse Daudet expressed his dismay at Gill's condition.[70]

Meanwhile, what should have been a joyous event was overshadowed by these misfortunes; Emile Cohl's daughter was born in May 1883. He named her Marcelle Andrée in honor of his friend.

In October Cohl took Gill out to dine with a few friends. Except for this small circle, the group of sympathizers was dwindling at an alarming rate. *La Ville de Paris* chided:

In Paris we always have an open hand. But daily cares make us forgetful and many people whom he had treated like friends gave Gill up for lost when the poor man was floundering between the extremes of his horrible malady. They finally abandoned him. It is thanks to Emile Cohl, who spared neither his time nor his effort, that we have been able to start a fund that will provide for the invalid's basic needs.[71]

Cohl and Gill were photographed together in Paris during a November outing. In one of these pictures (fig. 40), intended for friends only, we see Cohl sadly contemplating the listless figure of his master, who is staring with unfocused eyes.

Cohl organized a benefit performance of Gill's play *L'Habit* at the Gaîté-Montparnasse with Aristide Bruant, but only 400 francs were gained after expenses.[72] At the same time he personally organized an exhibition that opened on December 15 for one

38. Portrait of André Gill at Charenton, January 26, 1883.

39. André Gill: "Nouveaux Croquis" (three portraits of Emile Cohl), *La Nouvelle Lune*, March 4, 1883.

40. Charles Studio: Photograph of Cohl and Gill.

38

39

40

month at the Vivienne Gallery. The show, with sixty paintings, sixty drawings, and 250 caricatures, testified to Cohl's unrelenting energy in arranging loans and to the generosity of Gill's friends. Somehow he had even arranged to show "Le Fou," which had been sold to an anonymous Englishman at the January sale. Now, with pathetic irony, thanks to all the sensational publicity, the painting became the exhibition's macabre hit.[73] Cohl intended to raise money for Gill's cause primarily through the sale of the caricatures. It is almost certain that he had bought most of these himself at the January sale.[74] There were publications designed to stimulate interest in the show, including "André Gill et son oeuvre" by Cohl,[75] and in *La Nouvelle Lune* a poster showing the artist shackled to a symbolic ball and chain (fig. 41).[76] The exhibition was sketched by Robida (fig. 42) and well attended, but sales were so poor that Cohl had to buy back most of the works and still had to pay the gallery its commission. The financial strain was so great that three years later it was reported that "Cohl is still today paying to liquidate this bad deal."[77]

Gill's condition deteriorated into complete paralysis and loss of speech. He died with Cohl by his side in the early hours of May Day, 1885.[78] An 1885 portrait of Cohl included a symbolic vignette showing him following the hearse as it departed from Charenton (fig. 43). Clovis Hugues gave the eulogy at the funeral on May 4. The devotion of Cohl, who led the cortège, was noted in several obituaries, including one in *La Chronique Parisienne*:

> [Gill] vegetated, dreamed and suffered. Few careers have been as lamentable as this one in its decline. However, Gill had friends until the final hour. M. Emile Cohl was among this little number. A talented caricaturist and devoted student of his master, Cohl went to see him regularly at Charenton. It was he who arranged the funeral rites. This affection was the caricaturist's last consolation.[79]

Etienne Carjat, whose letter had brought the two together in 1878, also applauded Cohl at the dedication of Gill's tomb at Père-Lachaise.

> I would like to acknowledge the noble and touching conduct of another modest young artist who could not miss this last meeting. The name of Emile Cohl is on all your lips because you are aware of the affectionate, fraternal care that he administered during this long and lamentable malady. Cohl's faithfulness will be a consolation against the brazen ingratitude of those whom he pushed and overpraised in the early days.[80]

Throughout Gill's illness, Cohl had railed against the uncaring attitude of the government and the fickle public. Like Carjat, he believed that failure to recognize Gill's talent and his continual harassment had finally crushed him. Later Cohl wrote, "You do not have to search for the cause of his madness; it was the sadness of his situation that determined it. It was ingratitude, injustice and indifference, swallowed in silence, but

41

42

41. André Gill (or Emile Cohl): "En attendant,"
La Nouvelle Lune, December 15, 1883.

42. Albert Robida: "A l'exposition des oeuvres
d'André Gill," *La Caricature,* December 29,
1883.

43. Uzès (A. Lemot): Portrait of Emile Cohl,
Le Courrier Français, September 12, 1885.

43

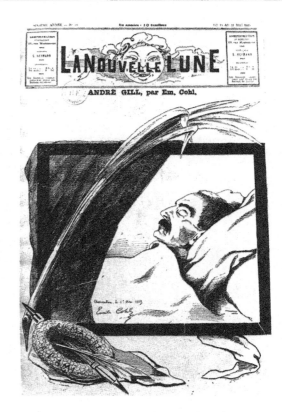

44. "André Gill," *La Nouvelle Lune*,
May 15–31, 1885.

chronically, that took Gill to Charenton."[81] Equally dismaying, the original large group of supporters had completely disappeared by 1885. For Cohl, the desertion by Gill's old radical friends, especially Vallès, was painful. Being alone with Gill when he died left a bitter memory that was never eradicated. He wrote in 1927:

> It is to these memories that I owe the comforting misanthropy that has taken over. It's no question of egotism, but a sort of sullenness, a protest directed at Gill's contemporaries who deserted him and left him all alone when he was floored by that terrible illness.[82]

Emile Cohl wrote no final tribute to Gill, nor did he make any funerary speeches. Instead he drew the deathbed portrait that *La Nouvelle Lune* published on May 15, 1885 (fig. 44).

That was the last Cohl drawing to appear there until June 20, 1886. Perhaps he counted the staff of the paper among the unsympathetic defectors and withdrew his collaboration. From 1885 to 1892, there were only eighteen original Cohl drawings (although the editors often reprinted his old works, effacing his signature). Without Cohl's stimulation, and with the death of the publisher Heymann in 1886, *La Nouvelle Lune* declined rapidly.[83]

Where did the death of Gill leave Cohl? Certainly after seven years of intimacy there was a profound personal and spiritual vacuum. He had become well known by 1885, but his reputation was linked to his master's. In addition to his loss, his marriage to Marie Servat was not going well, an indirect result of his attentions to Gill.

ANOTHER DUEL

At some point during Gill's final days, Marie left Emile Cohl and moved in with Henri Gauthier-Villars (1859–1931), the son of an established publisher of literary and scientific books, who, around 1887, would adopt the pseudonym "Willy" and become a favorite popular writer of the *belle époque*.

Cohl undoubtedly had first met Willy as a Hydropathe and had worked with him and photographed him while he was writing a musical review column under the name Gaston Villars for *Lutèce* in 1885. The strained relationship finally reached a crisis when Cohl and Willy fought a duel on October 25, 1886. Since it was considered less gentlemanly to fight over a woman than over "artistic" differences, the ostensible insult was in regard to Gill. Willy's notes, cited by his biographer, Caradec, recorded (not necessarily objectively) the tragicomic incident:

> One day I declared to this fervent disciple that the best poems of *La Muse à Bibi* were owed to the signature of Louis de Gramont, not to André Gill. Cohl was indignant. I held my ground. I should also say that a woman's involvement turned the atmosphere sour. The seconds on my opponent's side included the high priest of the Incoherents, the facetious Jules Lévy and I don't know how many other journalists. They interviewed my seconds, Beauvais-Devaux, celebrated duelist, and Lucien Normand, militant royalist and a practicing Catholic who dreaded being implicated in a mortal sin. We left for the Island of La Grande Jatte. It was a fight without interest, but while picking up Cohl's sword, I stuck my eye with its point and was bathed in blood. Doctor Devillers, renowned swordsman and my colleague at the Salle Miminque, shouted "Halt," walked over to me and pronounced gravely, "That's it." I was astonished. "Go on and you'll get just what you deserve. How many times have I told you to keep your head up."
>
> Cohl interrupted, rather concerned, "Doctor, I hope that his eye isn't gashed."
>
> After a quick examination the doctor replied, "No, just the eyebrow is cut." Then he continued his lecture on the importance of keeping one's head up when crossing swords.
>
> I returned to Paris with my seconds and Lucien Normand ran off to confession.[84]

The "procès-verbal" signed by the four witnesses (including Cohl's second, Georges Duval) tells a somewhat different story: "On the first engagement there were no wounds. On the second engagement Mr. Gauthier-Villars was struck above the right eye and on the right hand. In the opinion of the doctors, Mr. Gauthier-Villars was found to be in a state of definite inferiority, and the witnesses stopped the fighting."[85] In other words, Cohl won.

Marie would remain with Willy until her death, adding one more bitter twist to Cohl's memories of his life after Gill.

ALTHOUGH Gill had been able to provide little actual artistic guidance since 1881, his influence had been substantial. Now Cohl's independence was forced upon him. These events also left him, at the age of twenty-nine, embittered and sardonic. The directions his work took after Gill's death and the breakup of his marriage suggest that he was no longer restrained by others' expectations. Repeatedly he demonstrated his willingness to explore unorthodox areas of expression, even before the most surprising area—the cinema—was invented.

■

CHAPTER TWO

Art for Two Sous

PHOTOGRAPHY

Emile Cohl had served as official photographer for the 1885 Incoherents Ball. It was his newest interest, and his seriousness about pursuing it had been affirmed by renting a space in which to install a portrait studio. Among the few remaining examples of the work he did there are the tipped-in glyptographs that illustrate a very strange book called *Têtes de pipes* by "L.-G. Mostrailles," the pseudonym of Georges Rall and Léo Trézenick, the editor and publisher of *Lutèce*.[1] The title means "thumbnail sketches," and the album offered prose portraits of the leaders of various literary movements. Each personality was also represented by one of Cohl's photographs. But the strange thing is that Mostrailles's commentaries were all crudely derogatory. (Apparently the art of the backhanded compliment was in vogue.) Cohl himself was one of the celebrities:

EMILE COHL

Known especially as André Gill's pupil, whose moustache and hat he has successfully copied, but not his drawing style. Has caricatured here and there, from the late *Carillon* to the *Amusant*, by way of *Charivari*. That's why he launched *La Nouvelle Lune. Lune*, yes; *Nouvelle*—ha! ha!

One day when he had nothing else to do but reread Boileau, the verse, "Be a mason, if that be your talent," caught his eye. He understood the advice of the master—and followed it. That explains why this pen-pusher and scribbler (he has written two sonnets and they say that Lemerre hopes to assemble them in a volume of complete works) has retired—for now—and is doing photography, which the author of *L'Alluvion* is using to put butter on the spinach in his pictures. And he's doing it well. Cohl may have his esoteric caricature and his sugary poetry on his conscience, but his photography is excellent and hardly banal. His studios are already the rendez-vous of all artistic and literary Paris. He knows how to put life in his photos while his colleagues try only to catch the resemblance. Cohl has given up the pencil for the lens. He has the talent and the courage to be a mason and he has succeeded—an architectural triumph.[2]

Cohl protested that he had never caricatured in *Le Journal Amusant*, that he was not the founder of *La Nouvelle Lune*, that he could not be reproached if his moustache resembled Gill's, which resembled Nadar's, which resembled Van Dyck's, etc. But he acknowledged his admiration of Gill and that his photography studio was doing well:

> You state that my Art Photography studios (18, rue Saint-Laurent and 81–83 boulevard de Strasbourg, on the 3rd floor) are the rendezvous of artistic Paris. In fact I have been photographing all the young literary figures, the Ancients and the Unknowns, the Victor Hugos of tomorrow.[3]

In his own portrait (fig. 45) we see a slight, sensitive young man of twenty-eight. He is modishly dressed, but his expression is surprisingly serious. The other photographs reflect his personal friendship with most of the subjects. They are relaxed and intimate. He captured Norès's pranksterish twinkle, the intensity of the young Symbolist Moréas, and the self assuredness of Goudeau, founder of the Hydropathes (figs. 46–48). Verlaine's portrait is especially striking as he scowls directly at the lens (fig. 49). Laurent Tailhade and Léon Cladel refused to pose, so Cohl substituted pictures of a rose and an ear stuffed with cotton (fig. 50).[4] The Mostrailles book is a good example of the

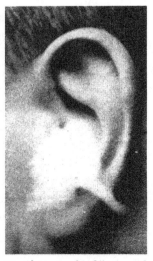

45. Self-photograph, 1885.

50. Photograph of "Léon Cladel."

46. Photograph of Edouard Norès, 1885.

47. Photograph of Jean Moréas.

48. Photograph of Emile Goudeau.

49. Photograph of Paul Verlaine.

cliquish schoolboy side of the Symbolist movement, and it is difficult to tell if the catty tone is the result of actual petty literary rivalries or practical joking. In any case, *Le Petit Bottin des lettres et des arts*, a literary *Who's Who* edited by Paul Adam, Félix Fénéon, and Oscar Méténier, retaliated by identifying Mostrailles as a "Bicephalic Monster."[5]

Cohl's interest in portrait photography was a natural outgrowth of his profession as a caricaturist. The goal of the two arts was similar, in that both strove to capture a likeness of the sitter that could be saved as a memento or, in the case of famous personalities, sold in the streets. It is significant that the vogue of the *portrait-charge* facial caricature coincides with the rise and fall of the popularity of the *carte de visite* photographic calling card in the 1850s and 1860s.[6] Many caricaturists had discovered at an early date that photographs provided an easy way to achieve a good likeness of the sitter in their drawings. Carjat and Nadar had both used them as the basis for their *portraits-charges*. There was a common belief, expressed by Nadar, that photography was a paradoxical medium; it could only render the nominal surface appearance of the sitter, while the caricaturist could transfigure "into *comicalities* these hundreds of different faces and conserve the unmistakable physical resemblance, the features, personality—the character, that is the moral and intellectual resemblance—of each one."[7]

The use of photographs gave many of Cohl's caricatures, especially some of his early ones, a strongly iconic aspect. The face of "Edouard Philippe," for example, is presented frontally and mounted on a symmetrical body (fig. 51). Because it approaches

51. "Edouard Philippe," *La Nouvelle Lune*, February 12, 1881.

photographic likeness, Cohl felt it was necessary to include symbolic "attributes" to alert the viewer to the subject's significance, hence the exploding firecrackers, which form a kind of radiance about the publisher's head and identify the titles of his publications.

Cohl must have quarreled with André Gill on the subject of photography because the older caricaturist held a conservative view, scorned the use of photos, and insisted on sketching from life or from memory. Once he explained in a monologue why he favored traditional caricature techniques.

> I have a thousand reasons . . . for preferring above all others this way [caricature] of reproducing the human face. Photography has neither consistency nor serious value. It will pass away and get lost. In short, it's nothing but paper.[8]

Though his social views were progressive, Gill's aesthetics were quite traditional where photography was concerned. His ideas were consistent with those of academician Charles Blanc, who in 1867 wrote in his influential *Grammaire des arts du dessin*: "Who does not know how deceptive is the truth of the photographic image, which pretends to be infallible? The painter, endowed with a mind, can evoke the mind of his model, but how can a machine evoke a soul?"[9]

A few months after Gill's death, Cohl's guilty feelings emerged when he and the ghost of Gill engaged in an imaginary dialogue on photography.

> The Shade: You have worked scarcely ten years and now you have been copying and recopying me for six months at *La Nouvelle Lune*. . . . What good was my advice? Look what it made you—I hardly dare to say it: a photographer. Yes, that's the dirty word. It makes me gag. I know what you'll say, that we could agree on some of its collodionesque qualities, but what does that prove? That your equipment is good.
>
> Me: Ah! Give me a chance. I'm not the only artist who has dipped his pencil in silver nitrate!: Nadar, Carjat, Bertall![10]

Whether it was because Gill's ghost finally won out or because photography was not as lucrative as he had hoped, Cohl's career as a portraitist was short-lived. No further mention of it is made after 1885, but in the course of this experience he acquired valuable technical knowledge that he would put to good use more than thirty years later. At the same time, we can surmise that Cohl would continue to brood over the doubts of Gill's ghost concerning the value of photography as a representational art form.

OTHER INCOHERENT ACTIVITIES

As long as Cohl was a driving force, the Incoherents continued their public ascent. By 1886 they had become identified with the decadent, almost maniacal pursuit of gaiety often associated with the *belle époque*. Their popularity extended far beyond the original small coterie, and all of Paris took note of their provocative activities.

Their second ball was in April 1886 (fig. 52): "All of young merry Paris is sentenced to it."[11] *Le Courrier Français* devoted a special issue to the Incoherents; there was an "Incoherent Revue" at La Scala, a "Café des Incohérents" on rue Fontaine,[12] and even an Incoherent novel by Charles Joliet, which was illustrated by Steinlen.[13] Many leading artists of the popular press were represented at the fall exhibition at the Eden-Théâtre (October 17–December 19). Among them were Henri Somm, Caran d'Ache, Henri Pille, Willette, Robida, and de Sta. Henri de Toulouse-Lautrec showed an "incoherent" work under the name "Tolau-Segroeg, Montmartre Hungarian."[14] The catalogue was designed by Jules Chéret, the leading poster artist (fig. 270), and the exhibitors' passes were strange works by Cohl (fig. 53). His catalogue entry contained an "Incoherent" portrait (fig. 54). In a piece that travesties the genre of critical Salon tours, Curty de Saint-Volfor was led through the exhibition by Cohl, for whom the exertion apparently was excessive:

> I came back and found Cohl lateral. He was admiring his own portrait made in five minutes by an artist who used only cold cream and collodion without being able to make Cohl look odious. While awaiting this stupefying image, the likable artist

52. Adrien Marie: "Souvenirs du bal des Incohérents," *Le Monde Illustré*, April 17, 1886.

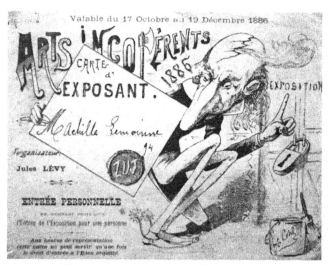

53. Carte d'exposant, Incoherent Exhibition, 1886.

54. Anon.: Portrait of Emile Cohl, *Catalogue de l'exposition*, 1886.

55. "L'Enterrement de l'Incohérence," *La Nouvelle Lune*, March 13, 1887.

passed out and fell to the floor. His landlord had found him there by chance and, having just been paid, was giving him caring attention. So I slipped into the next room for some air.[15]

Lévy and Cohl announced that the 1887 ball would be the last. "L'Enterrement de l'Incohérence" (The Burial of Incoherence) showed the masks of the organizers hung on a clothesline (fig. 55). The dancing clowns, lettering, and curvilinear graphic style show the influence of Chéret.

The Incoherent movement was not universally liked. One of its chief enemies was John Grand-Carteret, author of the first important treatise on late nineteenth-century caricature.[16] He regretted that the older generation of caricaturists (such as Alfred Grévin) were being neglected in favor of "this new process that we are seeing, this Incoherence." He equated the grotesqueness of the Incoherents' drawings with the literary Decadents whom he also disliked. The scolding continued:

Really, what is an Incoherent? What is Incoherence? Giving a portrait of this singular character who tends to be found in Montmartre, the *Revue Illustrée* said, "The Inco-herent is a painter or a bookstore clerk, a poet or a bureaucrat or a sculptor. But one thing distinguishes him: however he produces his incoherence, he would like to pass for something he isn't. The clerk becomes a tenor; the painter writes verse; the architect debates free love, all with great exuberance."

Incoherence is the result of a social state such as ours in which people who should know better are only affirming their impotence.[17]

His book became a standard reference work, as a result of which Grand-Carteret's anti-Incoherent bias had a disastrous effect on the appreciation of Cohl's career. He never mentions Lévy nor Cohl by name, but it is clear whom he means when he refers to the "Gill school."

Gill—scant satisfaction for him—has pupils and continuators. There are at least sev-eral who like to call themselves thusly, boys with restricted talent who know more or less how to draw but are possessed with the comic idea and, perhaps unconsciously, the intuition of the grotesque.[18]

It is significant that Grand-Carteret used the phrase "know . . . how to draw" because it was well known that Lévy had described the Incoherents as "people who don't know how to draw."

Although the movement had been "buried" in 1887, it was resurrected in full vigor in 1889. The exhibition catalogue featured another cover by Chéret (fig. 56). Lautrec mocked the Salon favorite Puvis de Chavannes by declaring himself a student of "Pubis de Cheval." Cohl's nine contributions were "normal" (that is, non-Incoherent) carica-tures such as "Francisque Sarcey" (fig. 57). His catalogue notice chided him for recently straying from the Incoherent path.

Cohl (Emile-Ernest) [everyone was cited as "Ernest," another *blague*]. Was devoted to Incoherence but for a while has dropped out with shocking offhandedness, but having no less talent because of having done so. Does caricature and lives at 20, rue Cadet, in the house he was born in.

Perhaps as a result of Cohl's temporary slackening of interest, there were no Incoher-ent manifestations again until the ball and exhibit at the Folies-Bergères in 1891. (There was no catalogue, so it is not known if Cohl participated.) But by 1893 he was back with eighty-seven entries at the Olympia Music Hall exhibition:

Cohl (Emile). To properly credit this name would take a quarter of the poster. How-ever, know that he lives at 92, boulevard de Clichy, on the sixth floor. Balcony on the boulevard and the Moulin-Rouge; Water and gas on every floor.[19]

One last Incoherent Ball was celebrated in April 1895, with invitations designed by Steinlen.[20]

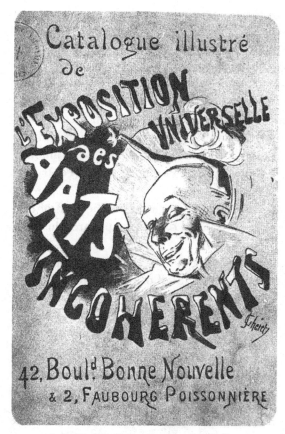

56. Jules Chéret: Cover for *Catalogue illustré
de l'exposition des arts incohérents*, 1889.

57. "Francisque Sarcey,"
*Catalogue illustré de l'exposition
des arts incohérents*, 1889.

Looking back at the Incoherents, we sense a certain desperation in their program as stated by Lévy. The movement was both defiant—assaulting the decorum perpetuated by the Salons and the Academy—and escapist, denying the problems of French society during the "banquet years" by drowning them in forced mirth. Similar generative mechanisms would produce the Dadaists and Surrealists in the next century. In addition to their antagonism to "seriousness," there was also an underlying fear of boredom implied in their frenetic activities. "Boredom," wrote Lévy, "there is the enemy of Incoherence."[21]

As Emile Cohl was a major force behind the Incoherent movement from 1881 to 1893, one would expect its aesthetic program to have profoundly affected his artistic endeavors. This is, in fact, the case. But to see its ultimate flowering, it is necessary to wait for his career in the cinema.

OTHER PUBLICATIONS

Cohl continued to live an active and varied life in the last decades of the nineteenth century.[22] His drawings appeared in some of the most important periodicals and reflected many contemporary changes in the art of caricature. His contributions to the established humor magazines diminished after the death of Gill, but a few of his major works appeared in the prestigious *Charivari.* "Quelques Envois au Salon (Section de sculptures)" (Some Salon Entries [Sculpture Section], fig. 58) posed various public figures next to their "follies." As a friendly gesture, he included Carjat and Lorin among the gallery of leading Symbolist and Decadent poets in "La Poésie en 1886" (Poetry in 1886) (fig. 59).[23]

Moloch included Emile Cohl in his large 1887 group caricature of the staff of *La Chronique Parisienne* (fig. 60), but in fact only a few Cohl drawings appeared in that paper.

The contribution to Robida's *La Caricature*, beginning in May 1887, is more important. Cohl's ambitious "Cadres de l'armée des peintres" (Staff of the Painters' Army)

58. "Quelques Envois au Salon (Section de sculptures)," *Le Charivari,* April 26, 1886.

59. "La Poésie en 1886," *Le Charivari,* June 17, 1886

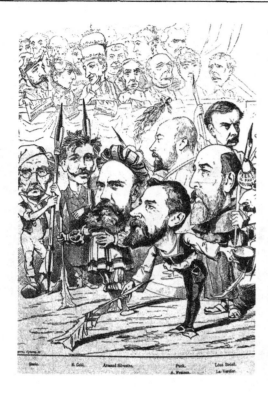

60. Moloch (B. Colomb): "Au bal costumé,"
La Chronique Parisienne, January 23, 1887 (detail).

and "Grand Revue des peintres passée par Gustave Boulanger" (Painters Reviewed by Gustave Boulanger, fig. 61) presented over fifty caricatures of contemporary Salon painters (now mostly forgotten except for Carolus-Duran, Cabanel, Puvis de Chavannes, and a few others). In all, there were ten drawings in *La Caricature* in 1887, eight in 1888, then no more.

Cohl's most traditional work was for *Les Hommes d'Aujourd'hui,* the periodical that Gill and the eighteen-year-old prodigy Félicien Champsaur had founded in 1876. Following the model of Carjat's *Le Diogène* (1856), they had published a caricature and a prose portrait of a celebrity each week. Following his first attack in 1881, Gill was unable to continue working on the magazine, after having illustrated the first 142 numbers. Charles Vanier acquired it in 1885 and farmed out drawing assignments to numerous artists, including Cohl, whose first caricature appeared in 1886.[24] The thirty-one issues he illustrated often contained caricatures of old friends from the Gill studio and from the days of the Hydropathes, including Champsaur (fig. 62).[25] He also drew people like Ernest Renan (no. 250), whom he admired but did not know personally. There were leading caricaturists, such as Robida (fig. 63). His 1898 drawing of Lautrec, significantly, depicted the artist as a caricaturist rather than as a painter or poster designer (fig. 64).[26] The drawing on the easel was derived from an actual self-caricature by Lautrec that Cohl must have seen at an Incoherents exhibition.[27]

61. "Grande Revue des peintres passée par Gustave Boulanger," *La Caricature*, May 21, 1887.

Cohl himself was the *homme d'aujourd'hui* (man of the hour) in number 288 (late 1886). Uzès, a fellow pupil of Gill, drew a caricature based on the 1885 Mostrailles photograph (fig. 65). The text, signed "Pierre et Paul," has provided us with much early biographical information.

Les Hommes d'Aujourd'hui reflected the prevailing avant-garde aesthetics, whether Symbolist and Decadent in the 1880s (represented by the contributions of Verlaine, Joris-Karl Huysmans, and Jules Laforgue), or Synthetist and Neo-Impressionist in the early 1890s. Number 373, for example, published Georges Seurat's portrait of Paul Signac, with text by Félix Fénéon (1890). Signac's portrait of Maximilien Luce appeared in number 376. In 1892 Emile Bernard drew Emile Schuffenecker (389) and Vincent Van Gogh (390). The Odilon Redon (386) and Paul Gauguin (440) issues had Schuffenecker drawings and texts by Charles Morice. Perhaps the most remarkable collaboration was number 387, devoted to Paul Cézanne, whose portrait was by Camille Pissarro, with an essay by Bernard.

62

62. "Félicien Champsaur," *Les Hommes d'Aujourd'hui* no. 327.

63. "Albert Robida," *Les Hommes d'Aujourd'hui,* March 27, 1897.

64. "De Toulouse-Lautrec," *Les Hommes d'Aujourd'hui* no. 460, 1898.

63

64

65. a) Uzès (A. Lemot): "Emile Cohl," *Les Hommes d'Aujourd'hui* no. 288, 1886. b) Uzès (A. Lemot): Original drawing for above.

From October 1886 to January 1887, Cohl and Georges Duval published *Les Chambres Comiques, Revue Satirique des Débats Parlementaires* (The Comic Senate, Satirical Review of Parliamentary Debates). Cohl illustrated the articles with caricatures and contributed political jokes. There were also numerous portraits of contemporaries and of the authors themselves. In one, Duval is sharpening his quill beside Cohl, who is testing the point of his pen. The publisher Lévy watches from the background (fig. 66). Elsewhere Cohl and Duval were shown as jacks-in-the-box or caught guzzling wine (figs. 67, 68).

Only seventeen numbers were published, so the reception of the little weekly paper was less than enthusiastic. Pierre et Paul's description may give a clue to its lack of success; apparently its political orientation was perceived by some to be ambiguous:

. . . a vigorous pamphlet published by Georges Duval in which some naive ones thought they saw an Orleanist conspiracy, as if the eighteen years of service to the

66. *Les Chambres Comiques*,
October 26, 1886.

67. *Les Chambres Comiques*,
November 16, 1886.

68. *Les Chambres Comiques*,
January 11, 1887.

Republic that Duval has to his credit and the antecedents of Emile Cohl do not quash
this grotesque supposition in advance.[28]

Cohl's toy-soldier caricature of General Georges Boulanger (fig. 69), who was then
courting Royalist factions, certainly seems to be devoid of Orleanist sympathies.

Cohl also tried his hand as a book illustrator. His most important work was Jules
Lermina's 1887 version of *L'Auberge des Adrets*,[29] for which he made forty-four caricatural and noncaricatural drawings (fig. 70). One of them contained portraits of Cohl and
Lermina (fig. 71). We can only speculate as to why Cohl showed the author (an old
friend of Gill) casting an ugly corpulent shadow behind him.

69. *Les Chambres Comiques*, October 12, 1886.

70. Illustration for Jules Lermina, *L'Auberge des adrets*, 1887.

71. Portraits of Jules Lermina and Cohl from *L'Auberge des adrets*, 1887.

Cohl drew caricatures of the actor and monologuist Félix Galipaux for the covers of two of his books, *Galipettes* and *Encore des Galipettes* (fig. 72).[30] He also illustrated a similar book by his friend Coquelin cadet, *Pirouettes*.[31] In one of the drawings (fig. 73) he made an "incoherent" visual pun by literalizing the expression *envoyer des postillons* ("to splutter," literally, to send out the escorts).

In November 1887 Vanier published the first monograph on Gill, *André Gill, sa vie, bibliographie de ses oeuvres par Armand Lods et Véga*. "Véga" was definitely Emile Cohl.[32] The extent of his collaboration on the text is unknown, but the biography draws on Cohl's feuilleton biography that had been published in *La Nouvelle Lune*. His 1883 Charenton portrait of Gill and the deathbed portrait were reproduced.

By 1890 Cohl's reputation was sufficiently established to warrant a biographical sketch in *Le Grand Dictionnaire Larousse*. The article emphasized his relation to Gill and declared his illustrations for Duval's *Les Chambres Comiques* to be his most important work.[33]

In 1891 he illustrated *Chansons fin de siècle* by Jules Oudot.[34] One picture shows Ernest Meissonier pursuing William Bouguereau on a hobbyhorse (a joking reference to the artist's well-publicized preoccupation with Muybridge's photographs) (fig. 74). *Chansons à la blague*, a book in a similar vein, was illustrated by Cohl in 1895.[35] Several

72. Cover for Félix Galipaux, *Encore des Galipettes*, 1889.

73. Illustration for Coquelin cadet, *Pirouettes*, 1888.

74. "Les Deux Salons," from Jules Oudot, *Chansons fin de siècle*, 1891.

illustrated song sheets, banquet menus, souvenirs from a magic act, and other ephemera from this period remain in the Courtet-Cohl collection.

COHL AND ANTI-SEMITISM

Like many of his countrymen, Emile Cohl became entangled in the contentious national debate that followed the treason conviction of Captain Alfred Dreyfus in December 1894. The incident raised serious questions about the role of the military and of religion in politics and launched an investigation into government corruption and freedom of the press. It also catapulted into prominence a small group of vicious anti-Semites who used the Jewish Dreyfus as the scapegoat for decades of pent-up race hatred. Cohl's opinions and the extent of his involvement are known only from one activity—his occasional contributions to the weekly newspaper supplement *La Libre Parole Illustrée*. Nevertheless, this collaboration places him in the anti-Semitic and anti-Dreyfusard camp.

The paper *La Libre Parole* was founded in 1892 by Edouard Drumont (1844–1917), who called himself "the chief rabbi of anti-Semitism."[36] Its illustrated supplement began in July 1893. Cohl's contributions began in November, several months before the Dreyfus story broke. According to his notebook, he appears to have submitted drawings every month until he quit in August 1895. He resumed his collaboration sporadically from August 1897 through August 1899.[37]

Cohl probably first became familiar with Drumont's name and anti-Semitic program from his 1886 best-seller, *La France Juive* (Jewish France), which blamed competing Jewish financiers for the collapse of the largest Catholic bank, the subsequent recession, and most of society's evils since the Middle Ages.[38] Cohl's published drawings indicate that he was in accord with Drumont's racist attitude toward Jews. His "Les qualités du Juif d'après la méthode de Gall" (Jewish Virtues According to [phrenologist] Gall's Methods)[39] represents the standard Jewish stereotypical traits as ironic attributes. Thus "Veneration" is illustrated by a man worshiping a giant coin; "Work" shows a Jewish boss supervising two laborers; and "Patriotism" depicts a businessman selling arms to a Prussian. All these vignettes are superimposed on a caricatural head with exaggerated Semitic features. Another drawing, Cohl's portrait of Drumont "settling" the Panama Canal scandal (fig. 75), indicates the artist's respect for Drumont. The historical reference is to the bankruptcy of the Panama Canal Company in 1892. *La Libre Parole* capitalized on the scandal involving two Jewish officers of the company. While not overtly anti-Semitic, Cohl's drawing clearly demonstrates the desire shared by many to turn to drastic measures and to extragovernmental heroes like Drumont for cures for the nation's ills.

Drumont's paper, which had a circulation of over 200,000, scooped the established press when it was the first to publish the news of Dreyfus's arrest in October 1894. While Dreyfus was exiled on Devil's Island, the facts of his false accusation and evidence of a military cover-up gradually emerged. But he was not pardoned and reinstated until 1906, and until then Drumont continued his nonstop diatribe against Jews in the military, in banks, indeed in all walks of life. Cohl's contributions to *La Libre*

75. "Edouard Drumont réglant la question du Panama," *La Libre Parole Illustré*, September 25, 1897.

Parole Illustrée reflected the mounting anti-Semitic fervor and Drumont-worship that the affair engendered during the "Dreyfus years."[40]

Late nineteenth-century anti-Semitism was widespread and arose from complex social, political, and economic circumstances.[41] Its origins were in left-wing causes and, to some extent, were an outgrowth of the anticlerical, revolutionary position of Marx in *On the Jewish Question* (1844). Anti-Semitism was incipient in many of the liberal and socialist issues of the 1880s. It is only necessary to examine the stereotypes in an anticapitalist cartoon such as Cohl's "Progrès" (fig. 28) to see the tendency to blame the social and economic crises on the prevalent myth of Jewish financial domination.

Michael Marrus has described three strains of French anti-Semitism: the socialist-Boulangist faction (those willing to place their faith in such unlikely figures as Boulanger, who committed suicide in 1891); conservative Catholics (for whom the Jews supplanted the Masons as favorite bogeys); and the nationalists (on the lookout for "the enemy within" and sympathetic to the writing of Maurice Barrès).[42] This third category was the one in which Emile Cohl fit. Witnessing the demoralizing scandals and corruption of the 1880s and 1890s, Cohl and hundreds of thousands of others rallied around Drumont's cry of "France for the French," and put the blame on anarchists, the Germans, the Protestants, and, increasingly, the Jews. In his analysis of the demographics of French anti-Semitism, Stephen Wilson found that blue-collar workers, artisans, and the military constituted the majority of anti-Dreyfus sympathizers.[43] Cohl was a fervent nationalist and promilitary. He remained a volunteer reservist until he was mustered out because of his age, and he produced an album illustrating the history of French military costumes.

When Emile Zola's open letter "J'accuse" appeared in *L'Aurore* on January 13, 1898, it exposed the injustice of Dreyfus's condemnation, split the country into bitter opposition, and redefined traditional political alignments.

Cohl was hardly alone among his colleagues in supporting Drumont. Many in Gill's former circle of old Republicans rallied to the cause, and many names associated with the popular press (especially the *Chat Noir* group) appeared in the pages of *La Libre Parole Illustrée*, including Adolphe Willette, Alphonse Allais, Job (Jacques Onfray de Bréville), Charles Huard, and Jules Jouy. Among the most prominent anti-Dreyfusard humorists were Jean-Louis Forain, Willette (who ran for a seat in the Chamber of Deputies as the candidate of the "anti-Semitic" party in 1889 and was Cohl's friend until his death in 1926), and Caran d'Ache, who founded the journal *Psst . . . !* in 1898 as a response to Zola. Stephen Wilson acknowledged the influence of these contributions:

> The pictorial representation of Jewish stereotypes by [Forain, Willette, and Caran d'Ache] and other artists must have been one of the most powerful and effective weapons of antisemitic propaganda, and to judge by the persistence of such images into the mid-twentieth century, they were an authentic reflection of popular antisemitism at the profoundest level.[44]

Although they were distinctly a minority, some humorists rallied to Dreyfus's defense, including Henri-Gabriel Ibels, who responded to Caran d'Ache's magazine with his own *Le Sifflet*. Among his contributors was the young Canadian artist Raoul Barré, whom we shall encounter later. Other artists, such as Steinlen, demonstrate the ambiguity of the times; he was pro-Dreyfus but continued to represent Jews as stereotypical bankers and landowners.[45]

As historians committed to the "warts and all" approach to biography, we must accept the fact of Emile Cohl's anti-Semitism, just as we cannot deny D. W. Griffith's racism and Leni Riefenstahl's Nazi association. At the same time it is necessary to contextualize and rationalize these ideological alignments in an effort to understand their motives, without condoning them. Linda Nochlin, in her study of Edgar Degas's anti-Semitism, observes that "although Degas was indeed an extraordinary artist . . . he was a perfectly ordinary anti-Semite" and "What effect did Degas's anti-Semitism have on his art? Little or none."[46] While the practice of not taking into consideration an artist's deep-seated beliefs is suspicious—for example, in separating biography from work in the examples of Griffith and Riefenstahl—perhaps Cohl's situation is closer to Degas's in its ordinariness. His prejudice did not control his life or influence his art, as it clearly did with Griffith and Riefenstahl.

There is one aspect of Cohl's involvement that remains puzzling: the fact that he did not sign his drawings with his professional name, Emile Cohl, but instead used his real name, Courtet (which only a few close associates would have recognized), or a pseudonym, J. Chanteclair (a pun meaning "I sing [or extol] clearly"). This is in contrast to his colleagues who signed their contributions to Drumont's journal with their widely recognized professional names. Should we interpret this as a sign of a personal commitment? Or does this concealment of his identity display Cohl's wish to keep his anti-Semitism from being associated with his public image, suggesting that he was not certain of his commitment to Drumont? Perhaps, like Guillaume Apollinaire's pseudonymous authorship of pornography, he indulged in this activity opportunistically to earn money. Unlike Degas, Cohl never made any public pronouncements about Jews or about the Dreyfus case, nor can one find any outright anti-Semitism in his other graphic art of the period, nor in his later films. Indeed, had Cohl not indicated his contributions to *La Libre Parole Illustrée* in his own notes, it is unlikely that these brief anti-Semitic activities would ever have come to light.

DIVERSIFICATION AND DISTRACTIONS

The decade of the nineties was characterized by serious disruptions in Cohl's personal life, of which a tendency to move to a new apartment every few months was perhaps symptomatic, and by rather directionless experiments in ephemeral art forms.

The diary entry for February 1889 is terse: "Tour Eiffel. Divorce." Marie-Louise

Servat Courtet, who was by then known as Germaine Villars, was pregnant by Gau-thier-Villars. The divorce became official on May 13, and on September 19, 1889, Willy's illegitimate son, Jacques Henri, was born.[47] When their son was only two, Marie/Germaine died, on December 31, 1891. Cohl recorded the event in his diary thusly: "† de Marie Servat ma divorcée qui m. empoisonnée." Although the death certificate does not state a cause of death, Michel Legros and Jacques Gauthier-Villars, in reconstructing their fascinating family history, determined from their surviving rela-tives that Marie did die by poisoning herself.[48]

Meanwhile, Cohl's daughter, Andrée, who had been living with him, was sent to live with relatives. Jacques Gauthier-Villars would be raised by Willy and his new love, Gabrielle-Sidonie Colette (1873–1954), whom he married in 1893. Colette's fame as a popular writer would much later eclipse that of her illustrious husband.

Despite these personal disturbances, Cohl's work in various media was to be found in numerous French and British journals throughout the 1890s. In 1891 he began sub-mitting picture stories to the London humor magazine *Pick Me Up*, which specialized in French artists. In December 1895 he moved to London to work there full-time. A small apartment at 21 Lisle Street became his new studio (fig. 76). His work began appearing regularly in *Judy: The London Serio-Comic Journal*, *Scraps*, *Cassell's Satur-day Journal*, and *Dawn of Day*.

Meanwhile, he continued to serve as a reservist and was promoted to lieutenant in 1892. Like millions of his countrymen, he was caught in the bicycle mania and made a trip from Paris to Toulouse in 1894, just before going to England.

His London stay was brief. He returned to Paris in June 1896 and married Suzanne Delpy. She was the daughter of Hippolyte-Camille Delpy (1842–1910), an engraver and landscape painter whom Cohl had first met at Gill's atelier. He had studied with

76. View from the studio on Lisle Street, London, 1895.

Camille Corot and Charles Daubigny and, since the Salon of 1869, had enjoyed a moderately successful career as the chief continuator of Daubigny's style.[49] On November 8, 1899, Cohl's second child was born, a son named André Jean.

The period was marked by a proliferation of contributions to diverse publications. His articles and caricatures appeared in periodicals devoted to the new sport of bicycling: *Auto-Vélo* and *Le Vélo Illustré* (fig. 77). Family-oriented magazines such as *Le Magasin Pittoresque, Lectures pour Tous, L'Illustré Soleil du Dimanche, La Vie au Grand Air, L'Almanach Hachette, L'Illustration, Fémina*, and *Le Grand Illustré* were frequently interested in his drawings and in his articles on the history of Paris, stamps and fishing (fig. 78). Since the 1880s publications designed for the children's market had been expanding, and this type of work attracted Cohl.[50] His juvenile entertainments appeared in *La Jeunesse Amusante, L'Image pour Rire, Polichinelle* (fig. 79), and—after 1906—*Nos Loisirs* and *Le Petit Journal*.

In July 1898 *L'Illustré National*, a cheap sensational weekly, began publishing his drawings. Soon (perhaps under Cohl's influence?) the paper began to replace its tawdry journalism (featuring, for example, photos of ax-murder victims) with humorous articles and cartoons. Cohl launched a series called "Les Gaietés de l'actualité" that commented upon the week's news events. By October 8, 1899, Cohl's work dominated the paper, and he began illustrating the cover each week. In the first half of 1900 alone,

77

77. "Partage de la galette des rois . . . du cycle," *Le Vélo Illustré* ca. 1900.

78. "Le Meilleur Moyen pour prendre beaucoup de poissons," *Le Grand Illustré*, 1906.

Et maintenant, allons déjeuner.

LE MEILLEUR MOYEN
POUR PRENDRE
BEAUCOUP DE POISSONS

Les figures ci-dessus montrent la manière dont on doit disposer les grains de blé et les asticots.

78

79. "Chez le coiffeur," *Polichinelle*, May 30, 1897.

over 150 of his drawings appeared.[51] There were also rebuses and assorted puzzles, but by far the majority of his contributions were of a genre that was relatively new to Cohl but whose popularity was rapidly building: the comic strip.

COHL'S COMIC STRIPS

Cohl's interest in the comic strip was the end result of a drift in his work away from the Gill-style caricature and toward more anecdotal, then fully narrative visual forms. Many reasons could be advanced for the decline in popularity of the older caricature: portrait photography was no longer a novelty; there was little motivation to celebrate heroes, as the cause of Republicanism had lost its allure; and the mores of French society were changing.

This shift away from the *portrait-charge* coincided with the rise of the *satire de moeurs* (satire of manners), or essentially nonpolitical comments on French social life.[52] Cohl's series "Les Avirons de Paris" (Rowing Clubs of Paris), which began in 1887, was the first sign that he was assimilating the principles of the genre (fig. 80). He experimented with a more polished, somewhat less caricatural style that reflects the influence of the Impressionists in composition and subject matter.

"Le Rêve de Félix" (Felix's Dream) demonstrates Cohl's further modification of the old iconic representations in the direction of anecdote (fig. 81). In contrast to the *por-*

trait-charge, in which everything seemed to exist in a timeless state, the *event* being represented here is more important than the subject's likeness for its own sake. In other words, the meaning of the work derives more from its mise-en-scène than from how well Cohl caricatured the president of the Republic. There are strong narrative implications: Faure is shown dreaming of his imperial coronation; before falling asleep, he had been reading the life of Caesar; from the tin of caviar, bottle of Kümmel, box of dominoes, and spats, we know he is returning from a diplomatic mission. There are also picturesque elements such as the open porthole, the half-visible chamber pot, and his gouty toe which add humorous touches.

The tendency to imply a rudimentary narrative prepared the way for Cohl's work in the picture story and the truly modern comic-strip. It is strange that Cohl's comic-strip art has not been discussed in any of his biographical sketches because it was his most important artistic activity in the years just before he entered the cinema. As we shall see later, it was his strips more than his earlier caricatures that often inspired him when he sought ideas. In this sense, they constitute a kind of overture to his later career.

Sequences of images were being used to tell stories long before Cohl became interested in the medium.[53] The Swiss artist Rodolphe Töpffer and the German Wilhelm Busch had both developed idiosyncratic and influential formulations in the early nine-

80. "Les Avirons de Paris," *La Caricature*, August 13, 1887.

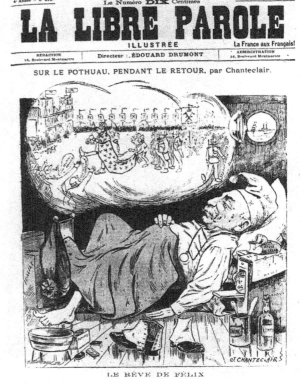

81. "Le Rêve de Félix," *La Libre Parole Illustrée*, August 28, 1897.

teenth century. The multipanel picture story was commonplace in German humorous papers such as *Fliegende Blätter* until it was given a more distinctly French definition by Caran d'Ache in the 1880s. By the 1890s there was scarcely a French caricaturist who had not experimented with the comic-strip format. Even such publications as *Le Figaro* and *L'Illustration* had begun running strips in their pages.

Cohl's comic strips appeared in many forms, with and without captions, usually reproduced according to the whims of his publishers. They can be classified in six different categories according to narrative structure.

The most common kind of strip was the *sight gag*, as in "An Absorbed Reader" (fig. 82). The structure of these strips corresponds to the verbal joke, with a premise ("set up"), elaboration ("build up"), and resolution ("punch line"). The preliminary panels are essentially nonhumorous and prepare the reader for the contrasting explosive burst of improbable, irrational activity in the last one. A sight gag can have as few as three panels, as in "Schampoing nouveau" (fig. 83), but this seems to be the minimum number. More often four or five panels are the rule, as in "Le Bottier" (The Boot Maker), "Big Bait for Big Fish," and "Un Remarquable Ronfleur" (A Remarkable Snorer) (figs. 84-86). One of these was extraordinary because it featured Cohl himself as the protagonist (fig. 87). In strips of six to eight panels, the longer length usually resulted from the

87. Strip containing self-portrait, *Judy*, January 15, 1896.

83

84

83. "Schampoing nouveau,"
*L'Illustré Soleil du
Dimanche*, March 4, 1900.

84. "Le Bottier," *L'Illustré
National*, January 8, 1899.

85. "Big Bait for Big Fish,"
Judy, March 18, 1896.

86. "Un Remarquable
Ronfleur," *L'Illustré
National*, March 19, 1899.

82. "An Absorbed Reader,"
Pick Me Up, October 3, 1891.

Big bait for big fish.   *Hooked.*   *Hooked again.*   *Landed—and watered.*

85

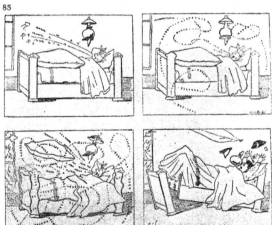

86

addition of expository details in the central section of the narrative. "The Dog-Hater and the Busby" (fig. 88) benefits from the added panels because it allows the intersection of two separate narratives—the story of the dog-hating man and that of the romantic guard. Cohl used the extra length of "An Improvised Mortar" (fig. 89) to elaborate a comic chase sequence.

Cohl's *pantomimes* are strips that illustrate a humorous story without the final visual surprise that is found in the sight gags. The action might be thought of as a record of a theatrical performance. The events depicted in "L'Ombre," "Wringing his Nose," and "Jeux de Clowns" (figs. 90–92) are stagy in conception. Nevertheless, the strips remain highly visual, with an apparent attempt to analyze phases of the movements. This conception of the strip as a performance is especially evident in those cases in which the protagonists address the "audience" directly in classic pantomime gestures (figs. 93–94). Others resemble vaudeville stage acts (figs. 95–96). "Penny in the Slot" (fig. 97)

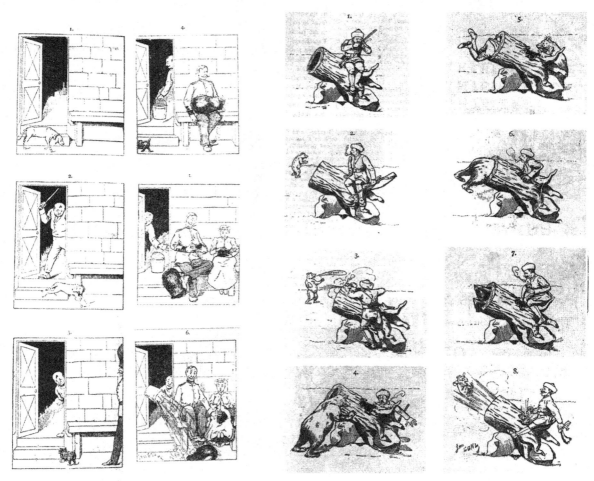

88. "The Dog-Hater and the Busby,"
Pick Me Up, November 28, 1891.

89. "An Improvised Mortar," *Pick Me Up*, January 23, 1892.

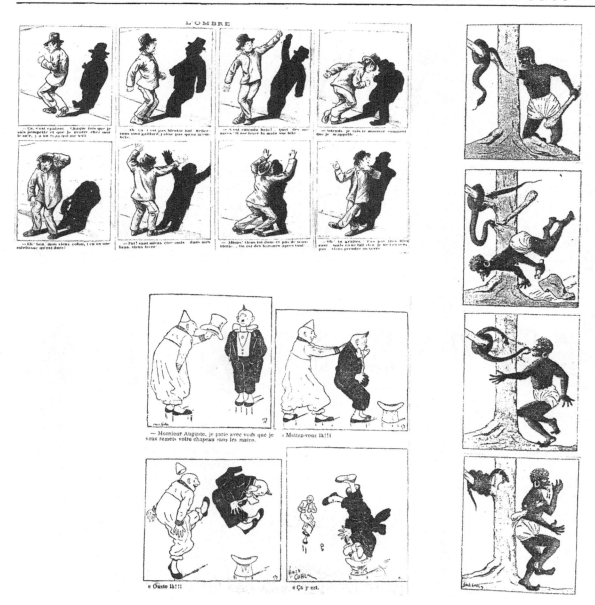

90. "L'Ombre," *L'Illustré National*, September 3, 1899.

91. "Wringing his Nose," *Pick Me Up*, June 6, 1891.

92. "Jeux de Clowns," *L'Illustré National*, January 22, 1899.

93. "La Perruque," *La Caricature*, May 21, 1897.

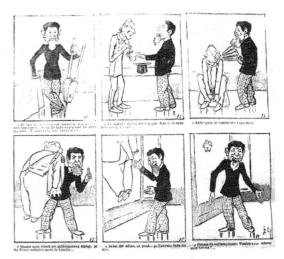

94. "Encore une invention américaine," *L'Illustré National*, December 25, 1898.

95. "Syncopation," *Judy*, February 5, 1896.

96

97

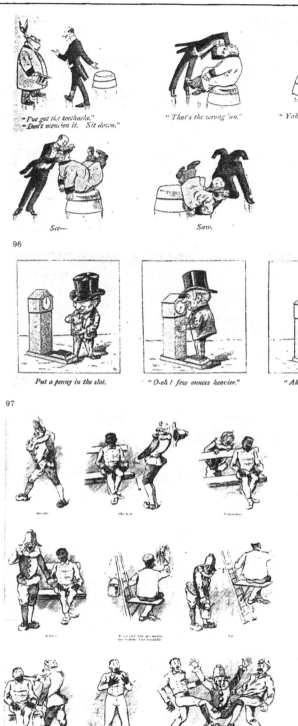

98

96. "Dentist," *Judy*, February 5, 1896.

97. "Penny in the Slot," *Judy*, January 15, 1896.

98. "Le Nègre blanc," *La Chronique Parisienne*, May 8, 1887.

99. "Le Voleur volé," *L'Illustré National*,
April 9, 1899.

102. "Une Mauvaise Farce," *Polichinelle*, January 23,
1898.

could conceivably illustrate a joke from a monologue in the style of Coquelin cadet or
Galipaux.

Cohl's *prank strips* and *fantasy strips* might, strictly speaking, be considered as
subcategories of either the sight gag or the pantomime as narratives, but they are
classed together here because of their specialized subjects.

The prank strips illustrate a mischievous joke perpetrated on someone. Cohl's first
comic strip, "Le Nègre blanc" (The White Negro), is one of these (fig. 98). Themes of
ingenious thefts and the tables turned on a thief are typical (figs. 99–100). "La Malheureuse Aventure du Beau Gontran" (Bumpkin's Misadventure) simply pictures two
mischievous boys (French cousins of Busch's "Max und Moritz") pulling the rug from
under a man (fig. 101). "Une Mauvaise Farce" shows a joke being perpetrated by mail
(fig. 102). The fourth panel registers the landlord's shock by showing him literally
knocked off his feet, with his glasses, hat, and umbrella flying, in anticipation of the
conventional way of showing surprise in the American comic strip several years later.

The fantasy strips illustrate dreams or bizarre stories. Many of these reflect Cohl's
fascination with the moon (fig. 103). His most important predecessor in the art of the
fantastic was J.-J. Grandville, from whom he borrowed the theme of the tormented
dreamer.[54] Cohl adapted Grandville's ideas to comic-strip formats, for example, in "Les

UN VOLEUR MALIN

LA PÊCHE

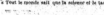

100. "Un Voleur malin," *L'Illustré National*, September 17, 1898.

101. "La Malheureuse Aventure du Beau Gontran," *L'Illustré National*, November 26, 1899.

103

103. "Comment sans le faire exprès
M. Bonneau arriva dans la lune . . .,"
L'Illustré National,
January 22, 1899.

104. "Les Suites d'un souper,"
La Chronique Parisienne,
January 30, 1887.

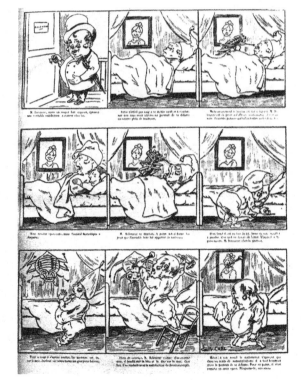

Suites d'un souper" (Aftereffects of a Late Dinner, fig. 104). There are no graphic clues provided to differentiate the dream imagery from wakefulness. It is only when the sleeper awakes in the final panel that the reader knows for certain that a dream has been presented. (The motif of the overindulgent dreamer and the device of the last panel awakening are prototypes of the American cartoonist Winsor McCay's "Dreams of the Rarebit Fiend," begun in 1904.) There were also visualizations of hallucinations, as when a painting comes to life and assaults a gallery visitor (fig. 105), and of drunkenness, as in the case of an elastic lamppost (fig. 106).

" Now, I wonder who the dickens this is ? No. 999."

" Oh, here we are—' William Sykes, Esq., Footpad.' What an ugly beast ! "

" Is he ? "
" Wha—a—t ! "
" Apologise, you scarecrow ! "

" May the Lord——"
" Apologise, I say ! You won't ? Then take that—

" —and that—and that ! From yours truly, William Sykes."

" Heaven be praised, he's gone back to his proper frame of mind."

" But I'll be revenged ! You take that, you ugly beast ! "

" But, my good Mr. Policeman, I tell you he's alive ; he——"
" Rubbish ! " said the Policeman. " Rubbish, hallucination and — DRINK ! "

105. "No. 999," *Judy*, March 11, 1896.

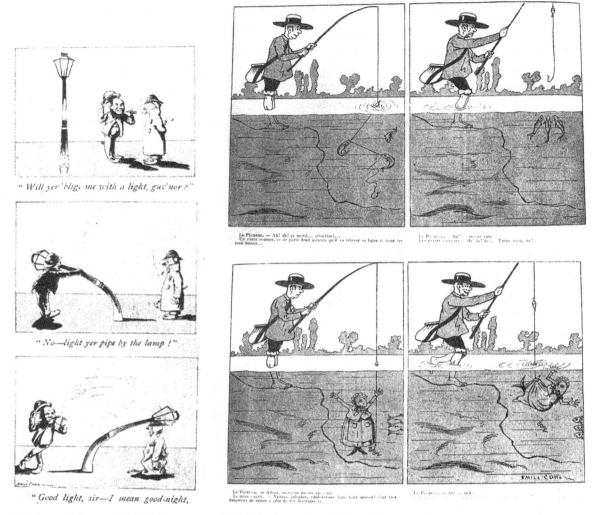

"Will yer 'blige me with a light, guv'nor?"

"No—light yer pipe by the lamp!"

"Good light, sir—I mean good-night,

106. *Judy*, February 26, 1896.

107. "Un Beau Coup de ligne," *La Caricature*, June 16, 1888.

Emile Cohl pioneered the *"bifocal" comic strip*, in which two separate points of view are incorporated into each panel. Some of these are variations on the theme of the fisherman seen from both above and below the water (figs. 107–108). Others exploit the idea of neighbors in an apartment house. The panel may be divided horizontally to represent a floor and ceiling (fig. 109), or vertically to represent a common wall (fig. 110). There were a few other cartoonists who apparently borrowed this idea from Cohl, but the bifocal strip remained his specialty.

The same is true of the sixth category, the *transformation strip*. Again the originator of the technique of sequentially metamorphosing one face or object into another through a series of panels was Grandville. Charles Philipon's adaptation showing the

"Not a bite yesterday."

"Plenty to-day."

Metal (?) more attractive.

Much more attractive.

Never satisfied.

108. "Never Satisfied,"
Judy, January 22, 1896.

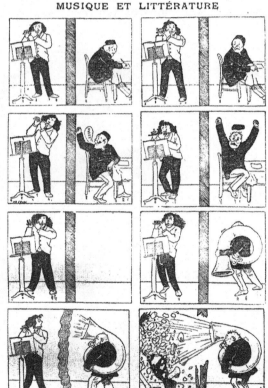

110. "Musique et littérature,"
L'Illustré National, February 19,
1899.

face of Louis Philippe gradually change into a pear had made the idea commonplace in the first half of the century, and it was this joke that was revived in "Comment on fait les jésuites," one of Cohl's earliest published works (fig. 111). He later used the technique for irrational effects, changing the outline of an elephant into that of a photographer without any apparent logical connection except their formal resemblance (fig. 112). An untitled 1896 strip used the device to give the "subjective" viewpoint of two men who think they see a clock tower in the distance (fig. 113). When they approach, it becomes a strange monklike person. Another variant demonstrated the progressive changes in a political candidate in a series of pseudoanthropological photographs and probably was influenced by William Hogarth's "Analysis of Beauty" (fig. 114). Cohl drew himself again in one especially ingenious application of the technique (fig. 115). His expression becomes increasingly miserable as his shirt becomes dirtier over a week.

The humor in Cohl's comic strips is primarily visual. It arises from the irrational, unexpected magnification of an everyday incident into an unreal, often oneiric, event. When occasionally a drawing does rely on a caption for its joke, at the heart of the humor there is frequently an ironic interplay between word and image, reflecting

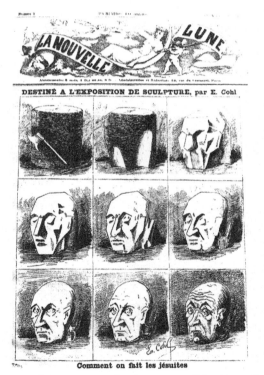

111. "Comment on fait les jésuites," *La Nouvelle Lune*, May 2, 1880.

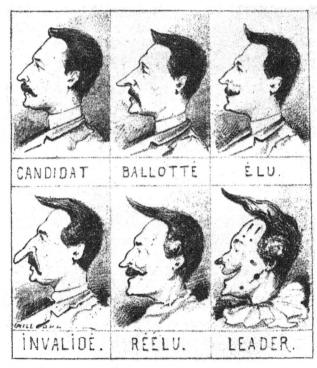

114. "Photographie d'après nature d'un représentant du peuple," *Les Chambres Comiques*, November 30, 1886.

112. "Distant Lens Enchantment to the View," *Judy*, February 12, 1896.

"*Lor'! what's that? The clock tower here?*"   "*I say!*"   "*What a lark!*"

113. *Judy*, February 29, 1896.

Sunday.   *Tuesday.*   *Thursday.*   *Saturday.*

115. "The Tale of a Shirt," *Judy*, January 22, 1896.

the influence of the Incoherents. In general, though, the captions are superfluous. This is typical of the French comic strip, which never incorporated captions or dialogue into the image until the influence of the American strip became strong. This was unquestionably a vestige of the European *imagerie populaire*, which rigorously segregated the captions from the little boxlike pictures. This heritage is apparent not only in works by Cohl (fig. 116) but by France's leading comic-strip artists, Christophe and Louis Forton.

Cohl employed graphic techniques that now seem advanced because they ultimately became standard comic-strip conventions. One of these was "spotting"—the repeated inking of one focal point in each panel to unify the composition, create an interesting

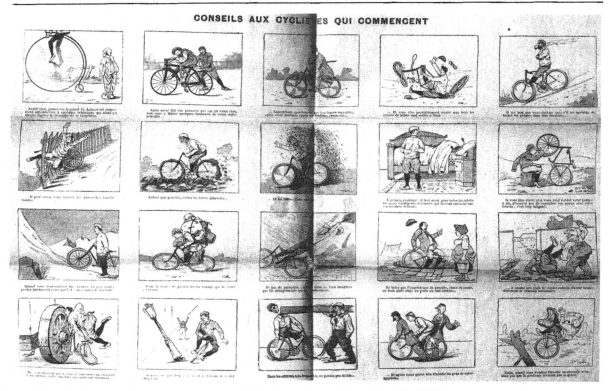

116. "Conseils aux cyclistes qui commencent," *Le Journal pour Tous*, May 29, 1895.

abstract pattern, and allow the viewer to locate the central figure. The "spot" may be a black area in the decor (fig. 83) or an article of clothing (figs. 92, 93, 110). Cohl's coarse slapstick humor, with its emphasis on burlesque violence, also anticipates later American comics.

His comic strips often suffered in reproduction. He was especially at the mercy of the editors of *L'Illustré National*, who crowded as many drawings as possible onto each page without regard for the artist's original layout. A case in point is the 1896 *Judy* strip (fig. 87). In the later *L'Illustré National* version the printing was poor, several graphic details were lost, and the size of the entire composition was reduced to less than one panel of the English original (fig. 117).

Yet Cohl was certainly aware that he was working in an ephemeral medium and had no illusions that he was creating great enduring art. Certainly there was very little monetary remuneration in it for him. One of the main reasons for continuing was simply because he loved the work for its own sake. He was a compulsive humorist, and he was motivated by a strong sense of curiosity about unexplored areas of expression, not limited to comic strips.

117. "Trop de zèle," page from *L'Ilustré National*, February 5, 1899.

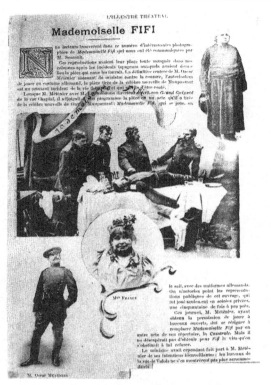

118. Scenes from *Mademoiselle Fifi*, *L'Illustré Théâtral*, 1896.

OTHER ACTIVITIES

In 1896 Cohl and Oscar Méténier collaborated on a production of Maupassant's *Mademoiselle Fifi* at the Grand Guignol (fig. 118). The performance generated controversy and considerable publicity when the producers went to court to win authorization for some of the actors to wear German military costumes.

In the meantime, Cohl's second calling as a philatelist was not ignored. From 1901 to 1906 he worked for the publisher and stamp collector Théophile Lemaire as a designer of his albums and editor of *La Côte Réelle des Timbres-Poste* (*Journal des Philatélistes*). Some curious postcards made for Lemaire were caricatures of national types which the collector was supposed to complete by pasting on the appropriate portrait stamp (fig. 119). While at Lemaire's, Cohl became a philatelic partner of Albert Coyette with whom he combined his own large collection. Together they devised a system of tiny perforations with which to identify their stamps.[55]

In 1906 he began exhibiting caricatures in the window of the High Life Tailor, which was located on boulevard Montmartre (until it went out of business in 1976). His drawings appeared there sporadically until the 1930s.

119. Four "Cartophilatélie" postcards, Lemaire, 1905.

120. "Un Conseil sérieux en riant," *La Nouvelle Lune*, August 27, 1882.

121. Maze, *Nos Loisirs*, October 15, 1906.

Cohl had always been fascinated by puzzles and had designed countless rebuses and brainteasers. An 1882 *La Nouvelle Lune* cover, for example, revealed the name of MacMahon when the maze was properly traced (fig. 120). He published an unusual volume of brainteasers under the pseudonym "Colibri" in 1887.[56] The almost obsessive intensity with which he created these curiosities continued to increase, culminating in the complex abstract compositions published in *Nos Loisirs* between 1906 and 1908 (fig. 121).

He was also an inventor. Sketches remain for an "Ombres chinoises de Séraphim," a shadow-puppet theater dating from around 1900 (fig. 122). One unusual aspect was a brace worn around the head that permitted the operator to work other puppets with his hands. The patented "Enveloppe mystérieuse" was a delicate Art Nouveau toy that made a portrait of Edward VII dissolve into Georges Clemenceau when the tab was pulled (fig. 123). In 1907 his "ABCD à la ficelle" won a prize at the Concours Lépine

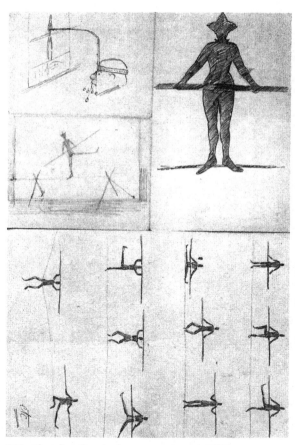

122. Sketches for shadow puppets, ca. 1900.

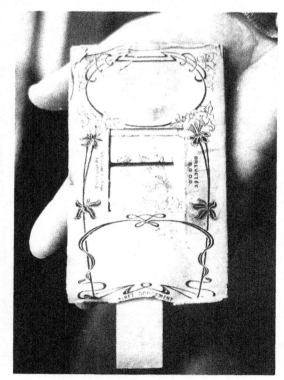

123. "Enveloppe mystérieuse," ca. 1905.

inventors' fair and was subsequently reproduced in *La Nature* (fig. 124). Greatly amused by wax matches, Cohl illustrated the various games that could be played with them (figs. 125–126).

When Charles Léandre and other artists of *Le Rire* formed the Society of Humorous Artists in 1904, they issued their first card to Cohl and honored him with a lifetime membership. At their first Salon three years later in the Palais de Glace (May 9–June 25, 1908), Cohl exhibited the result of yet another outbreak of creativity. In "Les Têtes de pipe," he took the colloquial meaning of the phrase literally and actually carved caricatural heads on pipe bowls (fig. 127).[57]

Cohl's expansive energies led him everywhere. It was this insatiable curiosity and boundless capacity for intellectual stimulation that made possible the biggest surprise for his contemporaries. While his carved pipes were on display at the Palais de Glace, he was just completing work on his newest plaything, a film called *Fantasmagorie*.

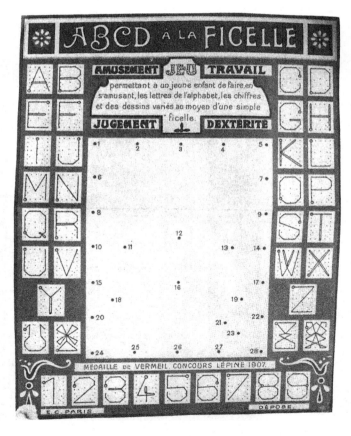

124. "ABCD à la ficelle," 1907.

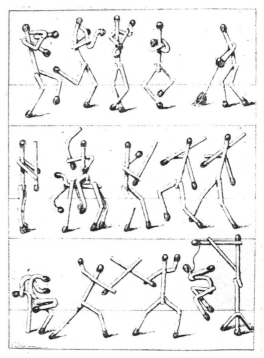

125. "Le Jeu des allumettes bougie," *L'Illustré National*, March 18, 1900.

126. "Amusement for the Winter Evenings," *Judy*, January 29, 1896.

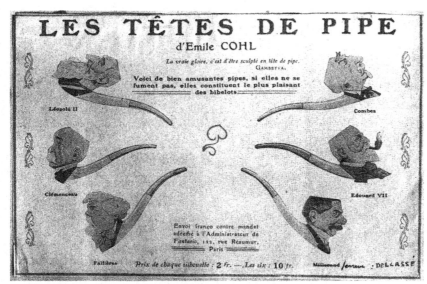

127. "Les Têtes de pipe," advertisement in *Nos Loisirs*, 1908.

PART TWO

The "Cinématographiste"

128. Léonce Burret: "Humoristes," *Le Rire*, January 11, 1908.

CHAPTER THREE

The Moving Image

As COHL'S CURIOSITY led him to more diversified—and more rarefied—interests, his income decreased commensurately. Although his comic strips, games, and puzzles may have been intellectually satisfying, they did not pay enough to allow him to support his family. By 1904 his fortunes had fallen so low that for three months he had to share the apartment of his employer, the stamp seller Lemaire. The situation deteriorated further two years later when Lemaire's *La Côte Réelle*, which Cohl helped edit, was acquired by another publisher. Once again he found himself unemployed and completely dependent upon his work in the illustrated press.

The great humorous papers were no longer interested in a caricaturist of the "old school," and, for his part, Cohl must have felt disenchanted with the direction taken by twentieth-century caricature. The "modern" tendencies exemplified by the social realism of *L'Assiette au Beurre*, the self-conscious eroticism of *Le Rire* and its imitators, and the general aestheticism of the once-satirical press probably struck him, as it had many of his colleagues, as decadent. Léonce Burret, for example, expressed this attitude when he portrayed the contemporary caricaturist as a pitiful figure so bourgeois that people laughed at him in the streets (fig. 128).

For Cohl, as for many other underemployed artisans, relief came from an unexpected quarter—the cinematograph. Although he did not become interested in film until later, there is little doubt that Cohl was aware of it from its earliest introduction in Paris, on boulevard Poissonnière (near his home) in early 1895 in the form of Edison Kinetoscope parlors, then in 1896 in the form of nearby Lumière Cinématographe exhibition sites. It is also possible that Emile Reynaud's protocinematic "Pantomimes Lumineuses," or the early projections of Georges Méliès in the Théâtre Robert-Houdin on boulevard des Italiens, or the showings in local musical halls and theaters might have attracted him. Several of Cohl's friends are known to have been interested in the cinematograph. Félix Galipaux was filmed by Reynaud in November 1896, and, in the same month, Coquelin cadet performed a new monologue entitled *Le Cinématographe*.[1]

There is an intriguing marginal note, "l'Egyptien," in his notebook for 1896. This may possibly refer to a visit to the Egyptian Hall in London where films were being projected during Cohl's stay there. Between 1895 and 1908 it was difficult for a moderately mobile Paris inhabitant *not* to encounter the cinema.[2] Nevertheless, establishing the precise circumstances of Cohl's initiation is not simple. In the early history of film it is often difficult to distinguish fact from legend. In the absence of corroborative films and documents, faulty memories and self-serving distortions sometimes have been elevated to gospel. In this field, rife with mythology, it is better to adopt a Cartesian method, examine the available information, and question the validity of everything until it is documented.

Legends abound concerning the circumstances by which Emile Cohl found himself making films for the Gaumont company. According to one of them, Cohl and the future director Robert Péguy invested in a traveling sideshow cinema and gave tent shows around 1904.[3] Cohl's own manuscript chronology and Péguy's memoirs show that this early partnership never existed. At the time Péguy first entered the cinema, he clearly stated that Cohl "had just discovered the principle of animated cartoons and was already working for a big company."[4]

Théophile Pathé, in his history of cinema, credited Cohl with the invention of the animated cartoon while working at the shadow-puppet theater of the Cabaret du Chat Noir: "Emile Cohl one day had the idea to cinematographically animate the shadow puppets, one of the cabaret's principal attractions."[5] Cohl knew many of the artists and technicians who worked at the Chat Noir, but he did not participate in any presentations there.

In the 1930s Cohl himself misleadingly told interviewers that he was already working for Gaumont in 1904 or 1905 when the idea for the animated cartoon came to him.

> About thirty years ago I was hired by Gaumont as a *truqueur* (trick photographer), the name then for those anonymous prestidigitators who intrigued so many of those kinds of people who love knowing how what they see is accomplished.[6]

The historian of animation, Giuseppe Lo Duca, dated the commencement of Cohl's "intense activity" as a filmmaker from 1906.[7] Jean Mitry agreed that Cohl entered the Gaumont studios in 1906, along with the directors Etienne Arnaud, Jacques Roullet-Plessis, and Roméo Bosetti.[8]

According to Jean-Georges Auriol (and those who repeated him, Georges Sadoul and Marie-Thérèse Poncet), Cohl's first contact with Gaumont was "during the year 1907."[9] It was also Auriol who first told the story of a plagiarism that drove the enraged caricaturist to demand redress from the studio.

> Emile Cohl . . . learned from a Gaumont poster about a film that had been made from one of his drawings on this subject: A worker puts an enormous screw through the ceiling of an apartment, piercing the floor above, while installing a chandelier. The screw also penetrated a trunk upstairs and the tenants there cannot figure out how to move it.[10]

Three years later another interviewer reported that

> a poster of an English film that had obviously been inspired by one of his drawings led him to Gaumont for more information. When he left, M. Emile Cohl was with what would later become—much later—the story department.[11]

Cohl told the same story, with great gusto, to *Comoedia* in 1936:

> In fact it was a quirk that got me into the cinema. One day I walked by a poster. I stopped, turned pale, turned red, I was furious. Someone had stolen my idea! I left, I ran, I flew to the Gaumont studio.
>
> The manager was amused, smiled, cracked jokes and spoke of the future marvels of the screen. He also proposed a contract as a kind of settlement. What to do?
>
> To make films! I always had a cinematographic turn of mind. I liked the idea, accepted, signed on the spot and the doors of the temple swung open before the neophyte.
>
> I wrote, I shot, I directed, I learned my trade.[12]

When René Jeanne quoted part of the above interview verbatim in *Cinéma 1900*, he inexplicably changed the plagiarized subject from a poster to an actual film that Cohl saw "one evening in a little Montmartre theater."[13]

The earliest physical evidence we have that documents Cohl's exposure to motion pictures is a simple entry in his notebook for March 1907: "Ciné with Marcel [a friend or relative] in Orléans." Although we may never know the absolute truth, it is very doubtful that Cohl worked for Gaumont before 1908. His chronology (MS II) and a surviving account book (Carnet I)[14] both provide a precise date of May 1 for *Le Mouton enragé*, "1er scénario Gaumont." The film was directed by Etienne Arnaud and released in July 1908.[15] Thus Cohl's career in the cinema did not begin as a director, trick photographer, or cameraman, but—like that of so many others—by submitting a scenario (a one-page story outline), for which he was paid twenty-five francs. The date of May 1 probably represents the payment of the author's fee. An entry in Arnaud's carnet for January 18 reads "Le mouton enragé (?)."[16] This indicates that Arnaud was considering shooting the Cohl scenario at that time and is thus the earliest proven date for any creative relationship with the Gaumont studios. Even so, Cohl's only activities were probably watching occasional shooting and talking with the employees. He was not formally hired as a salaried director until January 18, 1909 (significantly, exactly one year from the date of the Arnaud carnet entry, suggesting that he had passed a probationary period).[17] Until then he was paid for each work he submitted at the rate of twenty-five francs per scenario as a writer and 250 francs per film as a director. The first film for which he received the full director's fee was *Fantasmagorie* (cat. no. 1), which was completed in late May or early June 1908. Meanwhile, he did not work exclusively for Gaumont; several of his scenarios were produced by the smaller company Lux.

If the aging Cohl's memory of dates cannot be trusted, what about the stories of plagiarism? There is tantalizing, but inconclusive, evidence that the legend has substance. According to Auriol, the offending poster (or film) had shown a worker who, while installing a ceiling fixture, had drilled into a trunk on the floor above.[18] Cohl had, in fact, originally published this comic strip in a British periodical (fig. 129). However, a Gaumont film answering to this description has yet to be identified.[19] But there are other possibilities.

According to the memory of its author, Alice Guy, the Gaumont film *Le Matelas alcoolique* (dir. Roméo Bosetti, December 1906, Gaumont cat. no. 1550) told the story of a drunkard stumbling into a mattress factory.

> The bum wanted to go to sleep then and there on the material and just passed out. The mattress maker returned and innocently resumed her sewing. A porter arrived, loaded the mattress on his cart and went off. The wino, half awake, started staggering and there was a series of falls down the steps of Montmartre, over a little bridge, next to a laundry, in a urinal, etc., always with the delivery man in pursuit.
>
> Meanwhile a newlywed couple were waiting impatiently for their new mattress. Finally it arrived. The delivery man throws it down with all his might, gets his tip and runs off.
>
> Hastily the young couple make the bed while contemplating a pleasant night. But the crazy wino starts doing somersaults. The terrified newlyweds cry for help. The policemen arrive and take the lovers and the mattress to the station. Everything is explained and the film ended with the drunk going into his cell.[20]

This gag easily could have been stolen from an 1888 strip by Cohl showing a drunk being sewn inside a mattress (fig. 130). But Gaumont was not the only company to use the idea; Méliès borrowed it for *La Cardeuse de matelas* (1906, Star-Film cat. no. 818–820), and Pathé had made a version that more closely resembled Alice Guy's spicier plot (fig. 131).

There was still another Cohl source that may have inspired a Gaumont film. One of his 1901 cartoons showed a pedestrian being run down by a postman in a car (fig. 132). Louis Feuillade's film *L'Accident d'auto* revolved around a series of similar gags using a double amputee for comic effects. Cohl would not necessarily have had to see the film because a still from it was prominently displayed in the spring of 1908 on the cover of *L'Illustration* (fig. 133). Seeing this photograph on a Paris newsstand would have been sufficient cause to send Cohl to Gaumont.

The embarrassment of riches provided by these examples of possible borrowings from Cohl's work shows that his stories of plagiarism may have been substantially true, but since the practice was so rampant, there is no longer any way to determine exactly which of his strips and which Gaumont films were involved. In any case, we can add that Cohl's anger was more financially than ethically motivated because when he sub-

1.

"Screw it tight, now."

3.

" A splendid light, Maria, isn't it? "

2.

"That's it.

4.

"Oh !! —— ?? * !"

129. "The Thin Ceiling; or,
—A Lodging-House Mishap,"
Pick Me Up, June 20, 1891.

130. "Le Matelas à pattes," *La Caricature*, March 24, 1888.

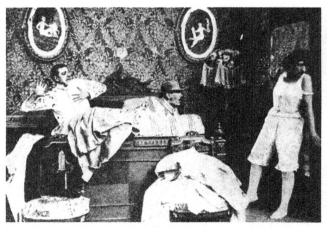

131. Georges Hatot: *Le Matelas de la mariée*, Pathé, 1906.

132. "Les Facteurs en automobile," *Polichinelle*, January 6, 1901.

133. Cover of *L'Illustration*, March 28, 1908.

mitted his first scenario, he did not hesitate to "borrow" the idea from "Le Mouton enragé," a picture story by his friend Moloch (fig. 134).

Cohl already may have been known—at least by reputation—when he arrived at the Gaumont studios. It was the job of "artistic director" Louis Feuillade to receive such visitors, as well as aspiring scenarists and actors. Before coming to Gaumont, Feuillade had also collaborated on papers that published caricatures.[21] Etienne Arnaud had also been a contributor to the satiric press.[22] It is likely that they would at least have recognized Cohl's name, especially since he had been honored by the Society of Humorous Artists in 1905.

Arnaud taught Cohl the rudiments of cinematography, and they quickly became collaborators and friends. For the next three years Cohl would labor on more than seventy Gaumont films that would, in retrospect, prove to be the most important of his career. But before these films can be fully understood by the modern viewer, there must be an understanding of the technical and artistic level of the cinema of that time and its economic and social roles—all of which were very different from our present conceptions of film.

134. Moloch (B. Colomb): "Le Mouton enragé," *La Chronique Parisienne*, July 27, 1883.

CINEMA 1908

Instead of saying that Emile Cohl discovered the cinema, it would be more accurate to say that they discovered each other. Although the circumstances were probably more or less accidental, the fact that he entered the cinema at the date he did was significant. French cinema was in a transitional state, and the year 1908 was a turning point in many respects. Considered as an industry, an art, and a social institution, cinema had progressed to the point at which the talents of a person like Cohl were increasingly valuable. By examining an abundance of documentary sources, we can survey this period in detail and sketch a panoramic background for Cohl's first film productions.[23]

By 1908 the cinema was already thoroughly integrated into Paris life, the heady cultural atmosphere of what Roger Shattuck called the "banquet years." Its rise had continued unchecked despite the 1897 Charity Bazaar disaster in which 150 socialites had lost their lives, owing—it was falsely rumored—to the inherent danger of the cinematograph.[24] (The fire had, in fact, made the novel attraction a household word and, to some, a titillating curiosity.) For those who had predicted its early demise, its ubiquity in 1908 was a source of irritation. The cinema had grown to such an extent that it was now considered a potential economic threat to the theater, music hall, and other forms of boulevard entertainment.

Emile Cohl would have been aware that film was also absorbing the audience and social functions of the illustrated family periodical.[25] His own publisher, Paul Lafitte (*Je Sais Tout, La Vie au Grand Air*), had participated in the founding of La Société des Cinéma-Halls in 1907 and, in 1908, helped launch the Film d'Art company.[26]

The rate at which the cinema was invading the private as well as the public life of France was astonishing.[27] According to Georges-Michel Coissac, it was obvious that cinema constituted a new social force to be reckoned with.

> It is an undeniable and universally accepted fact that cinema has definitely penetrated into our culture. In the provinces and in Paris, it is the king of the street, a very popular king who has courted and won the favor of all his subjects, the people, the bourgeoisie, the upper classes. In the grimiest street or the most fashionable boulevard, cinema has the key to the city. Its fantastic [outdoor] advertisements, veritable lighthouses with giant lamps, fascinate, hypnotize and subjugate the pedestrian, like a moth attracted to a bright light on a white sheet.[28]

Not everyone was as optimistic about this situation as Coissac was. *Le Cri de Paris*, for example, complained that the cinema constituted a national disease.[29] Some even worried that the moral climate of the colorful fairs such as the Fête Montmartre was threatened.[30] At some of these sideshow cinemas the entrepreneurs took in as much as 2,000 francs a day.[31]

Poet Georges Prud'homme best expressed the general situation with his witty paean to the omnipresent amusement, which ended with a pun [pâté] on the name of the largest film producer:

Trop de . . . Pathé
Pour mieux vendre ses broderies
Et ses mobiliers en thuya,
Dufayel, dans ses galeries,
Fit installer le cinéma.

Ce fut alors de la folie,
Le cinéma remplaça tout:
Au théâtre, la comédie,
Au concert, le joyeux Pitou.

Plus de bals, plus de brasseries,
Pas un cirque où l'on fait des tours
Sans défilé d'imageries,
Pathé partout! Pathé toujours!

Enfin, voici venir la fête
Qui, du boulevard Clichy
Au boulevard de la Villette
Met son joyeux charivari.

Oui, mais ô surprise nouvelle!
Marseille, Pezon et Bidel,
Se sont offert la fantaisie
D'imiter aussi Dufayel.

Pas un marchand de cacahuettes,
Bref, pas un seul de nos forains
Qui ne montre les silhouettes
Des sympathiques souverains,

Et qui ne nous fasse connaître,
Par les moyens du cinéma,
L'hospice de Kremlin-Bicêtre
Ou le muséum de Lima.

La chose est donc bien entendue,
Pathé triomphe en toutes parts:
Dans la plus misérable rue,
Et sur nos grands boulevards.

Mais, remarquez cette ironie
Qui dit que, seules, cet été
Les maisons de charcuterie
Ne nous ne servent pas de—Pathé.[32]

Too Much . . . Pathé
To better sell his embroidery
And his cedar furniture,
Dufayel equipped his showrooms
With a cinema.

What happened then was pure folly,
The cinema replaced everything:
In theaters, the play,
In music halls, the joyous Pitou.

No more balls, no more restaurant-bars,
Not one circus where one could stroll about
Without a procession of images,
Pathé everywhere! Pathé forever!

Finally the arrival of the fete
Whose joyous uproar could be heard
From Boulevard Clichy
To Boulevard de la Villette.

Yes, but what a new surprise!
Marseille, Pezon and Bidel
Also regaled themselves
By imitating Dufayel.

There was not one peanut vendor,
Nor carnival that was not showing
The silhouettes of these
Likable sovereigns,

And who, thanks to the medium of cinema
Acquainted us with
The hospice of Kremlin-Bicêtre
Or the Lima museum.

This, of course is well understood,
Pathé triumphs everywhere:
In the most miserable of streets,
And in our largest boulevards.

But, take note of this irony
That bears witness to the fact that
This summer only the butcher shops
Are not serving up any—Pathé.

Even conservative theater critic Edmond Sée grudgingly admitted that the cinema exerted an irresistible attraction. He recalled the street-by-street conquest of Paris during the past five years and his own secret afternoon pleasures as a "furtive specta-tor."[33] One barometer of the level to which cinema had saturated modern life may be seen in the already increasing nostalgia for the first naive surprises of the Lumière projections.[34] Films were being shown almost anywhere a crowd could be gathered, including in the streets. There were essentially four kinds of screenings:

1. *Advertising and promotional.* From the earliest days, films were used to lure clients into a variety of establishments or to advertise products, exactly as in the mod-ern "commercial." The most famous promotional cinema was the large department store on Boulevard Barbès, Les Grands Magasins Dufayel (fig. 135), where "the public is always pressing. These are the spectators coming to a screening of the cinematograph lining up at the entry."[35]

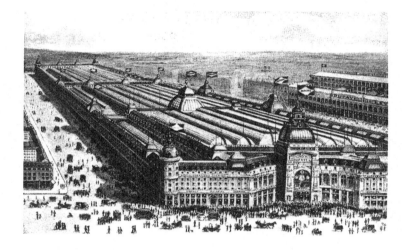

135. Les Grands Magasins Dufayel, ca. 1905.

2. *Traveling fair and carnival projections.* The year 1908, for reasons that will be seen shortly, was the apogee of this type of cinema. This *cinéma forain* was the most important means by which provincial audiences were first exposed to the new inven-tion. It rivaled the traditional amusements that appeared at the large annual fairs that ringed Paris, such as the Foire du Trône, Montmartre, and Pain d'Epice.[36]

3. *Supplements to theatrical programs.* In 1908 the defiant Janou, a café-concert proprietor near the Porte Saint-Denis, posted a notice: "I swear that I will never make the mistake of 'boring' you with the cinematograph."[37] He was reacting to a trend that had become more and more prevalent ever since the Châtelet and Olympia Music Hall had added regular cinematographic projections to their programs in 1896. Their lead had been followed by virtually every other music hall, popular theater, and concert (including Gill's old favorite, the Bal Bullier). Usually these films were "chasers," as their American vaudeville equivalents have been called. They appeared at the end, or

as an interlude, of a predominantly live program.[38] By 1905 the owners of many establishments were learning that their off-peak hours could be profitably filled by film programs. In 1907 and 1908 this trend reached explosive proportions. Even respected legitimate theaters were installing cinemas and, despite unusually hot weather and streets torn up by Métro construction, they were doing brisk business. The surprised writer in *L'Orchestre* commented:

> Do you like cinematographs? They are everywhere. It's a veritable invasion and all the [stage] theaters that are closed for the season are reopening, as if by magic, to offer the public a varied and always interesting program.
>
> There are two kinds of cinematographs, small and large, silent and musical, and make no mistake, the public is flocking to this new kind of spectacle.
>
> The "cinema" has progressed a lot in the past several months and it will progress more. For now the best one is the giant cinematograph at the Châtelet theater where, for a modest price, one can watch a truly marvelous spectacle and the variety of the program is not the least attractive aspect.[39]

Another writer proclaimed that cinemas, which one encountered "every 100 meters" on the boulevards, were the only amusements successfully battling the summer heat.[40]

An analysis of several periodicals in which entertainments were advertised between 1906 and 1908 corroborates these authors' statements. These summer peaks in the exhibition of films are evident in chart 1. In reality, though, the chart represents the "tip of the iceberg" because it includes only the larger theaters and music halls that advertised.

Of course, because a projector was installed did not necessarily mean that it was always a popular success. Too often, as one pundit remarked, "It does not seem likely that families will be comfortable coming to an establishment that is still impregnated with the smoke and musk of the night before."[41] The ramifications of this phenomenon were immediately apparent to a few. They predicted the cinema would soon enter legitimate theater—by the front door.[42]

4. *Cinema halls.* The first establishments that existed exclusively to project films were the "Cinématographes Lumières" on the *grands boulevards.* Architecturally these small converted cafés still retained their original decor, as well as many of the same customers. By 1906 the largest cinemas were concentrated around Emile Cohl's old neighborhood on boulevards Saint-Denis, Bonne-Nouvelle, and Poissonnière. But they became outmoded by the luxurious Omnia, the first modern motion-picture palace, which opened in mid-December 1906 (fig. 136). The Omnia was designed exclusively for film projection, its location and interior decoration carefully planned to appeal to a large, affluent, and sophisticated urban audience. It was strategically situated in the heart of the Paris entertainment district, next door to the Variétés and almost directly across from the Musée Grévin.[43]

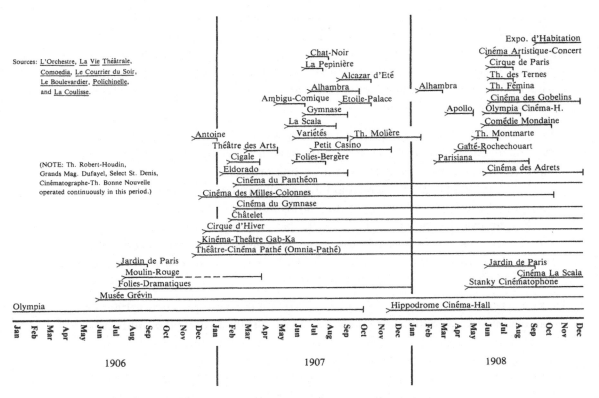

Sources: L'Orchestre, La Vie Théâtrale,
Comoedia, Le Courrier du Soir,
Le Boulevardier, Polichinelle,
and La Coulisse.

(NOTE: Th. Robert-Houdin,
Grands Mag. Dufayel, Select St. Denis,
Cinématographe-Th. Bonne Nouvelle
operated continuously in this period.)

Expo. d'Habitation
Cinéma Artistique-Concert
Chat-Noir
Cirque de Paris
La Pepinière
Th. des Ternes
Alcazar d'Eté
Alhambra
Th. Fémina
Alhambra
Cinéma des Gobelins
Ambigu-Comique
Etoile-Palace
Apollo
Olympia Cinéma-H.
Gymnase
Comédie Mondaine
La Scala
Antoine
Variétés
Th. Molière
Th. Montmarte
Théâtre des Arts
Petit Casino
Gaîté-Rochechouart
Cigale
Folies-Bergère
Parisiana
Eldorado
Cinéma des Adrets
Cinéma du Panthéon
Cinéma des Milles-Colonnes
Cinéma du Gymnase
Châtelet
Cirque d'Hiver
Kinéma-Théâtre Gab-Ka
Théâtre-Cinéma Pathé (Omnia-Pathé)
Jardin de Paris
Jardin de Paris
Moulin-Rouge
Cinéma La Scala
Folies-Dramatiques
Stanky Cinématophone
Musée Grévin
Olympia
Hippodrome Cinéma-Hall

Jan Feb Mar Apr May Jun Jul Aug Sep Oct Nov Dec Jan Feb Mar Apr May Jun Jul Aug Sep Oct Nov Dec Jan Feb Mar Apr May Jun Jul Aug Sep Oct Nov Dec

1906   1907   1908

Chart 1. Advertised Cinema Exhibitions in Paris, 1906–1908.

The Omnia's supremacy was soon challenged by the Cinéma Gab-Ka (whose unusual name was derived from that of its owner, Gabriel Kayser),[44] Le Cinéma du Gymnase (next door to the famous theater), and Le Cinéma du Panthéon (the first on the Left Bank). Pathé converted the Cirque d'Hiver (a permanently installed circus) to a full-time cinema in 1907. When it opened, however, there were complaints that the screen was too small. By mid-1908 there was a Cinéma des Adrets, Cinéma des Gobelins, Cinéma La Scala, and the Olympia Cinéma-Hall. Pathé's rival, Gaumont, operated a Cinéma-Palace on boulevard Bonne-Nouvelle and the Cinématographe-Théâtre at 7, boulevard Poissonnière.[45]

By far the most spectacular theater was the Hippodrome Cinéma-Hall at the Place Clichy (fig. 137). Its popularity as a showcase for circuses and pageants had declined since its construction at the turn of the century (during a period when Cohl lived across

136. Omnia-Pathé, 1914.

137. Hippodrome, after it
became the Gaumont-Palace,
1911.

the street). When it was purchased by the Société des Cinéma-Halls and converted in 1907, it could honestly claim to be, with 5,000 seats, "the biggest and most marvelous of all cinemas."[46]

These elegant theaters were far cries from their shabby nickelodeon counterparts in America. In 1909 a Chicago trade writer showed great prescience when he commented on the Hippodrome, "It is well worth the consideration of amusement capitalists whether a strictly high-grade, high priced show lasting as long as the usual theater performance would not be a success in this country."[47] A visiting French reporter, accustomed to Paris standards, was appalled by those he found in New York.[48]

The admission price at a French cinema was rarely less than one franc, and sometimes cost as much as four francs. The films were projected individually, with the houselights raised between each one. Music and synchronized sound effects were considered integral to every good performance. Films were presented in a definite "séance," or structured program, unlike the American "continuous performance" during which the spectators came and left as they pleased.

The French public was becoming accustomed to high technical standards of photography and projection. Not only were jittery, out-of-focus images whistled off the screen, but so were films with old trite plots. An editorial in *Ciné-Journal* signaled to producers and exhibitors that the quality of film subjects had to match that of the photography.

The public no longer goes along serenely. It continues to have a taste for the cinematograph, but in doses. Its stomach is full, it must have some order in its courses. It is the duty of the impresario to regulate this menu that we call the programme.[49]

The individual "entrées" offered on the typical 1908 cinematic menu were between 50 and 275 meters long. The average length of the films was 120 meters, or about six minutes. The program at one of the large theaters was normally two hours long. With one or two intermissions, as many as twenty films were sometimes shown. There were elaborate musical accompaniments and prologues, such as those provided by the Hippodrome's 200-piece orchestra and choir. As in a French dinner, variety was considered essential, and films of every genre were demanded. Producers aided in this selection by categorizing their films according to standard nomenclature, a practice that led to the conventionalization of genres.[50]

The films projected at the Hippodrome from February 27 to March 5, 1909, constituted a typically varied program.[51]

Juliano
Joyeux réveil
Mer en tempête

Les Dragonnades
Fatale méprise
L'Oncle d'Amérique
Marche des sports
La Fille prodigue
La Fête de la colonnelle
—Entr'acte—
L'Hirondelle
Corso fleuri
Amour et vendetta
Le Beau Tzigane
—Intermission—
Les Derniers Jours de Pompéi
Les Fitzgerald
L'Omelette fantastique
Rayons et ombres
Gribouille cherche un duel
—Intermission—
Le Carnaval de Nice, 1909
Bonsoir

Such a program resembled, in some aspects, those of the variety theaters and café-concerts. But in their obvious ambition to please the lowest common denominator of an average audience, the producers and exhibitors imitated the range of subjects found in popular family periodicals such as *Lectures pour Tous*. There were travelogues, humorous stories, educational and historical features, and "program lighteners" in the form of a *féerie*, or trick film. This was the function of Cohl's *L'Omelette fantastique* (cat. no. 17) on the above program: to round out a selection of subjects that would appeal to all and offend no one. Although some adjustment was made in programs intended for provincial audiences, it would be a mistake to accept the conventional wisdom that "serious" subjects on the program were aimed at the upper classes and trick and comedy subjects aimed at plebeians. There is some evidence that the opposite is more likely. Traveling in Europe in 1906, a British reporter noted:

There seems to be a free exchange of cinematoscope films between England and the Continent, for I have seen the same series in London, in Paris and in Amsterdam; and I have noticed invariably that, whereas the more expensive halls give farce only, at the poorer pathos is a necessary ingredient.[52]

Rivalry between the two major production companies that supplied these films motivated many of the changes that were taking place. Pathé was the giant. When two financial analysts, Binet and Hausser, examined the company in 1908, they discovered that profits from the film branch of the company had increased 15,722 percent in a decade![53] Annual turnover had doubled every year except 1907, when it had tripled. The Pathé studios in Vincennes and Joinville were the finest in the world, and in 1907 the company began distributing its films in the United States.[54]

Like his rival Charles Pathé, Léon Gaumont was also an entrepreneur who had prospered in the film business. The 1907 turnover for "Les Etablissements Gaumont" was 7,000,000 francs (compared to 12,162,000 for Pathé).[55] Profits were up 1,000 percent in the preceding five years. Binet and Hausser predicted a rosy future for the smaller company because it had just upgraded the studios in Belleville, but they revealed their fiscal conservatism by finally recommending Pathé as the safer investment.

Obviously the film business was booming. Many others hoped to cash in on this new industry, which promised an easy fortune. After Gaumont, the most important firm was Eclipse, the Paris branch of the Charles Urban Trading Company. Eventually it would prosper so well that it would absorb its London-based parent. Eclair was just beginning production in 1907.[56]

A major economic development during this period was Pathé's introduction of the rental distribution system. Most companies offered their new releases to exhibitors who bought prints outright, then sold them to "second run" exhibitors at reduced prices. Prints continued to make the rounds until they literally would no longer pass through a projector. To thwart this system, Pathé announced that films would be rented only to franchised Pathé exhibitors bidding for rights in six distribution regions.[57] By April 1908 the monopoly was already beginning to falter because illegal copies of Pathé films were readily available, and the legal force required to police the huge distribution network did not exist. Soon Pathé was forced to modify its distribution monopoly, but it continued only to rent its films.[58] Meanwhile, Gaumont profited from Pathé's partial failure by selling films to anyone, until they also converted to a rental system in 1910. The decision to rent films had the calculated effect of driving small exhibitors and the itinerant showmen out of business. Renting a film for one week was out of the question, since their livelihood depended on showing and reshowing only about 8,000 meters each season.[59] This also had an effect on the composition of the French film audience, which was already more homogeneous than the American nickelodeon counterpart. After the loss of the small itinerant venues, the French audience became even more uniform in its class and ethnic makeup.

Pathé's attempt to establish a monopoly was a repercussion of events in the United States which troubled European exhibitors. It was clear that exportation was essential, but the producers' efforts were restricted by the so-called Edison Trust, the Motion

Picture Patents Company.[60] Because their films had previously constituted a large share of the American market—perhaps more than half—this trust spelled potential disaster for the Europeans. Gaumont, for example, had to be content with signing a contract with the distributor George Kleine that allowed the licensed import of only two reels a week. The Europeans, despite constant effort, could not unite in a trust of their own, and it was not until it became clear that the MPPC was losing its power because of internal problems and the assault of the "Independents" that they could look optimistically to America.[61]

The international tribulations were compounded by a domestic crisis. The French market was being flooded with too many films of inferior quality. The year 1908 was the turning point, when the supply of films began to exceed demand and the large producers worried that the deluge of potboilers would jeopardize their own markets. Binet and Hausser urged self-regulation to prevent a glut.[62] Chart 2 was compiled from the releases listed in *Ciné-Journal* for a typical week in 1908 (the week *Fantasmagorie* was released). It shows that over 100 new films were added to the market. Half of them were French, and they were among the shortest films in the world.

Criticism about the triviality of film subjects came from everywhere.[63] An editor of *Filma* offered his criteria for a good movie: irreproachable photographic quality, good stability of the image, and enough "intrigue" to hold the audience's attention.[64] The author's suggestions were admirable, but his choice of an exemplary film reveals the bankruptcy of ideas: *Rover Drives an Auto*. To some, the crisis in subject matter was an unpleasant vestige of the cinema's plebeian roots. According to Georges Dureau, "That's the reason for its popularity and the cause of its weakness."[65]

In response to these complaints that the cinema was too much attached to the side-show, some producers experimented with "serious" subjects, such as Gaumont's filming of Carré and Wormser's *The Prodigal Son*. Its presentation at the Variétés in 1907 was only a limited success, owing mostly to the fact that the 1600-meter film was an unedited recording of the stage performance from a single wide-angle viewpoint.[66] When Le Film d'Art was launched in February 1908, *Le Matin* declared, "The duel between cinema and theater has just begun. We only hope that the former doesn't kill the latter."[67] The new company's series of filmed plays was highly acclaimed and sparked imitations such as Gaumont's "Théâtro-Film" series.[68] These "highbrow" productions did have the important effect of attracting not only more sophisticated audiences to the cinema for the first time but well-known actors and playwrights as well. Writers were dusting off their old works for film adaptations.[69] These authors' rights were assured after 1908 by a series of landmark legal decisions entitling them to royalties and damage claims for unauthorized use of their works.[70] At the same time, the Berlin revision of the Berne Copyright Law guaranteed copyright protection to cinematic works.[71]

Country and Producers	Number of Releases	Total Length (meters)	Average Length (meters)
France Pathé,* Gaumont, Eclair, Eclipse, Le Lion, Lux, Méliès, Mendel, Radios, Soleil, Théophile Pathé	50	6200	120
Italy Cines, Aquila, Comerio, Itala-Film, Croce	20	4200	200
United States Vitagraph, American Mutoscope and Biograph	17	3150	185
Great Britain Raleigh and Roberts/Continental Warwick (distributors of Hepworth, Ambrosio, Nordisk),** Cricks and Martin	18	2470	139
Russia Drankoff	9	1050	117
Total	114 Films	17,070 meters	

Source: *Ciné-Journal*, August 15, 1908
* Pathé releases were not listed individually because they were distributed directly to the members of their monopoly. For this chart, 8 releases constituting 1000 meters were estimated.

** Individual titles for Ambrosio (Italian) and Nordisk (Danish) were impossible to distinguish; therefore the actual British statistics should be slightly smaller.

Chart 2. Number of New Releases in Paris. Week of August 15, 1908

Close examination of the programs of the time reveals that the Film d'Art genre never threatened the traditional light subjects. Its rise actually reflected the producers' desire to annex a new audience of upper middle-class theatergoers who had formerly scorned the cinema. For this reason the "artistic" films were always kept separate from the everyday programs, which continued to flourish. It was here, in the regular programs, that more significant changes in subject matter were evolving that would ensure the vitality of the cinema in the future. An embryonic star system was being founded by vaudeville and music-hall personalities who made burlesque film series. Dranem, André Deed, and Prince Rigadin were the forerunners of Max Linder and Charlie Chaplin.[72]

The hegemony of the short French farces and chases was being challenged by longer, more serious productions from Vitagraph, Biograph (soon to release Griffith's first films), and especially Italian producers. Eclair began production of its Nick Carter series, directed by Victorin Jasset. The continuing exploits of the famous dime-novel detective were received enthusiastically, and the originality of the series was acknowledged: "The public adores this kind of show and Eclair should be congratulated for this innovation that foreign countries are already trying to copy."[73] It was being realized that what made good theater did not necessarily make a good film. It was possible, in the cinema, to relate a dramatic or comic narrative in a series of photographed scenes with a degree of clarity, fluidity, and intimacy that exceeded all traditional stage conventions.

This was slowly becoming understood by a growing number of intellectuals who were founding—but not in any rigorous way—a rudimentary basis for later film criticism. Most "reviews" in 1908 were little more than comments on plots or disguised advertisements. Even this meager recognition of a film's existence was much rarer in French periodicals than in their American counterparts such as *Moving Picture World*.

The first "criticisms" were only complaints by moralists condemning film for its tawdry associations.[74] Attacks on erotic content and warnings of censorship coincided with a wave of concern about pornography that prompted Senator Béranger to convene a 1908 world conference on the problem in Paris.[75] The best-informed and most influential voice for a socially conscious cinema was Georges-Michel Coissac in *Le Fascinateur*, published by the Catholic *La Bonne Presse*. Coissac, later an important early film historian, crusaded against immoral films and recommended good ones to his readers. He would chastise exhibitors for showing the *La Passion* to afternoon audiences and "spicy" subjects to evening crowds.[76] There was no question that films were becoming bolder in presenting taboo subjects. The police confiscated one that allegedly showed a man shooting himself in the head: "These images are cruelly and atrociously real, reproducing all the spasms of his agony in detail."[77] Small wonder that some psychologists were beginning to speculate about the effects of films on children.[78]

In opposition to those espousing a pragmatic, uplifting cinema that would "teach and delight," a few writers such as Maxime Leproust applauded cinema precisely for its "democratic" (what others were calling "vulgar") qualities:

It appeals to children as well as to grownups and thus addresses the enormous youth market which until now has been excluded from most spectacles.

Because of its moderate price, the most modest and numerous families can attend. . . .

The cinematographic theater is the democratic pastime *par excellence*.[79]

The need for programs suitable for children was obviously a factor that relates to Cohl's choice of career.

Leproust and others believed that cinema was of interest to the extent that it differed from the theater. The "realism" of film was frequently used to deride the "artifice" of the stage. The academician Rémy de Gourmont was astonished by the power of the cinematic image to elicit applause from viewers as though they were watching real beings.[80] Others, such as Edmond Sée, strongly objected to the implied denigration of the stage. For them the cinema could never replace the theater's power to create a unique performance every night.[81] The dual capacity of the cinema to produce a tangible illusion of reality while at the same time manipulating and distorting the audience's perception of the events shown on the screen seems to have confused and even induced a certain suspicion in some writers. The preservative powers of the film image were frequently commented upon, anticipating theorist André Bazin's 1945 hypothesis of a cinematic "mummy complex," as in this observation by Georges Dureau: "As the phonograph can revive 'the precious inflection of dead voices,' so the cinematograph will evoke the gestures, smiles and appearances of those dear beings who are no more."[82]

Others were quick to note the ambivalent nature of this apparent hyperreality. Fairy and trick films astounded viewers with their dreamlike fantasies, hallucinatory colors, and antirational special-effects photography. Spectators experienced near total identification with the screen images, as though they were witnessing real events. Travel films were popular, to a large extent, because they "transported" the viewer to the faraway places projected on the screen. But the lightning speed with which scenes and locations changed was at odds with this empathetic illusion. The result was a feeling of exhilarating giddiness.[83]

These early commentators saw no distinction between what later became the conflict in film theory between the "recording" and the "expressive" properties of the medium. Jules Claretie (Gill's defender) promoted the widely held view that all aspects of the visual environment provided potential cinematic subjects, be they historical reality or the fantasies of Jules Verne.[84]

Cinema was evolving into the popular apotheosis of the late nineteenth-century romantic ideal of the *Gesamtkunstwerk*, the total work of art. The fact that its illusions were achieved by a "formidable and invisible machine" further excited the public, hypnotized by the marvels of electricity and technology. The cinema was distinctively "modern."[85]

It was this same zeal and many of the same attitudes that formed the aesthetic basis of the so-called first generation of critics of the teens and twenties.[86] Ricciotto Canudo, Guillaume Apollinaire, Louis Delluc, Jean Epstein, Abel Gance, Germaine Dulac, and the art historian Elie Faure were seeing their first films and formulating thoughts about cinema during this period. Their ideas can often be seen as modifications of these earlier journalistic intuitions. Cinema was recognized as a profound social force that could redeem the human condition if properly channeled. It was a universal language and appealed to all classes and nationalities. Awe for the reproductive powers of the image coexisted with praise for the lyric, expressive, and "transportive" powers of the image. The association of cinema with popular science presaged the machine aesthetic of the 1920s, which would express itself in the writing of Jean Epstein as well as in the films of Fernand Léger and Marcel Duchamp. Finally the overpowering feeling of optimism that characterized later French criticism had already erupted in 1907 in an article by François Valleiry, the first critic to proclaim the "Age of Cinema."

> We are in the presence of the greatest transformation of the theater that our century has seen and the prodigious development of the cinematograph constitutes the principal event in the evolution of contemporary art. . . .
>
> The cinematograph is not a fad, but quite simply the beginning of a new age for Humanity.
>
> The Age of Cinema, the age of genuine documentation, the age when history and geography are becoming an industry.
>
> There was the age of the printing press, of gunpowder, etc. Each of these inventions changed the form of the world and human destiny.
>
> Now the cinematograph will transform everything. What we take for daylight is only the "rosy fingered Aurora."[87]

Many of these feelings about film were also being awakened in a small number of Parisian artists who had already encountered the cinema as a familiar adjunct to their cafés, bistros, and circuses, but who were just beginning to think about it seriously. Gustave Babin wrote in *L'Illustration* that artists were "intrigued and conquered" by the cinema.[88] Babin's statement that artists were enchanted by the cinema in 1908 is especially tantalizing because the author was in touch with some of the latest developments in avant-garde painting. He had been introduced to the cinema by his friend the poet Armand Sylvestre, a personal friend of the Lumière brothers, in 1895. At that time Babin frequented the atelier of the painter Maxime Maufra (1861–1918) in the ramshackle building on rue Ravignon that soon would be nicknamed the Bateau-Lavoir, the "Birthplace of Cubism."[89] Whether Babin still came there in 1908 is unknown, but there was definitely considerable interest in cinema at the time. The poet and dandy Max Jacob (1876–1944), Pablo Picasso's intimate friend, was an ardent aficionado of the new distraction. André Salmon recalled frequenting the Hippodrome-Cinéma with him between 1907 and 1911. Jacob's enthusiasm was so intense that Salmon wondered if it were not an affectation.

> I am speaking of a real film buff who went to the cinema in its primitive days, the cinema of Méliès's time. Whether Max Jacob was genuinely curious or just pretending, no one will know, but I think he was interested. I often thought he was pretending because of the very passion he would have when telling the stories. When Max led me against my protests to the outdoor cinema on rue de Douai, projected there for the edification of the pupils of the Jules-Ferry School, I stood contemplating these absurd melos transformed by the magic lantern. Perhaps Max wasn't faking after all.[90]

Though it is difficult to judge the extent of its impact, cinema must have influenced the nascent aesthetics of Cubism.[91] The mechanisms of the cinematic illusion seemed to provide a model for contemporary theories of visual perception that excited the artists. They were well aware that the "motion" of films was an illusion synthesized by the mind. Henri Bergson's influential writing would have guided their theorizing. Gilles Deleuze, who has applied Bergsonian aesthetics to modern cinema, traced the philosopher's interest in the problems of real and perceived motion back to his 1896 book, *Matière et mémoire*. Deleuze also argues that Bergson's more famous work, *L'Evolution créatrice*, of 1907, which explicitly discussed the "cinematographic illusion," was an effort to modernize and expand his earlier thoughts. The cinema yields a false movement because real movement can exist only in the present, as an act. "Immobile shots" (individual frames) can provide only memories of movement and not real movement. The single exposures record only one point in the continuum of movement, and the intervals between can *always* be further subdivided. The cinema can never equal natural perception, which is continuous, immediate, and irreducible. Yet the cinema provides an excellent model for understanding the paradoxical nature of time and movement as interval and as unity.[92] Bergson's ideas had been formed while attending films beginning at the turn of the century. He confirmed this himself when he tried to give a simplified explanation of his theory in a little-known 1914 letter to a trade journal:

> I went to the cinema. It was quite a few years ago already. I saw it at its origins. It is clear that this invention, related to instantaneous photography, can suggest new ideas to the philosopher. It can aid in the synthesis of memory or even of thought. If the circumference [of a circle] is composed of a series of points, memory is, like cinema, a series of images. Immobile, it is a neutral state; moving, it is life.

And *some may conclude*, or have already concluded, that life is movement. The essence of light, of sound is vibration. The living eye, is it not just like the cinematograph?[93]

Bergson's concepts—perhaps not always fully understood—were echoed consistently in the writings of Guillaume Apollinaire, Canudo, Futurist poet F. T. Marinetti, and others who were studying film and chronophotographs around 1908.[94]

The painters, poets, and writers of Montmartre often came in contact with cinema on a more down-to-earth basis as well. It was common knowledge that the Pathé and Gaumont studios paid well for a few hours of acting. All that was necessary was to line up at the gates early in the morning. Among the numerous artists and performers who took advantage of this extra income, at least one was an intimate of the Bateau-Lavoir.

Gaston Modot was a young painter who was friendly with the habitués of Gill's old cabaret: "I passed innumerable evenings, not to mention days, in Montmartre between 1905 and 1907 at the 'Lapin Agile.' . . . It was there that I knew Jehan Rictus, Mac Orlan, Modigliani, and Picasso."[95] Picasso's model and mistress Fernande Olivier recalled Modot from those days as one of the most amusing youngsters in their circle.[96] He turned to acting to subsidize his painting, and his name appeared, for example, on 1908 programs at the Folies-Dramatiques.[97] After his military service, like Emile Cohl and so many others who were unemployed, he began working full-time for Gaumont, in his case as one of Jean Durand's famous troupe, Les Pouites.[98] It was then, according to his friend Salmon, that "the nascent cinema seized him."[99] Later Modot became a distinguished actor in the French cinema, especially remembered for his films with René Clair and Jean Renoir (for example, as Schumacher in *Rules of the Game*, 1939).

The description of Modot ambling about Montmartre with nothing to do except act in films would have applied to his neighbor on the Butte, Emile Cohl. Of course, Cohl was a graphic artist, not an actor, and he was thirty years older. His career appeared to be behind him, not ahead.

Cohl's original interest in film may have been motivated purely by the need to supplement his income. Nevertheless, he could not have failed to be excited about the cinema, simply because of the controversy and enthusiasm it was generating among Parisians at the time. By coincidence, he had presented himself at the Gaumont studios just when they were undertaking major expansion of both their physical plant and their production staff. The trade and popular press were urging producers to ameliorate film quality or face disaster, so, to Louis Feuillade, Cohl's years of experience promised to inject fresh ideas into Gaumont films. In its efforts to attract huge audiences, the cinema was moving closer to Cohl's illustrated-press background as it consciously channeled its appeal toward middle-class families. His training as a professional photographer in the 1880s and his experience in the theater made him an excellent candidate for *metteur en scène*. His obvious aptitude for tinkering and experimentation was a further asset. In sum, his "cinematic turn of mind" made him and the cinema of 1908 a nearly perfect match.

Throughout Cohl's association with Gaumont, his films flowed into the stream, whose currents we have just described, which led to the awakening of cinematic consciousness among French intellectuals and the public. Cohl's films simultaneously reflected and contributed to that process. The changing circumstances of production, distribution, exhibition, and audience attitudes gave him freedom to make films as he chose, as long as they complemented other films in the program. But unlike Méliès, who had insisted on making films all by himself in the cottage-industry tradition, and whose career was already in rapid decline, the newcomer Cohl was learning the art of cinema within the context of Gaumont—a corporate structure dominated by principles of economy, efficiency, and streamlined production techniques.

CHAPTER FOUR

Cinema chez Gaumont

When he came to the Gaumont studios, Emile Cohl exchanged his past independence for a disciplined work environment. In 1908 the company was releasing about six short films each week, entirely conceived, photographed, processed, and edited within the La Villette studios or their immediate environs.

Léon Ernest Gaumont's personality dominated the company's productions, although he himself did not make films. Born in 1864, he had worked his way up in the photographic-supply business until, in 1895, he was able to borrow sufficient funds to buy out his employer and start his own company. As a sideline, Gaumont began exploiting a cinematograph-like camera and projection device that had been developed by Georges Demenÿ. In 1896 he started to concentrate on film production, but the legal transformation of his company into a corporation specializing in motion pictures (Gaumont Société Anonyme) did not take place until December 1906.

In 1908 Gaumont was forty-five years old (six years Cohl's junior). His reputation was that of a demanding employer known to be harsh with workers who incurred his displeasure. He was a private, self-restrained person. As a businessman, he was articulate, aggressive, and usually appeared "in a furia."[1] George Kleine, his American distributor, complained privately about Gaumont's "continually aggressive attitude."[2] He tended to be penurious in economic affairs and was endowed with a strict sense of propriety that was easily offended.[3] His personal puritanism often was reflected in the company's productions because he critiqued each of the new films in a weekly screening session. This "tribunal" was assembled in the presence of the staff every Tuesday promptly at 8:00 a.m. in a spartan projection room. As director Henri Fescourt later recalled,

Mr. Gaumont took his place to the left of the screen at a little table. In the first row were seated the company brass, the chief engineer, the head of camera sales, the director of the lab, the director of film sales and rentals, the director of the Gaumont-Palace, the newsreel director, etc. Behind these were seated, with their heads lowered, the film directors. They all looked more or less like the accused, or at least like people with guilty consciences. Then, on wooden benches, the actors and agents, and finally the staff. One did not make a sound without risking great unhappiness.[4]

It was under such circumstances that Emile Cohl made his only personal contact with Gaumont. The film of the most recently arrived director was projected first, and Louis Feuillade's latest film was shown last. Gaumont, regarded by the directors as an "homme au coup d'oeil sûr" (a sharp-eyed man), was especially attentive to the quality of the photography, for which the company had built an enviable reputation. He also watched for potentially offensive subjects. Adultery, violent crimes, and potentially controversial stories (for example, of corrupt military officers) were taboo.[5] But chase films that portrayed the police as comic figures or used amputees as butts of jokes were condoned. Typically burlesque subjects such as vomiting, enemas, and diarrhea were tolerated up to a point. Nevertheless, Gaumont's influence led to bourgeois standards in the films, according to Fescourt.[6] *Les Agents tels qu'on nous les représente* (The Police as They are Represented to Us, August 1908) exemplifies this moralizing tendency.[7] The first tableau portrays the popular media image of the police as ineffectual and possibly corrupt. Some officers watch idly as criminals flee the scene of a crime. The second tableau shows "the police as they are." When these gendarmes see a crime, they chase the culprit, and one of them is wounded in the line of duty. In the third tableau the officer is recuperating and receiving an award for valor.[8]

The majority of films bearing the Gaumont marguerite trademark were witty farces and chases improvised on location in the neighborhood streets or in the Parc Buttes-Chaumont. One of the best known and most typical is *La Course aux potirons* (The Pumpkin Race, February 1908).[9] Although frequently attributed to Cohl, the film was directed by Roméo Bosetti, based on a scenario by Feuillade, and probably had been completed before Cohl arrived.[10] The plot is simple: a peasant's cart collapses, and the giant pumpkins in it roll downhill, with him in pursuit. As more bystanders join the chase, the pumpkins take on life of their own and begin evasive actions. They go into a manhole, over a wall, up the chimney of a bourgeois dining room, and over the rooftops. Finally they return to the cart by themselves. Years later Feuillade recalled his films of this genre:

> They were eternal pursuits, chases without end, with a constantly growing crowd that would be chasing a flying pumpkin or a postage stamp blowing on the wind. The public was ecstatic about these burlesque fantasies.[11]

Although Feuillade disparaged these chases after wigs, pigs, barrels, cheeses, mothers-in-law, and other unlikely things, they were fondly remembered by later filmmakers ranging from Mack Sennett to René Clair to Jacques Tati.[12] They also established the reputation and fortune of Gaumont. Jasset, writing in 1911, noted their special qualities.

[Gaumont] was the first to create a specialty in a comic genre of a completely Parisian nature. It was not just a chase nor a comedy, but something witty and full of movement and spirit, using new ideas and techniques.[13]

Gaumont's ingenious trick films rivaled those produced by Ferdinand Zecca at Pathé. *Police magnétique* (August 1908) showed the gendarmes donning electric boots in order to chase criminals at lightning speed and even to scale telephone poles. In this scene an officer looks up the pole and prepares to climb it (fig. 138). Then, in long shot, he simply marches up the vertical pole, with his body extended horizontally toward the camera. The trick was done by spreading the painted backdrop onto the floor of the studio and photographing the actor from directly overhead as he pretended to balance on the pole.

Another trick film, *Le Ski* (March 1908), has also been incorrectly attributed to Cohl by Georges Sadoul and others. It demonstrates the ingenuity with which stories and tricks were improvised. During the expansion of the Belleville studios it was necessary to pull down an old chimney. Etienne Arnaud photographed the demolition and later superimposed the image of a skier flying through the air, timing it so that the skier appeared to collide with the chimney (fig. 139).[14]

138. Etienne Arnaud (?): *Police magnétique*, Gaumont, August 1908.

139. Etienne Arnaud (?): *Le Ski*, Gaumont, March 1908.

One reason why the spirit of improvisation reigned was the frugal Léon Gaumont's dislike of paying royalties to scenarists. Directors and actors were encouraged to make up stories on the spot and, as a result, films such as Bosetti and Feuillade's *Une Dame vraiment bien* (What a Lady, August 1908) still communicate their original unscripted spontaneity.

As long as they remained within general parameters, the directors were allowed to work as they pleased. Gaumont himself was too preoccupied with business affairs to exert constant pressure on them. Two projects in particular commanded his attention: the Chronophone and foreign expansion.

The Gaumont Chronophone was his sound-on-disc system for synchronizing songs and speech with projected images.[15] He was banking on it for the technological breakthrough that would finally gain an advantage for him over his archrival, Charles Pathé. It was successfully demonstrated at the Société d'Encouragement pour l'Industrie Nationale in 1907 to an audience of celebrated writers and scientists.[16] English-speaking Chronophone films were already being sold in London and in the United States, where Alice Guy Blaché, the artistic director of Gaumont before Louis Feuillade, and her husband, Herbert Blaché, were in charge. In the summer of 1907 Gaumont rented the prestigious Théâtre du Gymnase to premiere the Chronophone in Paris. But the system was plagued with all the usual problems of sound-on-disc—lack of synchronization and amplification, excessive background noise, and cumbersome mechanics. Despite a demonstration at the Academy of Sciences in 1910, Gaumont never achieved his dream of being the first to develop true synchronous sound films.[17]

At the same time, Gaumont was struggling to break into the American market. Since 1907, when Pathé had incorporated in the United States, Gaumont's nemesis had been supplying more than a third of all American film programs, while Gaumont titles amounted to only about two percent.[18] Gaumont had a modest studio in Flushing, New York, for producing Chronophone films, but he was planning to start local printing and distribution of his French-made films as soon as possible. These plans were aborted by the formation of the Motion Picture Patents Company, and he had to settle grudgingly for a contract with the licensed importer Kleine. His correspondence with Kleine, now in the Library of Congress, clearly indicates that Gaumont believed this arrangement would be temporary. During the years that Cohl worked for him, Gaumont was constantly crossing the Atlantic in hopes of establishing an American production branch. His letters to Feuillade from America reveal a shrewd businessman with his eye on American tastes in film.[19] At least one publication, *Cine-fono* of Milan, expressed the opinion—undoubtedly held by many in private—that Gaumont was too preoccupied with American affairs and that his Paris business was suffering.[20]

The everyday filmmaking business was supervised by Feuillade, who also acted as intermediary between Gaumont and the staff. He had been head writer from 1905 to 1907, when he replaced Alice Guy Blaché as artistic director (or, precisely, "chef du service artistique des théâtres et de la prise de vue"). He assembled a circle of gifted and efficient craftsmen. Foremost was Etienne Arnaud (1879–1955), an old friend from the south of France with whom he had previously collaborated on vaudeville scripts. Arnaud's first assignment at Gaumont was to direct Feuillade's *Attrapez mon chapeau* (Grab my Hat, 1906).[21] Among the other directors were the former actors Jacques Roullet-Plessis and Roméo Bosetti. Ben Carré recalled that, "having been an acrobat, Bosetti demanded that his actors perform difficult feats and neck-breaking stunts. If any of them hesitated, then he, himself, immediately demonstrated exactly the routine he was looking for."[22] Jean Durand and Léonce Perret joined Gaumont after Cohl.

These directors were not governed by the division of labor established in later studios. Neither were they *auteurs* in the modern sense, nor in the way that Méliès worked. They functioned as a team and could be called upon to provide a scenario, to direct, and even to operate the camera if necessary. It was not unusual for two or more directors to apply their talents to a single film, making it difficult now to attribute a film positively to only one of them. Arnaud's shooting carnet[23] shows that he assisted Cohl on many films, while Cohl's notes occasionally indicate "½ Arnaud" after a title. Cohl probably worked with Feuillade as well, but at present there is no confirmation.[24]

The scenarios Cohl submitted all fit comfortably within the usual Gaumont genres. There was a chase (*La Monnaie de 1.000 Fr.* [cat. S–11]), comedies (*Le Mouton enragé* [cat. S–1] and *Si nous buvions un coup* [cat. S–15]), and féeries (*Le Miracle des roses* [cat. S–8]).

When Cohl actually began directing, he supplemented Arnaud as a specialist in trick photography. He was responsible for the *féeries Le Docteur Carnaval* (cat. 19), *Les Chaînes* (cat. 48), and *La Lune dans son tablier* (cat. 38). These were inspired by traditional stage productions and, of course, by the films of Georges Méliès.[25] He also directed pageants, such as *Les Couronnes* (cat. 29), which presented scenes depicting the "crowning of different classes of people with varying laurels."[26] A decorative wreath framed each tableau. *Porcelaines tendres* (cat. 31) grouped live actors in compositions resembling pieces of Sèvres porcelain. They posed for a few seconds, then "came to life" and danced. As in *Les Couronnes*, each tableau vivant was enclosed within an ornamental vignette (fig. 140). Only a fragment of *Moderne École* (cat. 26) remains at the Cinémathèque Gaumont-Actualités.[27] In the excerpt the name of a historical personality is written on the left page of a large book. On the right page the character himself walks into view, salutes, and exits (fig. 141). Then the page turns, and the next actor appears.

Cohl also attempted a few comedies, documentaries, and even dramas, but his specialty was animation. By 1909 it was commonplace to speak of a "Cohl genre" or a "Cohl scene" at the studio. Even Gaumont once sent an idea for a "Cohl film" from America: "At this moment a big jewelry box opens and the jewels get out, run around the furniture and go back into the drawers. It's a scene for M. Cohl."[28]

140. *Porcelaines tendres* (cat. 31), 1909.

141. *Moderne Ecole* (cat. 26), 1909.

Out of necessity, Cohl kept to himself during his working day. There were occasions, though, as Ben Carré recalled, when Cohl would find time to chat with his colleagues:

During my six years that I was with Gaumont, one of the people I remember clearly was Emile Cohl. . . . Our conversations with Emile Cohl were centered more on painting than on motion pictures. He was married to the daughter of a well-known painter who belonged to the group of Corot, Monet, Boudin, and other moderns of that period.

What I remember about him is that he was a man twenty years older than [Robert-Jules] Garnier and I, who were then going on thirty. Our conversation was not austere. Our jokes were without offense. They would have amused anyone who overheard us in the restaurant. Emile Cohl teased us about our bachelor lives and advised us about the choice of a wife. According to him, one should marry a petite woman as he had done. A petite wife seemed like a miniature that one could put on a shelf when one wanted to work and you could keep her under your eye. . . .

The animation of Emile Cohl was the work of a single artist, not an organization like Disney's which I admire so much. I would have seen more of his films, but at Gaumont there was always some job which was needed at once, preventing me from viewing the projection of the film shot the day before.[29]

When Cohl finished these lighthearted luncheons, he would return to the special area set aside for his animation work in a corner of the studio. There, with the aid of an assistant assigned to him to operate the camera, he completed animated sequences for about four films each month which further enhanced the reputation of the Gaumont company and expanded its market. Alone in his corner he worked diligently with incredible patience. This monklike persistence won the respect of Léon Gaumont and the nickname he gave to this remarkable employee: "the Benedictine."[30]

ANTECEDENTS OF THE ANIMATED CARTOON

Moviegoers in Paris, London, the United States, and around the world saw a strange new film in the summer of 1908. Following the Gaumont trademark, a white line on a black background was drawn on the screen. The artist's hand quickly completed a child-like sketch of a clown. Suddenly the drawing seemed to come alive and the clown began to move in bewildering ways, changing his shape and encountering other equally strange moving beings. The film was *Fantasmagorie*, Cohl's first animated cartoon. Its projection time was less than two minutes, so short that most viewers undoubtedly were left puzzled by this curious apparition.

Fantasmagorie was the single most demanding task that Cohl had ever attempted as an artist. First he had made a drawing on white paper with black ink. Then he traced that drawing through a second sheet, changing nothing in the outline except for a minute alteration that would be perceived later as motion. Eventually hundreds of drawings were completed in this manner, then photographed in sequence. The result was printed in negative, so in the final film the illusion was produced of white lines moving on black. At the beginning and end Cohl's own hands appeared in positive, necessitating in these two shots the use of white ink on black paper to match the negative animation sequence.

The amount of work this film demanded was formidable, but Cohl tended to inflate it even more in his stories. He later claimed that the film contained 1,872 drawings and had taken a year to complete.[31] However, a close look reveals that only about 700 drawings—still an impressive number—were really used. Each was photographed twice in order to expose two consecutive frames of film. The live-action footage did not require any sheets of drawings. As for the amount of time required, Cohl had been frequenting the Gaumont studios only since the beginning of the year, so that would provide a maximum of six months for production. But it is very likely that the drawings were done in only four months. An early statement by him strongly suggests that the inspiration had come as late as March.

> The first strip of animated cartoon footage was released in Paris in June 1908 by the Gaumont company. Its title: *Fantasmagorie*. It scarcely matters how I first got the idea of making little stick figures move. It was in the month of March and all jokers know that March sun is dangerous. Let's just say then that the March sunshine is responsible.[32]

How did Cohl master the technique of the animated cartoon without any prior experience of cinematography? Although the "March sunshine" may have played its part, the basic technique was founded upon well-known principles. Cohl himself noted that the theory of animated drawings had been evident long before the invention of cinematography. Peter Mark Roget, Joseph Plateau, and Simon Stampfer had experimented in the 1830s with the physiological effect that came to be known as persistence of vision. The work of these investigators became vulgarized as various optical toys—Thaumatropes, Zoetropes, etc.—that were common in Victorian households throughout Europe and North America. Cohl anticipated many later animation historians when he argued that zoetrope strips showing a movement analyzed into its components were the original *dessins animés*.[33] Emile Reynaud's Théâtre optique, in operation at the Musée Grévin since 1892, was visible proof that drawings could be projected on a large screen with the illusion of movement produced by "une suite de poses successives" (a series of successive exposures, fig. 142).[34] It is more probable, though, that Reynaud's nonphotographic process of hand-painting the figures on transparent celluloid bands was of limited importance, compared to the influence of the chronophotographic studies of physiologist Etienne Marey.

Cohl himself acknowledged the importance of Marey's work and borrowed his vocabulary to explain the technique of animation:

> Every movement must be, so to speak, timed with a stop watch. If a salute is to last one second, you need 16 drawings for this gesture [fig. 143]. The projection, which lasts one second, uses 16 frames, the 16 different images that compose the salute.[35]

He modified Marey's "graphic method" to demonstrate the geometric abstraction of a cartoon figure's walk (fig. 144); Marey's moving-plate chronophotographs were the model for a study of a rotating statuette (fig. 145); and the study of multiple exposed fixed-plate chronophotographs led to a Futurist-like drawing of a running figure (fig. 146).

142. Emile Reynaud: "Théâtre optique," *La Nature*, July 23, 1892.

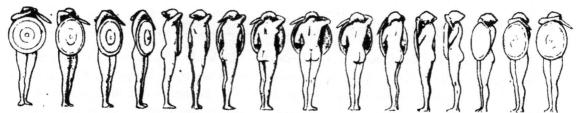

145. "Dessins animés," *Larousse Mensuel*, 1925.

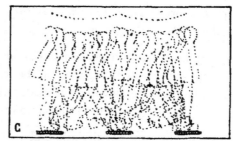

144. "Dessins animés," *Larousse Mensuel*, 1925.

146. "Dessins animés," *Larousse Mensuel*, 1925.

143. "Dessins animés," *Larousse Mensuel*, 1925.

There was also a lesson to be learned from the "flip books" ("thumb books") that had been popular since before the turn of the century. When these bound sheets of small sequential drawings or photographs were riffled with the thumb, the illusion of movement was produced. Schoolboys could easily simulate this effect by drawing in the margins of their books. Years later Cohl made some of these flip books with enlarged motion-picture frames (fig. 147).[36]

Given all these precursors and a basic understanding of the principles of cinematography, Cohl claimed that the principle of animation was simply a logical deduction.

Since the cinema is the decomposition of movement into 16 parts each lasting one second, instead of filming a living being moving about, I replaced him with 16 imaginative drawings of a fantastic being with two heads, six arms, and ten legs in front of the camera. Upon projection, I obtained the same results.[37]

He evaded the question when specifically asked about his sources, but told an interviewer that the idea had come to him gradually.

I don't know too much about how I first imagined reconstituting screen movement by means of a series of slightly modified successive drawings. The idea didn't come to me all at once and I think I recall being tortured by it for months. But the day came when I thought the idea had matured enough to submit it to my superiors. They liked it—which proves that the French cinema wasn't always in the hands of imbeciles—and I immediately set to work. The job was rather brutal and demanded patience and resignation. My first film cost me a few days that I would prefer not to remember.[38]

Although he did not choose to admit it, Cohl's experiments were also guided by contemporary developments in cinema. *Fantasmagorie* was released in the aftermath

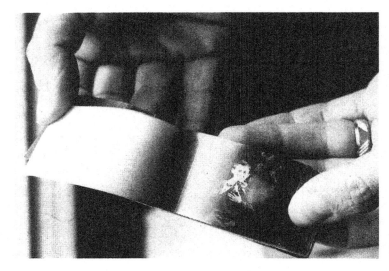

147. Flip book, "Premier cigar," ca. 1909

of one of the most sensational films to have appeared in Paris, *L'Hôtel hanté*. In February 1907 the American company Vitagraph opened its branch office in Paris at 15, rue Sainte-Cécile. In April they offered to sell a seven-minute film entitled *L'Hôtel hanté; fantasmagorie épouvantable*.[39] The film had been released in the United States in March as *The Haunted Hotel* and was directed by one of the founding partners of Vitagraph, J. Stuart Blackton (fig. 148). The film was replete with many favorite tricks, but there was also a long sequence using the technique of object animation.[40] Blackton had exposed a few frames of film in his camera, moved the objects, exposed a few more frames, and so on. The reception of the film in Paris alone made the effort worthwhile. It was the most successful American film distributed there, selling over 150 European copies.[41] It ran two shows a day at the Châtelet from July 17 through 29, 1907, and it appeared on Hippodrome programs (fig. 149).[42] By February 1908 Gaumont had purchased a print and was distributing it with another film by Blackton called *Lightning Sketches (Croquis au [grand] galop)*.[43]

Perhaps to generate some of the same kind of publicity that Vitagraph was harvesting, Gaumont invited the writer Gustave Babin to visit the studio. When Babin set out

148. J. Stuart Blackton, ca. 1908.

149. Hippodrome program, ca. 1907.

to reveal the various tricks of the cinema to his *Illustration* readers in April 1908, it was the secret of animation that he most wanted to divine.[44] He made a special visit to the Gaumont studios to interrogate Anatole Thiberville, Gaumont's chief cameraman, who responded that it was a trade secret only recently learned at the studio.[45] Babin expressed his own exasperation at trying to guess the secret of *The Haunted Hotel* and hoped an ingenious reader might succeed. The film Babin described was claimed to be Gaumont's *Le Travail rendu facile*. In fact it was *Work Made Easy*, another Vitagraph film with animation by Blackton, which had been released in the United States in December 1907.[46] Consecutive frame enlargements reproduced in the article provided striking visual evidence of the frame-by-frame technique (fig. 150).

150. J. Stuart Blackton: *Work Made Easy*, 1907.

Thiberville's statement that the discovery of the technique had vexed the technicians for a long time was echoed later by Arnaud:

There were three of us directors who had been assigned by the big boss, Léon Gaumont, the mission of going to find out by what really diabolical means objects could appear to be moving on the screen without any human intervention. We sat through three consecutive screenings [of *The Haunted Hotel*].

Finally, according to Arnaud, Emile Cohl unlocked the secret.

It was M. Cohl, author of almost 250 animated cartoons who explained the mystery of the haunted house . . . . The secret lay in the slowness of the taking: the camera having been adjusted so that each turn of the crank exposed one frame. This fractional operation allowed one to give the appearance of inert objects moving spontaneously, such as those that set a table to serve coffee. The cameraman turns the crank to photograph the set table, the director comes forward and moves the coffee pot a few millimeters and moves back out of the field of view. A second turn photographs this displacement and so on, continuing until after hundreds of new positions, one has the object in its new role as an animated being.[47]

Arnaud's account, which gives Cohl credit for the important discovery, leaves several disturbing questions unanswered. How far can Arnaud's account be trusted? If we combine his recollection with Thiberville's assertions and the known facts, we can reconstruct this scenario: *The Haunted Hotel* excited Paris in the summer and fall of 1907. Gaumont bought a print (along with other Vitagraph films, some of which contained animation), probably in December or January. It was duplicated for February distribution. These dates correspond to Emile Cohl's first appearance at Gaumont, so conceivably he could have participated in a close study of the film. According to Thiberville, the secret had been known for about eight months at the time of writing. Although we do not know when Babin interviewed him, nor by how much he exaggerated, a date near the end of 1907 seems to be indicated. The animated film *Work Made Easy* had obviously been "deciphered" by press time, which we may assume to have been about mid-March. Arnaud's account is possible, but is it plausible?

A serious challenge in the form of "negative evidence" is the fact that Emile Cohl himself, although he seldom hesitated to advertise his own achievements, never once claimed to have discovered the secret of *The Haunted Hotel*, even when he specifically discussed the film.[48]

Is it reasonable to believe that this team of experienced Gaumont filmmakers was unable to guess the technique, while Cohl, who had no experience in cinematography, was able to do so? It is true that Feuillade, Arnaud, and some of the others had backgrounds in writing and acting, but Anatole Thiberville had been a veteran technician at Gaumont for over a decade.[49] Their claim of complete ignorance seems even more baffling in light of the fact that the technique used in *L'Hôtel hanté* was almost as old as cinematography.

Like many aspects of early filmmaking, animation was discovered and developed more or less simultaneously in Europe and America. Credit for the first accidental application of the technique has traditionally been given to the director of *The Haunted Hotel*, Blackton, and his partner and cofounder of the Vitagraph company, Albert E. Smith.

Blackton was born in Sheffield, England, in 1875 and immigrated to the United States at the age of ten. By the time he was 21 he was eking out a career and trying to support his young wife by dabbling in several popular theatrical amusements. With Albert Smith and another partner, Ronald Reader, he entertained audiences in the New York City area with monologues, lantern projections, and "lightning sketches," an act in which the performer sketched at an easel while telling anecdotes. His main line of work in the summer of 1896 seems to have been as a "stringer" sketch artist for Joseph Pulitzer's New York *Evening World*. It was in exchange for publicity that he and Smith performed their variety act as a promotion for the paper's Sick Baby Fund. The paper also sent Blackton to meet Edison's crew to record three of his lightning sketches. The third one represented "the artist drawing a life-size picture of a female figure, in which the expressions of the countenance are rapidly changing."[50] This description strongly suggests that Blackton was using, in his very first appearance before a movie camera, a protoanimation technique visible in the surviving film made somewhat later, *The Enchanted Drawing*.

The Enchanted Drawing was copyrighted by Edison on November 16, 1900.[51] Composed in the knees-up framing, waist-high camera angle, and nine-feet distance that a few years later would be called the "American shot," the film depicted Blackton performing energetically at a large sketch pad in front of an oriental-rug backdrop. The Edison catalogue accurately described the film's action:

> Upon a large sheet of white paper a cartoonist is seen at work rapidly sketching the portrait of an elderly gentleman of most comical feature and expression. After completing the likeness the artist rapidly draws on the paper a clever sketch of a bottle of wine and a goblet, and then, to the surprise of all, actually removes them from the paper on which they were drawn and pours actual wine out of the bottle into a real glass. Surprising effects quickly follow after this; and the numerous changes of expression which fit over the face in the sketch cause a vast amount of amusement and at the same time give a splendid illustration of the caricaturist's art. 100 feet.[52]

The technical basis of the trick is the stop-action substitution effect. During shooting the camera was stopped while an assistant tore away the top sheet of paper to reveal the next drawing underneath (nearly identical, except for a change of expression; for example, a smile changes to a scowl). Drawn objects (a bottle of wine, a cigar) disappeared from the sheet and were replaced by real objects held up in the same position. Then the camera was restarted, and an instantaneous transformation would be produced during projection.

The 1896 Blackton sketch film has not been located, but the source of inspiration can be identified easily: Georges Méliès. The French magician and caricaturist had been filming his own lightning sketches since early 1896, and his films were readily available in New York.[53] Méliès did not invent stop-action substitution—Edison's *Execution of Mary, Queen of Scots* had used it in 1895—but he did perfect it and was the first to utilize it extensively. Blackton, who was in charge of the technical aspects of shooting, developing, printing, and illegal duping at Vitagraph, would have had no trouble in guessing Méliès's secret as he made copies. The earliest extant film that establishes Blackton's use of stop action is *The Vanishing Lady*, September 1898, which not only stole the Frenchman's technique but also plagiarized the American release title of Méliès's 1896 film. The film features Smith as the magician who makes the lady vanish, with Blackton behind the camera.

The stop-action trick was used again in *A Visit to the Spiritualist*, thought to have been lost but recently rediscovered. The Edison catalogue describes it as "the funniest of all moving magical films."[54] Smith dated the film 1898, but Charles Musser attributes it to December 1899. It is patterned closely on Méliès's 1897 film *L'Auberge Ensorcelée*. There are other entries in the 1900 Edison catalogue (both copyrighted June 1899) containing stop-action sequences perhaps by Blackton and Smith: *The Strange Adventures of a New York Drummer* and *Mesmerist and Country Couple* ("The mystical appearances and lightning changes are managed with wonderful cleverness"). Two additional extant early films contain numerous stop-action effects: *Hooligan Assists the Magician* (1900) and *The Mysterious Cafe* (1901). The September 1902 catalogue lists a "new" *Visit to the Spiritualist*, suggesting that the negative for the old one may have worn out.[55]

In his ghostwritten memoirs, *Two Reels and a Crank*, Smith cited (along with *A Visit to the Spiritualist*, implying that it was made at about the same time) *The Humpty Dumpty Circus*. He maintained that it was the first film in which the stop-action technique was modified into true object animation. "I used my little daughter's set of wooden circus performers and animals, whose movable joints enabled us to place them in balanced positions. It was a tedious process inasmuch as the movement could be achieved only by photographing separately each change of position."[56] This important film, alas, is another that seems not to have survived. Nor is there any documentation to confirm that it ever existed. This does not necessarily mean that the film was never made; indeed, there are several hypotheses. The first is simply that everything Smith said was true and the film is lost, like the vast majority of productions from this period. The second hypothesis is that the film was made, but not in 1898, as Smith recalled.

For legal reasons there was a hiatus in production at Vitagraph between January 1901 and March 1902. From 1902 to September 1905, there was only sporadic production,[57] but if the film really existed, it is likely that *The Humpty Dumpty Circus* dates from this period, perhaps from late 1904 or early 1905. (The title does not appear after the company reorganized and started advertising its films in the New York *Clipper*.)[58] During this three-and-one-half-year period of Vitagraph's relative dormancy, foreign films—especially those of Arthur Melbourne-Cooper, which probably contained true object animation—began to find American distribution.

British filmmaker Melbourne-Cooper's first experiment in object animation appears to have been *Matches Appeal*, a Boer War propaganda film said to have been released in 1899, although this date has not been confirmed. But either Cooper's *Dolly's Toys*, released in 1901, or *The Enchanted Toymaker*, of 1904, could have provided inspiration for Blackton if they contained true animation, since it is likely that they were both duped and distributed by Edison. The February 1903 Edison catalogue describes *Animated Dolls*, a film in which sleeping children are visited by a fairy.

> The dolls, which are dressed as boy and girl, come to life and begin to make love to each other. They make so much noise, however, that they wake up the children. Upon seeing the action of the little people, the children are very much amused, and sitting up in bed, they watch the performance. Finally the dolls, upon seeing that they are discovered, resume inanimate form, and the children jump out of bed to get them.

While this may have been a remake by Edison's special-effects buff, Edwin S. Porter, it seems more likely that the film was simply a retitled dupe of Melbourne-Cooper's original. The same may be said for *The Toymaker and the Good Fairy*, described in the September 1904 catalogue: "[The toymaker] is surprised to see all the toys he touches move as though alive. . . . [Toys] march along in rapid succession until all are inside the ark." This subject and its treatment resemble Melbourne-Cooper's *The Enchanted Toymaker*, which had been released earlier in 1904 by R. W. Paul. Circumstantial evidence exists in the fact that Edison did not attempt to copyright either film as his own, and that other R. W. Paul duped films can be identified in the Edison catalogue. We also know that Edison freely duped and distributed Pathé films during this period.[59] Paul's films were distributed in the United States by Williams, Brown and Earle and by Miles Brothers.[60]

The animated-toy theme in both Cooper films may also have been a likely influence on *The Humpty Dumpty Circus*. Unfortunately neither of the British films nor their American versions have been located, and some historians have questioned whether there were any truly animated British films before the technique was learned from Blackton.[61] However, pointedly, it now seems, Smith had referred to his Vitagraph film as "the first stop-motion film *in America*" [my emphasis], so the possibility of foreign inspiration should not be hastily dismissed. It is reasonable to conclude that the Blackton and Smith film, if it existed, was made around late 1904 and was patterned either directly on Cooper's films or, indirectly, on Porter's imitations.[62] This would explain the reason for Blackton's silence concerning his alleged status as the inventor of animation. He knew that it was not true.

In early 1905 animated films by Edwin S. Porter, who was by then the trick specialist at the Edison studio, started appearing with greater frequency. *How Jones Lost his Roll*, copyrighted in March, utilized animated title cards:

> From beginning to end the audience is kept in one continual state of expectancy

while the pictures show "How Jones Lost His Roll," the letters, after much effort and manoeuvering disentangle themselves at intervals and tell the story in words.

In May Edison copyrighted *The Whole Damm Family and the Damm Dog*, in the final scene of which we see parts of the dog's body "arrange themselves in shape, showing a dilapidated looking cur sitting up on his haunches. Presently his tail joins his body by piecemeal, the end having two tin cans tied to it."[63] In February 1907 Edison copyrighted *The "Teddy" Bears*, which has a remarkable sequence wherein Goldilocks views animated bears through a keyhole. All three films survive.

Europeans had plenty of opportunities to view these films. Porter's Edison films had been readily available in Europe since 1903 when a London sales office was opened. In early 1906 Edison strengthened its position when it opened a distribution office in London at 25 Clerkenwell Road, E.C.[64] However, it is not yet known which of the above specific titles were distributed in Europe.

To return to Vitagraph, when it resumed regular production in 1905, stop-action tricks were common (for example, in *Raffles, the Amateur Cracksman*), but there was no *verifiable* animated film until April 1906.

That was *Humorous Phases of Funny Faces*. By this time the technique of object and drawing animation was definitely established. The letters of the title form themselves on a blackboard (using reverse motion, as well as animation). Only Blackton's right hand appears. He sketches comic figures of a man and woman who "come to life," using a combination of the *Enchanted Drawing* protoanimation technique and true frame-by-frame animation. Early audiences were astounded when the drawings began to move:

> Suddenly the figure becomes animated with life, the umbrella is thrown up into the air, and making a complete turn, is deftly caught again by the sketch. After this astonishing occurrence . . . several of these mysterious and fantastic sketches appear, and each one is more surprising than the other, the whole film being extremely odd and unique, and causing considerable comment wherever exhibited.[65]

Other sequences animate cutouts of a clown and poodle and show Blackton rubbing out the picture with a wet sponge. The film has no narrative exposition; it is basically a catalogue of tricks.

Other 1906 comedies, such as *The Hand of the Artist* (August, now lost, and probably a dupe of Walter Booth's film of the same title), used similar effects. In December another narrative innovation was introduced in *A Midwinter Night's Dream, or Little Joe's Luck*. Joe dreams that he is sheltered by a wealthy family at Christmas. He goes to bed and dreams (within his dream) that his Teddy bear and circus toys come to life. (They are probably the toys that were in *Humpty Dumpty Circus*.) The animation sequence is "naturalized" by integrating it within the larger framing narrative. The film uses panning in astonishing ways, including panning back and forth between Joe and the animated scene on his dresser top.[66] Another significant aspect of this title is that Blackton was carelessly slow in retreating from the scene before the shutter tripped, thus "catching" him at work and potentially revealing the technique to astute viewers (fig. 151). *The Mechanical Statue and the Ingenious Servant* (January 1907), also used animation. Obviously by the time *The Haunted Hotel* was released in February 1907, there was a long list of animated antecedents.

In July Blackton released *Lightning Sketches*, a film that returns to his vaudeville roots. In the remaining fragment (about half of the original eight-minute film), we see Blackton sketching Smith at the easel, making some stereotyped racist caricatures, and there is some rather unwieldy paper animation.

Jon Gartenberg suspects, based on contemporary descriptions, that animation was used in these lost 1907 Vitagraph films: *The Disintegrated Convict* (September), *The Kitchen Maid's Dream* (November), and *A Crazy Quilt* (November).[67] *Work Made Easy*, the film that excited Babin so much when he wrote his article, was released in December. After this, Blackton began to lose interest in the technique. *The Thieving Hand* (1908) uses single-frame cinematography to reunite an artificial hand with its owner. *The Magic Fountain Pen* and *Princess Nicotine* (both 1909) contained animated inserts. Blackton's last effort seems to have been a sequence of clay animation in *Chew Chew Land, or the Adventures of Dolly and Jim* (1910).[68]

The influence of Blackton's films on European animators was enormous. In early 1906, just as Blackton's interest in the technique was strongest, Vitagraph contracted with Urban to supply prints to the European markets: "A negative is sent over [from the U.S.], so that the first performances can synchronize in England, America and Paris."[69] The studio opened its own London office in February 1907 at 10 Cecil Court. The prints they distributed became the primary source of technical knowledge for the first

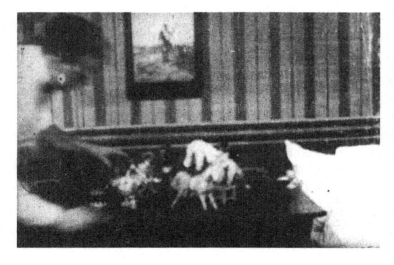

151. J. Stuart Blackton: *A Midwinter Night's Dream*, 1906.

generation of European animators. In summary, Jon Gartenberg is correct when he states that "Vitagraph's object animation films were the bridge between the stop-motion substitution films of Méliès and his contemporaries and the cartoons (animated films) of later years."[70]

Examples of animation made closer to the Gaumont studios would have been provided by another candidate for the distinction of discovering the technique in Europe, a Spaniard named Segundo de Chomón (1871–1929).[71] He had been making films in Barcelona when Ferdinand Zecca met him in 1902 and commissioned him to color and title some Pathé films intended for Spanish distribution. One day, according to his biographer Carlos Cuenca, Chomón was shooting titles and did not notice a fly on the sheets. When the film was processed, he was surprised to see the fly "jumping" about the screen and, after thinking this over, deduced the theory of object animation. A few more experiments led to the use of the technique in a seven-minute film, allegedly made around 1905, called *El Hotel electrico*. A couple is seen registering in a modern hotel. Among its unusual attractions are mysterious powers that cause the luggage to enter the elevator by itself and clothes to hang themselves up—accomplished by frame-by-frame exposures. The couple continue to marvel until a drunk downstairs interferes with the electrical system, causing them to be ejected into the street. They pick up their belongings and vow never to return. The film exists, but the 1905 date is dubious. Not only is the plot suspiciously similar to Blackton's hit film, but a check of the record shows that Pathé did not release it in Paris until 1907, when it competed with *L'Hôtel hanté*. In the United States it appeared even later, in December 1908.[72]

Chomón began working for Pathé in Paris in 1906 under the Gallicized name of Chomont. He contributed special effects to the films of Ferdinand Zecca and Gaston Velle, including *Le Théâtre du Petit Bob* (fig. 152).[73] In this film the boy Bob introduces

152. Segundo de Chomón and Gaston Velle (?): *Bob's Electric Theater*, Pathé.

his puppet-show stage to a few of his friends (in long shot). Then there is a long and very well done close-up animated sequence showing his toys cavorting before the little curtain. After the success of Blackton's *Haunted Hotel* in 1907, Chomón completed many films that utilized object animation. Cuenca argues that Chomón also made animated drawings before either Blackton or Cohl in the 1907 film *La Maison hantée*.[74] Unfortunately, so much of Chomón's work remains to be discovered, and the dating is so uncertain, that a final evaluation of his achievements must be postponed.[75]

The same might be said for another English developer of animation, Walter R. Booth. He had been a professional magician, who, like Méliès, recognized the potential of the cinema. Around 1898 he began to direct trick films produced by R. W. Paul.[76] His specialty was a type of transformation in which a drawing of a person changed into a living figure by using dissolves and stop-action substitutions. It was probably this trick that was used in *Hand of the Artist* (1906). Although it has been called the first British animated cartoon, nothing in the catalogue description suggests that the film used any true animation.[77]

Although he had already copied several of Blackton's films, Booth did not use animation when he made *Hanky Panky Cards* in June 1907, despite the seeming appropriateness of the technique.[78] The earliest existing actual animated film by Booth is *The Sorcerer's Scissors* (October 1907, fig. 153), in which a Teddy bear cuts paper with scissors.[79]

Meanwhile, in the United States, at American Mutoscope & Biograph, they were also trying their hand at animation by G. W. "Billy" Bitzer, who would become famous as Griffith's cameraman, and F. A. Dobson, a cameraman about whom little is known. The first known Biograph film with animation is *If You Had a Wife Like This* (also known as *How Would You Like a Wife Like This?*), photographed by Bitzer in February 1907 and released on May 23.[80] In the one animated sequence a bowling ball appears to pass through the pins without knocking any of them down. The following month Dobson filmed *Dolls in Dreamland*, in which "a luncheon is served by Teddy Bear to the now-animated Dolls, after each gives a dance peculiar to their character."[81] In *The Tired Tailor's Dream*, photographed collaboratively by Dobson and Bitzer in May 1907, a suit of clothes is sewn together by an animated needle and thread. "All this is accomplished without the aid of helping hands. The various articles seem endowed with human intelligence and go about their work in a business like manner. . . . This is undoubtedly the funniest film ever made, as well as the most mystifying."[82] (Emile Cohl would base a future film on a similar premise.) In May 1908 Biograph released *The Sculptor's Nightmare* (photographed by Bitzer, with D. W. Griffith and Mack Sennett as actors), in which clay busts metamorphose into political caricatures. Biograph had begun French distribution by this time, and it was almost certainly this film that was specifically described by Etienne Arnaud when he was interviewed in June 1908: "Take

153. Walter R. Booth: *The Sorcerer's Scissors*, Urban, 1907

a statue modeled in clay," Arnaud advised. "With successive touches of the thumb, deform it until it is only a mass, and with each change, expose one frame."[83]

The most surprising name on the list of animation pioneers is that of Léon Gaumont, who claimed a patent on the process. Whether inspired by Blackton's earliest examples or, more likely, a product of his own fertile technical imagination, Gaumont took out patent number 296.016 in 1900 for a "System of producing cinematograph films reproducing events, real or otherwise, by the representation of the simulated displacements of objects, bodies, masses, troupes, ships, etc., etc." Despite the tantalizing phrase "déplacements simulés," careful reading makes it clear that Gaumont intended his metal cutouts and figurines to be moved around with magnets.[84]

This brief survey shows that by the time Cohl arrived at the studio, animated films were abundantly visible. Blackton's films were distributed by the Paris office of Vitagraph, and Gaumont had purchased copies; Booth's Urban films were released through Eclipse; Chomón's Pathé films were seen regularly. Bitzer's, and probably Dobson's, animated films were known to Arnaud, and we presume that Cooper's and Porter's films were viewable. That the talented Arnaud and Thiberville did not know how to take single-frame exposures seems, in the light of their competition's efforts, suspicious, if not completely untenable. So why were there no animated Gaumont films before 1908, and why did both cinematographers deny knowing how to make them?

In *Before Mickey: The Animated Film 1898–1928*, I argued that producers and directors had little incentive to undertake the relatively high production cost and arduous exertion required to make such films because the return to them per meter was the same as for an ordinary film. It was not until the sensational success of *L'Hôtel hanté* that profits were assured and animation was considered a safe investment. Perhaps the strategy was concocted to save the faces of producers who had known the technique of animation all along but had simply blundered in not exploiting it earlier.[85] There is also evidence that an aura of secrecy was created deliberately to surround the technique of animation. The producers' rationale is revealed in this extract found in Edison's promotion of *How Jones Lost His Roll*. The 1906 catalogue appealed to exhibitors not to divulge the technique because "further description is unnecessary and would only detract from the interest and novelty, the same as exposing a trick before performing it. Everyone wants to know how it [i.e., animation] is done."[86] In *The "Teddy" Bears* the animated scene was not exploited by the studio catalogue: "[Goldilocks] unexpectedly discovers a peephole, through which she sees something that astonishes and pleases her. In the room beyond are a number of 'Teddy Bears' performing all sorts of tumbling, balancing and numerous other acrobatic feats."[87] The secrecy strategy was enormously successful for Vitagraph in Europe. No sooner had the London office opened than the advertising blitz to market *The Haunted Hotel* began in earnest, with ads explicitly provoking the audience: "Can you solve the mystery of THE HAUNTED HOTEL? A weirdly marvellous conception. Startling, Puzzling, Bewildering." Trade-journal editors rose to the challenge and (like Babin?) pretended ignorance:

> The Vitagraph Company's latest is called "The Haunted Hotel," and they ask, "Can you solve the problem?" In our opinion it would be a clever man who could explain some of the effects introduced in the course of the subject. . . . How all this is done we do not know, but it makes the film one of the best of the month, and one which should not be missed on any account. [88]

The cultivation of an aura of myth and secrecy is not unique to the origins of animation. Similar policies of secrecy were implemented during the beginnings of the star system. It is not surprising that technicians and producers have typically resisted applying new technology until they think that the marketplace warrants (or demands) the investment risk.[89] Furthermore, the "cult of secrecy" surrounding early animation could be taken as a mark of the producers' desire to commodify the subject matter of the films, to make the technique and the effects seem unique and valuable—as magic— rather than the simple mechanical operation which in fact it was.

According to Victorin Jasset, the secret of animation escaped when "some indiscretions brought the European directors up to date on the trick."[90] It was almost certainly Blackton, who often visited his London and Paris offices during this period, who disclosed the technique.[91] As soon as the cat was out of the bag, producers attempted to capitalize on their knowledge by getting free publicity. Animation was definitely in the public domain by April 1908 when "Stop Camera Tricks" was published in a British trade magazine:

> Un-natural scenes, such as tumbling cans, self-acting tools [i.e., *Work Made Easy*] etc., are made thus: take the marching battalion of toy soldiers. Put them in ranks and files, make one exposure and then move all of them little by little forward, between each movement making an exposure.[92]

In June the same periodical made public the technique of blackboard animation:

> Pictures of figures, etc., drawn on a blackboard without hands to guide the white chalk, are produced by the piecemeal process, i.e., a camera is used which is provided with the means for making one or more exposures at a given movement of the handle, and each time the handle is stopped some additional stroke is added to the drawing before the camera is started again. To keep the chalk in place the drawing is generally made on a board lying horizontally or nearly so, and the image is received by the lens of the camera after being once reflected. Hence the board being in a horizontal position, the chalk will rest on the board quite well.[93]

At the same time Arnaud was revealing the secret during an interview published in the June issue of a mass-circulation family magazine, *Lectures pour Tous*. In August 1909 the American exhibitors' trade journal *The Nickelodeon* revealed the various techniques used in *Princess Nicotine*.[94] We can conclude that by 1909 the original technical "mystery" of animation was well dissipated.

Sufficient proof that Cohl was aware of his cinematic precedents when he made *Fantasmagorie* lies within the film itself. Printing the animated footage in negative was probably motivated by the desire to simulate Blackton's chalk-line effect. Two of the characters who appear in *Humorous Phases of Funny Faces*, the clown and the bourgeois gentleman, return to Cohl's film in reincarnated forms. The most significant iconographic link between the two films is the motif of the artist's hand that creates the initial drawing before the camera on the black tabula rasa. When he borrowed this idea from Blackton, Cohl—perhaps inadvertently—situated his film in a tradition that originated in the popular stage act called "lightning sketches." In Europe music-hall performers such as Tom Merry and Little Stanley made a name for themselves drawing sketches on easels and blackboards. In the United States we have already seen young J. Stuart Blackton billing himself as a lightning cartoonist.[95]

Méliès was France's first "lightning cartoonist" on film. As the "Dessinateur express" in 1896, Méliès caricatured contemporary personalities in a style that looked very much like his earlier graphic art.[96] After Méliès, the "lightning cartoonist" films were always infused with magic. The sketches of the artists would take on a life of their own, obey their creators like somnambulists, or act rebelliously. None of these films contained any animated drawings. It was apparently Blackton who first realized that instead of making abrupt changes in the interval between exposures, gradual changes could be made that would produce the illusion of moving drawings. That theory, of course, was the basis of *Humorous Phases of Funny Faces*. The conception of the film was nevertheless still very close to the "lightning sketches" stage act, except that only the artist's forearm, not his full length, can be seen.

The "lightning cartoonist" motif was propagated by Booth when his imitation of *Humorous Phases of Funny Faces*, called *Comedy Cartoons*, was released in 1907. It also borrowed the two male and female faces, the smoking joke, and the figure of a clown.[97] Booth's *Lightning Postcard Artist* (1908) retained its association with the stage act in the title, but descriptions of the film indicate that neither the artist nor his hands appeared in it.[98]

Throughout the evolutionary change from the "lightning cartoonist" films to the true animated cartoon, there was a noticeable shift of emphasis from the performer to the drawings. At first the camera captured the artist's act in its entirety, and his full-length profile filled the screen. Later the camera was brought in closer to the easels and blackboards. Because only the arm of the artist was visible, his importance as an entertainer was diminished. With *Fantasmagorie* the artist's hand is seen in extreme close-up for only a few seconds. When it withdraws, the graphic work springs to life on its own. In the finale of the film the little clown rides away, as though asserting his liberation from the artist-creator. The drawings are now of primary importance and the hand is secondary—a mere vestige of the old vaudeville tradition that would completely disappear in Cohl's next films.

The Creation of Animation Techniques at Gaumont

Although *Fantasmagorie* was completed in June 1908 and screened for London buyers in July, it was August before the film was released in Paris. Cohl was fond of mentioning that his film was first shown at the Théâtre du Gymnase on August 17, 1908, when Gaumont had leased the prestigious theater during its annual summer closing. But a search of Paris newspapers and trade journals has failed to document any Gaumont public screenings at the Gymnase between mid-June and September of 1908. If there had been an unadvertised series of films, this would have been in sharp contrast to the heavy advertising for the program of Chronophone films presented there the summer before. Nevertheless, there is some circumstantial evidence, including the memoirs of the secretary-general of the theater, Léon Poirier, suggesting that screenings of some sort were taking place at the Gymnase.[99] One writer noticed that "theaters that put on serious plays in the winter (I refer to the Gymnase) have become cinemas for the summer."[100] This suggests that Gaumont had indeed leased the theater, but perhaps the unadvertised projections were restricted to potential buyers or were for the purpose of further testing of the Chronophone and not open to the general public.

Whatever the case, *Fantasmagorie* was added to the Gaumont program for the third week of August. By that time Cohl had already completed his second cartoon, *Le Cauchemar du fantoche* (The Puppet's Nightmare, cat. 2). It was also drawn in the chalk-line style of *Fantasmagorie* but was more than twice as long. No prints survive, so all that is known about it is the description published in the Gaumont catalogue:

> *Le Cauchemar du fantoche* is an amusing and bizarre series of humorous drawings in which the apparent neglect of form conceals a consummate art. Enormous success for this completely new genre.[101]

Rather than promoting Cohl's work vigorously, Gaumont's blurb was almost apologizing for its lack of "form." The writer was apparently puzzled by the drawings that moved in a state of constant flux.

Cohl was paid 250 francs for his third film, *Un Drame chez les fantoches* (A Puppet Drama, cat. 5), in August 1908.[102] The events unfold as quickly as in *Fantasmagorie*, but as the title implies, this film has some semblance of a plot. A stick-figure man pulls the bell cord on the facade of a house. From the window above the door a female figure looks down at her caller and dumps a bucket of water on him. A glimpse of another man in the room behind her shows us that there is a love triangle. The first man leaps through the open window and causes an explosion, then pursues the escaping woman while the lines of the house disintegrate. A policeman befriends her, and a bourgeois gentleman pins a medal for valor on the officer. The original jealous man is now sharpening a knife at a grindstone. It explodes and its pieces turn into bricks that build up a wall. He hides behind the wall and threatens the woman with a knife, but a snake concealed in a flowerpot takes it away from him. The policeman reappears and finds the man kneeling repentantly over the woman, who has fainted. The officer confines him in a salad basket, the outlines of which dissolve into a jail scene. The man, now a prisoner, stacks up the chairs and tables to gain access to the window, only to fall through and begin wrestling with another man wearing a broad-rimmed hat. The woman returns to separate them, and the two men melt into amorphous shapes on each side of her. As she kneels between them, a spider descends briefly, tethered on a strand of web. When she wraps the two deflated forms of the men about her neck like a boa, there is another incongruous happening as a shower head descends to drench her. The policeman returns carrying his nightstick. The two blobs—formerly the wrestlers—slither away but return when the woman kisses the policeman and hands him a heart. Everyone takes a curtain call, reminding the audience that these bizarre, irrational scenes began as though they were an ordinary melodrama.

These first three works may be conveniently called the "fantoche" films because they were all done exclusively in the white-on-black style and featured similar stick figures that were intended to represent puppets (*fantoches*). They form a separate group within Cohl's work and also represent the first stage of his development of the technology of animation.

Drawing animation. Cohl's earliest animation system, the one he used exclusively for the "fantoche films," created the illusion of moving lines from a series of individual drawings on paper. It is now called the retracing method. He constructed a light box, simply a wooden frame with a frosted glass top. Inside was an electric bulb for illuminating the sheets of paper from behind. In the first experiments the camera was aimed at the drawings horizontally, the normal arrangement used then for shooting titles. But this required a sheet of glass over the artwork to hold it up, and the cumbersome arrangement was quickly abandoned in favor of mounting the camera vertically above the drawings. In *Fantasmagorie* each image was drawn, photographed, then traced onto a second sheet before removing the original sheet from the light box. The advantage of this procedure was that image registration remained more constant than it would have if the drawings had been made and photographed separately. The technique also fostered spontaneous graphic improvisation, since there was no preplanned narrative.

However, there were great disadvantages. The rear light source produced a mottled background as the light passed through the uneven fibers of the paper. Each drawing had to be photographed before the next tracing was made, so there was no way to preview the animated sequence by flipping the sheets. The timing of the synthetic screen movements had to be calculated mathematically and by "animator's intuition." Cohl was also annoyed that the India ink he used tended to cockle the tracing paper:

> The transparent paper was very thin and without substance, in spite of the glass under it. It warped and offered no resistance to the pen full of india ink, however lightly used to trace the sketch. Another system had to be found.[103]

By far the greatest disadvantage was the length of time required to complete a film, which seemed, in 1908, like an eternity. In November Cohl had less than 200 meters of released film to show for seven months of hard work. This amount normally represented three to five days of shooting for a typical Gaumont film. And the three films had netted only 750 francs for the artist.

Nevertheless, Cohl was encouraged by the public reception of his films. A British correspondent wrote from Paris:

Two of Gaumont's productions are being well received this week. *Fantastical Transformations* [*Le Cauchemar du fantoche*] is a curious succession of tracings of a *fantoche*, and has evidently been made after the manner of "lightning sketches" lately issued by the American Vitagraph. It will certainly meet with great success here.[104]

His success was also indicated by the rapidity with which the first imitations appeared. Another film called *Fantasmagorie* (subtitled *Jeux divers*) was released in October 1908. Distributed by the British company Wrench, it amused audiences with "parts played by billiard balls, checkers and dominoes, without the appearance of any players."[105] The first explicit plagiarism of Cohl's technique was a Pathé film called (in the United States) *Bobby's Sketches*. According to its *Moving Picture World* description, the film

partakes of the character of "The Love Affair in Toyland" [*Un Drame chez les fantoches*] brought out by the same house [*sic*] some weeks ago. In this instance the sketches Bobby makes suddenly assume life and do a good many funny things. The sketches are funny and the action of the figures never fails to amuse the old folks and set the children wild with delight.[106]

Perhaps this animation was made by Segundo de Chomón. Cohl believed that "the first imitations came from Italy," and Chomón had been working in Turin with Carlo Rossi since early 1908.[107] His films were still distributed by Pathé.

Despite the popularity and alluring linear qualities of the "fantoche" films, Cohl could no longer sustain the heroic effort that their production demanded. Later he nostalgically regretted abandoning the original technique:

The drawing in these first films had the merit of visual suppleness. The smoothness of the penciled characters was remarkable, with no jerks or shocks. The sketches had been planned very carefully. The gestures, especially when foreshortened, were as exact as in reality. There was altogether a softness that later had to be sacrificed when the time required to make the designs had to be economized.[108]

The exigencies of the Gaumont studio required that he experiment with alternative animation systems.

Object animation. Cohl made surprisingly few films for Gaumont utilizing the object-animation technique of Blackton, Chomón, and others. The first was *Les Allumettes animées* (Animated Matches, cat. 6). It was also the first film to use economical live-action framing sequences preceding and following Cohl's animation. In the prologue a man buys some matches and blows up his room while trying to light his pipe.[109]

Etienne Arnaud probably directed this sequence. In Cohl's animated insert there is

> a box of matches on the screen; it opens and a match jumps out and stands up by itself; another follows and stands by the first, and a third places itself across the others, forming a letter H. Little by little an entire word is thus formed, or sometimes a geometrical figure.[110]

Cohl's skill at timing the movements allowed him to impart anthropomorphic qualities to the shoes in *Les Chaussures matrimoniales* (Matrimonial Footware, cat. 32) as they cavort about their owners' hotel room after the newlyweds have retired for the night. The aggressive "male" shoes chase the coquettish "female" shoes. The articles of furniture in *Le Mobilier fidèle* (Faithful Furniture, cat. 56) march back to their rightful owner like faithful puppies.[111] One scene in the film contains the first example of an "animated" human being when a man sitting on a piano stool is spun up and down by means of single-frame photography, a technique that would be called pixilation nearly a half-century later by Norman McLaren. *Le Linge turbulent* (Turbulent Laundry, cat. 27) was made with articles of clothing. Arnaud referred to it as "American laundry" because it was shot using "the American movement" animation.[112]

Les Quatres Petits Tailleurs (Four Little Tailors, cat. 61) illustrates how Cohl's animation sequences were planned as inserts in predominantly live-action films. The story describes

> the efforts of four tailors to win the hand of the master's daughter when he promises to give her to the one most proficient in his business. The love story gives a touch of life to some good trick photography. One sews without a thread, the second sews without a needle and the third sews the wings of a fly. The fourth merely does well what a tailor should do and gets the girl, putting the seal of approval upon the man who does his work well.[113]

The negatives at the Cinémathèque Gaumont-Actualités show that four separate sections were filmed originally. In the first the actor Lucien Cazalis is seen emerging from the doorway of a medieval building carrying a bundle of clothes. The second tableau is an interior set where tailors are hard at work. The third tableau shows the master tailor addressing the atelier. The fourth section consists of all the animation footage. Cohl's hand appears with a needle and thread. The thread crawls through the eye of the needle by itself, then goes to work on a piece of fabric. The hand opens a fold in the cloth to show that the needle has sewn it. In the final print this section would have been intercut with the previous tableaux to tell the story. Intertitles (not included in the archival print) would have helped make the transitions more fluid.

Le Champion du jeu à la mode (The Champion of Games, cat. 52) uses only the briefest insert of animation when the champion covers his puzzle with a handkerchief and the viewer sees the pieces moving magically into place. Léon Gaumont had sug-

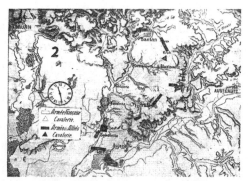

154. Cohl and assistant working on *La Bataille d'Austerlitz*, Gaumont studios, May 1909.

155. *La Bataille d'Austerlitz* (cat. 30), 1909.

gested the original idea after observing the jigsaw-puzzle fad on one of his American visits. This was apparently a fairly common practice because Cohl's *La Bataille d'Austerlitz* (cat. 30) was the realization of an idea of Gaumont's dating back to his 1900 patent. For this film, which "attempts to schematically reproduce on a map the movements of this grandiose battle,"[114] Cohl drew upon his childhood interest in cartography. He also supervised the construction of a special oversized animation stand (fig. 154). The scenario was adapted from actual movements of the famous battle (as recorded in the notebooks of Commandant Collin) at which Napoleon was victorious on December 2, 1805. The duration of the battle from 7:00 a.m. to 4:00 p.m. was indicated in the film by a clock face with animated hands (fig. 155).

Puppet animation. Eight Gaumont films were made by the specialized type of object animation that used articulated dolls or puppets. *Les Frères Boutdebois* (The Woodchip Brothers, cat. 9) and *Soyons donc sportifs* (Let's Be Sporty, cat. 12) had the puppets performing acrobatic feats. Vaudeville-trained animal acts were satirized in *Les Beaux-Arts de Jocko* (cat. 14), in which

> we find Jocko, a full size automatic monkey, taking a hand at the fine arts. He demonstrates his ability with the brush and palette—wins laurels as a sculptor, tries architecture and proves an apt scholar of music.[115]

There were many more animated animals in *Monsieur Clown chez les lilliputiens* (Mr. Clown among Lilliputians, cat. 28), one of Cohl's most accomplished puppet films. The audience is composed of about twenty dolls who move individually in response to the acts they are watching. Besides Mr. Clown, there are performing horses, bears, and elephants (fig. 156).

Three puppet animations were spectacular productions of literary classics. *Don Quichotte* (Don Quixote, cat. 39) condensed the familiar Cervantes story into a series of short tableaux. *Le Petit Chantecler* (cat. 54) was a diminutive version of Rostand and Le Bargy's *Chantecler*, then being revived in Paris. *Le Tout Petit Faust* (cat. 60) was not based on the original Faust but on the opéra-bouffe version that had been a favorite of Cohl's since he had caricatured Léa d'Asco in the role of Marguerite in 1882 (fig. 157). Cohl had background sets painted in grisaille, either by Gaumont's decorator Robert-Jules Garnier or by Ben Carré (fig. 158). The articulated dolls, which had to be repositioned for each exposure, were costumed by Cohl (fig. 159).

156. *Monsieur Clown chez les lilliputiens* (cat. 28), 1909.

157. "La Nouvelle Marguerite," *La Nouvelle Lune*, March 19, 1882.

159. a) Cohl working on *Le Tout Petit Faust*, April 1910.

158. Sets for *Le Tout Petit Faust* (cat. 60), 1910.

159. b) Cohl with puppets, ca. 1924.

In all the puppet films the fluidity of motion was restricted by the stiffness of the dolls, whose joints were incapable of lifelike movement. In some films, such as *Soyons donc sportifs*, the movement was so jerky that even early commentators noted that "to everyone it was too much of a wooden toy affair."[116] But these were Cohl's "superproductions" and his only all-animated films that equaled the length of Gaumont's normal releases.

Cutout animation. The use of cutout figures (*découpages*) was a labor-saving device for Cohl, as it had been for Blackton. *En route* (cat. 50) was probably the first film to use the technique exclusively. A fragment at the British Film Institute National Film Archive shows that the design of the two-dimensional figures was derived from primitive puppets (fig. 160). The story, however, is highly original. In each tableau a caveman watches an animal in motion. This scene is followed by a vision of man's application of that principle to modern transportation. The bird, for instance, forecasts the dirigible; the fish is the ancestor of the submarine. In the final climactic scene the earth is rotating on its axis propelled by rockets, airships, steamers, and balloons. When he wished to indicate water, Cohl placed a sheet of translucent celluloid over the scene. The system anticipated the later application of celluloid overlays in American animation, but the idea of drawing his figures on individual sheets of these "cels" (as in the Bray-Hurd process) did not occur to him.

Cohl used sketches of the cutout figures in *Le Peintre néo-impressionniste* (The Neo-Impressionist Painter, cat. 58) to demonstrate how they functioned as animation shortcuts (fig. 161).

Gradually, to avoid the long and, frankly, tedious work demanded to make thousands of drawings, one turned to silhouettes cut from bristol board that one could make go to and fro across the background by using registration marks.[117]

But with these articulated paper figures the movements were even more restricted than with puppets. Cohl was well aware of this potential flaw:

This intrusion of rigid cardboard led to real dryness in the character which, made in a block, moved its arms, articulated at the shoulders by a single pin, without having to shoot frame-by-frame. The work was economized, obviously, but to the detriment of suppleness.[118]

In several films he experimented with ways to turn this disadvantage into an aesthetic that profited from the flatness and artificiality of the cutouts. Each tableau of *Les Douze Travaux d'Hercule* (The Twelve Labors of Hercules, cat. 55) ends with the limbs of either Hercules or his adversary exploding and flying away from his torso. Cohl made no attempt to disguise the figures' two-dimensionality either by using trompe-l'oeil rendering or by hiding the pins that held the cutouts together. Sometimes limbs would spin around these pivots for purely humorous effects.

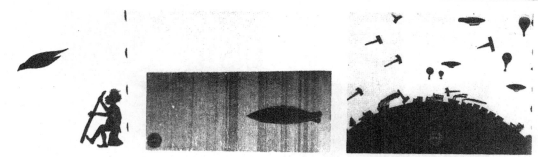

160. *En route* (cat. 50), 1910.

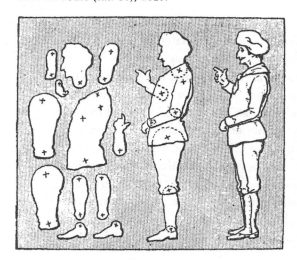

161. Cutouts for *Le Peintre néo-impressionniste*.

Le Peintre néo-impressionniste also toyed with the inherent artificiality of the system. In one sequence, for example, we see a camel moving across the sands of a desert (fig. 162). With the camel remaining stationary, the horizon begins to spin about a central pivot (actually just a pin stuck in the camel). As it comes to rest "upside down," the camel turns into a ship. The dark area that formerly represented solid ground is now seen as sky. The light area, which used to be sky, is now water. The trick was intended to dislocate the viewers' reaction to the representational gestalt formed by the arbitrary light and dark areas.

"Mixed" animation. In the majority of his Gaumont films, Cohl did not restrict himself to using only one technique. Animated lines frequently changed into cutout figures which in turn changed into solid objects or even into live actors.

The first film to combine several animation techniques was *Le Cerceau magique* (The Magic Circle, cat. 7). After a live-action framing sequence showing a little girl hanging her toy hoop on the wall of her room, a series of metamorphoses unfold within the hoop's magic boundaries. For the animation sequence a miniature hoop resting on a

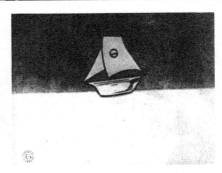

162. *Le Peintre néo-impressionniste* (cat. 58), 1910.

horizontal surface was used. Its image area was precisely calculated in order to matte drawings and three-dimensional origami paper chicks into its magic circle.[119]

Among his most important achievements in the art of animation was Cohl's development of a technique for combining live actors and animated figures in the same frame, first in *Clair de lune espagnol* (Spanish Moonlight, cat. 23). The existence of this film, released in May 1909, pushes the date of the technique back several years earlier than had previously been known. In the particular scene, "Broken hearted Pedro" is seen arguing with the moon, an animated cutout that hovers above the horizon against a black background (fig. 267). The moon responds by sticking out its tongue, grimacing, and rolling its eyes. Pedro throws rocks at it and bruises the moon's face, then peppers it with a shotgun, and, in the climactic scene, hurls a hatchet at it. Midway in its flight, the "real" hatchet changes to a drawing of a hatchet just before it is stuck in the moon's nose (fig. 267f).

In order to obtain this complex interaction between live and animated beings, Cohl had to plan the scene with split-second accuracy (see diagram 1). First he must have filmed the images of Pedro acting before the empty black backdrop. By close inspection of the developed footage, he could count the exact number of frames required, marking the ones in which the drawings had to be synchronized to the specific live events. Then he would have to complete the animation sequence, being careful to maintain frame-for-frame correspondence to the live-action footage. The white moon cutouts would be photographed on a flat black background, positioned in the upper right corner exactly as they would appear in the final film. Then the two strips of film could be combined, using the normal Gaumont matte process (double exposure) printing methods. There was one additional step in the final release prints: the moon was colored bright yellow by applying aniline dyes to each frame.

Cohl's next film was another technical success. In order to show simultaneous events in the adjacent apartments of *Les Locataires d'à côté* (Next-Door Neighbors, cat. 24), he divided the frame in half by a black line representing the common wall (fig. 163). In the apartment on the left a young magician and his friend are enjoying an amorous dinner, overheard by the old couple next door. The magician detects them peeping

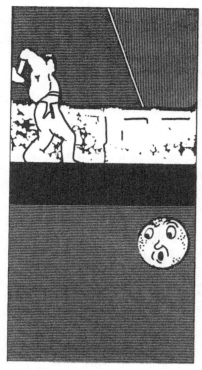

Diagram 1. Showing How Matte Effects
Were Made in *Clair de lune espagnol*,
Using Two Exposures.

163. *Les Locataires d'à côté* (cat. 24), 1909.

through a hole in the wall and goes into action. After an explosion, he changes himself
into various three-dimensional objects, including a dancing mannequin. Then he becomes an impish animated drawing who aims a rocket through the hole. This showers
fireworks into the apartment on the right, and the old couple hide in panic. Presumably
Cohl proceeded as in *Clair de lune espagnol* by filming the live action first and planning
the animation to match the developed footage. It would have been necessary to calcu-
late the field of the lens to ensure that the two images would matte together in the final
print.

   While he worked at Gaumont, Cohl had no practical examples to guide him in the
creation of animation techniques. He invented as he went along, and when special
equipment was necessary, he devised it himself, beginning with a primitive animation
stand. At first this was nothing more than "a table one meter long, well-leveled on its
four legs. On each side of the table were mounts for solidly fixing the camera."[120]

   For his camera he was fortunate to have the Gaumont Chrono-négatif at his disposal.
Although cumbersome as a field camera, it had a reputation for registration, and the
steadiness of its image made it excellent for animation work.[121] It held a 100-meter film
magazine, had variable shutter speeds, and provided reflex viewing through either a

fine Zeiss or Voigtländer lens. For special effects the film could be backed up into the magazine for lap dissolves and double exposures. It is likely that Cohl had modified the crank gears to produce one exposure per turn (as Blackton had done).

Cohl himself described the circumstances of actual cinematography (fig. 164):

> Most often the shooting was done in a darkened room with the drawings brightly lit by a bank of ten or twelve electric lamps situated between the lens and the table. Sometimes the artist used an operator whom he instructed when to turn the crank on the camera, but more often he shot by himself in order not to be distracted. Concentration was necessary at every moment if errors were to be avoided, and errors were often difficult to correct.[122]

This system required many modifications. The bank of lights made working under the camera uncomfortable and caused the paper to curl. Cohl solved this problem by replacing the standard 52 mm lens with a 75 mm telephoto lens that allowed the camera and lights to be raised.[123] But this created its own problems. The crank of the camera was too high to be easily reached, so he devised a system for exposing single frames by pulling on a cord. A technical description of this system and a series of carefully drafted

164. Cohl at animation stand, ca. 1909.

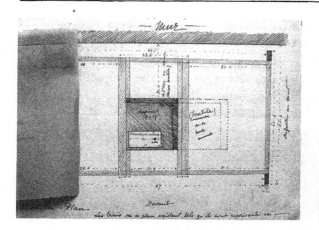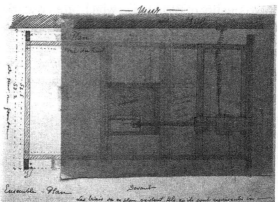

165. Drawings for shutter-tripping mechanism, with translucent overlay.

mechanical drawings, complete with transparent cellophane overlays, suggest that he eventually intended to patent it (fig. 165). Later he attached a small electric motor that could be activated by a remote switch to open the shutter and advance the film one frame at a time. With the electric drive, "the crank turned with perfect regularity and the images were exposed at the same speed and light intensity." This system was already in use during the filming of *La Bataille d'Austerlitz* in May 1909 and is essentially the same principle used on modern animation cameras.

In the back of his notebook, in 1910, Cohl compiled tables of aperture openings and depth-of-field calculations, a chart showing the viewing areas of lenses at various heights above the animation plane, and tables for converting the number of frames in an animated sequence into projection time (fig. 166). This compendium of data, still familiar to all animators, was signed "Emile Cohl, cinématographiste."

In less than three years at Gaumont Cohl had transformed the crude, jerky experiments of Blackton into a new cinema genre. Single-handedly he had created the technology and the art of the animated film and had brought it to the first plateau of development. The images of his films were photographed with the same clarity and steadiness that distinguished other fine Gaumont products. The motion was smooth and flickerless. Cohl had devised advanced, sometimes bold, techniques for diminishing the amount of time and labor required for their production. Had he not succeeded in doing so, it is unlikely that the animated cartoon would have survived in the intensely competitive economic environment of prewar cinema, once the initial novelty had eroded. In spawning a continual flow of over seventy films (almost all of which contained animated sequences), he kept the public interested in the genre and whetted its appetite. In effect, he created and sustained his own market for his work. But his achievement was more than technical. None of these films had the haphazard, pointless quality of Blackton's, which often resembled mere catalogues of special effects. Instead, each of Cohl's films was unified and disciplined, conforming to the developing criteria of uniform, institutionalized film production, although the content was often bizarre and inaccessible. These Gaumont productions laid down not only the technological foundations of the modern animated cartoon but its aesthetic basis as well.

166. Chart showing length, exposures, projection time, and number of revolutions required for various animated sequences.

CHAPTER FIVE

"Hollywood" in France and
New Jersey

PATHÉ, 1910–1911

Cohl left Gaumont on November 30, 1910, probably lured to Pathé by the offer of a better salary. The parsimonious Gaumont had also just lost Bosetti to Pathé's Comica branch, and Arnaud would join Eclair in 1911. After a brief vacation in the south of France, Cohl returned to his new apartment in Montmartre to begin working on his first two Pathé films: *Le Retapeur de cervelles* (Brains Repaired, cat. 80) and *Les Aventures extraordinaires d'un bout de papier* (Extraordinary Adventures of a Piece of Paper, cat. 81).

It was not long before he began to realize that signing with Pathé might have been a mistake. His diary for March 1911 noted a "Pathé quarrel,"[1] but since he probably had had no contact with Charles Pathé himself, the quarrel certainly must have been with Ferdinand Zecca, whose function at Pathé was analogous to Feuillade's at Gaumont and who was known for his hot Corsican temper.[2]

Perhaps the argument was about Cohl's new assignment as director of the burlesque series starring a performer from the opéra bouffe, Lucien Cazalis, as "Jobard." In all, Cohl directed ten of these films between March and May 1911.[3] It was the age of the first great screen comics, and Jobard joined his fellow comedians at Pathé: "Zigoto" (Lucien Bataille), "Calino" (Clement Mégé), "Little Moritz" (Maurice Schwartz), "Gontran" (René Gréhan), "Max" (Max Linder), "Rigadin" (Prince), and "Rosalie" (Sarah Duhamel). Judging only from the synopses of the films, the screen character of Jobard fluctuated from a henpecked bourgeois to a lecherous country bumpkin. The films were ground out at a frenetic pace and were very similar in spirit to the farces that Cohl had written in the 1880s. But they consumed all the time he would otherwise have devoted to animation, thus placing him in the predicament of his predecessor, Segundo de Chomón, who also had been allowed to make animated films only in the intervals between his other directorial assignments. In July Cohl made his last film for the Vincennes studio and embarked on a short vacation. It ended sadly when he learned that his daughter Andrée had died in an automobile accident. In mid-September Cohl signed an agreement with a man named Bates of Eclipse to make films for that company.

Le Retapeur de cervelles, the only Pathé film to survive as a viewable print, is similar to *Les Joyeux Microbes* in conception and structure. A bourgeois gentleman named Isidore Palmer is taken by his wife to call on Doctor Trepanoff for a senility cure. The celebrated doctor examines him with his latest invention, the "cephaloscope." To his amazement, the doctor sees (in a section of mixed animation) a pencil drawing of a bug change into a real insect. It divides into the two hemispheres of a brain, which then splits into six grimacing faces. These change into a dancing stick-figure drawing, a large black worm (fig. 167) and a drawing of the man's sick face. Obviously Isidore is being tortured by a brain parasite. In live-action again, the doctor drills a hole in the patient's head and extracts an enormous worm. He pins the beast to a blackboard, where it undergoes a series of transformations, generating the longest sequence of drawing animation since the 1908 "fantoche" films.[4] The white lines, animated by the retracing technique, move freely against a high-contrast, unmottled black background. After the "worm" has completed its fantastic metamorphosis, the doctor pronounces a cure and Mr. and Mrs. Palmer kiss happily.

One of the most popular "Emile Cohl" films now in distribution in the United States was made during this period. *Automatic Moving Company* (*La Garde-meuble automatique*) has been confused with Cohl's 1910 *Le Mobilier fidèle* (cat. 56), which is presently viewable only at the Cinémathèque Gaumont-Actualités. The film in distribution is actually a remake of Cohl's earlier Gaumont film and was released by Pathé in February 1912 after Cohl's departure. It begins with a postman delivering a letter which floats mysteriously (that is, with the aid of invisible wires) over to a desk where it is opened by an animated letter opener. In American prints it bears the incongruous return address of Kalamazoo, Michigan, but the setting is plainly Nice, France. This is known from the inscription on the moving van, the logo of the largest mover in Nice (who might have paid for the "product placement," as this ad strategy is now called). Next the

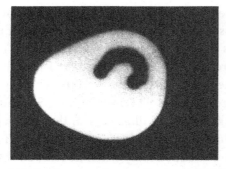

167. *Le Retapeur de cervelles* (cat. 80), 1911.

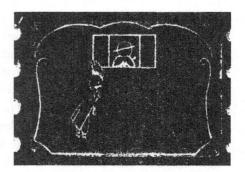

169. *Les Fantaisies d'Agénor Maltracé* (cat. 97), 1911.

furniture files out of the old apartment and into the new one in a series of excellent animated sequences. One highlight is a suggestive pas de deux between a small table and a coy lamp that is won over when the table opens its drawer. As much as one would like to attribute this film to Cohl, it was almost certainly made by Roméo Bosetti at Comica, Pathé's subsidiary in Nice. In one of his 1911 films, *Rosalie et ses meubles fidèles*, Bosetti had previously experimented with animated furniture.[5] A co-worker in the Gaumont studios, Bosetti obviously had enjoyed many opportunities to watch Cohl at work on *Le Mobilier fidèle* and other films. The existence of *Automatic Moving Company* demonstrates the early diffusion of Cohl's ideas and techniques and also their continuing popularity with audiences.

Excluding his "Jobard" films, Cohl completed only seven others in the eight months he was at Pathé (although another four have been tentatively attributed to him). Fortunately, scant traces of some of them remain in the form of short typewritten synopses and frame enlargements, which were deposited with the Cabinet des Estampes of the Bibliothèque Nationale to establish copyright priority.[6]

These documents reveal that Cohl returned to drawing animation during his stay with Pathé. *Le Cheveu délateur* (The Accusing Hair, cat. 83, fig. 168) showed a fortune-teller using a hair to predict the future. The "hair" was an animated line drawing. *Les Fantaisies d'Agénor Maltracé* (The Fantasies of Agenor Mistraced, cat. 97, fig. 169) was 110 meters long, one of his lengthiest all-animated productions. Agenor was a descendant of the early "fantoche" films a "character who always finds himself losing various parts of his body because the pencil has not drawn his silhouette completely."[7] *Les Bestioles artistes* (Beasty Artists, cat. 84, fig. 170) appears to have been made with animated spiders and other dead insects in combination with drawings. *Le Musée des grotesques* (cat. 82, fig. 171) seems to have utilized cutouts.

168. *Le Cheveu délateur* (cat. 83), 1911.

170. *Les Bestioles artistes* (cat. 84), 1911.

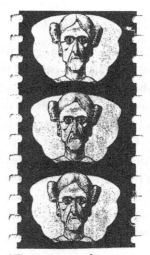

171. *Le Musée des grotesques* (cat. 82), 1911.

Cohl's last Pathé film was one of his most remarkable. *La Revanche des esprits* (The Spirits' Revenge, cat. 98) may have been the first film ever to combine live action with animation by superimposing the drawings directly onto the live footage without using a matte process. This conclusion is based upon a still in the Pathé catalogue showing a mischievous spirit thumbing his nose at the actor Cazalis (although the film was not part of the "Jobard" series) (fig. 172). However, because the photograph is a still and not a frame enlargement, we cannot yet be certain that it reproduces the effect as it appeared in the film.

172. *La Revanche des esprits* (cat. 98), 1911

ECLIPSE, 1911–1912

Cohl began working for the Eclipse company, Charles Urban's Paris branch, in October 1911. Only the titles of the eight or ten films made there remain, so little can be said about this brief period, which lasted until July 1912. Most of the films appear to have been object animations that recycled ideas first used at Gaumont.[8] At least once he shot a travelogue, *Dans la Vallée d'Ossau* (cat. 107), while vacationing in the Pyrenees.

Cohl's agreement with Eclipse was not exclusive, so occasionally films were distributed by other companies. Lux, for example, released *Fruits et légumes vivants* (Living Fruit and Vegetables, cat. 117). More important for Cohl's future was *Campbell Soups* (cat. 105). It is unknown whether this was an advertising film or a comedy, but it was his first contact with the Eclair company, with whom he would be associated for the next decade.

ECLAIR I: COHL IN AMERICA, 1912–1914

Etienne Arnaud probably introduced Cohl to the director of Eclair, Charles Jourjon. In July 1912 Arnaud had written to Cohl from America, thanking him for sending some amateur footage Cohl had shot of Arnaud's father.[9] It may have been at that time that a meeting was suggested.

In August Cohl was added to the roster of Eclair employees; he had made only a few twenty-meter commercials when the exciting news came that he, too, was being transferred to work at the studio in Fort Lee, New Jersey. He sailed with Suzanne and André first class from Le Havre on the steamer *La Lorraine*. When the family disembarked at Ellis Island on September 29, Cohl had his first disillusioning experience in America. The authorities requested that, "for sanitary reasons," he shave off the magnificent handlebar moustache that he had first grown in emulation of André Gill (fig. 173). While in America, he would find that its people were frequently inhospitable to foreigners. New York even had a law forbidding the hiring of aliens as motion-picture projectionists.[10]

Nevertheless, Cohl and the small band of French cinéastes at Eclair remained enthusiastic about the prospects of American life. Arnaud, for example, declared that New York was "altogether Paris . . . without the Parisiennes."[11] Cohl explored the city's famous attractions, such as Coney Island, where he had a trick photograph made (fig. 174).

The migration of directors and technicians to the United States was a by-product of the continuing meteoric rise of Eclair. The phenomenon was all the more startling

173. Cohl in Fort Lee, 1913.

174. Trick photograph, New York, 1913.

because the company had been founded only five years before, in 1907, by Charles Jourjon and Marcel Vandal.[12] Soon they had acquired the estate of Etienne de Lacépède in Epinay-sur-Seine. The celebrated naturalist had cultivated exotic plantings that served as excellent exterior locations for the first Eclair productions. Jourjon and Vandal also showed good judgment in hiring Victorin Jasset, who had been working for Eclipse. In September 1908 Jasset's first episode of "Nick Carter, King of Detectives" was released. *Le Guet-Apens* was an overnight sensation.

Like other French producers, Eclair coveted the American market, which the Edison Trust—soon to become the Motion Picture Patents Company—had sealed off to the smaller foreign producers in mid-1908 (possibly in collusion with Pathé, which benefited from this blow to its competitors).[13] However, by 1909, as the power of the MPPC drained away, Eclair films found their way into the United States via the Chicago-based Unique Film and Construction Company and Anti-Trust Film Company.[14] At the same time negotiations were under way with John J. Murdock of the Western Vaudeville Managers Association. It was the resulting "Murdock affair" that propelled Eclair into American production.

Murdock had set up the International Producing and Projecting Company in February 1909, with the aim of importing films from uncommitted European producers, including Eclair, in defiance of the Trust's quotas and tariffs. Murdock impressed the foreigners with his successful congressional lobbying efforts to maintain relatively low import tariffs on foreign film stock. Unknown to the European producers, though, and despite its apparently strong connections to B. F. Keith and Carl Laemmle, the IPPC was a very shaky consortium. It faced enormous legal problems in its fight against Edison, as well as technical problems in supplying noninfringing projection equipment. As the Europeans began to get wind of Murdock's difficulties, they threatened to find another American outlet. Murdock departed for Europe to explain the situation to his contacts there. But while he was overseas, the company dissolved and all of the Europeans' investments were lost. Murdock fell mysteriously "ill" in Paris, then disappeared altogether. He reemerged in the United States to become president of an independent trade association, the National Independent Moving Picture Alliance, which would go bankrupt in less than six months. J. J. Murdock, a seldom-studied figure in vaudeville and film history and a classic wheeler-dealer, became the powerful manager of the Keith vaudeville circuit in 1913 and, in 1928, cofounded RKO with David Sarnoff and Joseph P. Kennedy.[15]

Murdock's disappearance so disturbed the European producers that they decided to travel en masse to New York in the fall of 1909 to investigate the situation for themselves. Eclair was joined by representatives from Itala, Le Lion, Pathé, Gaumont, Promio, Théophile Pathé, and Raleigh. Ciné-Journal predicted that they would not regret their seasickness.[16] Most of Murdock's former producers, including Eclair, joined a new alliance, the Film Import and Trading Company. Jourjon and Vandal returned to Paris in November, depressed at the realization that only American-made films could be successfully distributed in North America as long as the MPPC was in power. Within two months Vandal confirmed that Eclair was opening an office at 31 East 27th Street in New York as one of Laemmle's Independents. It was predicted that "the Eclair Company should prove equal to the task of selling their own films in America, where they have won general appreciation."[17] Their first release was scheduled for February 7, 1910. The films were shot in France but printed and titled in the United States. When Laemmle founded the Motion Picture Producing and Sales Company, Eclair joined, along with Ambrosio, Itala, Lux, and other Europeans. Meanwhile, Eclair was establishing its reputation for films with no murder, adultery, or seduction, "which American audiences neither like nor understand."[18] Sensing a lack of comic subjects in the American market (since the old European sources of comedies had been partially dried up), Eclair announced that beginning in 1911, they would offer at least one split-reel comedy (that is, six to eight minutes) per week. This decision would later be strong motivation for sending Cohl in order to help meet the rising American demand for comedies.[19]

Announcing his intention to build an American studio in the fall of 1910, Vandal later chose a lot in Fort Lee on Linwood Avenue near Main Street (now buried under the approach ramps of the George Washington Bridge) for the site of his American studio and laboratory. By February 1911 construction of an ultramodern factory was in progress.[20]

In the midst of shooting the first Eclair-American feature, the French director Gaston Larry suddenly died on September 13.[21] It was the resulting need for a replacement that brought Arnaud (and subsequently his friend Cohl) to the United States.

Arnaud arrived in Fort Lee on January 6, 1912, and was found to be "an interesting personnage and, though unfamiliar with American customs and manners as yet, he promises to be a quick student and a man who will readily adapt himself to new conditions."[22] Under his leadership, the studio became efficiently organized. Owing to Arnaud's connections, the majority of these craftsmen were former Gaumont employees. "The personnel of this American branch is most notable," reported *Moving Picture World.* "Wherein the French excel there is a most capable Frenchman and wherein the American may excel, there is to be found a native."[23] With this nationalistic division of labor, it was natural to pick a Frenchman like Cohl to be involved with the production of comedies, for it was widely believed that the French had a special genius in that domain.

Eclair again signed a distribution contract with Carl Laemmle when he formed the Universal Film Manufacturing Company in June 1912.[24] By the time Cohl and his family boarded the *Lorraine* on August 29, 1912, Eclair had grown to be one of the most prestigious and prosperous names on the American filmmaking scene.

In October Cohl rented a modest house at 47 Hoyt Avenue and furnished it in the fashionable Mission style (at a total cost of $230). The family settled in and quickly adjusted to American life (fig. 175). Cohl spoke English well enough from having prac-

175. Cohl with Suzanne and André in Fort Lee, 1912.

ticed with his friend Norès, the expatriate American architect, and from working in London. This gave him an advantage over most of his colleagues, who relied on a Swiss named Grisel to translate instructions and other communications, including Arnaud's when he was on the set directing.[25] Cohl's first day of work at his new job was on October 16.

There was already a large French colony in New Jersey working for Pathé, Peerless/World, Royal, and for Alice Guy Blaché, who was opening her Solax company in Fort Lee in September 1912. Among the other French technicians working for Eclair were the cameramen Henri Maire, M. J. Guisac, Georges Benoit, and René Guissart, the assistants Lucien Andriot and Henri Deau, and, arriving in November, Benjamin Carré. Carré (1883–1978) had been a scenic artist at the Amable Studio, then the Menessier Studio, which supplied sets for the Opéra and other theaters. He had been hired by Alice Guy Blaché at Gaumont in 1906 and had become one of Cohl's friends. He was a neighbor in Montmartre and a Sunday painter who shared Cohl's interest in art. He was hired by Jourjon early in 1912, and in November 1912 he arrived in New York to became the chief set designer and art director at Fort Lee.[26]

There were also Francis (né François) Doublier and his wife, who became good friends with the Cohls. Born in Lyon in 1878, Doublier had traveled about Europe and Asia as a cameraman for the Lumière brothers. Between 1902 and 1911 he managed a photographic manufacturing plant in Burlington, Vermont, where antitrust Lumière film stock was made. When the Eclair laboratories were established, he was named head of the negative department. According to Cohl's notebook, he lived at nearby 2011 Lemoine Avenue.[27]

While in the United States, Cohl worked on dozens of newsreel subjects and a series of animated cartoons called "The Newlyweds." Virtually nothing is known about the long list of titles he identified as "weeklies" in his filmography, except that they were journalistic reportages produced for the Animated Weekly. This newsreel was begun by the Sales Company in March 1912, then continued by Universal (Eclair's distributor). Cohl's titles refer to topical news events, and his contributions were so short that they were not even included in the published lists of releases. He described them in 1920:

> These little films, only 30 or 40 meters long, almost always underlined some comic or salient news item. We never saw them here [in France]. They were too specialized and of interest only where they were made. They had nothing in common, neither in work nor importance, with the films of 120 or 150 meters that we ordinarily film here. I should add that the work was rather restful and I adored that! I shot them every week in New York between 1912 and 1913.[28]

We do not even know if these films used any animation. It is sad that none survive because, besides the personal amusement they afforded the artist, their subjects would now be of great historical interest. *Les Cubistes* (cat. 145), for instance, was released in June 1913 in the aftermath of the New York Armory Show, which first introduced European Cubism to America. No doubt the film could be added to the long list of satires railing against the new movement.

Cohl's major activity in Fort Lee was the creation of the "The Newlyweds" in 1913-1914. Although the existence of this series has been universally ignored by historians, it was not only Cohl's most ambitious project to date but would also prove to be crucially important to the development of the American animated cartoon.

Whose idea was it to produce an animated version of the popular comic strip "The Newlyweds and Their Baby"? Perhaps it was Cohl's inspiration. He would have known the strip in its French version, "Le Petit Ange," because it ran next to his own contributions in *Nos Loisirs* (fig. 176). That the strip was well liked in both France and America would have been a favorable factor. Or perhaps the project was suggested by the author of the strip, George McManus (1884–1954; fig. 177). It had been his first real success as a cartoonist for the New York *World*.[29] Perhaps McManus's friend and fellow comic-strip artist Winsor McCay had encouraged him to look for a producer. McCay himself had already experimented with animating some drawings based on his own "Little

176. George McManus: French version of "The Newlyweds" in *Nos Loisirs*, April 26, 1908.

177. George McManus: Self-portrait with "The Newlyweds," 1908.

Nemo in Slumberland" strip, which Blackton had supervised at Vitagraph in 1911. In 1912 he completed *The Story of a Mosquito* and was already planning his most famous cartoon, *Gertie*.[30] Finally, someone at Eclair may have suggested the project. After all, adapting a comic strip to cinema was an old idea. There had been Blackton's turn-of-the-century "Happy Hooligan" series, some episodes of Outcault's "Buster Brown" in 1904, and in 1911 David Horsely (of the Nestor company) had contracted with cartoonist Bud Fisher for the rights to his "Mutt and Jeff" characters.[31] As in the previous attempts, Fisher's stories were staged with real actors playing the parts. The real novelty of the Eclair production was that it was the first to attempt to transpose a comic strip to the screen using animated drawings.

The stories of the cartoons were to be very similar to the "situation comedies" of the original strip. "The Newlyweds" were a young naive couple blessed (or cursed) with a truculent baby named Snookums who burst into tantrums if he did not get his way. Cohl began the actual work of animation in November 1912. But it was not until February that Eclair was able to proclaim: "Snookums Brought to Life."

> This series will undoubtedly make a genuine hit, since the cartoons are actually brought to life and made to move by trick photography. Several of this series have been shown to a number of prominent exchange and newspaper men who were really enthusiastic about the pictures, announcing them a real "scream."

For the first time Eclair used a term that would be employed henceforth to describe this new genre: "animated cartoons."

> We will present the comedy HIT of the year—a series of animated cartoons based on the famous Newlywed pictures of George McManus.[32]

The first release was supposed to be on March 5, 1913, but it was not ready until March 16. In *When He Wants a Dog, He Wants a Dog* (cat. 133) the devilish Snookums throws a tantrum for a dog he sees in a passing motorist's car. Papa attempts to steal the dog to mollify his baby, but the dog refuses to cooperate and tears off Papa's clothes. When he returns home, Snookums has forgotten the whole thing and has gone to sleep anyway. The ultimate futility of the father's efforts became the standard moral of the films, as in the strip.

The publicity for the series was the most ambitious ever undertaken for any of Cohl's films. Eclair repeatedly stressed the genuine novelty of the technique of animation.

> The Newlyweds are not real people dressed up to imitate the famous McManus cartoons, but are *drawings that move*! The trick photography required to produce such wonderful effects is the work of the "Eclair" people.[33]

Eclair also explained that the cartoons would be released at much slower intervals than normal films because "it takes two weeks to make a half reel." But in none of their advertising was Emile Cohl's name ever mentioned. Instead, all the credit for the series went to McManus, whose popularity, it was hoped, would attract the public. In modern advertising jargon this tactic would be called a "tie-in" to a "presold" commodity.

The series became an instant success. Cohl's animation technique elicited specific praise from reviewers.

> [*When he Wants a Dog, He Wants a Dog*] . . . is a unique little comedy which has been very cleverly worked out, evidently with pasteboard designs and figures. The peculiar manner of its progression and the whimsical play of the different designs which eventually resolve themselves into the figures of two men, a woman, a baby and a dog, will no doubt prove most entertaining and laughter provoking.[34]

This description shows that Cohl had adapted some of his transformation and metamorphosis effects for use as transitional devices between scenes. Reviewers of the second film, *Business Must Not Interfere* (cat. 134), also singled out its unusual graphic qualities.

> A sure laugh-producer. Drawn by George McManus, creator of the Newlywed cartoons. The baby, Snookums, is seen in all his glory, and the eccentric effects of the line drawings in motion are irresistible. A splendid little novelty.[35]

Until recently we could judge "The Newlyweds" cartoons only from surviving stills. The compositions of most of the tableaux appeared to have been transposed from the original strips, for Cohl emulated McManus's simple linear style (fig. 178). But in others he rejected McManus's influence in favor of a white figural style that more closely resembled some of his early caricatures (fig. 179). Once, in *He Doesn't Care to be Photographed* (cat. 164), he may have experimented with fully modeled figures (fig. 180).

The recent discovery of the tenth film in the series, *He Poses for His Portrait* (cat. 153), indicates that Cohl was experimenting with new techniques while forging an uneasy compromise with McManus's original strip. The film is relatively "talky" for Cohl, with much of its exposition being delivered by dialogue in speech balloons. In order to clarify who the speaker is, Cohl tried the novel approach of darkening the entire scene, thus highlighting the speaker. The film is organized around a recurring tableau that could have been drawn by McManus: Mother and Father are shown on the left; Snookums is in an armchair on the right; and the artist is in the center at his easel. The entire film is drawn in white lines on black (from printing the negative as positive), and the animation is a combination of line and cutout work.

The plot is simple: the parents try to quiet the screaming Snookums; the artist gives him a cat in the hope of distracting him; Snookums instead chases the cat under a chest of drawers. Finally the parents leave the studio in frustration, while the artist has com-

178. Stills from "The Newlyweds," 1913.

179. *He Loves to Be Amused*
(cat. 160), 1913.

180. *He Doesn't Care to Be
Photographed* (cat. 164), 1914.

181. *He Poses for His Portrait* (cat. 153), 1913.

pleted only a sketch of Snookums's face (fig. 181). After telling his artist friends his terrible tale and wondering about his sanity, the artist is shown in the last scene being consoled by his friends. Throughout the film there are seemingly gratuitous intrusions by animated metamorphic segments. For example, our first view of the family is introduced by the image of an eye that becomes an octopus, out of which a blob materializes that gradually forms the outlines of the family members. One finds almost no traces of Hollywood classicism influencing this film; it is unrelentingly nonlinear, and its imagery is very difficult to interpret. Although the film must have seemed exceedingly strange to its original audiences, it nevertheless received good notices and the entire series was a success.

"The Newlyweds" was the first modern animated cartoon series. Each installment presented a self-contained episode in the continuing adventures of the same characters, analogous to the weekly comic strip. The significance of this innovation, as we shall see shortly, was not lost on American artists and producers. But first it should be noted that the series did not consume all of Cohl's time.

Bewitched Matches (cat. 142), the only other American film by Cohl known to have survived, provided some diversion from Snookums, as well as the opportunity to put his favorite matchstick figures through some stunts. *Clara and Her Mysterious Toys* (cat. 156) was a vehicle for Clara Horton, "The Eclair Girl." The toys were shown reconstituting themselves out of torn bits of paper, using animation combined with reverse-motion cinematography. This film was followed by the remarkable *A Vegetarian's Dream* (cat. 159), in which fruits and vegetables acted out a melodrama (fig. 182). The film was accompanied by hyperbolic advertising:

A high-salaried artist labored patiently with the pen and scissors for a *whole month* to evolve nearly 80,000 [!] drawings which were required to produce this unique reel. Thus you may consider "The Vegetarian's Dream" a "bonus offering" of the month, for the half-reel costs close to the production figures of a regular single reel.[36]

The less-biased *Moving Picture World* also mentioned some drawings: "Moving drawings of vegetables, egg cups, peanuts, frogs, etc. Some amusing effects are achieved. The love drama enacted by the young onions was especially funny."[37]

Unforeseen Metamorphosis (cat. 161) seems to be Cohl's lost American masterpiece, judging by its reviews. *Moving Picture World* called it "A highly original and entertaining series of moveable drawings, introducing animals, street parades, fruits and the like. One of the best series of this kind we have seen."[38] In the sequence that astounded and delighted viewers the most, Cohl had modified a technique first used in *Les Beaux-Arts mystérieux* in 1910. Photographs and moving-picture footage somehow transformed themselves into unexpected scenes and objects.

> Again, very many beautiful scenes of New York's waterfront and view [*sic*] of interest throughout the country are flashed, only to resolve themselves into some astonishing shape or form. From the flash of a gun we see a canoe floating peacefully down the water and this disappears to be replaced by a single line, which forms itself into a beautiful prism and then gives way to something equally startling.[39]

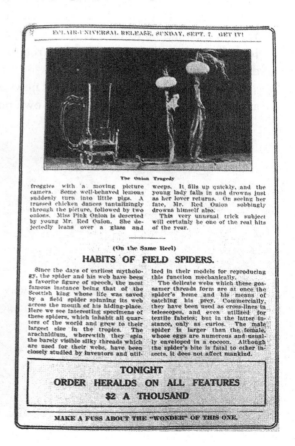

182. *A Vegetarian's Dream* (cat. 159), 1913.

Cohl unfortunately was not able to fulfill his career's early promise in America. For unknown reasons he moved from Fort Lee to an apartment on Nicholas Avenue in October 1913.[40] He did continue to make films. Then, after a stay of nearly eighteen months, the family departed for France on *La Savoie* on March 11, 1914, soon after learning of a death in Suzanne's family. It is not known if Cohl intended to come back to resume his film work, but in fact he never did return to America.

On March 19, the day after his arrival in Le Havre, a disaster occurred that has contributed to Cohl's neglect as a film pioneer. Back in Fort Lee, a fire broke out in the "joining" (editing) rooms of the Eclair laboratories. The wooden-frame studio buildings, as well as all the positive prints on the premises, were destroyed. Francis Doublier made an effort to rescue the negatives, but most of them were also lost. The damage to the studio was $125,000, but the value of the lost films was incalculable.[41] This fire must have completely destroyed all of Cohl's American work, including several as yet unreleased films in "The Newlyweds" series (fig. 183). Charles Jourjon left Paris to investigate the calamity. Upon his arrival on March 30, he announced that Eclair would rebuild its production facilities in Tucson, Arizona, and restore the Fort Lee site only as a laboratory. After reassuring the stockholders in Paris, "Your New York branch has continued to progress normally in 1913 and will continue to do so," Jourjon conceded that the fire had retarded business. Nevertheless, he praised the devoted directors in Fort Lee.[42]

Cohl arrived in Epinay to find that news of the fire had disrupted the normal routine at the Eclair studios and had left his own position in a state of limbo. In April 1914 he

183. Theodore Huff and Mark Borgatta: *Ghost Town: The Story of Fort Lee*, ca. 1935 (frame enlargement).

184. Cohl and Eclair staff, Epinay, August 4, 1914.

wrote in his diary: "Help from J.J. finally! Bayard Contract." "J.J." means Jourjon, who was still in America; Bayard was an assistant manager of the studio. Secure again with his contract, Cohl commenced work on *L'Enlèvement de Déjanire Goldebois* (The Kidnapping of Déjanire Goldebois, cat. 169), *L'Avenir dévoilé par les lignes des pieds* (The Future Revealed by the Lines of the Feet, cat. 170), and *Le Ouistiti de Toto* (Toto's Wistiti [monkey], cat. 171). Again an unexpected disaster intervened. The first two films would not be released until 1917 and the third was never released at all. The reason, of course, was that Germany declared war on France on August 3, 1914.

When the war broke out, Cohl and several members of the Eclair staff were photographed together on a set in Epinay (fig. 184). The movie industry greatly underestimated the length and severity of the conflict, as did almost everyone. Eclair at first believed that its American branch would be able to supply France with sufficient releases to carry them through. Besides, they confidently pointed to an eight-month supply of unreleased French negatives (which included Cohl's American films). This optimism quickly dissipated. When every able-bodied man under forty-five was called up, Jourjon found himself in the 113th regiment and Vandal in the 156th. The new

Eclair office building on rue Gaillon was given over to the Red Cross. The Gaumont and Pathé studios were also requisitioned as hospitals. By August 11 the film industry had suffered an eighty-percent loss of staff. Actors were giving their autos to the war office. Cafés were closed, but cinemas continued to reshow old films at reduced prices for the benefit of the Red Cross. *Moving Picture World* correspondent John Cher reported that audiences in the theaters sat through the films in depressed silence. [43]

Since Cohl was too old to serve with the French forces, the mobilization of practically the entire industry personnel assured him of a job. He had tried to enlist but, after being unsuccessful, volunteered to serve in the Red Cross. After the initial shocks, the Eclair-Journal newsreel resumed production and Cohl rejoined its staff in late September 1914.

THE BEGINNINGS OF THE CARTOON INDUSTRY

During the first years of World War I the animated cartoon was transformed from a rare novelty item on occasional programs to an important new branch of the film industry. Although the site of most of the activity was in the United States, the importance of Emile Cohl's contribution must nevertheless be emphasized.

Cohl's Gaumont films had arrived long before he came in person. *Fantasmagorie* was released in the summer of 1908 under the title *Metamorphosis*. However its exact date of entry is unknown because Gaumont's importer, George B. Kleine, was then embroiled in an important patent-infringement trial with Edison. [44] After Kleine's import agreement was worked out, Gaumont films (including Cohl's) were released in the United States at the rate of two each week. *Le Cauchemar du fantoche* was first shown on October 16, 1908, as *The Puppet's Nightmare*. *Un Drame chez les fantoches* was singled out for special mention when it was released (as *A Love Affair in Toyland*) on November 21.

> A unique and exceptionally attractive Gaumont film. It cannot be described, but a game common many years ago known as "geometry at play" comes nearest to it. It is funny and in such an unexpected and unique way that it wins rounds of applause wherever it is shown. [45]

Cohl himself also noted the enthusiasm for his first films.

> It was around 1909 and the Americans were still searching for their way around cinematography. They received "with open screens" the first animated cartoons that arrived from France. [46]

Cohl's animation tricks were quickly recognized as highly successful audience-pleasers, and his films added to Gaumont's reputation. A reviewer attending a New York screening of *Japon de fantaisie* reported:

We overheard considerable guessing among the audience at Keith's Bijou Dream as to how the clever transformations were accomplished. Gaumont's man is up to all the tricks of the camera.[47]

Clair de lune espagnol received one of the most unusual reviews given any production of this period:

The man who prepares the plays for the Gaumonts, or the one who selects them, perhaps, seems afflicted with a perpetual liver difficulty and selects generally only those more or less lugubriously inclined. Perhaps this [film] was sneaked in without his knowing it. If that is the case, more sneaking should be done. It is a welcome change.[48]

Of *Génération spontanée* it was reported that "the Gaumont studios have sent out a number of excellent pictures of this character, of which the one shown this week is not the least."[49] The animation sequences in *Les Lunettes féeriques* were "all worked out in the admirable manner for which Gaumont's films of this character are famous. Some of the magic films produced by this house rank among the very best anywhere."[50]

Cohl's films attracted what probably were the first notices ever in the trade press on the subject of animated cartoons. In August 1909, for example, *The Nickelodeon* published a strange story.

Trick pictures are rather expensive to make. . . . Furthermore, many of them especially those pictures of inanimate objects in motion, require a great deal of time. It is reported that one French manufacturer consumed seven months in working out a single trick picture and then was overcome by a mental malady due to the continued close application. But this, of course, must have been an exceptional picture.[51]

This apocryphal anecdote may have been planted in the Chicago-based journal by Kleine as a publicity stunt to call attention to the sensational new films being exported by Gaumont. Two months later Cohl's *La Bataille d'Austerlitz* became, as far as we know, the first animated film to have an entire article devoted to it, in *Motography*.[52] It was even illustrated with a production still and was the most important recognition of Cohl's early career in film. Equally important from the standpoint of his influence was the revelation in the article of all the technical details of his single-frame animation system. With the obvious popularity of his films and the vulgarization of his techniques, it was inevitable that commercial interest in animated films would increase.

Cohl's techniques were disseminated in an early how-to-do-it manual, *The Handbook of Kinematography*, in 1911. The author, Colin Bennett, described how to make "self-forming" titles, how to use the "downward pointing camera," and, referring to a specific Cohl film, how to achieve the "step-by-step" effect:

The particularly puzzling and odd step-by-step effect exhibited by the film of the

"Affair of Hearts" [*sic*] [i.e., cat. no. 45, 1909] order, in which purely mechanical arrangement and re-arrangement of geometrical areas of black and white follow up each other in a sort of kaleidoscopic sequence, are also produced by means of the vertical camera, combined with infinite pains on the part of the artist operator. By the same means also automatic writing, drawing, etc., of all sorts is produced, the camera being stopped after each picture or two for a few more short strokes to be added or taken away.[53]

Bennett also described "double printing," or the traveling matte devised by Cohl, in which "two negatives produce one positive."

Among those whose interest was whetted was the best-known comic-strip artist, Winsor McCay (1871–1934), who for years had been justifiably famous for "Hungry Henrietta," "Little Sammy Sneeze," "Little Nemo in Slumberland," and "Dreams of the Rarebit Fiend," as well as for his vaudeville appearances as a lightning cartoonist. There can be little argument that McCay's art was influenced by the early cinema, which was already a ubiquitous entertainment in New York when he moved there in 1903. One of his "Dreams of the Rarebit Fiend" had been adapted to a movie scenario by Edwin S. Porter in 1906, and he was acquainted with J. Stuart Blackton of Vitagraph because of their common background in journalism and as neighbors in Sheepshead Bay, Brooklyn. He must have been cognizant of Blackton's animation experiments as they progressed.[54] Blackton himself had responded to the influx of Cohl's films by making his first two animations since 1907: *The Magic Fountain Pen* (July 17, 1909) and *Princess Nicotine* (August 10, 1909). In one section of the latter, Blackton plagiarized Cohl's *Les Allumettes animées*, which had been released in the United States in December 1908. A review of Blackton's film suggests that animation had already come to be regarded as a French specialty: "Although we look for little of this class of work from Americans, the Vitagraph Company has here proven that it is not from lack of ability that we do not produce more of it on this side."[55] McCay wrote in 1927 that he "established the modern cartoon movies in 1909,"[56] and although he acknowledged only his son's flip books as his inspiration, Blackton's influence and the vogue of the Gaumont films must have been key factors in persuading McCay to try his own hand.

McCay set to work on the project of making some experimental drawings of the characters in "Little Nemo in Slumberland." Despite claims that McCay was using the completed footage in his vaudeville act by 1909, contemporary reviews state clearly that when the film opened at Williams' Colonial Theater in New York on April 12, 1911, "the idea was being presented for the first time on any stage."[57]

When McCay finished his drawings, probably in late 1910, he brought them to Blackton to photograph. Vitagraph released the film under the title *Winsor McCay* on April 8, just a few days prior to its vaudeville premiere (fig. 185). (Today the film is better known as *Little Nemo*.) Emile Cohl saw it in Paris when it was released there by

185. Winsor McCay: *Little Nemo*, Vitagraph, 1911.

Vitagraph in June 1911 as *Le Dernier Cri des dessins animés*.[58] A special preview took place at the Pathé studios, where Cohl was then working.

> I recall perfectly that Mr. Zecca, who was then the director of production at Pathé, took me into his office to show me the latest film of Winsor McCay when it arrived. This was in 1910 [*sic*].[59]

When Nemo first appears on the screen, his outline coalesces from a swirling array of dots. It was a technique Cohl had used many times, for example, in *Un Drame chez les fantoches* and *Les Joyeux Microbes*. In another sequence there is a metamorphosis of a rose into the figure of a princess—a trick that could have had precedents in metamorphic tricks in *Fantasmagorie*, *Génération spontanée*, or numerous others. But despite some similarity of technique and specific effects, McCay's artwork was original. The American artist had transferred his comic-strip characters to the film without modifying their appearance or sacrificing linear detail.

Nevertheless, the impact of the film was not as immediate as might be expected, especially considering that a practical course in animation by the retracing method had been provided in the prologue. Part of the reason was that McCay's contract with W. R. Hearst severely restricted the venues where the cartoons could be shown. *The Story of a Mosquito* (also known as *How a Mosquito Operates*, 1912) could not be shown in American movie theaters without McCay's presence.[60] Therefore, the major impact of these first two films was felt in Europe, not in the United States.

Ironically, because Cohl was in the United States at the time, he could only have seen *The Story of a Mosquito* as part of McCay's stage routine at Hammerstein's, where it was reported that the "moving pictures of his drawings have caused even film magnates to marvel at their cleverness and humor."[61]

This second film was also drawn by the retracing method. It is the story of a gluttonous mosquito who explodes after indulging in too much blood. Again there are reminiscences of Cohl's films when the mosquito sharpens his proboscis on a grindstone, recalling the grindstone in *Un Drame chez les fantoches*, and when the insect expands as the clown had done near the end of *Fantasmagorie*.

Between the completion of *Little Nemo* in the spring of 1911 and the release of the first "Newlyweds" cartoons in March 1913, the only other animated films on American screens were the old Blackton and Cohl films still in circulation.[62] By contrast, as soon as the "The Newlyweds" began to appear on screens across the country, there was an immediate jump in the number of other cartoonists adapting their works for the cinema, including Richard Outcault, Henry "Hy" Mayer (*Life* and *Judge*), and several Chicago cartoonists: Sydney Smith of the *Tribune*, Charles Bowers, Andy Hettinger, and Wallace A. Carlson, a sports cartoonist for the *Inter-Ocean*.

Meanwhile, Winsor McCay had been at work on his third and most memorable film, *Gertie*. As was the case with his first two, this one was also intended to be integrated into McCay's vaudeville act.[63] Just before he left for France, Emile Cohl attended McCay's stage act in which the sensational film was featured. Later he described the performance:

> McCay's films were admirably drawn, but one of the principal reasons for their success was the manner in which they were presented to the public.
>
> I remember having been at one of these public performances at the Hammerstein Theater in New York. The principal—I should say, the unique—character in the film was an antediluvian animal, a kind of monstrously large diplodocus.
>
> At the beginning there was a scene with rocks and trees. On stage, before the screen, was Winsor McCay, very elegant, armed with a short trainer's whip, and

making a speech like a circus animal tamer. He called to the beast who jumped from between the rocks. Then, it was like an exhibition of *dressage*; always obeying the artiste's commands, the animal danced, turned around and at the end curtsied to the public who applauded the artist and the work of art at the same time. It was very successful for Winsor McCay who never left the theater without stopping by the cashier to be laden with some pretty engravings from the National Bank Note Company, that is, some merry dollars.[64]

In the stage version that Cohl saw, McCay stood by the screen and spoke with Gertie as though she were standing beside him. Once he pretended to toss a pumpkin to her, coordinating his movements with the appearance of a pumpkin on the screen. This interaction between performer and the animated film might have reminded Cohl of the sequence in *Clair de lune espagnol* in which the actor fights with the animated moon.

Gertie, Winsor McCay's masterpiece, will remain one of the great landmarks in animated history. But now it is clear that its importance as a stimulus to early American animation has been overemphasized because the "film rush" on the part of America's best-known prewar cartoonists had actually begun earlier. By the time Gertie took her first steps on the screen, Snookums had already plagued his parents in thirteen cartoons. Certainly it was the success of the Cohl-McManus series that was more important in encouraging other cartoonists to go ahead. That also explains the prominent role given to McManus in the version of *Gertie* released to theaters, in which McManus is specifically introduced as the creator of the "The Newlyweds" comic strip.

Despite the fact that only two of Cohl's American films are extant, *He Poses for His Portrait* and the unexceptional *Bewitched Matches*, it is nevertheless certain that he acted as a powerful catalytic agent. Because of his early return to France and the war's interruption, he was able to observe the fruits of his labor only from a great distance, after a long delay, and without much satisfaction. In his absence the industry was revolutionized by several technological developments. Because they touched his career indirectly, it is only necessary to outline them briefly here.

The success of the "The Newlyweds" demonstrated that strong audience appeal existed for continuing episodes of cartoon characters. It is significant that this change in animation subject material coincided with the contemporaneous rise of the star system. Audiences returned to see their cartoon favorites, just as they did to see Max Linder or John Bunny week after week. But the primary obstacle to cartoon production on a regularly scheduled basis was that the work was too time-consuming. Obviously the retracing method, which had required over a year of work in making *Gertie* for an artist even as skilled as McCay, was too impractical. Cohl's cutout system seemed to have only a limited potential, and, besides, it was almost as tedious to cut out figures as to draw them. It was during the run of the "The Newlyweds" that two animators working independently arrived at practical solutions to the mass-production problem.

Raoul Barré (1874–1932) was born in Montreal, studied art in Paris in the 1890s, and made extra money by contributing to *Le Sifflet* and other illustrated periodicals (fig. 186).[65] In 1903 he moved to New York in hopes of becoming a successful commercial artist. By 1912 he had become known for his "Noah's Ark" comic strip, which he signed "Varb." He was also acquainted with William C. Nolan (1894–1954) at the Edison studios, where he made some short advertising films. About this time he saw his first cartoon—whether by Cohl or McCay is unknown—and left the theater determined to try animation himself. Did Barré seek out Emile Cohl for advice? This intriguing question is posed by an anecdote Cohl told about two unnamed New York visitors:

I was told by my superiors that I had to admit to my studio a person still [i.e., around 1920] very important in the film industry. After being introduced in this rather brutal fashion, he told me of his curiosity concerning my work and of his impatience to know "how I did it." He was accompanied by a young man with glasses who did not say a single word. But I could see that behind those lenses no aspect of my equipment was escaping his view. I was burned up. Animated films were popping up here and there, as I've already said, but I had nevertheless protected certain methods and devices that were personal. Shortly after this regrettable visit, I saw that a new series of perfected animated cartoon was being distributed.[66]

— Et pourtant! nous avons combattu pour les droits de l'Homme !...

186. Raoul Barré: "Quatre-vingt-treize," *Le Sifflet*, March 3, 1898.

Were these men Nolan and Barré? It would seem natural for them to wish to confer with the creator of the most successful series, especially since the work was being done only a few miles from the Edison studios. It is also entirely possible that Barré and Cohl may have know each other by reputation in France, since Barré was contributing to the pro-Dreyfus *Le Sifflet* at the same time that Cohl was drawing anti-Dreyfus cartoons for *La Libre Parole Illustrée*. If either party was aware of these past associations, that alone might have been cause for animosity.

The technical strategy that Barré devised was almost the inverse of Cohl's. Instead of making cutout figures, he used a cutout background. Cohl's moving figures were photographed on top of their background drawings; Barré, on the other hand, drew simplified linear backgrounds on white cardboard, then cut a space out of the center. The moving parts of the picture were drawn on separate white sheets by the retracing method. The composition was planned so that the drawings would show through the hole in the cardboard when it was laid over each one during photography. The advantage was that the background did not have to be redrawn and, unlike Cohl's system, complicated cutout figures did not have to be made. However, the system had the disadvantage of falling into monotonous compositional patterns because the moving figures tended to remain centrally located. They could not obscure any of the background lines, so they floated in large white areas. To ensure proper registration of background and drawings, Barré used perforated paper. Each sheet fit over pegs when placed under the camera, exactly as is done today.

Barré and Nolan realized that no single person could produce cartoons in sufficient quantities, so they established in the Bronx what would become the first animation "studio." Assembly-line techniques were developed in which employees were trained for one specific task. Barré himself eventually acted only as coordinator and supervisor. With many apprentices working on a single cartoon, it was necessary to schematize the drawing style to maintain uniform consistency. To save time, each drawing was sometimes photographed three or even four times to "stretch" the footage, often resulting in jerky and repetitious movements on the screen.

Despite these production shortcuts, the first in the "Animated Grouch Chasers" series did not appear until 1915.[67] Each one begins with a live-action prologue and includes three or four short animated sequences. *Cartoons on the Beach*, for example, includes four separate cartoons. Barré's debt to Cohl is evident. The baby boy in *The Kelly Kid's Bathing Adventure* closely resembles Snookums (fig. 187). The stars of *A Sand Microbe Flirtation* are relatives of Cohl's *Joyeux Microbes* and are seen inside the same circular vignette (fig. 188). Perhaps Cohl was referring to Barré's films when he recalled:

> I wasn't in the least surprised when I saw short funny American films arrive in France after the War in which I had the rather melancholy satisfaction of rediscovering every

187. Raoul Barré: "The Kelly Kid's Bathing Adventure," in *Cartoons on the Beach*, 1915.

188. Raoul Barré: "A Sand Microbe Flirtation," in *Cartoons on the Beach*, 1915.

once in a while some gag that I knew well, having used it myself a dozen years earlier in *La Lampe qui file* or in *Les Joyeux Microbes*.[68]

Cohl had no reason to be jealous of Barré, whose career had almost as many peaks and valleys as Cohl's. After retiring from animation, Barré returned temporarily to assist Pat Sullivan and Otto Messmer on several "Felix the Cat" cartoons in 1926, but when he died in France in 1932, he was an all-but-forgotten figure in the history of early animation.

The permanent contribution of the other important pioneer of the animation industry was primarily technical. John Randolph Bray was born in Michigan in 1879 (d. 1978) and later moved to New York to seek his fortune as a cartoonist for *Judge* and other great humor magazines.[69] He claimed that the idea of animated cartoons came to him around 1908 or 1909, but it may well have happened closer to 1912.[70] Although the date of completion of his first film, *The Artist's Dream*, is uncertain, we know it was released on June 12, 1913, three months after the first "Newlyweds." Charles Pathé, whom Bray had met on a New York visit, signed him to a contract to produce one film each month. Bray initiated an assembly-line system similar to Barré's to meet this demanding schedule. But more importantly he invented his own method for rendering the backgrounds and applied for a patent on January 9, 1914. It was granted on August 11, giving him the rights to a streamlined production system that borrowed ideas from McCay's practice.[71] In 1915 Bray met another young animator, Earl Hurd, who had in June of that year patented a process using transparent glassine sheets that would eventually revolutionize the animation industry. The background was rendered normally, as in Cohl's system. Anything that moved was drawn on the individual clear sheets. These were placed sequentially over the background during photography. Hurd's registration system apparently infringed on Bray's patent, so they decided to become partners and formed the Bray-Hurd Process Company. By that time sheets of cellulose acetate had replaced glassine, and these "cels" became the standard commercial animation process, which remains in use today.

Like the Barré studio, the Bray studio became an important training ground for later animators. Paul Terry began his "Farmer Alfalfa" series there; later Walter Lantz joined. Max and Dave Fleischer's "Out of the Inkwell" pictures were released by Bray beginning in 1919. By the end of World War I the Bray-Hurd cel process had become virtually the only one used in the United States.

ECLAIR II: COHL IN FRANCE, 1915

Cohl was not aware of any of these developments as they were happening because he was back in France on the staff of the Eclair-Journal (fig. 189). The studio was struggling to remain open during 1915 despite the difficulties caused by the mobilization of Jourjon and Vandal and disagreements with the management of the American branch.[72] Cohl contributed several patriotic and propagandistic films to the Eclair-Journal and some trick films, such as *La Blanchisserie américaine* (American Laundry, cat. 177) and *Fruits et légumes animés* (Living Fruits and Vegetables, cat. 178). Both were remakes of earlier successes. The only animated drawings were the maps he made showing the

189. Eclair identification card.

moving battle lines. There were often long delays between completion of the films and their release because Eclair, formerly the shining star of the smaller French producers, was now in deep financial difficulty.

In November 1915 Cohl had to look for a *pension* in Nice because Suzanne Courtet was suffering from an illness. He returned to Paris in January and resumed work on films that seem (on the basis of their titles) to have been little more than uninspired versions of his Gaumont pictures. These shorts made at the ailing Eclair studios might well have been an inglorious end to his career had he not received on July 17, 1916, a letter from Benjamin Rabier saying, "I have a proposition that you may find interesting."

COHL AND RABIER

The wave of enthusiasm about the animated cartoon that swept the United States in 1913 and 1914 reached France in 1916. Eclair had begun importing Cohl's "Newlyweds" on the eve of the war, renaming Snookums "Zozor." The second American series was that of Barré. Gaumont had purchased the "Animated Grouch Chasers" from Edison and scheduled the first of them for April 7, 1916.[73] Unlike the prewar days when Gaumont had advertised Cohl's animations only as "scènes à trucs" (trick shots), the new imports were given unprecedented publicity, including full-page advertisements with frame enlargements and a portrait of Barré (fig. 190). Privately Cohl must have been bitter about Gaumont's advertising campaign, doubly so if it is true that Barré was the cartoonist who had visited his studio in Fort Lee.

Chez le coiffeur (formerly *Cartoons in a Barbershop*) met with immediate success in April. *Sur la plage* (*Cartoons on the Beach*), said one reviewer, "attests once more to the virtuosity and varied imagination of this able artist."[74] Barré's "Grouch Chasers" played the role in France that Cohl's "Newlyweds" had in the United States. They triggered an immediate rush to capitalize on cartoons while they were still a fresh novelty item. Gaumont, Pathé, AGC, and other distributors signed contracts to import American animated films. It was inevitable that France would respond to this sudden invasion by initiating domestic production. Just as Cohl's "Newlyweds" had shown American cartoonists the possibilities of animating their works, so these American films stimulated French caricaturists. At first only minor figures like Pierre de Léka were interested. Nothing is known about him except that he announced the opening of a studio at 6, rue Saulnier to compete with Barré's films. Like Barré, he contemplated weekly releases, but his first film, *Marius Blagford et le serpent boa* (fig. 191), was apparently also his last.[75] The caricaturist Seavois began a "semaine humoristique" (weekly humor review) featuring animated drawings in the Gaumont-Actualités newsreel, in direct competition with Cohl's Eclair-Journal shorts.[76] *Le Film* announced that its artist, Henri Debain (creator of caricatures of movie personalities and also a future

190. Gaumont publicity materials for "Les Dessins animés de Raoul Barré," 1916.

191. Pierre de Léka: *Blagford et le serpent boa*, 1916.

actor), was about to launch his own series. The increasingly nationalistic attitude toward cinema in general and cartoons in particular was revealed in the announcement:

> Animated cartoons: We will see excellent ones appear soon, and made by a Frenchman. That is a surprise, no doubt, because until now the Americans have made a specialty of these "cartoons" that are now so much in vogue here. Like the other arts, this one was born in France; it's time it returned. [77]

By emphasizing the French origins of the animated cartoon, the author, who may have been Louis Delluc, indirectly paid tribute to Cohl's Gaumont films and the Eclair films that had been appearing regularly before the arrival of the American imports. Those knowledgeable about the French cinema still remembered Cohl's work and recognized its importance.

It was also in 1916 that Benjamin Rabier decided that he, too, wished to have movie versions of his works. Rabier (1869–1939, fig. 192) was one of those artists who, like Cohl, had realized the potential of the expanding market for children's literature at the turn of the century. He was the first to transform the Caran d'Ache album into a form directed toward a specifically juvenile audience. In such books as *Pages folles* (Richard, 1898), *Tintin-Lutin* (Juven, 1898), and *Maman Cabas* (Max, 1900), he adapted Caran d'Ache's precise linear style to his animal stories. The traditional *imagerie d'Epinal* (the popular French picture story) was another early influence.[78] Rabier's drawings appeared in many of the best satirical periodicals, where Cohl undoubtedly first encountered his work. These *histoires sans paroles* still show Caran d'Ache's influence in their

192. Benjamin Rabier and "Flambeau."

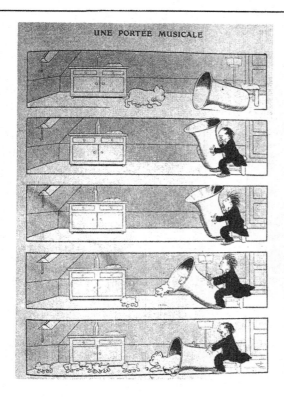

UNE PORTÉE MUSICALE

193. Benjamin Rabier: "Une Portée musicale,"
Sans-Gêne, 1904.

careful redrawing of each panel from an unchanging point of view. Rabier used the
effect to signify the passage of time (fig. 193). His interest in cinema may have begun as
early as 1910 when he wrote children's plays, such as *Bonhomme de neige; conte féeri-*
que en 20 tableaux lumineux (The Snowman: Fairy Tale in 20 Luminous Tableaux),
which were influenced by Méliès's films.[79] Rabier had already been honored by a special album in Juven's series "Les Maîtres humoristes" and was nearing the height of his
celebrity at the time he wrote to Cohl in 1916.[80]

The discovery of Rabier's intact correspondence with Cohl permits us accurately to
establish the chronology and extent of their cooperation.[81] Rabier's plan was that Cohl
would animate his drawings just as Cohl had done for McManus. Rabier was to take
care of the business aspects of the partnership, leaving the artistic side to Cohl. They
needed capital and a distributor for the cartoons, so Rabier approached Film National
with the idea, suggesting to Cohl that he might pass by their office "to activate their
decision."[82] But Cohl demonstrated his independence by visiting Gaumont instead,
who, much to everyone's surprise, advanced an offer.[83] It was rejected, and further
assistance did not arrive until September. But when it did, it came from Fantomas!

René Navarre had brought the hero of Pierre Souvestre and Marcel Allain's serial-
ized novella to life on the screen in Feuillade's famous Gaumont series in 1913 and
1914. Navarre's adroit depiction of the sinister criminal, a master of disguises, had

194. René Navarre, 1917.

made him a matinee idol. Now, in 1916, the actor (fig. 194) was a producer and became interested in this cooperative venture between the popular children's artist and the filmmaker whose reputation still must have haunted the Gaumont studios when Navarre began working there. Near the end of September Rabier sent a message to Cohl requesting advice:

> I've seen Navarre—it seems to be working out. We only need to work out the percentages. What % should I ask for above the 2500 francs up front? I have to phone Navarre between 2:00 and 2:25 with an answer. You could say it's urgent! Come by before noon or if that's a problem, send me a *pneu* [pneumatic telegram] with the information. I have no idea what royalty to ask for.[84]

Rabier returned from his meeting with the conditions. The filmmakers would receive 2,500 francs minimum with an additional five percent royalty on sales and rentals. Navarre would furnish Cohl with the raw stock for shooting. It was expected that six cartoons would be completed in at least six months. Rabier was pleased with the deal and signed the contract. Immediately there was an ominous development for Cohl. He was informed by Rabier that his name was not going to appear on the credits, as had been promised. Obviously Rabier and Navarre felt that the addition of the caricaturist's name would do little to attract the general public, who no longer remembered him since he had become an anonymous filmmaker. Cohl's role in the production, Rabier continued, would be properly credited in the advertising.

> For some reasons that Navarre gave me which I will explain to you, having your name on the film will not be possible, but you'll have the satisfaction of getting your way in the end. There will be a place for you in the advertising. I will give you some assurance that you'll be satisfied. And something more, we have to do good business and be successful. [85]

Cohl was infuriated. He protested to Rabier, who sent the letter to Navarre. Navarre responded by inviting Cohl to his office, where the artist must have been placated because work on the film continued. [86]

Trade editors received the news happily that a new French cartoon series was in production.

> We are happy to learn that some excellent new cartoons will be presented soon, thanks to one of our best caricaturists. It is astonishing that no one has thought sooner of putting the remarkable talents of a great number of artists of the pencil into the service of the French film industry. [87]

Le Film also thought the announcement of "Rabier's" project was "excellent news."[88] But there was no mention of any collaborators.

The project proceeded with a clear division of labor. Rabier negotiated with Navarre, designed the preliminary drawings, and wrote the scenario. Cohl was responsible for all the technical aspects, including the photography. While Cohl worked on the graphic art in his apartment at 48, rue des Abbesses, Rabier would occasionally play the role of cheerleader when his partner did not seem to be working fast enough. In the first week of November they were ready for the photography, which had been contracted for with the Eclair studios in Epinay. The title of this first film was *La Journée de Flambeau* (Flambeau's Day), and it starred a dog that Rabier had introduced in an album called *Flambeau, chien de guerre* (Flambeau, War Dog). [89]

Navarre proved to have transferred some of Fantomas's mischievous traits to his own real life. When he saw the results of the first day's shooting, he wrote an angry letter to Cohl demanding that the main title be reshot. Had Cohl included his own name in the credits? It is possible because Navarre stated precisely what should appear on the screen: either the series title *Les Dessins animés de Benjamin Rabier* or the title of the individual film followed by "Par Benjamin Rabier." Navarre's trademark, a shamrock in a circle, was also to be included in all titles. Navarre exercised his prerogative as producer and suggested changes in the content of the film.

Don't you think that it would be interesting, at least for the first film in the series, to show Benjamin Rabier himself sketching a design? . . . I am writing him to ask his opinion about this. . . .

I am counting on this series, and I am certain that with your collaboration we will attain perfection.[90]

It seems fairly clear that both Rabier and Navarre knew that they needed Cohl but were nervous about keeping his interest alive. Then there was a disaster. For unknown reasons, all or part of the footage that had been shot was destroyed, probably during its development at the Eclair labs. Rabier tried to console his partner.

I'm sorry about what happened to you. I hope that there is nothing more than the negligence of the company or the subcontractor and no malice.

You are right. It would be better to begin again and not to compromise our arrangement.[91]

So they agreed to work quickly on the proposed second film in the series, *Flambeau au pays des surprises* (Flambeau in the Land of Surprises). Understandably suspicious of Eclair, they decided to move the lab work to the Paris studios of Navarre's distributor, AGC, on rue Grange-Batelière. Despite shortages of coal and electricity for lighting, Cohl prepared Flambeau for the underseas adventures he was to have in his second film. But the artist was dissatisfied with the drawings and with the story. He criticized Rabier for being too prosaic, and his partner agreed.

You're right; we have to be a little outrageous. I think that the shipwreck scene needs to be more exaggerated. Make the waves higher to carry Flambeau to the top of the screen then dash him down until he capsizes.

I'm going to exaggerate, overdo it and enter more into fantasy. The next film will take place at the bottom of the sea. There will be a scene with Flambeau, a saw fish and a lobster. The saw fish will rescue Flambeau while sawing the lobster's claw off, etc. . . . See you later.[92]

Obviously Cohl was not working as a passive copyist but rather exerting determinant influence on the final product. Later Rabier protested, again defending himself from Cohl's criticism, that there would be plenty of opportunity for fantasy in the next film, *Flambeau dans la lune* (Flambeau on the Moon): "In this film all extravagances will be permitted."[93]

Flambeau au pays des surprises was shot in December 1916 and the footage sent to the laboratory. Instead of the expected congratulations, the two filmmakers did not receive any word at all from their producer. Nor did they receive any money. Rabier met with Navarre two weeks later and was given a cool reception. It was not that he was disappointed with their work, Rabier wrote, but rather that Navarre's wife was ill and the film business was suffering because of the war.[94] On December 19 Cohl's lab announced, "Your film is ready," and Navarre met with them the following day to view it. For some reason the film was found to be unsatisfactory. Its release was delayed to allow Cohl to make revisions, but meanwhile work continued on the next one, *Les Fiançailles de Flambeau* (Flambeau's Wedding). Rabier submitted the sketches in January 1917.

There was another move to the south for the health of Mme. Courtet. Neither Navarre nor Rabier was pleased that their animator intended to shoot the film there and argued that no risk should be taken that would jeopardize its quality. Rabier wrote, "This time we have to knock them out."[95] He also passed on the producer's message: "Navarre tells me again that he is counting heavily on the third film, *Les Fiançailles de Flambeau*. He hopes that it will convey the impression of absolute perfection."[96] Eventually Rabier realized it was futile to argue with Cohl and resigned himself to trusting him: "So, do your best; your renown as resourceful will not be diminished by these events."[97] There was a delay in installing the camera in Monaco, causing further annoyance to Navarre, who urged Cohl to work quickly without sacrificing quality: "I'm relying on you, dear friend, to animate as many of Rabier's drawings as possible without falling into the exaggeration of the Americans."[98] At the same time Navarre asked him to lower the production costs while increasing the length of the films.

Les Fiançailles de Flambeau and *Les Aventures de Clémentine* were completed in Monaco and screened for Navarre in April 1917. *Flambeau au pays des surprises* remained unfinished because Cohl still found Rabier's revised sketches unacceptable. In mid-May the two filmmakers were given their first payment after insisting on it several times.

On June 15, 1917—almost one year from the beginning of the project—*Les Aventures de Clémentine*, the first of the new series, appeared in theaters. Guillaume Danvers summarized it:

> Clémentine is a mother duck protecting her ducklings against the dangers that threaten them. Great success for Benjamin Rabier's cartoons, which are the funniest. It is a good beginning for our witty caricaturist's series.[99]

Les Fiançailles de Flambeau was released in July. Both films were advertised extensively to compete with Barré's cartoons. There were drawings by Rabier (fig. 195) and even his smiling portrait, but Navarre did not live up to his promise to include Cohl's name in the advertising.

It was the last straw for the rapidly deteriorating relationship, and Cohl quit. He had shot four films, but only two of them were ever released. Rabier, who had learned the technique of animation from Cohl, easily found an assistant to make two more films in

195. Benjamin Rabier: Advertisement for the "Flambeau" series.

the series, *Clémentine et Flambeau* (released September 1917) and *Misti le nain de la forêt* (Misti, the Troll, November 1917). Nevertheless, Rabier apologized to Cohl in October and invited him to rejoin him on new terms.

> I am always willing to get back together with you, as soon as you have the means to compose new films. Certainly, if you would like to, it is with you that I would like to try out some interesting innovations. But to do that we'll have to get rid of some old habits.
>
> I've "invented" a cartoon system that allows me to shoot a scene [as fast as it can be drawn]. (I just shot 20 meters in five minutes!) But to continue in this direction, to take full advantage of my "invention," I need an intelligent collaborator. That's why I would be happy to chat with you one of these mornings if it's OK.[100]

Although Cohl was assured that "nothing remains of our previous conditions," he spurned the offer. He believed that his talent had been exploited and, when he submitted an advertisement to the 1917 *Annuaire général de la cinématographie française*, a trace of bitterness entered his description (written in the third person): "Cohl is an artist at once knowledgeable, methodical and a fantasist. He is a true encyclopedia that his friends 'like to leaf through.' "[101]

Rabier continued to make cartoons using his "new" technique, which was actually nothing more than a simplified version of Cohl's cutout system (fig. 196). In 1919 Eclipse released *Un Rude Lapin* (March), *La Journée de Flambeau* (April, which might have used some of Cohl's 1916 footage), and *Caramel* (May). A Pathé series of Rabier films appeared during the early twenties.[102]

Rabier's letters reveal that there was much friction in their relationship. He was aggressive and domineering, while Cohl was adamant about his own conception of cartoon production. Cohl insisted that the pace of the films be fast and lively; Rabier wanted the movement to be slow and naturalistic, once demanding, "We need our animals to be acting out a comedy." Cohl wanted to use speech balloons for the dialogue like those in American comic strips, but Rabier preferred to have the dialogue appear in a caption below the drawings (as in *imagerie d'Epinal*). Whenever Cohl proposed an experiment or an innovation, Rabier opposed it with a more conservative idea. Given the temperamental differences between the two filmmakers, it is hardly surprising that so few films were completed.

The remaining sketches from *Les Fiançailles de Flambeau* have preserved a record of how Cohl and Rabier made their films.[103] The scenario agreed upon, Rabier would

196. Benjamin Rabier at work on a Pathé film using his homemade animation stand, ca. 1920.

prepare a design for each scene, for which Cohl would render a background (fig. 197a). Then Rabier sketched Flambeau in a variety of poses to demonstrate the range of his expressions and the phases of motion (fig. 197b–c). Cohl was free to modify Rabier's drawings to facilitate the animation. There was an exchange of ideas during the formative stages of the film, as shown by the sketches of Flambeau inflating a friend with a bicycle pump. They were based on a suggestion by Cohl and are reminiscent of the inflating sequence in *Fantasmagorie* (fig. 197d).

The only surviving print of *Les Fiançailles de Flambeau* (Cinémathèque Française) shows that the cutout figures were executed with great finesse. Their movements on the screen are fluid, supple, and convincingly puppy-like. This reflects Rabier's taste and Navarre's admonition to avoid the "exaggerated" movements of American cartoons. Illusionistic space is shallow, with no attempt to show depth recession. The "cuteness" of Rabier's animals (which anticipated Disney's style) is offset by the coarseness and morbidity of humor, which is perhaps attributable to Cohl. In the scene for which the sketches remain, the dog mischievously grinds up a friend in a sausage machine, a gag that Cohl had used in *He Poses for His Portrait* in 1913.[104] But generally speaking, the quality of the cartoon is superior in both technique and content to one of Barré's "Animated Grouch Chasers."

LES PIEDS NICKELÉS

Throughout Cohl's collaboration with Rabier, he had continued to work at Eclair. During 1916 he completed about one film a month, but the company was sinking into greater difficulties and could not release them until 1917. There are indications that the quality of these films was not high. *Jeux de cartes* (Card Games, cat. 198), for example, was criticized for poor photography.[105] *Les Victuailles de Gretchen se révoltent* (Gretchen's Food Revolts, cat. 192) elicited the hope for "something more substantial."[106] The only film to receive praise was *L'Avenir dévoilé par les lignes des pieds* (The Future Revealed by the Lines of the Foot, cat. 170), which was inspired by a 1907 Gaumont film of the same title. In a nearly complete print at the Archives du Film, a man comes to consult a lady fortune-teller who practices the unusual specialty of reading the soles of feet (fig. 198). The client's future is displayed as a series of animated transformation drawings. There is to be a marriage, but its blissful images give way to a monstrous mother-in-law, a policeman, and other harbingers of unhappiness. But when the scenes of marital bliss finally return, the man is so happy that he proposes to the fortune-teller. Obviously all her predictions will become self-fulfilling. *Le Film* rejoiced that this success proved that Eclair was still in business. The editors did not realize, however, that Cohl had completed *L'Avenir dévoilé par les lignes des pieds* almost three years earlier, before the war. As often happened in 1917, Cohl's film was the only one released by Eclair that week. Danvers, of *Le Film*, reacted to this situation:

197. Benjamin Rabier: Drawings and sketches for *Les Fiançailles de Flambeau*.

A good little film that should have been accompanied by one or two others. To ration the programs like courses in a restaurant—is it good commercial politics? I think not.[107]

The sad state of Eclair was a reflection of the general wartime crisis atmosphere hovering over the French film industry. Once the suppliers of films to the world, the studios now struggled to stay in business. Theaters were ordered closed every Tuesday and of course during Big Bertha's bombardments. Meanwhile, American movies—almost all feature length by now—flowed into all of Europe in unprecedented numbers.[108] Raw stock was scarce, but even had it been available, demand for exports had virtually disappeared.[109]

Near the end of Eclair's history as a producer, what was possibly one of its most interesting achievements took place—"Les Aventures des Pieds Nickelés." These five cartoons may also have been among Emile Cohl's greatest accomplishments.

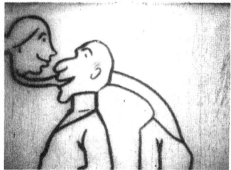

198. *L'Avenir dévoilé par les lignes des pieds*
(cat. 170), 1917.

It was probably his frustration with Rabier and Navarre that prompted Cohl to begin working on a new series of his own in December 1916. He could not have chosen a more promising subject. "La Bande des Pieds Nickelées" (The Leadfoot Gang) was a series of comic-strip adventures that began in *L'Epatant* in June 1908. Understanding the nature of the periodical helps us to understand that of the strip. It was published by Offenstadt Frères, a firm specializing in juvenile literature. The company also published *Le Petit Illustré*, *Fillette*, *Cri-Cri*, and *L'Intrépide*. Each of these was directed toward a specific demographic market, and *L'Epatant* was aimed at the children of the Parisian working class. A major part of its appeal was that it was written in argot. Because of its slang dialogue, street-smart situations, and antiauthoritarian attitude, it was under constant attack by the Catholic press, whose own children's magazines competed with Offenstadt's. Louis Forton's comic strip was consonant with the general tenor of *L'Epatant*.[110]

Its protagonists were three scruffy characters named Croquignol, Ribouldingue, and Filochard. They roughhoused through six lively adventures in what some considered a disturbingly anarchist manner. Georges Sadoul aptly described them: "bad boys, practical jokers, sneak thieves; the Pieds Nickelés were a sort of comic version of the [anarchist] Bonnot gang."[111] Although the comic strip was ostensibly written for children, many adults followed the gang's activities. Their popularity was at its height when

Forton was mobilized in 1915. He continued to send drawings from the front, and the Pieds Nickelés joined in the fighting.[112] Meanwhile, the original *Epatant* drawings were reissued as albums between August 1915 and June 1917. Just as the albums ceased, Cohl's film version began. The timing was perfect.

Regrettably, all that remains of the entire series of cartoons are two short fragments.[113] It is doubly sad because these fragments contain the best French animation that had yet been made.

Cohl adhered closely to Forton's style, as he had with his adaptations of McManus's and Rabier's drawings. The art in the original strip was self-consciously childish, and Forton had imitated the layout of *imagerie d'Epinal* by confining the pictures to little square boxes above verbose captions. Cohl's rendering of the characters was slightly less juvenile than Forton's, but their roguish nature was unchanged. The major differences were found in the adventures themselves.

Forton's stories were rooted in the real world. Contemporary events were incorporated into the strip and imparted to it a sense of immediacy and reality. In the film versions, on the other hand, the characters were transported to Cohl's world of fantasy, which was unlike anything they would ever have encountered in Forton's strip. In *Filochard se distingue* (cat. 221), for example, the villain is asleep in a room that fills up with water (accomplished by means of a translucent overlay) (fig. 199a). As he floats out the window, Filochard uses his sleeping body as springboard. He bounds into the air, causing a woman to exclaim, "That must have been a 'boche' [German] plane!" His flight across Paris continues until he is snagged on the Obelisk at the Place de la Concorde, which sways under his weight. Elsewhere, he escapes from a room by curling into a scroll and slipping through a crack in the shutter (fig. 199b).[114] This trick destroys the illusion that the figures are anything but two-dimensional cutouts. In other films in the series, Filochard's profile materializes as a piece of string thumbing his nose at a police inspector (fig. 200a). In one remarkable moment the villain is struck by a piece

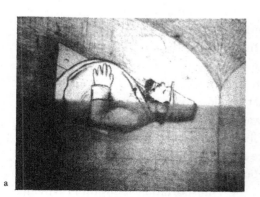

199. *Filochard se distingue (Pieds Nickelés* no. 4; cat. 221), 1918.

200. Unidentified films in the "Pieds Nickelés" series.

of falling fence and momentarily turns into a walking "Cubist" drawing (fig. 200b). Cohl used comic-strip speech balloons to indicate dialogue, but the action was primarily visual. In the final shot of one film the three heroes are walking from a strange mausoleum-like structure (fig. 200d). To show their progressive foreshortening, Cohl used cutouts of steadily decreasing size.

In contrast to *Les Fiançailles de Flambeau*, *Les Pieds Nickelés* was innovative and improvisational. The figures move quickly without too much regard for "naturalism." The result is a lively cartoon that captures the spirit of the original strip. This was precisely the quality that Rabier had wished to banish from his own cartoons when he told Cohl, "What we should do is so far from Les Pieds Nickelés."[115] Cohl's primary interest clearly was in creating a product that would satisfy the amateurs of Forton. Judging from these surviving fragments, he was successful.[116]

Perhaps there would have been more than five episodes had the war not intensified. In August 1917 the Eclair-Journal studios were occupied by the Cinematographic Services of the American army under the direction of one Lieutenant Miller.[117] André Courtet joined the Americans as an attaché to the Transportation Division in November. On May 11, 1918, Emile Cohl also offered them his services, as a volunteer in the

Air Service Supply (fig. 201).[118] Finally the war ended, and in December 1918 Jourjon asked him to return to work for Eclair-Journal in Epinay.

There Cohl stayed until May 1920, when he quit to begin work on *Fantoche cherche un logement* (Puppet Looks for an Apartment). It was completed and released by AGC as *La Maison du fantoche* (The Puppet's House, cat. 239) in April 1921.[119] The only notice of the short cartoon was in the form of three words in *Ciné-Journal*: "divertissants dessins animés" ("amusing cartoon"). It was his last significant film, but now it is lost.

Cohl did not retire from filmmaking, but practically speaking his career ended with the war. The reasons are not difficult to ascertain. Eclair never regained its prewar stride, despite the reorganization of the studios as Union-Eclair in 1919. The company leased its Epinay studios and concentrated on manufacturing equipment after 1920, when Charles Méry designed the "Cameraéclair," the prototype of the Eclair camera for which the firm is now known.[120] Other producers relied heavily on American imports instead of investing in domestic production. Beginning with the reincorporation of Pathé Frères as Pathé Cinéma in 1918, the major studios attempted to cut their

201. Cohl as U.S. Army volunteer, 1918.

losses by merging with smaller distributors and integrating with foreign interests.[121] Léon Gaumont, now humble in 1918, appraised the new situation: "Those distant times when we were a few resolute beginners, all with equal chances, are gone and will never return."[122] Success now depended on amassing huge capital reserves to produce features. With these requisites, producers were hardly interested in animated shorts that were expensive and had little promise of competing with American productions.

Emile Cohl was sixty-one years old in 1918 and suffered bouts with illness more frequently. For ten years he had labored without assistants. No longer could films like his be expected to hold their own on the market against those of Barré, Bray, and other industrialized studios. The first American "Mutt and Jeff" cartoons were introduced to France in April 1919; renamed "Dick et Jeff," they would become one of the most popular animated series in the early twenties for reasons that *Ciné-Journal* explained:

> These cartoons compete with the best of their kind; their extreme originality, their fantasy subjects and the irresistible characters of Dick and Jeff all show the animator's incomparable talent and unmatched wit. The spontaneous comedy of our two heroes surpasses all the buffoonery that our best humorists might imagine.[123]

The once-a-week frequency of the cartoons enhanced their audience appeal. In contrast, an Emile Cohl "Pieds Nickelés" film one third as long could be released only after

202. Advertisement for Chaplin series animated by Otto Messmer, 1916.

months of hard work. Meanwhile, the films of other talented Americans poured into Europe. Chaplin's popularity was exploited by a number of cartoon versions of his films, including Otto Messmer's early imported work (fig. 202). "The Adventures of Sammy Johnsin" by Pat Sullivan and Otto Messmer followed, and their "Felix the Cat" arrived in 1927. F. M. Follet's popular "Fuller Pep" cartoons came from the Powers studio. Competition even came from Sweden. Torsten Jungstedt has brought the active Swedish animation industry to light in his study of Victor Bergdahl, Emil Åberg, M. R. Liljeqvist, and Paul Myrén.[124] Bergdahl's first "Kapten Grogg" cartoon was imported to France by AGC in June 1918.[125] Liljeqvist's 1916 cartoon *Negern och Hunden* was released in Paris as *Le Nègre et son chien* (The Negro and His Dog) in July 1919. Ultimately the Swedish animation industry suffered the same fate as the French, dwindling under American domination and finally disappearing after about 1922.

But ironically it was the victorious assault of American cartoons upon the European market that opened a new and unexpected avenue in the career of Emile Cohl.

CHAPTER SIX

The Father of the Animated Film

EMILE COHL'S reputation was known to those in the French film business. Thus when the first detailed account of the American mass-production animation system appeared in French translation, the editor of *Ciné-Journal*, Georges Dureau, and the editor of *Ciné-Tribune*, Edmond Benoit-Lévy, both asked Cohl for his reactions. The article in question was written by Bert Green, one of the animators working for Pathé News in New York.[1] Green described the assembly-line organization, the use of "cels," and Barré's system. Several animators were discussed, including Winsor McCay, whom Green credited with the invention of the cartoon.

Needless to say, Cohl was incensed by Green's claim. In an introduction to his response, Dureau noted that Cohl's achievements were common knowledge:

> The creation of animated cartoons is generally attributed to our compatriot, the caricaturist Emile Cohl, student of André Gill who, some time ago while on a long sojourn in America, demonstrated this genre to our Allies.[2]

Cohl's letter was written with his usual colorful panache:

> The author of this article, Bert Green, presents Winsor McCay as the inventor of animated cartoons.
>
> Excuse me, I think there's been a mistake. I know as well as can be known the unfortunate forsaken one who had the vexing notion of finding pleasure by replacing living beings with drawn chaps. One only has to look in the programs of those days for the date of the first of these films that was called *Fantasmagorie*—right, Mr. Gaumont?[3]

Cohl knew that McCay was exaggerating the date of his film *Gertie* in order to claim priority, and he cynically dared someone to substantiate it:

> When will they give us the release date of the famous *Gertie* which, it seems, took three years of work? [Untranslatable joke]: Un travail bluff. . . . pardon, boeuf. — We'll see.

Cohl warned that, although he had made hundreds of cartoons, he was not too tired to put up a fight. He generously confessed his sincere admiration of McCay, "the most skillful and gracious graphic artist in the United States," but his admiration did not extend to his own self-effacement.[4] The technique of animation, he maintained, had undergone characteristic changes.

It was Americanized, that's to say, industrialized, until now it takes a troupe of thirty to produce what one artist used to draw here, working alone and shooting by himself.

Promising to discuss the "shady deal" again in the future, he closed confidently with "A moi, les adjectifs!" (the adjectives belong to me!).

In fact, Cohl was to dedicate most of the next decade to defending his own position as creator and promoter of the cartoon. Dureau had been the first to call him "le père du dessin animé" (Father of the Cartoon), a label that Cohl liked and adopted. It is not true, as some have implied, that Emile Cohl became a forgotten figure after the war— he was far too vociferous to be forgotten. The record shows that he frequently presented his case in public and gradually embroidered the facts as he grew older, helping to create his own legend.

Benoit-Lévy met with Cohl in May 1920 and showed him the translation of Green's article that *Ciné-Tribune* would publish on June 24.[5] Just before the article appeared, either by design or by coincidence, Cohl was invited to give a lecture on animation to the Ciné-Club at the Pépinière-Cinéma. Cohl's talk, the second in the series (the first having been by André Antoine, founder of the Théâtre-Libre),[6] began with a curious comparison of cartoons with other genres:

Cartoons belong to those kinds of films made by trick photography, a domain in which the workers are far removed from the psychological studies, somber dramas, slapstick comedies or those more or less bright plays that constitute the basis of cinematic art. These trick films, when one sees them, are a puff, a nothing, a few minutes of attention extracted from a population thirsty for the mysterious vicissitudes of New York, disguised hands, lace gloves, bloody teeth, diabolical horse rides into the chasms of Eternity . . . or Incomprehensibility![7]

Using Gaumont's old nickname for him, the Benedictine, Cohl stressed the difficulty of making these films:

These few minutes represent, however, an amount of work that I would call colossal—in spite of the bad connotation of the word—before which many a Benedictine would pale. . . . In spite of Benedictine [liqueur].

Drawing diagrams on a blackboard, he illustrated the theory and technique of animated cartoons and their relationship to ordinary cinematography.

There was a whole technique to find, a particular shooting angle to discover, lighting to try, etc. But we had something new and that was an accomplishment.

If the drawings for just one film were laid side by side, he joked, they would form a path from the Pépinière-Cinéma through the Arc de Triomphe on into the Bois de Boulogne. Then he added a remark that he would often repeat: "For the artist, there's one more thing; this path leads nowhere. No, I'm wrong. It will lead him to Charenton if he doesn't watch out." After his talk, the two films made in collaboration with Rabier were projected.[8]

When his response to Green's article appeared in *Ciné-Tribune*, Cohl's vehemence was toned down, but his wit remained sharp. He maintained that the incident was one more example of the famous "American ingenuity," which, "[while] charming, is generally accompanied by an almost complete misunderstanding of anything happening outside of the United States."[9] After having lived with Americans and served with them in the army, Cohl was convinced of their deep-rooted provincialism, of which Bert Green's claim that McCay invented the cartoon was simply another manifestation. Once again he chafed at the American studio system:

> While we work on our films alone in our studio, there they work in teams of fifteen or thirty who earn 50–1500 francs a week! My god, how much these cartoons must earn! Enough to make the French distributors tremble and to incite the poor artists here to pick up the timetables for the next transatlantic boats bound for this dreamland.

Cohl's articles and lectures caused him to be grouped among the "most notorious" filmmakers by the end of 1920, when *CinéMagazine* polled several filmmakers about their projects for the new year. Cohl answered with a bizarre letter reminiscent of his "incoherent" days:

> What am I working on for 1921? Well I'm embarrassed to tell you that several serious projects are engaging me: railroad crossing schemes, a way to imitate fake Gruyère cheese, and a scheme for hydropathic devulcanization. Business is business. As long as our French movies are almost completely in the hands of gents as circumlocutory as circumspect . . . it is difficult for a trick specialist, such as me, alas, to find a receptive company. Therefore . . . I will fly with my own wings.[10]

He took the opportunity to repeat his new "title" and to attribute his difficulties to exploitation at the hands of the Americans:

> Creator, that's to say, Father of animated cartoons, today I see my offspring returning from America resurfaced, gilded, thanks to the fabulous Dollar and I am floored by the many reject products that are oversaturating the public. They say we must resist. . . . Well, this is what I am doing, and since I do not wish to be a bother, I'll

close this jeremiad with a list of my intentions for the next year. There's Fantasy, Comedy, and more Drama than one might think. Here it is: *Her Pearl, Hip! Hop! Ettkom, Nègra, The Frenchwoman's Daughter,* etc.

His serious remarks about the difficulties of finding a producer reflect problems with *La Maison du fantoche,* which was complete, or nearly so. It is curious that he did not mention *Pages d'Histoire,* a mysterious film known only by a printed advertisement (fig. 203). Supposed to be about the reign of Napoleon, it was only 200 meters long; no record of its release exists.

203. Advertisement for *Pages d'histoire.*

In January 1922 Cohl entered the hospital for a prostatectomy. Complications prevented his leaving until March 15, but meanwhile his celebrity increased with the publication of *Le Cinéma pour tous,* a book by his friend Etienne Arnaud,[11] which devoted ten pages to Cohl's work. As we have seen, it was Arnaud who promulgated the story (probably apocryphal) of Cohl unveiling the secret of animation at the Gaumont studio. Arnaud quoted extensively from his friend's article in *Ciné-Tribune*[12] and agreed with his pessimistic assessment of current French animation.

This attention ushered in a brief period of optimism and satisfaction, as Cohl found himself basking in the unaccustomed limelight. During this period he relied on his expertise as a stamp collector to support himself. After 1924, when the cinema no longer provided any income for him, Cohl worked in the Pouillet stamp boutique on the Avenue de l'Opéra and remained there until 1929, "when a discussion between one of my colleagues and me made me leave." With all the new publicity, it appeared that at last his cinematographic achievements would be recognized.

Mon Ciné, a new publication by Offenstadt patterned on American fan magazines, saluted Emile Cohl in its inaugural issue of February 22, 1922. Twice referring to him as "the ancestor," the laudatory article announced that he was nearing completion of his three hundredth film.[13] *Ciné-Journal* also announced that Cohl's health was improving after submitting to his "delicate operation."[14] He was flattered once more as the "Father of the Cartoon" and as "our dean." There was also the news (premature, as it turned out) that he had contracted with a large producer to make scientific and instructional films.

Actually his next job was with Publi-Ciné, an advertising agency founded by the animator Lortac. From December 1922 to September 1923, Cohl made dozens of theatrical commercial trailers. Known only by the names of the products advertised, such as "Jacobino Vermouth," these were probably insignificant potboilers. Cohl quit in 1923 over some "difficulties of payment."[15]

A great honor was accorded him in 1924 when the Musée Galliera asked him to participate in its Art in French Cinema Exposition. He exhibited an "initial sketch from the creation of animated cartoons," which purported to be a drawing from *Fantasmagorie* (incorrectly dated 1907). There is no proof that this was an original drawing, and no verifiable originals are now known to exist. Also shown was a "Strip of 16 drawings (statuette revolving) representing the work of the artist for a one-second projection" (fig. 145). There were drawings for some of the didactic films that had been announced in 1922: *La Circulation du sang chez l'homme* (The Circulation of the Blood in Man, fig. 204) and *L'Oreille (Comment nous entendons)* (The Ear, a.k.a. How We Hear). Maps from *The Battles of Napoleon I* (which may have been an alternate title for *Pages d'Histoire*) and some "Studies and Projects for the formation and growth of Paris before the eyes of the spectator: *Paris through the Centuries*" were included. There were three puppets from *Le Tout Petit Faust*.[16]

In January 1925 the Larousse company asked him to write an explanatory article on animated cartoons for their encyclopedia. The 2500-word essay appeared in the *Larousse Mensuel* in August.[17] In order to avoid appearing immodest when discussing his

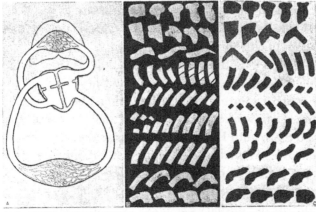

204. Project for *La Circulation du sang chez l'homme*, ca. 1921.

own accomplishments, he signed the piece "J.-B. de Tronquières." The animated cartoon was described as "a series of drawings (ordinarily of childlike characters, executed by hand, brush, pen, etc.), that analyzes the phases of a motion and that, when filmed and projected, appears to have all the mobility of living beings." There was a brief history of the discovery and development of animation, with considerable space devoted to "a Parisian artist, Emile Courtet, better known in the illustrated weeklies under the pseudonym Emile Cohl." He mentioned the Swedish cartoons in passing but conceded that "the best cartoons come from New York." His account of industrialized production in America relied on Green's despised article, concluding, "This Taylorization allows the release of one film every five or six days." He also described the use of "cels" but dismissed the process as too expensive for French animators: "It is a faster process, but rather costly, and it is an expenditure that for now only our former allies can bear." Cohl finished by describing *L'Oreille* (The Ear, cat. 242) and emphasized the significance of such films: "All the phenomena that are impossible to film in nature are here *translated* into very clear, analyzed drawings." Public instruction, not entertainment or advertising, was the future direction of the medium:

Aside from the amusing fantasies reserved presently it seems for advertising, it is certain that the future of animation will be found in education. It will more and more be a clear and precise adjunct to the teacher's voice.

In the same year Georges-Michel Coissac singled out Emile Cohl in his *Histoire du cinématographe*, the most important work on film history to have been written by 1925:

In a very special category of directors, we mention the famous caricaturist Emile Cohl, nicknamed the "ace's ace" of animation. He had the idea of putting art to the service of the cinema before anyone else.[18]

Coissac noted the explosive rise of the American cartoon but maintained that, because of Cohl's parentage, the medium was "rigorously French, like the cinema."

The following year brought further recognition, but not related to his films. The High Life Tailor, which had begun to exhibit Cohl's drawings twenty years earlier, held a retrospective showing of its best contributors. Many caricaturists—legendary or forgotten—appeared with Cohl: Albert Guillaume, Charles Léandre, Moloch, and Robida. Of all of them, only Cohl was still something of a celebrity. The exhibition was undoubtedly a nostalgic event, but it was soon followed by a more touching one: the publication in 1927 of Charles Fontane's deluxe two-volume monograph on the life and work of André Gill.[19] Cohl assisted Fontane, as he had Armand Lods in 1887, by supplying information and documents from his collection. He wrote a letter of dedication and contributed a drawing of Gill's tomb. Many of the items listed in the catalogue raisonné were from Cohl's collection. Fontane thanked him in the text and dedicated the catalogue to him.

On December 16, 1929, Cohl was invited to attend the Gala Méliès, organized by Paul Gilson and Jean-Georges Auriol.[20] The affair celebrated the almost miraculous discovery of a dozen "lost" Méliès that had belonged to M. Dufayel, the turn-of-the-century department-store magnate. Georges Méliès had been living in much more obscurity than Cohl during the 1920s. While the latter was earning a pittance at the stamp shop, Méliès was operating a candy stand at the Gare Montparnasse, where Cohl must have encountered him on his travels to and from Saint-Mandé. Whether Cohl attended the gala is unknown. Within a few weeks Auriol also paid homage to Cohl in an article for *La Revue du Cinéma*.[21] It was the first time a serious study of his films had been attempted.

Auriol classed Cohl with Méliès as a worker in the "domain of the marvelous" and claimed he was the forerunner of the "supernatural poetry" of Winsor McCay, Pat Sullivan, and Dave Fleischer. The "fantoche" films were highly praised, but Auriol took the artist to task for using cutouts:

> The work degenerated rapidly and gave birth to articulated characters with disagreeable gauche gestures who moved all of a piece. The cutouts were no longer capable of the charming lifelike flexing seen in the image by image treatment that we admire in the supple and gentle American cartoons and which Emile Cohl used for his fantasmagoric transformations.[22]

Then came the surprising statement: "The animated cartoon has been lost in France since Emile Cohl. His films have disappeared. His imitators have met with only mediocre success." Never before had anyone suggested that he was such an important figure. Auriol concluded with the suggestion that Cohl should found a school:

> Should not Emile Cohl be able to found a society or—something even more French—a school, where those who are now struggling desperately and others who might profit by his experience, from his achievements and his ingenuity, might work in peace and quiet on a body of work on which we cannot resign ourselves to give up?

Auriol's article was a fitting capstone to one of the most gratifying decades of Cohl's life. Now he was generally recognized as the "Father of the Cartoon." True, he had taken some liberty with historical facts and did not object when others tried to create legends for him, but like many aging artists, he welcomed the relative happiness and knew he deserved it. This happiness, it turned out, was only temporary. The elation of the 1920s gave way to sadder times in the 1930s.

The first crisis to be faced was the sudden loss of his stamp collection, the youthful hobby he had never abandoned.[23] He was still known in philatelic circles, especially since his friend Verrier (brother-in-law of the dealer Arthur Maury) had bequeathed his important collection to Cohl in 1912. Thinking that he was making a sound investment, Cohl had combined his collection with that of an old friend, Albert Coyette, when they had worked at Lemaire's between 1901 and 1906. Unfortunately both Coyette and Suzanne became ill at the same time, and the hidden risk of the scheme became obvious. Eventually the entire collection, including Cohl's share, which had taken nearly seventy years to gather, was sold off to pay the medical expenses of his wife and his partner. Jourjon rescued Cohl with a job offer in March 1930, but he had to leave Epinay and return to Paris in April because Suzanne was now gravely ill.

Suzanne Delpy Courtet-Cohl, who had been in poor health for some time, passed away in September 1930. In his notebook, Cohl simply entered a touching "Alas." Seventy-three years old and without resources, he was forced to leave his Montmartre apartment to live with his son, André, his daughter-in-law, and two grandchildren in the suburb of Saint-Mandé. A note sets the tone for this final period: "My tribulations date from this time. I was obliged from this moment to bear the burden of the adventure that befell me."

ANIMATION IN FRANCE: THE "COHL SCHOOL"

One might expect any traces of Emile Cohl's influence on his own countrymen to have been drowned in the sea of American cartoons that overwhelmed France in the immediate postwar period. But in fact this is not quite the case. His frequent pontifications as the "Father of the Cartoon" kept Cohl in close personal contact with the pioneers of the struggling industry, although his actual physical contributions were minimal. His most important connections can be traced back to the prewar days when there were only his Gaumont and early Eclair films to entertain French cartoon buffs.

Cohl had known O'Galop (Marius Rossillon) when he was a popular contributor of picture stories to *La Caricature*, *Le Rire*, *L'Illustré National*, and other humor magazines (fig. 205). He is now immortalized as the creator of the "Bibendum" tire-man, the Michelin trademark.[24] After Cohl left Pathé in 1911, O'Galop went to work there animating a series of didactic films. The first was *Le Circuit de l'alcool* (The Course of

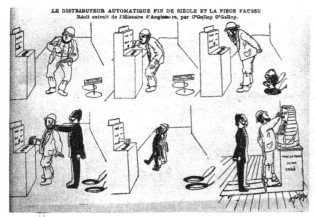

205. O'Galop (Marius Rossillon): "Le Distributeur automatique fin de siècle et la pièce fausse," *La Caricature* no. 647, 1892.

206. O'Galop (Marius Rossillon): *Le Circuit de l'alcool*, 1912.

Alcohol, fig. 206), which was released in 1912.[25] The film shows some technical influence of Cohl, who in all likelihood collaborated on the content as well. The subject—the degenerative effects of alcoholism—was one of his recurring themes, and the film ends with a remarkable sketch of the painting "Le Fou," labeled "after André Gill."[26]

O'Galop paid his respects to "my old comrade, Cohl, the initiator of the genre."[27] Commenting on his friend's address to the Ciné-Club, O'Galop agreed with the melancholy conclusion that animation could open the doors to Charenton: "Obviously he exaggerated a little . . . just a little . . . almost not at all." Cohl, he reported, showed no such tendencies because he was at work on his 245th film and "still has a full deck."

Cohl also knew Lortac (1884–1973), the other important French animator (fig. 207). Robert Collard (his real name) was a student at the Ecole des Beaux-Arts before deciding to devote his career to caricature. Cohl and Lortac met for the first time about 1916, and they may have worked together on a few episodes of the Eclair-Journal newsreel.[28] Lortac made a brief visit to New York and upon his return founded the first American-style animation studio in Montrouge in 1921, inviting Cohl to participate as "technical adviser." This was probably little more than an honorary designation for publicity purposes. However, Lortac's team constituted the first generation of commercial animators in France: André Rigal, Raoul Guérin, Cavé, and Cheval trained there.[29]

Lortac tapped Cohl again when he founded Publi-Ciné. In addition to advertising films, the studio produced "Le Canard en . . . ciné" (punning on the famous radical paper *Le Canard Enchaîné*). This series, "the first animated happy newsreel"[30] was modeled on Cohl's Animated Weekly and Eclair-Journal shorts. The "Canards" were issued irregularly until 1923, but the extent of Cohl's cooperation—if any—is unknown. Unable to compete with the Americans, Lortac quit in the 1930s to pursue painting and write novels.[31]

It is legitimate to speak of the animators clustered around Lortac and O'Galop as a "Cohl School," in the sense that they tempered the American influence with his methods and his fundamental aesthetic assumptions that defined the genre. This partially explains the tenacity of the cutout technique in France. Certainly there were shortages of celluloid caused by the war, but economic factors alone cannot account for the fact that all but one animator still relied on cutouts as late as 1930.[32] *La Tuberculose menace tout le monde* (TB Threatens Everyone, fig. 208) is a film from Lortac's studio that demonstrates its anachronistic reliance on Cohl's system. The cutout figures of a lecturer and an articulated skeleton are the only moving elements. After a didactic hygiene lecture delivered with the aid of speech balloons, as in "Les Pieds Nickelés," the skeleton symbolically knocks over dolls in a sideshow booth who represent people from all classes and occupations. The idea may have been inspired by one of Cohl's nineteenth-century drawings (fig. 20).

Cohl's influence was evident in the unusually strong emphasis placed on the cartoon as a journalistic item. In fact, he apparently came to believe that it would (or at least

207. Josbert Lormard, caricature of Lortac
(Robert Collard).

208. Lortac Studio: *La Tuberculose menace tout le monde*,
ca. 1912.

should) eventually become an ideological tool for promoting French culture. After the
war he claimed that entertainment cartoons were best left to the Americans. His experiences on the Animated Weekly and the Eclair-Journal led him to write that it was the
domain of the newsreel that was proper for animation, and this idea was drummed into
his younger colleagues. The journalistic-didactic emphasis was a distinctly French formulation of animation in the early 1920s.

In all his printed and spoken statements, Cohl endeavored to differentiate American
and French animation on the basis of fundamental economic and cultural factors. He
painted a picture of Easy Street for the American cartoonists, focusing on the Bray
studio's practice of "in-betweening" (the animator sketching the beginning and end
points of an action, with the intervening movements drawn by assistants):

> The minds of the artists and the understanding of the public favor the diffusion of
> animation better in America than here. Since the cartoonist has a comfortable con-
> tract with a production company, he can work undistracted. He creates or borrows
> a popular character, furnishes ideas, the scenario and and a few drawings, then a
> team of six, eight or ten artists set to work based on his models and directions. Differ-
> ent parts of the story are done simultaneously. Then the cameramen photograph the
> drawings piecemeal in the order in which they left the hands of the workers. The
> director preserves his serenity and respect and is always in a good mood to work.[33]

His picture of the French animator, on the other hand, was essentially romantic. Economically deprived, the native artist had to struggle to succeed with the public:

> Each of these artists brings his particular style, his wit, his handicraft to the camera.
> In every case we have a work that is a whole, that reflects its *auteur* as an emanation

209. Albert Mourlan (with assistant), ca. 1921.

of his personality and his individual originality. It's a consolation for the French artist, who always has had a hypertrophied ego and who would rather drink in a movie studio.[34]

Finally, Cohl, in his self-appointed role as spokesman for the French animation industry, was calling for his countrymen to resort to their traditional national genius. His argument was a version of the old cliché: the worse the soil, the better the wine.

In the mid-twenties promising animators were at work in France. Foremost was Ladislas Starevitch (1882–1965), the reclusive Russian emigré who lived outside of Paris and had been producing animated puppet films since 1919. The illustrator Albert Mourlan (1887–1946) set up a studio in Montfermeil in 1921 (fig. 209). His first films were apparently sold to an American distributor and have disappeared. During the twenties he worked in both drawing and puppet animation modes, but without achieving any great success.[35]

The battle against American domination was lost by the mid-twenties. Audiences in France—as everywhere else—cared only to see more of Felix the Cat, Koko the Clown, and, after 1929, Mickey Mouse. When French intellectuals began to notice the new genre, the films of Cohl and his followers were forgotten or, at best, remembered as prehistoric fossils.

One of the first important assessments of the cartoon was Gus Bofa's article "Du Dessin animé" (On the Cartoon), which appeared in the special 1925 cinema issue of the art magazine *Les Cahiers du Mois*. Bofa, a caricaturist himself, advanced an argument that was consistent with the prevailing tenets of film criticism. He praised the cartoon's antirealist capacity and its potential for obtaining that elusive goal of cinematic "rhythm." It substantiated his belief that "the cinema has at last furnished to man the power to create something new in the world."[36]

Felix the Cat's emigration to France in 1927 elicited remarks from Marcel Brion, later an academician and historian of abstract painting. In "Félix le Chat ou la poésie créatrice" (Felix the Cat, or Creative Poetry), he became the first to link the cartoon with Surrealism.[37] Felix was a *sur-chat*, a supercat distinct from everyday cats. Brion's discovery that the cartoon was an unintentionally Surrealist art form influenced most later writers, including Maurice Bessy. Writing on *Steamboat Willie* (1928, released in France in 1929), the first released film featuring Mickey Mouse, Bessy recognized the revolution that synchronous sound was bringing. Mickey, he said, "was the first to reveal the striking original poetry of sound cartoons. . . . Because this new genre singularly enlarged the profoundly cinegraphic domain of the dream and the unreal."[38] Jean Morienval, writing in *Le Cinéopse*, did credit "Emile Courtet (whose professional name is Cohl)" as the inventor of moving drawings but preferred the more recent work of Starevitch.[39]

Gregory Waller has pointed out the apparent paradox in criticism of the animated film in the early 1930s. Authors equivocated between praising cartoons' plastic qualities, as though they were Cubist paintings in motion, and praising them for the appeal they held for the masses. Critics, according to Waller, "disagreed about whether Disney was more akin to Marcel Duchamp or to Mack Sennett."[40]

Emile Cohl took a predictably dim view of the glorification of American cartoonists by French intellectuals. When Pat Sullivan died in 1933, Cohl clipped an obituary notice that described the American as one of the inventors of the cartoon. He protested in the margin: "Pat Sullivan *invented* cartoons ten years after me!"[41] He was deeply wounded by the injustice of French critics who praised the "Surrealist" world of Sullivan, Disney, and the other Americans while ignoring the irrational world of dream and fantasy that he had created years before in his own films. It seemed as though the critics finally had caught on to what Cohl's animation was about, but they insisted on crediting the marvelous discovery to the wrong people.

THE 1930s

The manuscript from which much of our biography has been based (MS. II) ends abruptly in July 1931, leaving unknown most of the facts about Cohl's subsequent private life, at least from this primary source. His financial condition continued to deteriorate as the worldwide Great Depression took its toll. Gradually he became more bitter and felt cheated when he was ignored by the government and the film industry, especially after Georges Méliès was awarded the Legion of Honor medal in 1931. When a reporter from *Pour Vous* came to call, Cohl made a dismal prediction:

> I strongly fear, and some experiences have confirmed this, that it won't be many years now until the French will not know that Mickey, Flip the Frog and Felix the Cat are only the "industrialized" descendants of the puppets that a Parisian caricaturist used to draw in a modest studio in Montmartre.[42]

He reiterated his horror of being forgotten by historians in a letter written to the newspaper *Paris-Soir* in 1934:

> These drawings, multiplied by merry dollars, have acquired some deserved popularity, but all the same have left behind the old trickster who first imagined this branch of cinematography.[43]

The plight of the aging cartoonist came to the attention of Jean-Marie (né Giuseppe Maria) Lo Duca and his young friend, the animator Pierre Bourgeon. Lo Duca was preparing a book on the history of animation and was producing the films of Bourgeon

210. Cohl with Lo Duca and Pierre Bourgeon (center) at DAE studio, 1935.

and Mimma (Léontina) Indelli for his company, Les Dessins Animés Européens (DAE). They thought they could help Cohl by hiring him as a "consultant" for the film *La Conquête de l'Angleterre* (The Conquest of England). Cohl's only collaboration turned out to be chatting, drinking coffee, and posing for some publicity pictures (fig. 210).[44]

Cohl found his staunchest defender in Jean-Pierre Liasu, a young writer for *Comoedia*, who was as articulate as he was ardent. Reacting to the forwarding of the Legion of Honor medal to Disney, Liasu reminded readers of the trade journal that if Walt Disney was Mickey Mouse's father, then Emile Cohl must be his grandfather.[45] Curious to discover what had happened to the old man, Liasu searched him out. A few days later he published the shocking news that "Emile Cohl has lost everything. He is not simply poor, he is—forgive me—he would be in a state of destitution except for the devotion of a young friend. I did not dare knock on his door."[46] Cohl was subsisting on the one hundred francs he received each month from public assistance. Liasu noted with irony that the inventor of a most popular and lucrative branch of cinematography could no longer afford to go to a movie, and he called for aid from all those making profits from films. Meanwhile, he arranged an interview that was published two weeks later.[47]

The first thing Cohl wanted to know was why *Comoedia* was taking such an active interest in his case. Liasu told him that René Brest of *Paris-Soir* and the actor Albert Préjean were campaigning on his behalf. After Liasu had been introduced to André and kissed the cheeks of the grandchildren, Cohl told his story, but with more bitterness than ever before:

> After the war I tried in vain to make financial contacts. In France, it's useless. I threw in the towel. You have to live.
>
> I did survive and I'm still living. But I protest with all my last strength against those who don't respect the truth.
>
> It's hard to give a damn anymore. France likes its artists, scientists and intellectuals dead and chilled, with flowers and marble overhead.
>
> What I thought to be a pastime gave birth to a noble cinema, of quality. The clock has struck eighty for me. And I have nothing, nothing more. It's the crisis.

But the interview ended on a less gloomy note when Cohl told of the joy that his grandchildren, Pierre and Suzanne, had brought him (fig. 211) and of his hopes for the cinema because of all the young people taking an interest in it.

Cohl's misanthropy against those who controlled the film industry was not yet translated into his other personal relationships. One day he discovered that the aging Georges Courteline—recalled from the Gill days—frequented the café in the center of Saint-Mandé. Cohl came every day thereafter to chat with the playwright and the other customers. The proprietor later remarked on his timid demeanor:

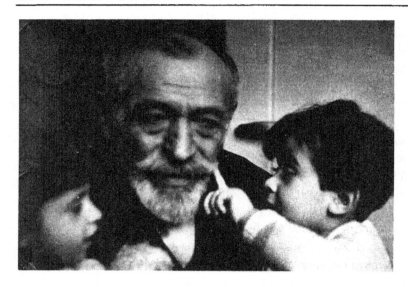

211. Cohl with his grandchildren, Suzanne and Pierre, ca. 1936.

[He had] an admirable nature. We only knew him when he was already old, but what an exquisite being. Not only did he not earn anything, but he gave away what he had if someone asked him. No sense of reality. He was timid, but a marvelous conversationalist once you were in his confidence. He wouldn't sit down without asking whether he was bothering the other customers at the table. He regularly drank coffee or chocolate with croissants. That's all I ever saw him drink.[48]

The barkeeper also suggested that Cohl was developing a mild persecution complex and that he spoke of a woman "who spent millions to have me shut up."[49] He also believed that he was an intolerable burden on his family.

Lo Duca and Bourgeon cheered him up in 1936 when they mounted a celebration of the cartoon's "thirtieth" anniversary. (They dated *Fantasmagorie* from 1906.) Actually most of their effort went to promote DAE productions, but Lo Duca had discovered prints of two of Cohl's films in Rome (where the Centro Sperimentale was just being organized), and they were to be included in the program. (In 1930 Auriol had believed that all of Cohl's works had been destroyed in the war, so the discovery was important.) *Fantasmagorie* and an unidentified film called *Santippe* (cat. 77, possibly the 1921 *Fantoche* film) were well received. Both, according to Liasu, "are white lines on a background and are naive and forceful."[50] There was also the inscrutable remark that "the captions [*légendes*, i.e., Italian intertitles?] on the two films will be redone by Emile Cohl."

Bourgeon wrote a flattering letter to Cohl predicting the end of the great injustice he had encountered:

You should not content yourself with [just being credited with] an invention, in the mechanical sense of the word, but also with having given the cartoon its soul. The humor of today's animated cartoons is of the same spirit as the first. The same feeling for the satirical and the improbable.[51]

Cohl sent his young colleague some publicity drawings in his old "fantoche" style (fig. 212a and b).

Bourgeon's prediction came true in the spring of 1937 when Léon Gaumont nominated Cohl for the annual award given by the Société d'Encouragement pour l'Industrie Nationale.[52] On March 13, 1937, the assembly convened in the same auditorium at 44, rue de Rennes where Lumière had first projected his Cinématographe films in 1895, and where Gaumont had demonstrated his Chronophone in 1907. The president congratulated Cohl on receiving the medal for the year 1936 and presented him with a stipend of 4,000 francs.

Be assured that our Society is well within its traditions in recognizing the creator of a branch of industry that, while flourishing today, has not rendered all that it should toward he who gave so much to it. But alas, such is the case for a great number of precursors.[53]

Un Drame chez les fantoches and *Les Joyeux Microbes* were screened for the assembly, followed by Disney's *Three Little Pigs* and Amedee Van Beuren's *Sunshine Makers*—to demonstrate the industry's progress.

The happiness brought by this award was short-lived. In mid-April the newspapers reported that Cohl had been admitted to the hospital La Pitié for burn treatment.

212. a) Cohl drawing a stick figure, ca. 1937. b) Publicity drawing for *La Cinématographie Française*, September 26, 1936.

Exactly what had occurred is unknown, but there are several versions of the story. The proprietor of the café in Saint-Mandé thought that Cohl had set his apartment on fire during one of his imagined persecutions.[54] One often-repeated version of the accident states that he set his long flowing beard on fire while working by candlelight. But as a picture taken during a visit to Méliès at Orly plainly shows (fig. 213), Cohl kept his beard neatly trimmed. The origin of this story can be traced to "a ruddy-faced little guy in an overcoat" who allegedly told it to a journalist named Roland Bouvard.[55] The most plausible version is Robert André's in *Le Figaro*.[56] The fire was caused by an overturned oil lamp. Such lamps were still used in old suburban houses only partially wired for electricity, and of course oil lamps were widely used in the 1930s to save money. The burning fuel spread quickly to newspapers and curtains in Cohl's room.

Cohl was placed in a forty-bed charity ward of La Pitié called the Salle Berger. He was suffering from extensive burns, which made all movement agonizing. As he told Robert André, "I am nothing but a broken marionette." The 4,000-franc award was spent quickly, but film historian Marcel Lapierre made an appeal for aid in *Paris-Soir*.[57] The newspapers politely indicated that the family was poverty-stricken and that André Courtet could do little to help his father.[58]

213. Cohl (right) visiting Georges Méliès at Orly, 1937.

In October 1937, after six months at La Pitié, Cohl was transferred to the departmental hospital Paul-Brousse in the suburb of Villejuif. This was essentially an indigent hospital, where conditions were even worse than at La Pitié (fig. 214). Robert André reported, with a not-too-thinly veiled jab at Gaumont:

It is truly pitiable to state that after all appeals for charity, and that's the right word, directed toward a corporation that owed him so much, not a single individual would honor him by defending his cause.[59]

Appeals for help also came from an unexpected source, *L'Intermédiare des Chercheurs et des Curieux* (Bulletin for Researchers and the Curious), a periodical that answered (and still does) esoteric questions submitted by readers. The question "Who is the Oldest Parisian?" was answered by Charles Fontane, Gill's biographer and Cohl's friend since the 1920s.[60] Fontane used the question as a platform from which to publicize Cohl's pathetic condition and to appeal for a place for him with Méliès at the industry's retirement home at Orly, La Maison du Retrait du Cinéma. He took to task the unsympathetic public:

The oldest Parisian, Emile Courtet, so esteemed, so loved by all who know him, is suffering at Villejuif on his bed of sorrow. It is not only for the film industry to come

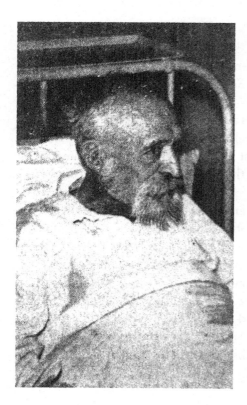

214. Cohl hospitalized at Villejuif, 1937.

to his aid, but for all Parisians, his juniors for whom all his drawings, animated or not, so often brought a little comfort and joy.

Simultaneously A.-P. Richard called for state recognition of Cohl's contribution:

> Let us state that the [medal of the] Legion of Honor, if one can still attach some importance to this distinction, should be placed firmly on the breast of Emile Cohl.[61]

Also among those responding was René Jeanne, a young journalist and future historian of early cinema, who organized a benefit screening at the Champs-Elysées Cinema on January 19, 1938.[62]

The first tangible assistance resulted from an article in *L'Epoque* on Cohl's worsening condition:

> He was atrociously burned in a fire in his modest apartment. Poorly treated and still suffering, he can no longer pick up the pencil by which he earned his living.[63]

A burn specialist, Dr. Raoul Leroy, read this alarming notice and called Norpois, the author, to volunteer his services. But it was too late. Norpois wrote:

> Doctor Raoul Leroy and I looked again all over Paris for the old Parisian. We learned that bronchial pneumonia had taken him, at the age of eighty-one. Dolorous pleas are no longer necessary now that he is dead. The doctor who made this moving gesture to save him can feel less bitter for it.[64]

Cohl died during the night on January 20, 1938, shortly after his eighty-first birthday, and was cremated at Père-Lachaise four days later. Elsewhere in Paris, audiences were attending the opening of *Snow White and the Seven Dwarfs*, Disney's first feature-length animated cartoon.

The trade press expressed its loss, and notices appeared in the *New York Times* and the *Journal des Débats*.[65] *Le Figaro*'s obituary echoed one of Cohl's refrains: "It is the lot of inventors and thinkers to die poor. At least it is here."[66] *L'Illustration* and many other periodicals combined Cohl's obituary with that of Georges Méliès, who died a few hours after Cohl on January 21, 1938.[67]

For his grieving family, the suffering did not end with Cohl's death. They were the victims of a cruel swindle. A committee for a Cohl-Méliès monument was established under the leadership of Jean-José Frappa, with such notables as Louis Lumière, Abel Gance, Jean Renoir, Germaine Dulac, and Marcel Vandal on its committee of honor. Gaumont was a major contributor, and Walt Disney sent 5,000 francs. The committee commissioned sculptor Amerigo Montagutelli to make a plaster model of the monument, which ultimately was to have been erected at the Porte Dauphine (fig. 215). But plans were disrupted by the outbreak of World War II and the death of Frappa. Then in 1940 it was learned that Montagutelli had absconded with all the funds. Nothing more was heard of him until 1972, when Madeleine Malthête-Méliès discovered an amazing newspaper story. Montagutelli had just fled Haiti—accused of swindling the heirs of "Papa Doc" Duvalier![68]

It was not until after World War II that the city of Paris designated a little park in the twelfth arrondissement the "Square Emile-Cohl." Located across from the "Square Georges-Méliès," it is used, appropriately, as a playground by the children of the neighborhood (fig. 216).

In 1895 Cohl drew a revealing self-portrait for *Le Chat Noir* in which he pictured the past, present, and future stages of his life (fig. 217). Again he expressed his love for André Gill and his commitment to graphic art. He whimsically sketched the Pantheon as his final resting place by the time of his centenary. Unfortunately the glory and recognition for which he always longed did not materialize until after his death. As an old man he saw himself in Gill's final position, overcome with anger and frustration, abandoned by his friends, and ignored by his profession.

Much of Cohl's misery was not so much the result of malevolence toward him by persons in the film industry, as he implied, or even because of his independent creative spirit. Rather it was the result of the times in which he worked. If his career had begun and ended earlier, there would never have been any expectation of recognition because no one could have dreamed of the future importance of the cinema. A few years later and he might have emerged from the anonymity that was normal in the film business before 1915.

215. Amerigo Montagutelli: Model for a Cohl-Méliès monument, 1938.

216. Square Emile-Cohl, 12th arrondissement, Paris.

A few years before his centenary, in 1953, Emile Cohl achieved some recognition of his talents and contributions. Several of the journalists who had assisted him in his final crisis later chronicled his achievements in their books on French film history.[69] The importance of his early graphic art was being assessed by Jean Adhémar and others.[70] A serious scholar, Marie-Thérèse Poncet, became interested in his films and published a long list of titles in her book *Dessin animé, art mondial* (Cartoons, the Worldwide Art).[71] Since then, his films have been screened with increasing frequency at international animation festivals in Annecy, Montreal, Ottawa, New York, Paris, Perpignan, Pordenone, Italy, and Chicago. Gradually Emile Cohl's pipe dream of glory is being fulfilled by his elevation to a pantheon that did not even exist in 1895—one dedicated to the pioneer artists of the cinema.

217. Self-portrait, *Le Chat Noir*, May 4, 1895.

PART THREE

Toward an "Incoherent Cinema"

CHAPTER SEVEN

Graphic Humor and Early Cinema

FILM AND COMICS

Emile Cohl left behind a massive corpus of art executed in many different media. The questions we wish to examine in this section are: to what extent were those different media interrelated, and by what processes did Cohl's nineteenth-century graphic art affect his twentieth-century cinematic art?

The significance of these questions extends beyond their applicability solely to the work of Emile Cohl. The early cinema was an intertextual system par excellence, and very much a hybrid of various technologies and disparate aesthetic models derived from other popular arts. Conventional wisdom has it that comic strips were in some vague way the forerunners of cinema in general, and of animated cartoons in particular. Because Cohl was a successful practitioner of both arts, a study of his career should provide us with an excellent test case by which to evaluate and clarify the issues concerning the general relationship between comics and early film.

Most of what has been written on the subject can be consolidated under three general arguments: Movies and comics were born at the same time; the formal elements of cinematic narrative construction were perfected first in the comic strip, then integrated into films; and comic-strip art and film art share a "final cause" because they tend toward the same cultural and aesthetic ends. Each of these statements will be considered separately.

The simultaneous genesis of film and the comic strip. "The cinema and the comic strip," wrote Francis Lacassin, "were both born toward the end of the nineteenth century, and they have experienced a similar initial reception: disdain from the intellectuals, enmity from critics, and immense public acclaim."[1] Pierre Couperie agreed that the "animated cartoon, the movie, and the comic strip were born simultaneously."[2] According to John Fell, "Newspaper comics rivaled dime novels as early, mass circulated ephemera. Their appearance accompanied the development of the motion picture," and "As movies grew in length and shot-to-shot complexity, the comics progressed from 'one-shot' graphics, such as editorial cartoons, to multipanel successions of imagery, measured by the limitations of an unfolded newspaper page."[3] Maurice

Horn repeated the presumption that the two arts "were both born around the same time" and added the often-heard comparison, "The comics come closer to the movies than to any other art form."[4] It was the same assumption that motivated Jean Mitry to include a chapter on turn-of-the-century comic strips in his *Histoire du cinéma*.[5]

The historical fallacy of these statements has already been demonstrated by David Kunzle, who, in his erudite history of the comic strip, examined the form when it thrived in the seventeenth and eighteenth centuries.[6] Even if one objects that we are dealing only with the "modern" comic strip, then one must concede that its mature form was already widespread by the early 1880s, at least a decade and a half before motion-picture technology. If one insists on defining the comic strip in the restrictive terms of its American newspaper variant only, then one arbitrarily ignores the vigorous traditions of *Puck, Life, Judge, Punch, Fliegende Blätter*, and the numerous French publications to which Cohl contributed in the eighties and nineties. An empirical examination makes it clear that the comic has a much longer history than cinema, and that most of its narrative conventions were fully established by the time film was invented.

Film derived its "cinematic" narrative techniques from comic strips. Horn succinctly expressed the view that "many techniques which have come to be called 'cinematic' have originated in the comics."[7] Among these are montage, cutting, framing, panning, and "audio" effects that anticipated the sound film. More importantly, Horn continues,

> Even the grammars of the comic and the movies are almost identical: the concepts of "shot" (as opposed to the static "scene") and of "sequence," and the attending variations of angles and perspectives, the unlimited possibilities of tracking forward and backward, are present in both forms.

Lacassin's formulation is very similar:

> In both [cinema and the comic strip], the language is composed of a succession of "shots" (that is to say, images with variable framing) in a syntactical arrangement or *montage*. The comic strip demonstrably corresponds to the film sequence, or the act of a play, except that the background tends to change more often. The daily comic strip of three or four images is comparable to the cinematic scene.[8]

For him, the exemplary comic-strip artist was Christophe:

> This much is certain: it was Christophe who, between 1880 and 1892, discovered all the rudiments—save the extreme close-up and low-angle shots—of a language, which the cinema did not master (and yet claimed to have fathered) for many years after its birth.

Kunzle, in his addendum to Lacassin's article, added examples of "close-ups," "pans," and "dolly" shots gleaned from his study of Rodolphe Töpffer, "subjective camera" effects in Gustave Doré's *Histoire de la Sainte Russie*, and "extreme close-ups" in the work of Wilhelm Busch.[9] Fell cited formal correspondences in cramped framing, commonality of length, a common pool of gesturing and posturing conventions, and the tendency to use "topical introduction" shots. For Fell, the most "cinematic" graphic artist was Winsor McCay, in whose drawings he found trucking and aerial shots, as well as montage sequences that predate those in *Un Chien andalou*.[10]

Are these formal similarities significant? Do they even exist?

At the most basic level, the analogy between the individual panel of a comic strip and a shot in an ordinary film is clearly erroneous. The panel is conceptually a "snapshot" of a represented action that normally obeys traditional pictorial norms of showing one space from one point of view in one instantaneous glance. A shot in a film may share the optical and spatial properties of a drawing, but it always has temporal duration (whether or not anything is moving on the screen). It also possesses the potential of changing the optical view within the shot, or of changing the spatial representation by moving the camera.

Consider Emile Cohl's strip "On Fire," containing nine panels (fig. 218). This lively picture *story* of a man awakening to find the tip of his nightcap ablaze was published in 1891, so it obviously predates film narrative. The champions of formal similarity between the comic strip and film, cited above, might analyze the strip as follows: It shows one "scene" that Cohl has divided into two subsegments representing the cause and the effects of the action. Panels one through three are the causal establishing pictures, grouped together by the formal device of their repeated viewpoint. (Are we to interpret this as forecasting one filmic shot or as three?) The remaining six panels show the effects. Unlike the first three panels, each one in this group shows the action from a different viewpoint and, although the activity is confined to one room, it would be difficult to reconstruct the floor plan. Between panels three and four there is an oblique change of angle, and again between panels four and five, when we see the bed in "long shot." For this reason, the strip might be called "cinematic" by the above authors.[11] Perhaps they would go so far as to suggest that the last six panels forecast fast cutting across several angles of view, *in six brief shots of the sort that one might find in a Soviet montage sequence of the 1920s.*

As a "filmic" practice, Cohl's comic-strip technique of changing angles within a scene is advanced indeed. This type of editing style, as Barry Salt has documented, was quite slow to develop as a film practice: "It is also possible to break down a scene into more than one shot by changing the camera angle across the cut, as had already happened in a few films in the previous period [pre-1906]. This kind of cut continued to be quite rare until 1913, unless the camera was forced away from the standard move straight down the axis by the physical nature of the set or location."[12]

But there is something wrong with our breakdown of the strip. If the first three panels can stand in for one film shot, could not the final six panels also be represented adequately by one continually moving take? Or, for that matter, could not all nine

218. "On Fire," *Pick Me Up*, May 23, 1891.

panels of the strip be filmed in one take as a theatrical mise-en-scène? In other words, although the strip gives us nine definite "pictures," it is impossible to say exactly how many "actions" it represents. A potential filmmaker might wonder long and hard whether this strip should be adapted in one, two, or six "shots."

The definition of "cinematic" is not the constant unshifting term these authors would like us to believe. Invariably they evoke the "classical Hollywood cinema" as their norm, but comparisons to earlier cinema forms and practices reveal problems. Rather than shifting points of view and moving the camera, the first generation of filmmakers tended to shoot continuous actions as a self-contained tableau, regardless of whether the source material was "original" or a comic-strip adaptation. Tom Gunning has called this the "noncontinuous style" of filmmaking, "which maintains the separateness of [a film's] component parts, instead of absorbing them into an illusion of a continuous narrative flow."[13] For the first fifteen years of the movies, this was the predominant way of filming a scene. These authors would have to argue that early cinema was somehow "uncinematic" because they assume that the term means editing and manipulative formal devices. The classical cinema model that is being projected here onto primitive cinema was not in place until around 1917. Meanwhile, as Kristin Thompson has observed, the conventions for representing spatial relationships were not used consistently, nor did they develop in a linear evolutionary pattern, nor was their meaning automatically understood by audiences (supposedly, it has been argued, tutored by decades of comic-strip reading).[14] This answers the question as to why, if there were so many alleged affinities, did it take cinema so long to discover its "language" when it was there waiting for it all along in the comic strip? Quite bluntly and simply, the early filmmakers, such as Griffith, had very little to learn from comic-strip form when it came to solving their own narrative problems.

Comic strips and cinema share the capability of pictorial narration, but the desire to press the formal analogy further may be akin to the same naive enthusiasm that in the past has prompted comparisons between cinema and Greek vase painting, Chinese scrolls, Trajan's Column, and the Bayeux Tapestry. These narratives have their own conventions for signifying the passage of time, for representing objects in motion and changing points of view. Similarly the cinema relies on complex systems and codes, rallying them to create an illusion of natural perception and spatiotemporal continuity. While these arbitrary codes may overlap, often they do not. Here are some examples of differences.

For the comic-strip artist, dividing the page into panels was not a decorative effect but an essential narrative device. The represented action is divided into its significant moments. Each panel is a successive step in the story, demarcating where one narrative element ends and another begins. A problem arises when the artist wishes to denote the passage of time. One convention that was popular in the nineteenth century (and that survives in "Doonesbury") was repeated panels, as in one through three in Cohl's comic "On Fire," which indicated that little was happening—dead time in the narrative. This device became the trademark of Caran d'Ache and was copied by other comic-strip artists such as Théophile-Alexandre Steinlen in his exceptional "Puisqu'ils ne veulent pas se laisser manger, 'suicidons-les!!' " (Since They Won't Let Themselves Get Eaten, Let Them Commit Suicide, fig. 219). The repetitive drawing (with time indicated by the rising and setting sun) is a sign of the fisherman's boredom (as well as of the artist's patience). Each panel represents an equally spaced interval in the course of the day.

The filmmaker need not observe such arbitrary formal narrative markers. He or she has a choice between breaking down an event into its component parts or simply filming the event in its entirety. And the shot or sequence of shots can be long or short. This alternative is not available to the comic-strip artist because there is no formal convention equivalent to the "long take" or "sequence shot." An excellent comparison is provided by Cohl's four-panel strip "Nos Grandes Inventions: Le Lit réveil-matin" (Our Great Inventions: the Alarm Bed, fig. 289) and the film version made by Cohl and

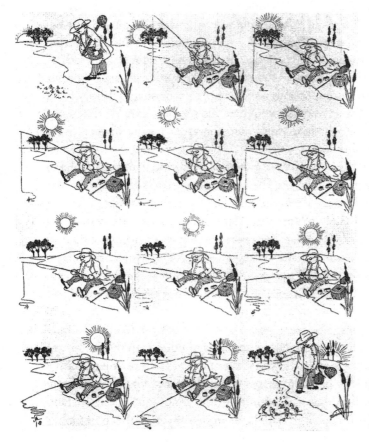

219. Théophile-Alexandre Steinlen: "Puisqu'ils ne veulent pas se laisser manger, 'suicidons-les!!' " *Le Chat Noir*, June 28, 1884.

Arnaud. The 1900 comic strip shows the traveler receiving instructions from the hotelier, setting the clock on the bed, anticipating the alarm, and being ejected from the bed—each panel corresponding to four irreducible components of the narration. In the 1908 film, *L'Hôtel du silence* (fig. 288), the bed sequence is filmed in its entirety in one take. In fact, it is one of several loosely strung-together gags in this one-reel, single-take film. Cohl the comic-strip artist had to draw multiple panels (with progressing clock hands) to represent the passage of night, but Cohl the film artist could resort to profilmic tricks like accelerating the hands of the clock. For the comic-strip storyteller, "montage" was a necessity for narration; for the film artist (after ca. 1907), montage was an option, but one that was typically not chosen, since stories could be told quite effectively without it. Indeed, for nearly two decades, this tableau style was the "cinematic" way of telling a story, not the classical montage style singled out by the above authors.

When looking at these two examples of Cohl's comics, one might be tempted to compare each panel of a comic strip to a single-frame enlargement rather than to a complete shot. But even this analogy has problems. Unlike panels, in actual projection the individual movie frames are invisible to the viewer. And of course the image in each frame is a mechanical temporal division of a motion (an arbitrary moment), while a picture in a panel indicates the artist's representation of a "significant" moment.

The array of panels printed on a page calls for a "reading" that is quite different from the way film narrative is perceived. Comic strips (and their closest cinematic equivalent, storyboards) cannot escape their textuality and remain bounded as a discursive narrative form. Even if they do not contain words, they still must be "read." Movies, on the other hand, are, in Raymond Bellour's well-known aphorism, "unattainable texts" that resist quotation and atomization. The perceptual and social experiences of watching a film image are of quite a different order from those of perusing a comic strip.

One questions the assumption that the shot is the "basic unit of filmic narration." Recent studies suggest that these reductive generalizations are misleading.[15] Furthermore, if these authors err in their comparison of comic-strip narration to a false "cinematic" ideal, it should be pointed out that it is also a mistake to assume that all comic strips rely on sequential narrative panels. An intriguing example is to be found in "Une Petite Femme passe dans la rue" (A Girl Passes by on the Street, fig. 220). Rather than relating a story, the strip by Kober presents the various male reactions to a passing prostitute ("There's where they should stick a taxi meter").[16] Louis Feuillade and Roméo Bosetti filmed their version, *Une Dame vraiment bien*, a few months later and replaced the verbal jokes with sight gags, each filmed as a tableau with the woman entering the shot, disrupting the males' activity, then exiting. In the strip there is no particular order in which the reactions should be read; in the film the viewer must watch the successive tableaux in the linear sequence in which they are presented. In the strip one drawing of the woman is sufficient; in the film the image of the woman walking in each new location must be repeated in each shot.

220. Kober, "Une Petite Femme passe dans la rue," *Le Rire*, September 19, 1908.

This example shows that even when a specific strip was the source of a film adaptation, as in Cohl and Arnaud's *Hôtel du silence* or in Porter's *Dream of a Rarebit Fiend*, the filmmakers instinctively used the tableau style and the tricks of the *féerie* (double exposure, dissolves, invisible wires, stop-action substitution) rather than the so-called "cinematic" montage seemingly available in Kober's, Cohl's, and McCay's comic-strip archetypes.

The desire to represent geographical distances led comic-strip artists to devise ingenious formal devices for orienting the reader in space. In his "Up in a Balloon; or, —a Miraculous Voyage" (fig. 221) Cohl attempted to create the impression of following the action over a great distance by repeating views of objects. The chimney in the background of panel two is repeated in the foreground of panel three. In panel four it is shown dropping away, while a church is visible on the horizon. Its steeple will be central to the action in the next panel. The eighth panel reveals the uppermost leaves of the tree whose trunk will be seen in panel nine. These conventions were intended to suggest that individual sequences of the Munchausenesque story were unfolding over vast—but contiguous—geographical distances. The same strategy easily could have been adapted to the cinema, as it was in Méliès's *A Trip to the Moon* (1902) when we first see the moon over the horizon, followed by a closer shot, followed by a shot of the spacecraft landing on the moon's surface with the earth in the sky. But such exam-

221. "Up in a Balloon; or, —A Miraculous Voyage," *Pick Me Up*, August 15, 1891.

ples are rare. The simple reason is that cinema developed many other conventions to suggest off-screen space and spatial contiguity without having to resort to such literal constructions.[17] For example, a character pointing or staring off-screen, followed by the object of the glance, connoted a subjective view. The fluid transitions between interior and exterior spaces in Griffith's Biograph films established spatiotemporal continuity through match-action cutting, screen direction of movements, and repeated camera angles.

One compelling reason why some of the authors cited wish to associate the formal means of comics and cinema is to invent a critical taxonomy for comics. The cinema, unlike comics, has developed an extensive practical language that enables its technicians to communicate with one another, a descriptive language of production practice that is also available to critics and analysts. Comics, which were traditionally made by one or two artists working in a small studio, had less need to develop an extensive descriptive vocabulary. It is a great convenience then for critics of comic strips to borrow from film discourse such terms as flashback and extreme close-up. There are dangers, however, in applying the jargon of one medium to another. A kind of visual ethnocentrism results from viewing the work of artists in other times and cultures through the "cinematic" eyes of the mid-twentieth century. There is a risk that formal devices cultivated in other media might be overlooked because they have no counterpart in the modern cinema.

We should not overreact and dismiss all comic-strip influence on film narration. One attempt to solve the problem of the film's lack of dialogue was to experiment with speech balloons and subtitles, both in animated and live-action films, around 1910. That this practice derived from comics and that it produced only an unsatisfactory temporary solution are obvious observations.

The historical evidence shows that comic-strip artists were developing their narrative conventions and formal syntaxes before, and without regard to, the influence of cinema, and that the resemblance of certain formal devices of film narrative to comics may be only superficial, or even misleading.

Comics and cinema share a "final cause." The writers on the subject often speculate that similarities in the two media are the result of common underlying technical, cultural, and populist bonds. Fell saw comic-strip artists and filmmakers linked by their pursuit of formal and technical problems: "A number of additional relationships emerge between film and the comics if we broaden our perspective to view the strip artist and the filmmaker as confronting common problems of space and time within the conventions of narrative exposition."[18] As an example, he equates the artists' attempts to master color lithography with the early filmmakers' restriction to popular entertainment subjects. According to Horn, comics and cinema "both tend to the same end: the creation of dialectical movement either through optical illusion (cinema) or through kinetic suggestion (comics).''[19] Lacassin cautiously avoided insisting on any actual direct interchange between the two arts but does not give up the idea of a common cultural source:

> With a few rare exceptions, the comic strip gathered most of its basic expressive resources without recourse to the cinema, and often even before the latter was born. But it would be rash to deduce that the latter is a tributary of the former.
>
> For priority does not necessarily mean influence. It is more reasonable to suppose that comic strip and cinema have both separately drawn the elements of their respective languages from the common stock accumulated in the course of the centuries by the plastic and graphic arts. The comic strip owes its lead over the cinema to the fact that printed pictorial narrative was already mature many years before moving photography was born. It is therefore more judicious to suppose that the two media are autonomous, at least in the technical domain.[20]

Gunning wrote that "film's borrowings from comic strips embrace both form and content. Foxy Grandpa, Happy Hooligan, Buster Brown and the Katzenjammer Kids are some of the characters from comic strips found in films made by the Edison and Biograph companies.''[21]

One ulterior motive behind the argument for simultaneous genesis of the two media is to imply that the connection is more than chronological; it is also an ideological final cause, as though film and comics generated spontaneously from a common cultural source in the working class: "This popular turn-of-the-century sibling [of cinema, the comic strip] was parented, like movies, by industrial technology, mass distribution, and commercial appeals to semiliterate audiences.''[22] Aside from the historical distortion inherent in such a statement, there is also the problem of audience composition. Just as we cannot definitively say that early film audiences were illiterate laborers (especially in France), or that the films represent lower-class values,[23] we are at risk if we assume that comic-strip readers were semiliterate, lower-class types. Looking through the work of McCay, Opper, Töpffer, Christophe, and Caran d'Ache, one wonders to what extent the uneducated person would comprehend these sophisticated stories and why an illiterate person would buy a newspaper to begin with. Could Cohl's comic strips really be characterized as "proletarian images"? One important change had taken place in the audience for the comic strip, as compared to the political *portrait-charge* of an earlier generation. Though socially marginal, comics constituted a marginality that was encouraged by and contained within middle-class boundaries.

All these authors sense that these arts were closely related at the turn of the century, but their insistence on formal influence, either direct or through a collective consciousness, forces them to fall back on the vague romantic concept of "correspondence" to explain the phenomenon. However, the fact that both comics and films present short narratives to a popular audience primarily through pictorial means does not in itself provide evidence that the media were related, or that they shared a final cause. The same description applies to many popular entertainments and spectacles of the nine-teenth century.

This fact was noted by Pierre Fresnault-Deruelle in his structural-semiotic thesis on French-language comics, a book that wisely avoids many of the above pitfalls.[24] The fact that the image is drawn is enough to distinguish it from other "analogical" representations, such as film, photography, tapestry, and painting. Among the many specific codes available to the comic-strip artist, but not to the filmmaker, is that of the dynamic frame. "While the cinema has only one unique frame, the projection screen, the comic strip has the possibility of varying its frame. The artists choose it as a function of its subject to vary the tabular composition of the page. The size of the image corresponds to the subject treated, large scale for decorative images . . . , small scale for close-ups" (p. 22). He also emphasizes the importance of the "significance" of each panel. "Each drawing is a reconstructed whole, perfectly univocal, and made all the more so by the balloons which combat polysemic tendencies. The world of these images, absolutely different from ours—in the sense that it isn't equivocal—is a revenge against reality" (p. 25). Fresnault-Deruelle successfully shows the narrative and formal complexity of the modern comic strip, but he ignores the content and ideological context of the comics he analyzes.

The primary shortcoming of this entire line of argument is that the search for optical and narrative formal analogies has actually obscured several important relationships. There was indeed an active and free exchange between the early cinema and popular graphic art, but not in the form of a common "grammar" of narrative conventions or in some predestined social function.

Comic Art as an Avatar of the Cinema

As early as 1877, when Edison's talking machine was demonstrated to the editors of *Scientific American*, the idea of combining this device with the latest advances in photography struck the reporter covering the event:

> It is already possible by ingenious optical contrivances to throw stereoscopic photo-graphs of people on screens in full view of an audience. Add the talking phonograph to counterfeit their voices, and it would be difficult to carry the illusion of real presence much further.[25]

The staggering implications of this invention were not lost on the artists of the nine-teenth century either. The caricaturist Albert Robida grasped the potential for a kind of realistic representation hitherto only dreamed of by a few visionaries. In the very first issue of *La Caricature* in 1880, he transformed Edison's invention into a satire against Zola's naturalism by picturing Nana with one of his imaginary "photo-phonographs" (fig. 222). These machines "photograph everything that happens and report it to *naturaliste* novelists."[26] Robida's vision of life in the twentieth century, as seen from his 1892 book, was of a society permeated by an even more advanced machine, the "telephonoscope." This apparatus was a sort of large-screen projecting television that carried public information, news of scientific progress, educational and entertainment programs into private homes. A decade and a half later the first apologists for the cinema drew on this established body of opinion and optimistically foresaw the same socially ameliorative functions for the newest technological marvel.[27]

At the same time that Edison was perfecting his phonograph, Eadweard Muybridge was photographing galloping horses on the ranch of Leland Stanford, the governor of California.[28] His plates showing the analyzed phases of the horse's motion became famous around the world when they were disseminated in all the important scientific and popular periodicals.[29] When they were printed as zootrope strips in *L'Illustration* on January 25, 1879, readers were invited to cut them out, view them at home, and thereby reconstitute the original motion that Muybridge had photographed. By that date it was generally realized that motion, like speech, could be mechanically (photographically) recorded, stored, and reproduced.

Muybridge's sequential photographs provoked a flurry of excitement among artists, who debated their validity and usefulness.[30] The flamboyant Muybridge himself pro-

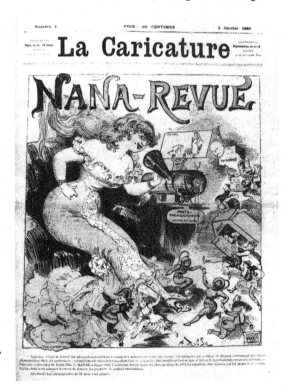

222. Albert Robida: "Nana-Revue," *La Caricature*, January 3, 1880.

jected zoopraxiscopic images of galloping horses for artists gathered at Ernest Meissonier's studio. (A close friend of Gill and Cohl, Edouard Detaille, who later incorporated Muybridge's lessons into his large canvases, also attended these demonstrations.) Muybridge's books *The Horse in Motion* (1882) and *Animal Locomotion* (1887), documenting the "consecutive phases of animal movements," have since provided a storehouse of visual information profoundly influencing the history of modern art. Muybridge's work also affected the "minor" art of the comics.

Caricaturists satirized the photographic strips and lampooned Meissonier for his interest in them. Even Cohl invariably pictured the artist on horseback (fig. 74). Nevertheless, the results of Muybridge's work (and that of his French continuator, Etienne-Jules Marey) were studied closely. One of the most interesting cases in point is Caran d'Ache (Emmanuel Poiré, 1859–1909). Before 1882 he had earned his reputation as a satirist of polite society in the style of Alfred Grévin. After that date he concentrated on wordless comic strips (*histoires sans paroles*), the sequential panel picture story for which he was so much admired and imitated.[31] Critics have accurately noted that he borrowed the format from German sources, particularly from Adolf Oberländer, but the "photographic" precision, the layout of the strips, and the fact that the date of his change of genre coincides with the vulgarization of Muybridge's work strongly suggests that motion-study photographs were also responsible.

The comic strips of Caran d'Ache are sight gags or pantomimes distinguished by an absolute clarity of draftsmanship. The backgrounds were carefully retraced for each of the nine or twelve panels, introducing minimal alterations to suggest changes in point of view or the passage of time. Each story was restricted to one humorous incident of short duration, usually observed from an unchanging angle. The action in "Une Poule survint" (The Dame Arrived Unexpectedly, fig. 223), for example, was analyzed into the successive phases of the girl's movements as she walks from foreground to background (as in motion studies). (There is a change in view between the first and second panels.) The phases of the battle she leaves in her wake are also frozen into panels that are analogous to Muybridge's individual frames. "Aux Prises avec trois jeunes anarchistes" (Three Young Anarchists Stand Together, fig. 224) decomposes the phases of two continuous motions, the simultaneous fall of the boys and of the guardhouse. Although the artist's ideas were conceptually related to Muybridge's work, the iconography remained that of the traditional military picture story. An early biographer recognized that Caran d'Ache's achievement was the adaptation of the comic strip to the "modern" format resembling the chronophotographic display. He aptly called this technique the "successive anecdote":

Caran d'Ache has . . . replaced the old charades and improbable adventures with simple subjects sketched from life and comprehensible on first glance. Certainly he shows everything to its best advantage and does not hesitate to draw another frame

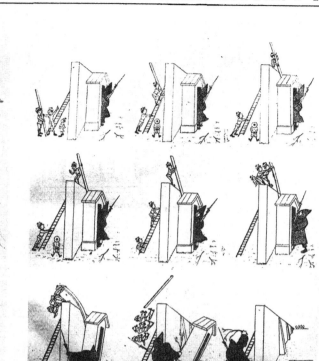

223. Caran d'Ache: "Une Poule survint," *La Vie Militaire*, April 26, 1884.

224. Caran d'Ache: "Aux Prises avec trois jeunes anarchistes," *La Caricature*, January 3, 1885.

in order to express a slight transition. But every movement is so right! And every nuance is so precise![32]

His 1885 series, "The German Hussards," testified to the influence of motion studies by copying a horse poised at the exact instant at which, according to Muybridge's startling revelation, all four hooves were aloft (fig. 225).

Other artists, Moloch, for instance, looked at these photographs with a more traditionally satiric attitude. "Courses de propriétaires: l'entraînement" (Landlord Races: In Training, fig. 226) is like one of Muybridge's horses running amuck. Moloch also preserved the silhouette effect of the original photographs.

One of the most striking examples of motion study converted to comic-strip humor is "Voilà comme nous tirons . . . à Toulouse!!" (How We "Draw"—in Toulouse, fig. 227). This 1892 strip was inspired by Marey's fencing photographs, which had been published the previous year (fig. 228). It was drawn by O'Galop, Cohl's friend and the future animation pioneer.

225. Caran D'Ache: "Les Hussards allemands,"
La Caricature, January 10, 1885.

226. Moloch (B. Colomb): "Courses de
propriétaires," *La Chronique Parisienne*,
April 26, 1885.

Emile Cohl's debt to Caran d'Ache was obvious when he began drawing wordless comic strips in 1887. He practiced his colleague's draftsmanship and had learned to freeze motion in such strips as "A Phenomenal Weight" (fig. 229).

By the advent of the cinematograph, the artists of the popular press had already anticipated its materialization in two ways. First, since the beginning of the 1880s, Robida and a few other visionaries had excited the public's imagination about a machine with certain idealized social and technological functions, a preconception that would shape the popular definition of cinema as an institution. Second, the diffusion of knowledge concerning the scientific analysis and reconstruction of motion made it all the more possible to comprehend and rationalize the invention. Comic-strip artists, particularly Caran d'Ache and his followers, took a keen interest in photomechanical reproduction processes, both as potential satirical subjects and as serious aids to improving their observation. When this protocinematic technology evolved into film, the artists, in a sense, evolved along with it. They were prepared for, and had prepared their public for, the first projected moving pictures. Thus André Bazin's hypothesis that

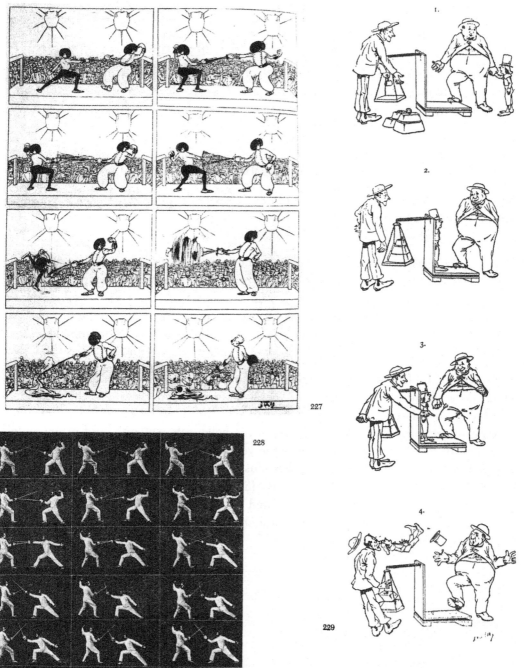

227. O'Galop (Marius Rossillon): "Voilà comme nous tirons . . . à Toulouse!!" *La Caricature* no. 647, 1892.

228. Etienne-Jules Marey: "L'Escrime français," *Paris-Photographe*, 1891.

229. "A Phenomenal Weight," *Pick Me Up*, August 22, 1891.

there was in the nineteenth-century a "myth of total cinema," which impelled scientists and savants to invent an idealized cinema apparatus capable of a complete simulacrum of reality, may even be extended to include the works of these popular graphic humorists.

THE SHARED MILIEU OF CINEMA AND THE HUMORISTS

When Henri Flamans, a popular writer in *Le Magasin Pittoresque*, saw his first Kinetoscope (actually a pirated version of Edison's original), he instinctively sensed that the device belonged with other quasi-scientific optical amusements:

> [Edison] transformed a scientific demonstration into a very amusing spectacle, the Kinetoscope, that is today attracting large crowds in the cities of the United States. The highly ingenious apparatus is a sort of black box wherein one peers through a lens and sees a photograph of various characters gesticulating, marching, and fighting, exactly as in life. Even with the colorlessness of photography and the minuteness of the beings, one can believe it is a vision of reality.[33]

As he wrote, the first Kinetoscope parlor was opening at 20, boulevard Poissonnière. The early promoters of the cinema were naturally attracted to the district that had been devoted to visual spectacles for at least half a century: the *grands boulevards*. The curving streets provided cafés, theaters, music halls, café-concerts, and promenades for a spectrum of Parisian classes. Over the years they had sheltered an assortment of spectacles including magic theaters, wax museums, panoramas, dioramas, magic-lantern projections, and itinerant peepshows (fig. 230). The area was also the obvious choice for Auguste and Louis Lumière and their father, Antoine, when their new Cinématographe was ready for its public debut. Their business office was one floor

230. Draner (Jules Renard): "Les Panoramas automatiques," *Le Charivari*, January 13, 1899.

above the Théâtre Robert-Houdin on boulevard des Italiens, where Méliès had performed since 1888. They had considered the Musée Grévin (the irregular site of Emile Reynaud's *Pantomimes lumineuses* since 1892), and also had weighed an offer from the Folies-Bergères. But finally they decided upon the Indian Salon, a former billiards room in the basement of a luxurious hotel across from the Opéra (and around the corner from the Pouillet stamp boutique) at 14, boulevard des Capucines. The first screening was on Saturday, December 28, 1895, at 8:00 p.m.[34]

As it spread up and down the boulevards, the cinema also entered the boyhood neighborhood and the adult professional world of Emile Cohl. The offices of the satiric press still clustered around this area. The same customers who bought these papers also frequented these optical amusements. One of the earliest and most striking instances of the intersection of the world of cinema with that of comic-strip artists exists as an article explaining the workings of the Cinématographe to the readers of *L'Illustré Soleil du Dimanche*. It was by Georges Colomb, the real name of the legendary comic-strip artist Christophe.[35] Frame enlargements from the Lumière film *Le Déjeuner de Bébé* (fig. 231) illustrated the article. (Curiously, though, the caption misdirected the reader to view the images left to right instead of, correctly, top to bottom. Was this error instinctive by the artist who assumed that the pictures should be read like comic-strip panels?)

Many early references to film in the popular press were essentially journalistic, but caricaturist Henriot combined his report of an 1896 presentation of the Cinématographe at the Academy of Sciences with an anti-Naturalism joke that recalls Robida's jab at the phonograph (fig. 232). By April 1896 a humorist in *Le Courrier Français* was already discussing the ubiquity of the cinema and predicting that it

> would soon be instantaneous and long distance. Combined with the "theaterphone," it will bring spectacles into the household. Subscribers can have the ballet at the Folies-Bergère, or *Messidor*, which ever they please, projected on a screen, if photographers have time to take the pictures.[36]

There were unexpected prejudices and misunderstandings about the new apparatus. "Le Reportage au cinémato" (Newsreel Report, fig. 233) speculated about how a film called *The Bather* might have been shot without the knowledge of the unfortunate victim. The joke was in reference to the "piquant" movies made by the photographer and manufacturer of naughty "French" postcards, Eugène Pirou. Soon after the Cinématographe was installed, Pirou began exhibiting *Bain de la parisienne* (The Parisienne's Bath) and similar spicy attractions at the Café de la Paix, just next door.[37] The cartoon expresses the underlying suspicion that the cinema might constitute an invasion of privacy and thereby represent a potential menace to bourgeois society. A contemporary popular novel by Jean Joseph-Renaud, *Le Cinématographe du mariage*, also exploited the public's concern that films were capable of private revelations.[38] The

Fac-simile d'une bande pelliculaire qui passe dans le Cinématographe de MM. A. et L. Lumière.
(Voir les images de gauche à droite).

231. Louis Lumière: *Le Déjeuner de Bébé*, 1895, from the Georges Colomb (Christophe) article cited.

Le 2e Académicien :
— D'ailleurs, messieurs, nous allons faire, grace au cinématographe, la reconstitution de quelques scènes de *la Terre*...

232. Henriot (Henri Maigrot):
L'Illustration, February 22, 1896.

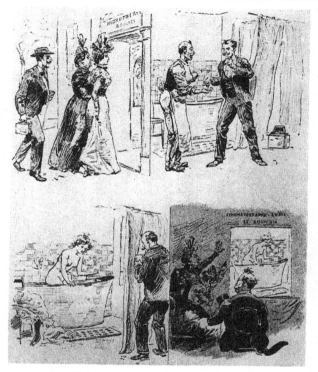

CINÉMATOGRAPHOMANIE
— Toi... chez le dentiste... J'ai tenu à ce que le cinématographe enregistrât
cette belle opération...

233. Anon.: "Le Reportage au cinémato," *La Caricature*,
July 31, 1897.

234. Henri Somm: "Cinématographomanie,"
Le Rire, February 22, 1902.

camera even invaded the sanctum of the dentist's office, to the embarrassment of the
patient's middle-class wife, in Henri Somm's "Cinématographomanie" (fig. 234). Many
factors contributed to this distrust. Viewers could plainly see their neighbors caught
off-guard in the local views that usually accompanied Lumière programs.[39]

These cartoons provide a clue to the nature of the first film audiences, for the readership of these journals was by no means the illiterate laboring class that has been claimed
for early film. On the contrary, these periodicals were purchased and read by the same
"respectable" middle classes who sat at the expensive café terraces on the boulevards.
From its origins, in France cinema was defined as an urban, middle-class phenomenon,
competing for the same market that constituted the readership of *Le Rire*, *La Caricature*, and other great French humor magazines.

Although "respectable" classes may have claimed to disdain the cinema because of its
boulevard associations, there is no reason to believe that this was anything more than
hypocritical piety—and thus an obvious target for the barbs of the humorists. As with
its neighboring amusements on the boulevards, there was an obvious appeal to prurient
interests in early film. Art historian Erwin Panofsky recalled a favorite from his youth,
perhaps Pathé's *Le Bain des dames de la cour* (fig. 235): "I remember with great pleas-

235. Pathé: *Le Bain des dames de la cour*, ca. 1906.

ure a French film of *ca.* 1900 wherein a seemingly but not really well-rounded lady as well as a seemingly but not really slender one were shown changing to bathing suits."[40]

Pirou's *Coucher de la mariée* (The Bride's Bedtime), starring Louise Willy of the Olympia music hall, was by far the most famous such production—perhaps the first film "smash." Its popularity was satirized by Henri Avelot in "La Lanterne magique amélioré ou cinématographe" (Improved Magic Lantern; or, Cinematograph, fig. 236). The male crowd before the Pirou film is clawing through the screen trying vainly to enter the room with the demoiselle, but when Lumière's *Une Charge de cuirassiers* (Charge of the Cuirassiers, fig. 237) flashes on the screen, everyone flees in terror.[41] Georges Méliès made an imitation called *Le Coucher de la mariée ou triste nuit de noce* in 1899; later Georges Hatot made two remakes for Pathé (fig. 238). One component of the audience to which such films appealed has been recorded in "Les Merveilles du cinématographe" (The Marvels of the Cinematograph, fig. 239), in which two boulevard types are watching still another "bride" film in a Mutoscope-like peep show. They are descendants of the middle-class flaneurs who patronized similar attractions in the precinema epoch. One says to the other, "God, what I wouldn't give to get into this box."

These documents show that the cinema's appeal was demographically varied and by no means exclusively patronized by lower classes. The audience in Avelot's drawing includes a respectable middle-class woman, a bourgeois gentleman with an umbrella, a soldier, a nanny, a child, and an adolescent. The movie parlors also were trysting places for the worldly upper classes (fig. 240). It was urbane, often risqué entertain-

LA LANTERNE MAGIQUE AMÉLIORÉE OU CINÉMATOGRAPHE

Impressions de la foule devant : « Une charge de cuirassiers ».   Impressions de la même foule devant : « Le coucher de la Parisienne ».

236. Henri Avelot: "La Lanterne magique améliorée ou cinématographe," *Le Rire*, July 28, 1906.

237. Louis Lumière: *Une Charge de cuirassiers*, 1896.

238. Georges Hatot: *Coucher de la mariée*, Pathé, ca. 1906.

239. Jean Frinot: "Les Merveilles du cinématographe," *La Caricature*, January 12, 1901.

240. Destez: "Cinématographe," *Le Sourire*, February 8, 1908.

ment, certainly no place for a provincial type like the stereotypical M. Nigaud pilloried in S. d'Alba's 1907 drawing (fig. 241). This bumpkin was so shocked by the scenes of Paris life he witnessed in a cinema that he boarded the next train out.

The darkened rooms in which these films were projected could not be photographed, so we rely on artists of the illustrated press for our only eyewitness views of actual presentations. In January 1898, for example, a giant screen was installed at the Palais de Glace ice rink on the Champs-Elysées. *Le Courrier Français* reported that "bravos and foot stamping lasted long every night . . . at the curious Lumière Cinématographe."[42] Respected critic Francisque Sarcey even mentioned it in *Le Temps*:

[To see the Cinematograph] you only have to walk to the Palais de Glace between five and six o'clock. Darkness falls in this vast enclosure. The Cinematograph rolls down its vast white sheet and the most varied views succeed each other: a trainer in a tiger cage, a voyage of the President of the Republic, a cavalry charge, a procession of Turks. All the images and movements have a marvelous sharpness and precision. It is a very interesting spectacle.[43]

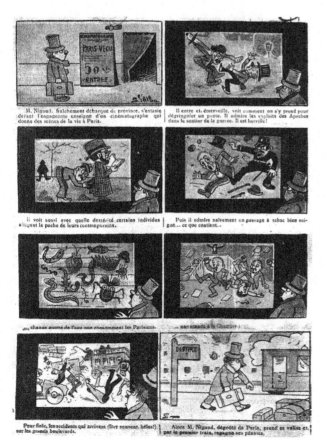

241. S. d'Alba: "Le Cinématographe," *Polichinelle*, January 13, 1907.

Despite all the excitement, the only remaining visual evidence is a sketch by the illustrator W. Tilly (fig. 242) that captures better than words the strange beauty and fascination of these images hovering over the skaters—a vision later recalled nostalgically by Marcel Duchamp, Jean Cocteau, and countless others who visited the rink. Appropriately, the subject shown in Tilly's drawing is identifiable as Lumière catalogue no. 101, *Bataille de neige* (Snowball Fight).

Another drawing by Avelot in *Le Rire* reveals the startling extent to which cinema had invaded boulevard life by 1901 (fig. 243). It shows a night scene in the district illuminated by electric-light advertising and outdoor film projections. Avelot has frozen the moving signs and thus fragmented their messages in almost Cubist fashion. The film image (an advertisement for a painless dentist) has been executed in wavy lines to suggest its flickering appearance. This electrified, animated view of the modern city not only shows the dynamism that cinematography brought to the streets of Paris but also anticipates Fernand Léger's view of the city in his monumental Cubist painting *La Ville* in 1916. Already, in 1901, popular illustrators and authors regarded the cinema as the very image of modernity. That the cinema was symbolic of twentieth-century life is explicit in the caption for the drawing:

Cinematographic projections. Advertisements. Electric inscriptions with illuminated letters light up (but not always) one by one. Very modern ensemble.[44]

243. Henri Avelot: "Les Grands Boulevards," *Le Rire*, June 29, 1901

242. W. Tilly: "Au Palais de Glace," *Le Courrier Français*, February 6, 1898.

CINEMA AS AN INFLUENCE ON THE COMIC STRIP

While there has been much discussion of the influence of comics on early cinema, there is evidence that the flow of influence was actually stronger in the other direction. Comic-strip artists frequently looked to other entertainments for their subject matter and for compositional innovations. Their tendency to borrow was visible, for example, in the revival of the silhouette graphic style during the vogue of the Chat Noir shadow theater in the late 1880s. In a similar spirit, Jacques Villon attempted to simulate the visual effect of a Loie Fuller-like exotic dancer when the stage lights were doused in the "Cabaret du Néant" (fig. 244).[45]

At first the mass media were more influenced by the appearance of films as they were reproduced in periodicals than by their appearance when actually projected. The two panels of "Dans les fumeurs" (In the Smoking Car, fig. 245) were probably intended to resemble the adjacent frames of film strips as they had appeared in articles like the one by Colomb. The artist has noticed that a characteristic of Lumière stock was the absence of a distinct frame line; instead the images blended together at the top and bottom.[46] The motive for mimicking this filmic trait in the cartoon might have arisen from

244. Jacques Villon: "Au Cabaret du Néant," *Le Courrier Français*, October 10, 1897.

245. Noël Dorville: "Dans les fumeurs," *La Caricature*, January 9, 1897.

246. Jean Frinot: "Un Mariage manqué," *La Caricature*,
September 1, 1900.

the artist's desire to be trendy, or even to associate the woman of questionable morals
in the smoker with the types that one might encounter in a cinema. A strip by Jean
Frinot (fig. 246) not only eliminated the frame line but added an Art Nouveau border
suggestive of sprocket holes that enhances the resemblance to film stock.[47]

One need only leaf through the periodicals of 1896–1901 to be struck by the definite
increase in the use of heavy black borders around comic strips and cartoons. Perhaps
this decorative edging was sometimes intended to imply that the stories were taking
place on the movie screen. M. Radiguet's "Pris au piège" (Trapped, fig. 247) and
O'Galop's "En Découverte" (Discovered, fig. 248) both have this black outline with
typically rounded corners. The framing of the full-length figures with the tops of their
heads touching the frame was also a characteristic of many French films shot around
1900 in the so-called "French foreground" style.[48]

Only rarely did any artists attempt to render the visual effect of screen movement.
But two drawings by that extraordinary cinephile Avelot illustrate how this effect might
be achieved (fig. 249). One humorously tried to show both sides of a cow as it might
appear from a fast-moving train; the other illustrated the "fusion" of passengers, objects, and mechanical parts at the moment of impact during a train crash. Both drawings
look forward to the serious preoccupations of the Cubists and the Italian Futurists, who
would explore ways of signifying motion by "lines of force" and other experimental
means derived from chronophotography and film.

247. Maurice Radiguet: "Prix au piège," *La Caricature*,
September 17, 1898.

248. O'Galop (Marius Rossillon): "En Découverte,"
L'Illustré National, August 6, 1899.

249. Henri Avelot: "Croquis des trains et des gares," *Le Rire*, January 26, 1901.

— De la violette, patron! — De la violette, mon baron? — De la violette, mon prince? . — Va donc, citoyen!
— Merci... — Non, merci... — ... — ...
Dessin de MARKOUS.

250. Markous (Louis Marcoussis), *Le Rire*, June 27, 1908.

A surprising number of artists who contributed drawings to these periodicals would later become famous, not as cartoonists but as Cubist painters.[49] Juan Gris, Franz Kupka, Jacques Villon, Marcel Duchamp, Louis Marcoussis, and others occasionally satirized the cinema, as in one drawing by Gris that shows a cameraman filming a man falling over a cliff. The caption reads, "With a film like this, I'm not afraid of competition." Another drawing signed "Markous" (the pen name of Marcoussis) demonstrates the formal influence of cinematic style on the Cubists (fig. 250). The four panels show a boulevard scene in which a working-class type tries to sell a violet to a fast-walking gentleman. The close cropping, pseudo-chronophotographic analysis of movement, and the way in which the man gradually exits the panels on the right suggest that Marcoussis was trying to simulate the visual effect of a fast panning shot. Not even Caran d'Ache had experimented with close analysis of a motion as fleeting as this. Marcoussis's friend, Marcel Duchamp, later would readily admit that films and motion studies influenced his early work, including his *Nude Descending a Staircase* (1912), but this particular drawing is perhaps the earliest datable proof of when the Cubists were studying cinematic movement and trying to synthesize it pictorially.[50]

COMIC STRIPS AS AN INFLUENCE ON EARLY FILMS

The exchange of ideas between cartoonists and early filmmakers worked both ways. Besides speech balloons, already mentioned, another example of modifying a pictorial compositional convention for use in the cinema was the "dream balloon." A common device in popular illustration (fig. 81), it was perhaps first adapted for film by Ferdinand Zecca in 1901 in *Histoire d'un crime*. Wishing to show that the prisoner was dreaming of his past, Zecca constructed a boxlike space above the scene in which the actions of the "past" were acted out. Soon the double-exposed matte shot replaced this crude technique, and it was effectively used in 1907 by Lucien Nonguet in *L'Affaire Dreyfus*. A vision of his children back in France hovers above Dreyfus's head as, imprisoned on Devil's Island, he looks longingly out to sea.

The dream balloon, however, was a simple convention with limited usefulness for both the filmmaker and the comic-strip artist. "Termes nautiques" (Nautical Terms, fig. 251) by Gino shows one of its more sophisticated applications, with decorative vignettes representing the thoughts of the characters.

These graphic solutions to the problem of representing subjectivity are quite different from the conventions developed by Griffith, Feuillade, and others. The "subjective" shot for visualizing thought became a point-of-view narrative structure: showing the person in close-up, then cutting to the object of his or her thoughts—a syntax that audiences quickly learned and understood.[51]

The screen adaptation of Emile Cohl's specialty, the bifocal comic strip, can be examined as another attempt to transfer graphic conventions directly to the screen. The composition of a typical strip divided each panel in half to represent two separate, but adjacent, spaces (fig. 109). One of Cohl's colleagues, M. Mauricio, demonstrated an even more complex application of the prevailing convention in "La Sonnerie révélatrice" (The Revealing Ring, fig. 252). He showed bells ringing in four different offices by dividing one panel into four smaller subpanels, presuming that his readers would

251. Gino: "Termes nautiques," *La Caricature,* January 18, 1890.

252. M. Mauricio: "La Sonnerie révélatrice," *La Caricature,* October 21, 1892.

interpret this as a sign of narrative simultaneity. It was Méliès who first adapted the split-panel idea to the cinema with his *Voisins irascibles* (Irascible Neighbors, fig. 253). As Zecca had done with the dream balloon, Méliès chose the essentially theatrical technical solution of constructing an unwieldy double set representing a cross section of the apartments. Cohl's later film version, *Les Locataires d'à côté* (Next Door Neighbors, fig. 163), used a matte technique for simulating the composition of the comic-strip panel.

253. Georges Méliès: *Les Voisins irascibles.*

   As filmmakers, at least in the case of the split screen, both Méliès and Cohl reacted instinctively as comic-strip artists when faced with the necessity of showing simultaneous actions in separate spaces. Essentially they divided the screen into graphic panels rather than using alternating views or Porter's technique of repeating action. Soon displaced by montage, the split-screen technique did linger on to show, for example, both ends of a phone conversation in *Max et son chien Dick* (Max [Linder] and His Dog, 1912) and in Phillips Smalley and Lois Weber's *Suspense* (1912). These narrative systems operated concurrently with the Griffithian crosscutting system, which would eventually predominate. Neither the dream balloon nor the split panel became assimilated into the classical cinema; on the contrary, they constituted anachronistic alternatives that became obsolete when other roads were taken.
   Inarguably the most important way in which the comic strip interacted with the early cinema was by serving as a source of comic characters, stories, and gags. In 1911 the director Victorin Jasset discussed the practice:

The general length of films in 1898–1899 was still about twenty meters. One could make humorous scenes, but not very long.
   At this time the journal *Chat Noir* had absorbed the spirit of Montmartre graphic artists for a decade. Even the supplements to the *Gil Blas* were made to contribute.

The wordless drawings of Steinlen, Villette [*sic*], Doës, Guillaume, Caran d'Ache, etc. spawned comic scenes for a long time.[52]

This borrowing was evident from the beginning of cinematography. Georges Sadoul, in the course of his research into nineteenth-century juvenile literature, was the first to discover that the 1895 Lumière film *L'Arroseur arrosé* was related to a picture story by Hermann Vogel in an 1887 Album Quantin.[53] But Sadoul did not realize the extent to which it was already an old joke by 1895.

Besides Vogel's version, there was one by A. Sorel in the *Chat Noir*-inspired shadow style (fig. 254). Two years later what was certainly Lumière's direct source was published in *Le Petit Français Illustré*. It was Christophe's "Un Arroseur public" (Public Gardener, fig. 255). The differences between the film and the strip appear to be minor, but they demonstrate once again that the filmmaker had little use for the "cinematic" montage that, some might argue, existed in the original strip. When Christophe inserts a "close-up" in his second panel, it is to show the boy's contemplation of the scene while he forms his mischievous scheme. Lumière achieved the same end by having the boy stand close enough to the camera to see his face (fig. 256). The filmmaker borrowed the

254. A. Sorel: "Fait Divers," *La Caricature,* March 12, 1887.

255. Christophe (Georges Colomb): "Un Arroseur public," *Le Petit Français Illustré,* August 3, 1889.

gag and its setting, but typically left behind the narrative conventions of the comic strip and recorded the joke in a continuous take.[54]

Many specimens of late nineteenth-century popular art served as archetypes for cinematic adaptation. The most conspicuous was the police chase. Films like Zecca's *Slippery Jim*, in which the criminal always eludes the police, recall strips like "Après le grand prix" (After the Prize, fig. 257) of the previous decade. The comic image of the Paris police in the Gaumont productions *L'Agent a le bras long* (The Long Arm of the Cop, fig. 258) and *Police magnétique* (fig. 259) were reminders of their origins in the satiric press as well as in the music hall (fig. 260). The idea of multiplying their

256. Louis Lumière: *L'Arroseur arrosé*, 1895.

Deux gendarmes, l'au're dimanche.
Poursuivaient un joueur de bonn'teau

L'aut' filant comme un' souris blan he,
N sanblaiu pas d' v ir été pris d si tot !

Ils courrai'nt p'tet' tous trois encore...

Mais un mui barrait l'horizon.

Pourtant l'un et l'aut' Pandore
N'eur'nt qu'un' veste et qu'un pantalon !

257. Nicholson: "Après le grand prix,"
L'Eclipse, June 25, 1896.

258. *L'Agent a le bras long*, Gaumont, 1909.

259. *Police magnétique*, Gaumont, 1908.

260. Deslaw, "La Musique adoucit les moeurs," *L'Illustré National*, July 31, 1898.

uniformed numbers for comic effects, in both the strips and these early films, laid the groundwork for the police gags that reemerged years later with Linder, Sennett, Chaplin, and Keaton.

Alice Guy recalled from her days as a Gaumont director-scenarist:

At this time, we could not have cared less about author's rights and looked everywhere for inspiration. Personally I was inspired by:
 —Grand Guignol plays for: *L'Asile de nuit, Le Paralytique, Lui, Au Téléphone*;
 —Comic strips by Guillaume for *Amoureux transis*, and [a spicy film] *Professeur de langues vivantes*. (For this last film Mr. Gaumont demanded severely to know how I knew about this milieu.) And *La Fève enchantée*.
 —Theater plays, fairy tales and novels for: *Lèvres closes, La Légende de Saint-Nicolas, Conscience de prêtre.*[55]

Movies were, in Panofsky's apt words, "craving for narrative," and it was primarily to satisfy this need that filmmakers rifled the great illustrated periodicals. But bear in mind that we are speaking of content—gags—rather than a transposition of narrative form, and that there were two important pragmatic considerations: adapting a comic-strip story meant one less writer to be paid; and the audience's foreknowledge of a popular strip or character added appeal to the subject, perhaps making the story and gags easier to understand.

Certainly the most direct way in which popular graphic artists influenced cinema was by joining the "enemy." Caricaturists, cartoonists, and comic-strip artists made up a surprising number of the personnel of early cinema. Méliès, besides practicing magic, was an able political caricaturist.[56] In the United States virtually all the early animators began as popular graphic artists. And of course we recall that it was probably the practice at Gaumont of plagiarizing the stories of comic strips that brusquely launched Emile Cohl into his new career in 1908. When he began working, he had technical skills learned from photography and his practice as a graphic artist. But his move to film was not an easy transition. Less than a decade after the invention of cinema, Cohl would have discovered that the techniques and narrative conventions of the new medium were already becoming codified, and that these methods of telling a film story were seldom informed by anything he had done as a practicing graphic artist. On the other hand, he found that his memories of early work provided him with a vast repertoire of stories, jokes, characterizations, sight gags, and, in general, a platform for his distinctive hydropathic and incoherent humor.

CHAPTER EIGHT

"Incoherent Cinema"

WHEN Emile Cohl's films are viewed, one is struck not only by their technical ingenuity but also by their bizarre humor. Even in comparison with the slapstick comedies of Zecca, Feuillade, Bosetti, and other contemporaries, Cohl's films are extraordinary in their outrageousness, their outlandishness, and, frequently, their incomprehensibility. They do not imitate the physical knockabout gags of the vaudeville stage or the domestic farces of the type that Cohl himself had once written. They rely instead on a peculiar dry, cerebral wittiness that makes his films stand out alone in pre-World War I cinema. This quality is so pervasive that it may be said to constitute Emile Cohl's unique world view.

In order to examine the roots of this sensibility, let us look once again briefly at the Incoherents, that group of artists, journalists, and bon vivants led by Cohl and Jules Lévy from 1883 to 1891. Cohl's films resurrected the Incoherents' playful anarchy; his attitude recalls their antibourgeois, antiacademic manifestations.

Cohl's aesthetic roots, we remember, were put down in direct personal contact with the literary leaders of the 1880s. At the Hydropathe meetings and elsewhere he had consorted with, photographed, and caricatured representatives of the various cenacles. Their common ancestor was Baudelaire, but at least three separate movements were discernible: the Symbolism proper of Mallarmé, Rimbaud's *poésie fantastique*, and Verlaine's Decadents.[1] The Incoherents absorbed the general aesthetic program of linguistic renewal proposed in varying formulas by these divergent groups but reacted strongly against their seriousness, introversion, and morbidity. Lévy's motto, "Frères, il nous faut rire" (Brothers, we need to laugh), was an implicit rejection of the Symbolist catch phrase, "Il nous faut mourir" (We all must die).

The distinction was also geographical, with the Symbolists occupying the Left Bank and the Incoherents entrenched on the Right. Cohl and his compatriots were devotees of the cabarets and typified the Right Bank Montmartre spirit commonly associated with Willette, Steinlen, and Lautrec (to mention only graphic artists). Across the river, in their Latin Quarter enclave, the Symbolists "disdained the Chat Noir and the Montmartre artists." Mallarmé's biographer Camille Mauclair described them as "Left bankers, hermetics, rather pontificating, and while they conceded humor, laughing at jokes made them indignant."[2] In this respect at least, the Incoherents were the antithesis of the Symbolists.

THE PURSUIT OF THE IRRATIONAL

The Incoherents placed high value on spontaneous artistic expression. They were nihilists who adamantly refused to adhere to rules or conventions or to temper their creations in order to conform to standards of respectability. Like the Dadaists and Surrealists, whom they anticipated in many ways, they also refused to impose any rational order or unified structure on their art. Charles Joliet, the author of *Le Roman incohérent*, proudly noted that the chapters of his "novel" were written without any intention of combining them, and that the order in which they were eventually assembled was accidental.[3]

The Incoherents were also attracted to the grotesque, distorted images that the Surrealists would later claim had originated in the subconscious (fig. 261). Steinlen, for example, populated his "Palace of Incoherence" (fig. 262) with hideous hybrids of animals and humans that seem to have been inspired by nightmares or hallucinations. It was the same principle of subconscious imagery that guided many of Cohl's films, beginning with *Fantasmagorie*, his first.

The title of the film refers to an elaborate illusion constructed by an eighteenth century French showman named Etienne Gaspard Robertson. His "Fantasmagorie" projected hovering apparitions before its startled spectators by means of a magic-lantern device called a fantascope.[4] Cohl's evocative title, by associating his film with this well-known spectacle, alerted his viewers to the strangeness of the images they were about to see. But even with the explicit warning, few would have been prepared for the rapidity and complexity of the visions. Fewer still would have grasped the content at a single showing.

For one second the viewer sees a short white line on a black background (fig. 263). The hand of a lightning-sketch artist begins to draw a stick-figure clown who will become the protagonist (frames b–c). No sooner is he completed than he begins to move (d). The activities that follow may be segmented into three episodes in this picaresque adventure:

The man at the movies (40 seconds). When the clown releases it, the white line modifies itself by growing a shallow triangular extension at the top that might be interpreted as wires from which the "line," or bar, is suspended, or as lines indicating perspectival recession. At the same time, a rectangle begins to descend, obscuring the figure of the clown (e). When it is fully descended, we see inside it a bourgeois gentleman wearing a top hat and carrying an umbrella. We recognize this as the iconography

261. "Aux Arts incohérents," *La Nouvelle Lune*, November 1, 1884.

262. Théophile-Alexandre Steinlen: "Le Palais incohérent," illustration for Charles Joliet, *Le Roman incohérent*, 1887.

of a type with which we are already familiar from Cohl's comic strips.[5] As the lines forming the rectangle recede, the top hat and umbrella reshape themselves into a theatrical decor (j–k). On the right is a proscenium arch, and in front are two chairs.[6] The man settles into one of them, but the other holds a surprise. It is not really a chair but a jack-in-the-box concealing the little clown (l–m). The clown startles the man once again by descending as a spider and causing his wig to fly off (n–o). Then the clown ushers in a lady wearing a large plumed hat to watch a film of a marching soldier that has already begun (p–q). We know that it is not a stage play because there are no footlights or receding floor lines to indicate a deep space. The woman sits directly in front of the man, who gesticulates angrily because she has obscured his view (r–s). But she is already absorbed in the movie and alternately sheds tears and laughs. One by one the man plucks the plumes from the hat and finally, exasperated, he "tears" a slit in the black background and inserts one of the plumes through the trompe-l'oeil hole (t–w). The spatial ambiguity of the tear destroys the illusion of depth that the clown had just created by swinging in from the background. Meanwhile, another movie has commenced, consisting of abstract shapes in motion. As a last resort, the man lights a cigar and, while its smoke curls upward, he touches it to the woman's hair (x–z). To his surprise, the woman's head expands into a sphere. The little clown floats inside it in embryonic form. He continues growing into a balloon, becoming so large that he completely engulfs the man (a'–c').

263. *Fantasmagorie* (cat. 1), 1908.

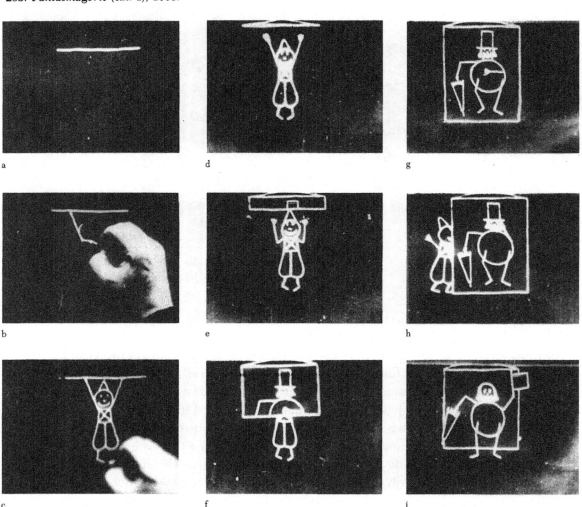

a

b

c

d

e

f

g

h

i

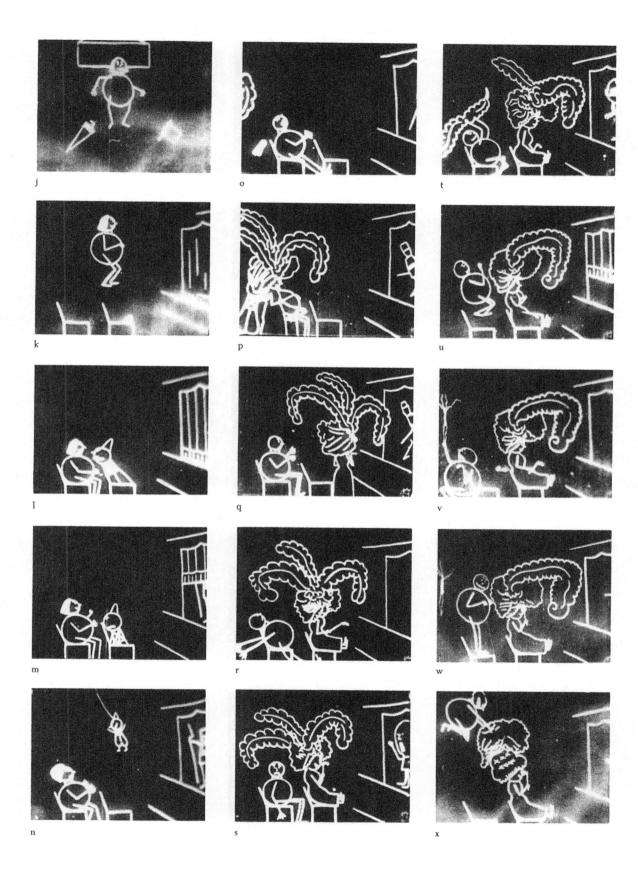

j

o

t

k

p

u

l

q

v

m

r

w

n

s

x

y

d'

i'

z

e'

j'

a'

f'

k'

b'

g'

l'

c'

h'

m'

n'

s'

x'

o'

t'

y'

p'

u'

z'

q'

v'

a"

r'

w'

b"

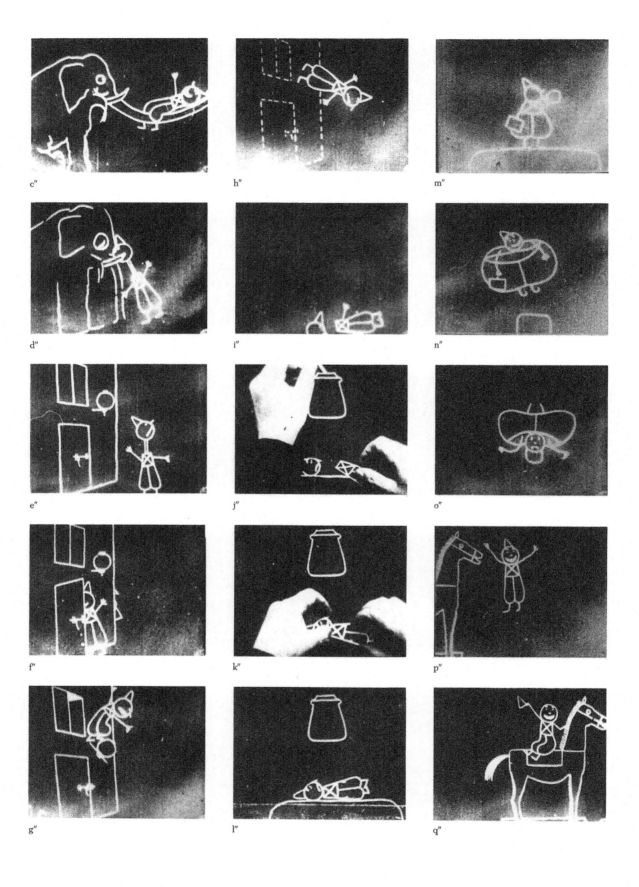

c″

h″

m″

d″

i″

n″

e″

j″

o″

f′

k″

p″

g″

l″

q″

The clown's trials (47 seconds). The tables are now turned. The clown is no longer the mischievous tormenter but is himself the persecuted one. He changes from his balloon shape back into his original form and plummets into his jack-in-the-box (d'–h'). As he spins, his body rotates 180 degrees, revealing his two-dimensionality. (For two frames, when viewed obliquely, he is only a single straight line.) His first adversary is the Michelin "Bibendum," the man made of tires (i'). The Bib throws two heavy weights onto the box, but they do not restrain the clown. He punctures the tire-man with his pointed hat (j'–l'). One of the falling weights has changed into the top hat of a gentleman who is now seen rising slowly from the bottom edge of the screen. He doffs his hat and exits, but the clown quickly produces a fishing pole and snags his coat (m'–p'). To his dismay, he sees that the swinging coat has struck an off-screen soldier, a giant with a triangular hat. When the angry soldier pokes at him with his sword, the clown lights it with a candle. First it burns like a fuse, then it causes the soldier to evaporate (q'–r'). Next the clown sniffs a flower. But it spurts into growth, lifts him up by his nose, and pops off his head (s'–t'). As his torso rotates around the flower stalk, his head is captured by a strange bottle-shaped man who bounces it up and down in a cup as though it were a rubber ball in the game of Diabolo, a 1908 fad (u'). The bottle-man changes into a champagne bottle on a cannon mount and fires its cork at the clown, whose head has been restored. Then the bottle "walks" toward the clown and sucks him inside (x'–y'). The lines of the bottle metamorphose into a lotus blossom. Its petals open, leaving the clown standing on its stalk—which turns out to be not a stalk but the trunk of an elephant (z'–c"). The whole elephant becomes visible just before it changes into a house. Its legs become the wall and door, its ears the upstairs window, and its eye the light by the door (d"–g"). The clown opens the door and enters. Immediately a policeman rounds the corner and locks him inside. The clown leaps through the upstairs window to escape but falls to the ground, breaking his head once again (f"–i").

The clown is repaired (18 seconds). The little figure lies immobile for a second before the artist's hands return with a paste pot to glue him back together. After a few tentative movements, the clown ducks out of sight, then returns carrying a jug and a valise, as though prepared for a voyage. He drinks from the jug until his body inflates like a wineskin or a balloon; then he floats away, coming to rest on the back of a hobbyhorse. Smiling and saluting the audience, off he rides (q").

The short film fulfills the promise of the title. Its images are as fleeting and evanescent as those of a dream, defying attempts at rationalization. They succeed one another without logical connection in a manner reminiscent of the arbitrary technique of Joliet's Incoherent novel or, looking toward the future, in anticipation of Surrealist "automatic writing." Nevertheless, there are identifiable recurring themes and motifs. Cruelty and torture dominate most of the actions. The clown and the woman torment the man at the movies, and the man in turn sets the woman afire. The clown is repeatedly confined to small spaces—the jack-in-the-box, the bottle-flower, and the elephant-house. There is a paranoid aspect to the oppressiveness of the authority figures (the soldiers and the policeman) and menacing representatives of contemporary popular culture (the Diabolo player and the Michelin man). The treatment of the woman is particularly misogynistic, since her symbolically castrating punishment, being set afire, is excessive in comparison to her "crime," which was only that of wearing a hat that blocked the view of the male. But the cruelty is more apt to be seen as whimsical rather than frightening. The clown, like so many cartoon characters later, can be decapitated twice in a minute with no harmful effects. All of these aspects—the illogical narrative, images of cruelty and revenge, evocations of claustrophobia and paranoia, the act of floating in an undefined spatial void, painless violence—substantiate the analogy to dreams. Furthermore, the film tends to incorporate hybrid monsters (as in Steinlen's drawing above), demonstrating the Freudian concept of condensation.

The movie-house setting and the little cartoon-within-a-cartoon also lead us to speculate on self-referential possibilities of the scene. Do the frustrations of the man trying to watch the films reflect the frustrations of the viewer who is trying to comprehend the actions in this strange movie?

In Cohl's next film, the oneiric content was explicit. *Le Cauchemar du fantoche* is now lost, but a drawing after a scene in the film seems to capture its spirit (fig. 264). Another stick figure is interrogated by a sphinxlike monster with a tiger's body, a man's head, the ears of an ass, and a cyclopean eye in its tail. Such nightmarish conflations of bestial imagery were common in Cohl's Incoherent drawings of the 1880s. "Abus des métaphores" (untranslatable pun on "Metaphor Abuse," fig. 265), for example, is a

264. Drawing after *Le Cauchemar du fantoche*.

265. "Abus des métaphores," *Catalogue illustré de l'exposition des arts incohérents*, 1886.

grotesque composite birdlike creature. The effectiveness of this chthonian imagery results from the shock value of the juxtaposition—a deliberately disjunctive strategy promoted by Cohl's Incoherent colleagues, as well as by Lautréamont in his famous savoring of the chance encounter between an umbrella and a sewing machine on a dissecting table. When this imagery flowered in Cohl's films, it linked them to the tradition of the fantastic, and to the visionary art that extended beyond the Incoherents to Bosch, Breugel, Goya, Grandville, Redon, and Moreau.

Le Songe du garçon de café (cat. 53) was another film explicitly made in a dream mode. A waiter falls asleep in a quiet café (fig. 266). The murmurs of the customers are assimilated into his dream as gypsy violinists, whose soothing strains cause him to levitate from his chair. The reverie ends, however, when Cohl's hand enters the picture and squeezes the waiter like a sponge. The tormented character then experiences Saint

266. *Songe du garçon de café* (cat. 53), 1910.

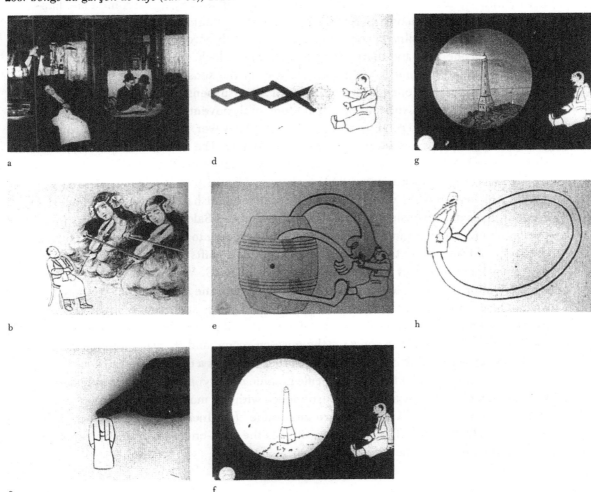

a

d

g

b

e

h

c

f

Anthony-like visions that are all variations on alcoholic themes. A demon in a wine barrel plagues him by ejecting a stream of bottles. The *garçon* expands into a giant grape. The monster sucks him into the barrel, but he escapes through the bunghole. Seated before a circular screen, he witnesses a series of transformations that suggest delirium tremens. Other moving images have no readily apparent interpretation, such as the picture of a lighthouse beam revolving in the night. At one point the man's limbs become elastic, and he repeatedly kicks himself, a sort of masochistic out-of-body experience. The gypsies, who have proven themselves to be more like sirens, return in the form of a decorative fountain. They spray the waiter, who wakes up only to find that the customers in the café are all squirting him with seltzer. Instead of the process of condensation, as in the above films, here the mechanism is sublimation, the inscription of everyday activities into the bizarre imagery of the dreamwork.

The events of *Clair de lune espagnol* (Spanish Moonlight, fig. 267) do not resemble a nightmare as much as they do a hallucination. The film tells the story of the matador hero Pedro's quarrel with his paramour, his kidnapping by a flying machine that "happens to pass" (quoting a title in the film), and his subsequent fantastic adventure on the moon. Not only is the film one of Cohl's most technically accomplished, it is also one of his most "Incoherent" and therefore deserves a closer look.

Clair de lune espagnol is a slapstick comedy in the sense that it operates on the principle of excess: it depends on distortions of logic (suspension of causality), exaggerated physical plasticity, disruption of spatiotemporal conventions, and unexpected juxtapositions of images to produce its comic effects. However, the extent of its mixing of precinematic sources to produce comedy is remarkable. The result is a chaotic mélange that the spectator must read either as very funny or as not at all legible.

The film begins and ends with a tableau showing a Spanish cabaret where Pedro's girl friend (who looks like she wandered in from Manet's Spanish period) is dancing (a). The scene derives its "Spanishness" from the iconography of Salon painting, popular illustration, opera, and the music hall—now being inscribed into the early cinema. During the scene of transport to the moon the genre suddenly shifts to science fiction and the flying machines of Albert Robida, Jules Verne, and H. G. Wells, and their adaptors, Zecca, Walter R. Booth, and others (b–c). On the moon the arrival of star-women and Pierrot again transforms the film, at this point into a *féerie* such as one might see performed at a fête forain, the commedia dell'arte, the Châtelet Theater in Paris, or in a Méliès film.[7] However, the concept, the mise-en-scène, and the gag motif (an assault on the moon's face) all derive from Cohl's earlier career as a comic-strip artist and, like many of his films, can be traced to specific graphic prototypes that preceded his entry into filmmaking. In this case Pedro's experience with the moon was anticipated in one of Cohl's comic strips, "Une Aventure incroyable" (An Incredible Adventure), published in 1899 (fig. 268). The strip approximates the mise-en-scène of the film and the motif of the assault on the moon's face.[8]

267. *Clair de lune espagnol* (cat. 23), 1909.

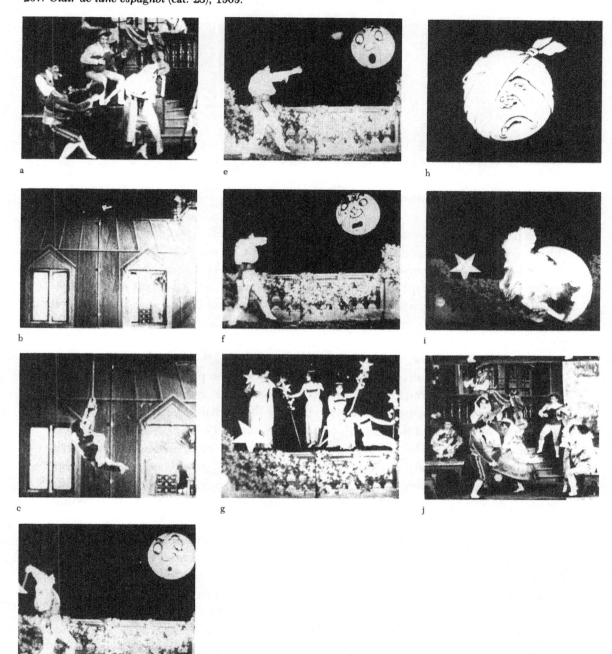

268. "Une Aventure incroyable," *L'Illustré National*, May 7, 1899.

The progression of the narrative through these various changes in genre is responsible for much of the disjunctive humor of the film, but, on a serious level, the progression also exemplifies the state of cinematic specificity in early film. In *Clair de lune espagnol*, theatrical, graphic, and cinematic conventions are tried out, momentarily incorporated, then discarded, having served their purpose of narrating a comic episode. In this particular example the sources not specific to film are still strongly marked.

Clair de lune espagnol, despite its early date and its length of less than half a reel, is a "classical" linear narrative structured in three "acts": the protagonist's quarrel with his lover, their separation, and eventual reconciliation. The opening is a symmetrically composed scene of dancing and domestic balance that is disrupted by Pedro's sudden departure. At the end of the film this balance is restored: Pedro and his lover reunite; the dancing resumes. This closure exists formally as well: the scene is restored to the initial "master shot" composition as though nothing had happened in the interval; also, Pedro's departure upward has been canceled by his return downward. Indeed the reestablishment of narrative symmetry is so abrupt and complete as to produce a comic effect in its own right by its suddenness.

More interesting than this simple romance is, of course, what happens during the second segment, which may be read as a reenactment of the quarrel but displaced into an imaginary realm. The film provides a powerful visual device for showing the audience that the segment is Pedro's fantasy: the image of a melancholy person staring out a window—a prevalent motif in nineteenth-century art (best illustrated in several paintings by Gustave Caillebotte). It is an image perhaps better known to film historians because it was travestied in the opening sequence of *Un Chien andalou* when the protagonist-filmmaker Buñuel stares out the window at the moon before committing his violent act, slicing an eyeball. Pedro's anger with his girl is recast as a male conflict with femininity on a cosmic scale.

Pedro's capture by the flying machine is an appropriate metaphor for showing that he is "beside himself" with jealousy and that his mind is taking leave of his body on this flight of fancy. When Pedro is set down on the moon, Cohl takes full advantage of the hallucinatory potential of the *féerie* genre. The moon was particularly suited as a setting because of its double association in the nineteenth century with both eros and insanity. In the popular arts of the *fin de siècle* the moon frequently played the role of commentator on man's erotic life, as in the 1886 cartoon "Fantaisie lunaire" (fig. 269). Pedro transfers his anger to the moon, attacking it as a traditional symbol of female inconstancy by means of a violent (and symbolically phallic) assault with ax and gun. Pierrot intervenes and shows Pedro that he has wounded the moon, upsetting the order of the universe. The Pleiades (personified by women in star suits) arrive on comets, change into acrobats, and throw Pedro to earth, where he is welcomed back by his lover. He apologizes for his jealous rage, having learned to accept fickleness as "natural" for women. Pedro's amorous frustrations have made him a lunatic. His temporary insanity is indicated spatially and by conventional iconography.

The space of the moon, as represented in the film, is impossible for the spectator to comprehend, since it defies a reading from a single viewpoint. Pedro is supposed to be standing on the surface of the moon, yet he can see the moon's face in the "sky."[9] Then, when Pedro touches Pierrot with the sword, the androgynous clown is replaced by another representation of the moon as an actor in a crescent-shaped costume, the

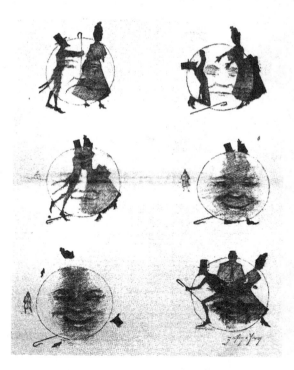

269. D'Yvrony, "Fantaisie lunaire," *La Chronique Parisienne*, December 2, 1886.

change of shape suggesting the moon's unpredictable "feminine" mutability. Perhaps Cohl's Parisian contemporaries, the Cubist painters, might have appreciated this irreconcilable "simultaneous" vision; for other viewers it was (and is) a playful spatial disjunction that suggest's Pedro's being "carried away," a *dépaysement* that André Breton later might have applauded.

Emile Cohl's use of the moon to convey Pedro's *amour fou* is consistent with similar uses throughout the late nineteenth century, especially within the Incoherent context. It was because of its association with insane laughter that the moon was chosen as the mascot of the Incoherents, when, as early as 1882, Cohl drew his "Lunes politiques et incohérents" (Political and Incoherent Moons, fig. 30). It was also natural for Chéret to depict Jules Lévy as a lunatic, shown in three stages of being devoured by the moon on the cover of the 1886 exhibition catalogue (fig. 270). The Incoherents explored madness as a source of artistic inspiration, and Emile Cohl, throughout his career, was preoccupied with the theme of insanity and its relation to laughter. This can be traced back to his association with Gill, whose publications *La Lune Rousse* (April Moon) and *L'Eclipse* had lunar evocations in their titles. On its masthead *La Nouvelle Lune* repre-

270. Jules Chéret: Cover for *Catalogue illustré de l'exposition des arts incohérents*, 1886.

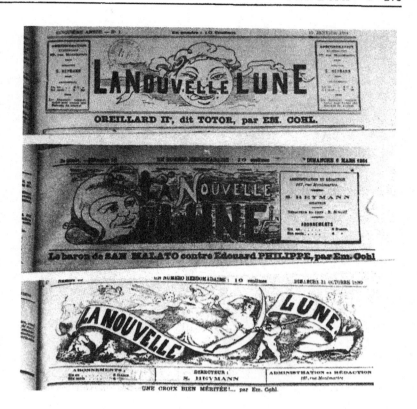

271. Mastheads for *La Nouvelle Lune*.

sented the moon in three successive personifications: first as a reclining female (Phoebe), emphasizing the traditional erotic implications of the image; then as a jester hovering over the Parisian skyline; and finally as an insane laughing face, perhaps signifying the lunacy of the caricaturist's art in general (fig. 271), or perhaps making a specific reference to Gill's insanity. Cohl's frequent remark in later life that animation would inevitably lead to Charenton was simply an extension of this earlier cliché regarding caricature, which, in the case of Gill, was demonstrably true.

THE WORLD OF THE CHILD

The Incoherents often modeled their exhibition entries on the drawing style—or nonstyle—of children. In part this gesture constituted a further rejection of academic quality, and partly it was a genuine manifestation of fascination with the art of children, graffiti, and other "primitive" art forms that had been developing since mid-century.[10] Besides the iconoclastic aspects, Lévy had emphasized the feeling of satisfaction obtained by these artists who "did not know how to draw." A work like Cohl's "Page de dessins trouvée dans la case d'un député" (Page of Drawings Found in a Deputy's Case, fig. 272) is both an antibureaucratic political statement and simply an excuse to indulge

272. "Page de dessins trouvée dans la case
d'un député," *Les Chambres Comiques*,
January 4, 1887.

in juvenile scribbling. Emile Cohl's love of childish pastimes carried into the twentieth
century when he found that youth-oriented periodicals were willing to pay for such
contributions. When he became a filmmaker, Cohl saw his new profession as the perfect opportunity to continue creating juvenilia. When asked in one of his late interviews
why he first became interested in cinema, he gave this reason:

It was simply because I was born a trickster. For more than sixty years I have poured
out a stream of brain teasers, contests, rebuses, and puzzles for the multitude of large
and, especially, small magazines that reserve space for things for youngsters, who are
always interested in this sort of thing. It is a trade that may seem bizarre, but which
nevertheless, in my opinion, is very engaging. But to practice it, you have to have
started very young. The habit of constantly racking your poor brain to find something
novel and unpublished, as quickly as possible, makes it almost mechanical the way

the more or less ingenious ideas flow from this kind of work, which must be uninterrupted and, naturally, which is less remunerative than one might wish.[11]

Many of his films demonstrate implicitly the infantile regression that Cohl first associated with his art, then with cinema.

Cohl looked to the world of children, first of all for his subjects. The children in his films, whether in one of his early scenarios (*La Force de l'enfant*) or in his mature "Newlyweds" series, always dominate adults. Cohl's childish world was very similar to the one imagined by Maurice Ravel in his 1908 operetta *L'Enfant et les sortilèges* (The Child and the Magical Happenings). Magical happenings were everyday events, and fantasy blended indistinguishably with reality.

This is certainly true in *Le Cerceau magique* (cat. 7), which begins with a little girl playing with her hoop in the park. A young man offers to mend her broken hoop, and, as in fairy tales, he turns out to be a magic prince. In the next scene she has learned some magic herself and can make animated visions appear inside the circular frame of the hoop.

In *Rêves enfantins* (cat. 49), in contrast, Cohl explicitly enters the dream world of a little boy, who, after being tucked in for the night, is led by his little stuffed dog through animated visions of dancing toys. Unlike McCay's "Little Nemo in Slumberland" strip, to which there is thematic similarity, Cohl's dreams are not picaresque adventures but rather are nonnarrative transitions between bizarre and unrelated images.

Children's toys constitute much of the iconography of Cohl's other films. As in a child's wishful fantasy, toys come to life and move in *Les Jouets animés* (cat. 101), *Clara and Her Mysterious Toys* (cat. 156), and *Les Braves Petits Soldats de Plomb* (cat. 179). The animated wax matches that play in four of Cohl's films (cats. 6, 102, 142, and 193) are descendants of those that cavorted in many of his nineteenth-century journals (fig. 273). This tendency to anthropomorphize objects was quite common for Cohl. *Japon de fantaisie* (cat. 16), "in which a Japanese lantern, several dolls, chickens, mice and grasshoppers play a prominent part,"[12] was an adaptation from a "Fantaisie japonaise" (fig. 274) with an "animated" doll and mouse, which was published in 1885. It may be possible to generalize that object animation as a genre—with the illusionistic self-locomotion endowed by the cinema—provides a visualization of the child's primitive pantheistic belief that all objects are endowed with life.

"The Newlyweds" series must have provided Cohl with a special challenge, since the protagonist, Snookums, is not a lovable tyke but a squalling hellion. In *He Poses for His Portrait* the baby refuses to cooperate with his doting parents when they take him to sit for his portrait. The transformation sequences that interrupt the film seem to represent, at first, visualizations of Snookums's thoughts (fig. 275a). The artist's head becomes a boat, which becomes a balloon drifting over the horizon, which becomes the outline of the family. When Snookums is given a cat to distract him, there are images

273. "Les Allumettes animées," unidentified clipping, ca. 1899.

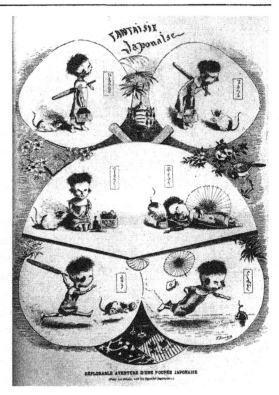

274. Bainsin: "Fantaisie japonaise," *La Chronique Parisienne*, November 1, 1885.

of notes appearing on the kitten's whiskers (drawn in a childish style, fig. 275b) that represent the sound of its meowing, and a scene of its being ground up in a sausage grinder. But later in the film the metamorphosing images clearly are the visions of the artist, whom Snookums is driving mad. Snookums's head swells up to show the intensity of his crying, and he drags the cat's tail with an enormously long arm. Near the end of Snookums's visit, the raving artist looks into a cannon, out of which a white liquid pours and covers him. Then a threatening vision of a cigar (?) wearing a baby bonnet hovers over his head. Although the meaning of these pictures in this most bizarre film is difficult to fathom, Cohl does seem to be making a comparison between the free-flowing imagery of the child's "normal" way of seeing the world and the mimetic aspirations of the traditional portrait artist, for whom Snookums's vision represents insane hallucinations. Near the end the artist cries out, "Can it be I am sane, or is it ze dream!" (fig. 275c). In fact, it is neither; it is the world of childish imagination, which the artist can no longer understand. His insensitivity seems to be confirmed in the final tableau when he shows Snookums's portrait to his artist cronies, explaining, "And all ze time zat terrible brat bawl like zat and zey want me to paint ze picture." One friend responds,

275. *He Poses for His Portrait* (cat. 153), 1913.

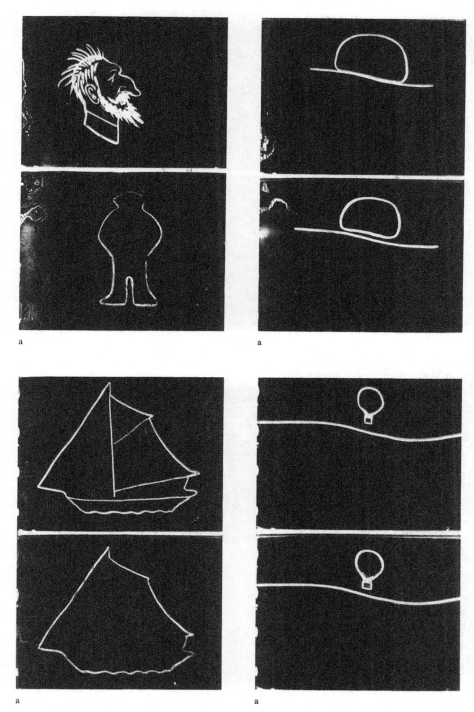

a   a

a   a

275. *He Poses for His Portrait* (cat. 153), 1913.

275. *He Poses for His Portrait* (cat. 153), 1913.

c

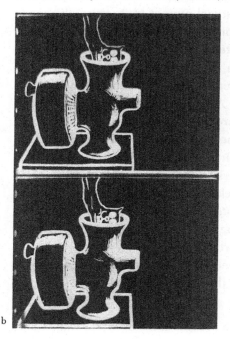

b

"The Phillistines [*sic*] have no soul for ze art!" and the other says, "Zey make me tired." Snookums has the last laugh as his portrait smiles and winks at the viewer.

Traits of the world of children also surface in imagery borrowed from the circus and the puppet theater. *Monsieur Clown chez les lillputiens* (cat. 28) presents an entire circus mounted by animated toys. The *guignol* puppet theater exerted an even more pervasive influence. Cohl's enthusiasm for the puppets undoubtedly dated back to his youth, which coincided with the revival of the art, dormant since Edmond Duranty's popular shows in the Tuileries. Cohl grew up only a few steps from Holden's theater at 11, Faubourg Poissonnière, the most popular puppet show in Paris in the 1870s. In the next decade the Guignol Lyrique and Petit Théâtre competed with the "fantoches" of Dickson and Hewelt at the Théâtre Robert-Houdin and the Musée Grévin.[13] Even the Chat Noir featured a *guignol* before it was replaced by the better-known shadow theater.[14] Cohl readily assimilated this imagery into his caricatural art, and then into many of his films.

A few of them, such as *Le Tout Petit Faust*, can readily be seen as transpositions directly from the puppet stage to the miniature animation set. Cohl's version follows the scenario of an ancient "Parodie de Faust," one of the most popular plays in the puppet repertoire.[15] Similarly, Hercules and his tasks were familiar pieces on the puppet stage, long before Cohl's *Les Douze Travaux d'Hercule*. The cutout figures Cohl made for that film closely resemble the primitive Epinal puppets that children cut from broadsheets in the nineteenth century.[16] The vestigial puppet traits were also made obvious by enclosing the action within an ornate proscenium arch.

The "fantoche" films represent an especially interesting example of puppet adaptation. Originally the word "fantoche" was used to distinguish wire-operated puppets from hand puppets, both called *marionnettes* in French. Around the turn of the century the word came to refer to a special kind of puppet. An actor would tie a small doll torso around his neck, so that when he poked his head through a hole in the stage curtain, the audience was given the illusion of a dwarflike puppet with a human head (fig. 276). One of the most successful of these acts was recorded on film by Pathé (fig. 277). In order to conceal the actors' bodies, the actions in these plays necessarily required a black backdrop, a visual effect incorporated into the black background and shallow space of Cohl's films. Of the first three, *Un Drame chez les fantoches* is the most guignolesque in pictorial and narrative conception. The plot, a melodramatic love triangle, is typical Punch and Judy fare, ending with the troupe's curtain call.

Children's drawing was responsible for stylistic elements of Cohl's images, as well as for the iconography. Once he acknowledged that the "fantoche" films were originally conceived as a kind of animated childish graffiti:

> I had an eight-year-old child pose for my camera in front of a very white wall. Using charcoal, the budding artist drew for me a stick figure of the famous general [Napoleon] with the classic triangular hat on its head. Then the young artist went away leaving his work on the wall. In an instant the charcoal character descended from the wall and jumped into the imaginary world where he met his fellows and, naturally, palavered, scuffled, etc., etc. The animated cartoon was born.[17]

276. "Fantoche" puppets, *Le Pierrot*, 1903.

277. *Le Théâtre des fantoches parisiens*, Pathé, ca. 1906.

278. Louis Feuillade and Cohl: *Les Chefs-d'oeuvres de Bébé* (cat. 75), 1910, with René Abelard.

LES PREMIÈRES

279. Cul-de-lampe figures, *Tout-Paris*, 1880.

Les Chef-d'oeuvres de Bébé (Baby's Masterpieces, cat. 75, fig. 278) began as an attempt to realize exactly this idea.

The graphic prototype of the animated stick figures had appeared thirty years before the "fantoche" films in a cul-de-lampe sketch for *Le Tout Paris* (fig. 279). Chances are that it was also Cohl who drew an eight-panel picture story with little figures (fig. 280), signed "Tata." Its simple linear background is a precedent for that of the future films.

The stick figures were more than a mark of children's style. At least as early as 1845, when J.-J. Grandville pictured himself signing his name above one of these crude drawings, the childish, graffiti-like image had been used as the signifier of the caricatural artist (fig. 281). Cohl paid homage, perhaps unconsciously, to Grandville's drawing when he reinterpreted it in a scene in one of the "Pieds Nickelés" films, signing it again with the childish pseudonym "Tata" (fig. 282). But the most telling images are the ones in which he actually represented himself drawing the figures. In these pictures (figs. 283, 284) he proudly displayed the scribble as the sign of his profession. In other pictures caricaturists were cast as bohemian types separated from normal society (fig. 285), scorned by respectable artists (fig. 61). By transferring this iconography to the "fantoche" films (and to several others in which the stick figures appear), Cohl implied that the traditional alienation of the caricaturist had now become that of the animator, whose labors were difficult and for whom appreciation was nonexistent.

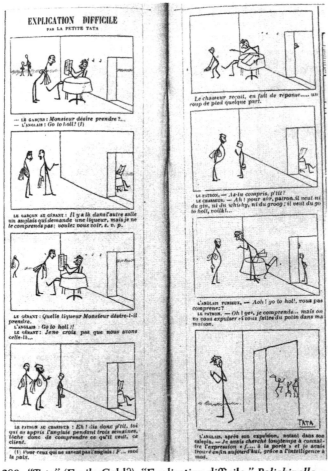

280. "Tata" (Emile Cohl?): "Explication difficile," *Polichinelle*, May 30, 1897.

282. Unidentified film in the "Pieds Nickelés" series.

284. Self-portrait, *Les Chambres Comiques*, October 12, 1886.

281. J.-J. Grandville: from *Cent Proverbs*, 1845.

283. "La Rédaction du *Tam-Tam*," *La Nouvelle Lune*, May 29, 1881 (detail).

285. Untitled drawing, *Les Chambres Comiques*, January 4, 1887.

THE CINEMA OF SATIRE

Throughout his thirty years as a caricaturist, Cohl satirized his targets with a barrage of witty and often grotesque imagery. It is therefore not surprising to find traces of the same turn of mind in his films. Almost certainly the most relevant examples of the adaptation of Cohl's social commentary (*satire de moeurs*) to the cinema would be provided, if any of them still existed, by his short films made for the Animated Weekly and for Eclair-Journal. We can guess that titles like *The Subway* (cat. 125) and *The Police-women* (cat. 129) commented on topical New York subjects, and that *Ce qu'ils mangent* (What They Eat, cat. 175) reflected current war developments in France. Films of this type were carryovers from Cohl's "journalistic" caricatures, analogous to his documentation of the drought of 1881 and his "Gaités de l'actualité" (Gaiety in the News, figs. 286, 287). In his other films we need discuss only two favorite subjects to demonstrate his satiric spirit in action.

287. "Les Gaietés de l'actualité," *L'Illustré National*, December 25, 1898.

286. "Paris sans eau," *La Nouvelle Lune*,
July 31, 1881.

288. *L'Hôtel du silence* (cat. S-9), 1908.

289. "Nos Grandes Inventions: Le Lit réveil-matin," *L'Illustré National*, February 11, 1900.

Science. Cohl had aimed his barbs at science in the cinema even before he completed his first film. In one of his early scenarios he conceived the ultramodern *Hôtel du silence* (cat. S-9) as a marvel of electricity, furnished with modern devices like an alarm bed that was supposed to wake the guest at a designated time. The bed, like all the other gadgets, received a burlesque treatment, went berserk, and threw the sleeper onto the floor (fig. 288).

The inspiration for several gags, including the alarm bed, came from a 1900 series of picture stories drawn for *L'Illustré Nationale* called "Nos Grandes Inventions" (Our Great Inventions, fig. 289). The overall conception of the film was borrowed from his friend Robida's book *Le Vingtième Siècle; la vie électrique* (The Twentieth Century; Electric Life).[18] Its hero had also constructed a modern hotel that used complicated electrical devices for servicing the guests and calculating their bills (fig. 290). But Robida's hotel differed from Cohl's in the very important respect that it worked. *L'Hôtel du silence* is essentially a parody of Robida's progressive vision of technology. Cohl viewed the subject with cynicism and as another opportunity for a joke.

This was also the case with *Les Joyeux Microbes* (cat. 22). The film begins with a live-action prologue that borrowed its mise-en-scène from a strip called "A diagnosis; or, Looking for a Bacillus" (fig. 291). In both, a gentleman visits a bacteriologist for some medical advice. In the film the doctor draws a blood sample and invites the patient to peer at it through the microscope as he exclaims, "My god, you're full of microbes!" (fig. 292). The doctor identifies five distinct microbes, each of which is illustrated with animated sequences showing them coalesce from moving lines and dots: the microbe of pestilence (or the politician), laziness (or the bureaucrat), rabies (or the mother-in-law), cholera (or the chauffeur), and tetanus (or the wino). The "chauffeur" sequence is typical. It begins with moving microbes in the shape of dismembered

290. Albert Robida: "La Bonne à tout faire," *Le Vingtième Siècle; la vie électrique,* 1892.

291. "A Diagnosis; or, Looking for a Bacillus," *Judy*, March 11, 1896.

pedestrians. They come together to form a cutout automobile that drives around the circular vignette representing the viewing field of the microscope. The picture changes to an animated drawing of the car's outline, then to a toy auto with the chauffeur inside. Once more around the circle, then he explodes. After viewing the other four microbes, the patient is reduced to a raving lunatic and paces the office, crying, "I'm so sick!" Finally he smashes a framed picture of a microbe over the head of the doctor and stalks out.

292. *Les Joyeux Microbes* (cat. 22), 1909.

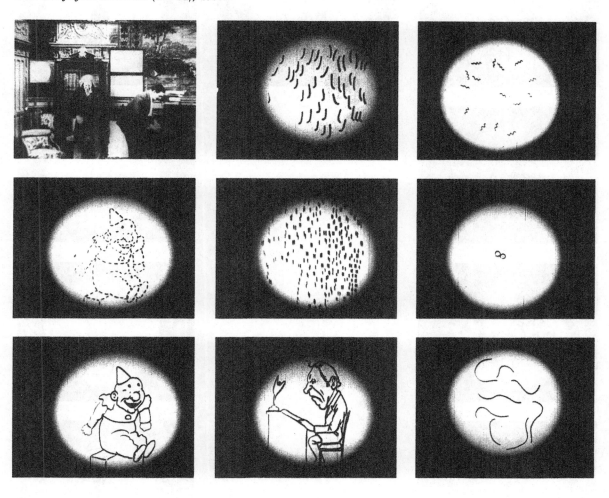

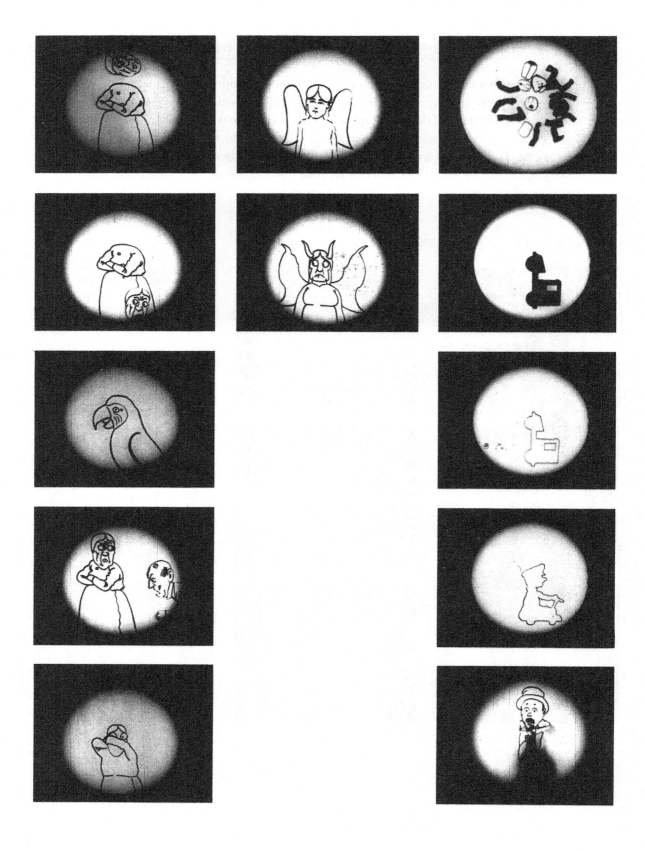

The Age of the Microbe had been a long-standing joke for caricaturists. At least as early as 1883 the humorist Draner had attributed various social ills to their respective microbes (fig. 293). Cohl's conception is similar. It is as though the caricaturists were transferring the traditional "humors" that had been thought to rule the body to this new scientific discovery. In the graphic arts the microbes themselves were always pictured inside circular frames and were usually drawn as grotesque little sea creatures (fig. 294). Microbiology (like cinematography) entered the domain of public awareness largely through its representation in the popular press.[19]

A closer look at *Les Joyeux Microbes* suggests that Cohl had a specific personality in mind for the role of the bacteriologist. At first one might suspect Jean Comandon as the target. His pioneering work with Pathé had brought him fame as a macrocinematographer.[20] However, his first presentation to the Academy of Science did not take place until October 1909, about six months after Cohl's film.

It is much more likely that Cohl's doctor was a caricature of the publicity-loving Dr. Eugène Doyen, who had been a favorite butt of the caricaturists' jokes since 1899, when he had been the first to record a surgical operation on film.[21] In 1903 he published *Le Micrococcus néoformans et les néoplasmes*, illustrated with photographs taken by an

293. Draner (Jules Renard): "L'Age du microbe," *Le Charivari*, November 15, 1883.

294. Albert Robida: "Découverte du bacille de la santé," *Le Vingtième Siècle; la vie électrique*, 1892.

assistant named Clément-Maurice.[22] Few laymen would ever have heard of this treatise had the doctor not become embroiled in a sensational trial. Maurice's entrepreneurial instincts had gotten a little out of hand, and he had been peddling the surgery footage to carnival sideshow cinemas. Dr. Doyen sued and won in February 1905.[23] The highly publicized testimony rejuvenated Doyen as a subject for caricaturists such as Henri Somm, who pictured him advising a patient that she has "a terrible microbe, the troublesome *micrococcus néoformans*" (fig. 295). Although the famous doctor was not identified by name in *Les Joyeux Microbes*, few Parisians would have failed to see a caricature of him in Cohl's goateed bacteriologist.

Other scientists appeared in Cohl's films, including the one in *Un Chirugien distrait* (The Distracted Surgeon, cat. 40), the "old and learned doctor" of *Génération spontanée* (cat. 36), whose discovery of the secret of life was heralded by a huge comic explosion; and the burlesqued psychoanalyst of *Le Retapeur de cervelles*.

At the same time, a few films seem to have been intended as paeans to scientific progress. One of these equivocal films, *En route*, celebrated the triumph of modern transportation, and the other, *Rien n'est impossible à l'homme* (cat. 69), was explicitly intended to celebrate Napoleon's homily, "Impossible is not French" (fig. 296). The author of Gaumont's catalogue description wondered: "What would [Napoleon] say today if he came back and saw passing in review, not vast armies and soldiers, but all the unbelievable progress accomplished in less than a century?"[24] Apparently the progress of science was so exhilarating that even the pessimistic influence of the Incoherents could not prevent it from being taken at face value once in a while. It must have seemed as though Robida's predictions were coming true. Much later this attitude prevailed when Cohl turned to planning his own didactic science projects.

295. Henri Somm: "Chez le docteur Doyen," *Le Rire*, March 25, 1905.

296. *Rien n'est impossible à l'homme* (cat. 69), 1910.

Art and Artists. Cohl had first hinted at his attitude toward the fine arts when he had a monkey travesty each of them in *Les Beaux-Arts de Jocko* (cat. 14). His definitive statement, however, was made in his best-known film, *Le Peintre néo-impressionniste* (cat. 58).

A young painter wearing the traditional beret is seated at his easel before his "classically" draped model (who holds a broom for a spear) (fig. 297). He has just begun to daub a "fantoche" stick figure on his canvas when a collector interrupts, asking to see some pictures. One by one the painter displays blank canvases and announces their titles. By using animated inserts, each picture draws itself. The jokes arise from the interplay between the ridiculous titles and the colors in which the various pictures originally would have been tinted. The title "First we have a picture showing a cardinal eating lobster with tomatoes by the Red Sea," for instance, preceded a scene tinted entirely red. A few seconds of black leader were spliced in for the picture of "Negroes making shoe polish in a tunnel at night." After submitting to a few more outrageous jokes, the collector begins to rave deliriously and agrees to buy everything in the studio.

Le Peintre néo-impressionniste links the cinema to the tradition of satire that began with Daumier's parodies of the Salon of 1840.[25] The Incoherents, quite expectedly, had added their own personal send-ups to this extensive subgenre of caricature. The motif of the wily artist outsmarting the stupid collector in Cohl's film was a standard gag that, for example, Paul Bilhaud, a fellow Incoherent, had treated in "L'Art appliqué à l'industrie" (Art Applied to Industry, fig. 298). In Cohl's own comic strips, artists always succeeded in duping bourgeois patrons like "Monsieur Duputois" and the one in "Une Epreuve concluante" (A Definitive Proofsheet, figs. 299, 300). In all the early drawings, as in the film, the artists are invariably presented as sympathetic young bohemian stereotypes.

The joking intertitles also connect Cohl's film with the art of the Incoherents. Cohl's colleagues were especially infatuated with the dissonances that could be created between words and images. Their ideas originated with the Symbolists' interest in wordplay, practiced by poets such as Jules Laforgue, but of course the Incoherents modified the Symbolists' solemn theories for their own witty purpose. Lévy explained the Incoherents' goals:

As language only has a certain number of words available to express its thinking, the erudite writer is forced to create words not found in the dictionary. As classical painting and drawing only permit the use of certain lines, the drawing records only the strokes of the pen and faithfully interprets the text.[26]

To illustrate his notion of the graphic equivalent of the neologism, Lévy cited one of Cohl's 1884 Incoherent exhibits (fig. 301): "Let us cite a classic example of a drawing representing 'A Minister having the government's ear' or, better, 'A criminal choking on the voice of his conscience.'" The method called for literalizing idiomatic expres-

297. *Le Peintre néo-impressionniste* (cat. 58), 1910.

297 a

297 b. "A canvas representing a cardinal eating lobster with tomatoes by the banks of the Red Sea"

297 c. "Little fish offering forget-me-nots to a lavender-seller blueing her linen on the Côte d'Azur"

297 d. "Chinese transporting corn on the Yellow River on a sunny summer day"

297 e. "[Green] devil playing billiards with green apples while drinking absinthe on the lawn"

298. Paul Bilhaud: "L'Art appliquée à l'industrie,"
1884 Incoherents Exhibition.

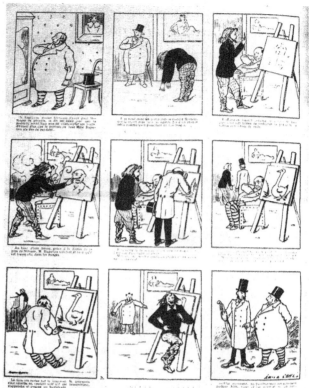

299. "Pourquoi M. Duputois n'aime pas
les peintres," *La Chronique Parisienne*,
November 14, 1886.

300. "Une Epreuve concluante," *L'Illustré National*, November 14, 1899.

301. "L'Assemblée était suspendu à ses
lèvres, il avait l'oreille de la Chambre,"
1884 Incoherents Exhibition.

sions, exposing the oxymoronic figures they frequently conceal, as well as their underlying irrationality. The most flagrantly Incoherent creation was Cohl's 1886 "Abus des
métaphores" (fig. 265), which visually concatenated seventeen idiomatic figures of
speech, mostly untranslatable:

> A level head; hair of flax; alabaster forehead; Lotto ball eyes; marmot paw nose; calf's
> ears; pastry mouth; boot chin; gingerbread complexion; swan's neck; round back;
> windmill arms; hippopotamus belly; horse's ass; rooster legs; violin case feet.[27]

"Un Général hors cadre" (fig. 302) is another example. The military meaning of *hors
cadre* (away from the regiment) was literalized as "out of the frame."[28]

302. "Un général hors cadre," 1886 Incoherents
Exhibition.

There is no question that Cohl intended the painter in his film to represent an Incoherent artist. His punning pictures revived the spirit of the work Paul Le Bouillant had
enigmatically entitled "Vitrail opaque pour décoration de chambre d'aveugle" (Stained-
Glass Window for a Blind Man's Room, fig. 303). Even more specifically, Cohl's basic
gag was borrowed from a cartoon by Draner in *Le Charivari* that showed a young
Incoherent displaying his blank canvas to a dealer while announcing the title, "Police
repulsing a nocturnal attack" (fig. 304).

Then why did Cohl not call his film *Le Peintre incohérent*? Because, by 1910,
the ephemeral Incoherents had been completely forgotten. Neo-Impressionism, on
the other hand, although it had faded from the public's mind since 1895, was, in 1910,
at the height of its so-called "second flowering."[29] The paintings and color theories
of Georges Seurat and his followers were being studied by the next generation of mod-

303. Paul Le Bouillant: "Vitrail opaque pour décoration de chambre d'aveugle," 1884 Incoherents Exhibition.

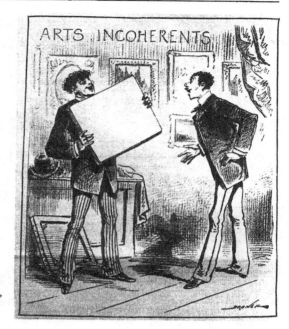

304. Draner (Jules Renard): "Arts incohérents," *Le Charivari,* October 30, 1884.

ernists. Cohl (or perhaps Louis Feuillade) must have realized that the film would have more popular appeal if it were tied in to this latest "ism." The paintings in the film have no relation—not even satirical—to actual Neo-Impressionist works, except in the vague sense that they have something to do with colors. But we must remember that Cohl was well aware of the aims and methods of the movement because the ideas of the original painters and theorists had been aired in the pages of *Les Hommes d'Aujourd'hui* while he was there during the editorship of Charles Morice. But the aesthetics of that movement were of little interest to Cohl; his real motive was to establish a parodic situation in which to exhibit his playful puns and image-word jokes. The same attitude had prevailed in his "Essais d'Impressionnisme—Synthétisons!" (Impressionist Experiments—Let's Synthesize!, fig. 305). Like the film, it is mainly the stage for more "incoherence" and has little relation to Impressionism or Syntheticism.

In 1916 Cohl remade this Gaumont film under the title *Les Tableaux futuristes et incohérents* (cat. 188), but the reference to the Incoherents was dropped from the title when the film was released. Although the film has disappeared, we know that it also contained verbal-visual jokes because an unappreciative reviewer noted dryly, "The irony of the titles and subtitles is not understood."[30] Many other films could be singled out to demonstrate Cohl's love of wordplay. His two object animations, *Les Chaussures matrimoniales* (Matrimonial Shoes) and *Un Drame chez la planche à chaussures* (A Drama in the Shoe Rack), were inspired by the idiomatic expression "Il a trouvé chaussure à son pied" (He's found a shoe that fits), meaning idiomatically that a man has found a good marital match. The significance of one scene in *Un Drame chez les fan-*

305. "Essais d'impressionnisme," *Le Courrier Français*, August 9, 1885.

toches depends on a pun that might escape English-speaking viewers. Before the protagonist is put in jail, he is momentarily enclosed inside a salad basket—an image that visualizes "panier à salade," the slang equivalent of "paddy wagon."

One of Cohl's favorite jokes was to insert a paste pot in a corner of one of his drawings (cf. fig. 53). "Colle" is almost a homonym of "Cohl," so the image is his *visual* signature. The appearance of the paste pot at the finale of *Fantasmagorie* should also be interpreted as Cohl's punning Incoherent signature to the film.

A BOUNDLESS UNIVERSE

Cohl's graphic works had little in common with the nineteenth-century positivist view of reality as finite, mensurate, and orderly. Instead he was more interested in expressing the inner reality of the Symbolists, which was delineated only by the imagination. One is tempted to say that he would have been more sympathetic toward turn-of-the-century psychoanalysis than toward physics. Often his subjects, his fantasies, were reflections of the darker regions of consciousness, untempered by any rational pretensions (fig. 306). At the same time, his Incoherent horror of seriousness prevented him from following the Symbolists in their deification of hermetic philosophy.

When Cohl began making films, it was natural for him to continue to embrace these attitudes toward art. Thus the world in his films is never the bright exteriors of Paris that one sees in the productions of his contemporaries, but rather they are evocations of an interior universe always in flux and responding continually to the whims of the animator.

His favorite, and most characteristic, animation effects were the metamorphosis sequences in which images coalesce briefly from moving lines, then decompose and reform themselves into another image. The idea obviously was an extension of the technique that Cohl had used in his nineteenth-century transformation comic strips, which had revived the basic formula established by Grandville. Even in these graphic works the logical relationships between the images before and after the transformation are often difficult to guess. How is an elephant like a photographer? The expected metaphorical relationship that would rationalize the juxtaposition does not exist. This ambiguity was compounded in the cinema when Cohl discovered, with obvious delight, that metamorphoses limited to a few panels in the comic-strip format could be protracted indefinitely in the movies.

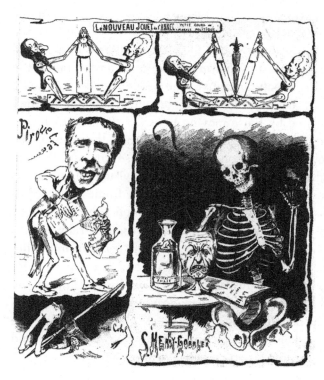

306. "Fantaisies," *Le Courrier Français,*
September 13, 1885.

The metamorphosis sequences in *Le Retapeur de cervelles* are the longest ones that survive, and they contain some of Cohl's most remarkable animation feats. In one section, for example, there is a drawing of a man viewed from behind (fig. 307). Cohl repeated the action of doffing his hat four times in order to establish a rhythmic repetition not unlike the repeated image of the woman climbing stairs in Léger's *Ballet mécanique* (1924). Then the man's outline breaks up and continuously reforms itself into the following staccato images: a flowerpot from which a blossom grows, a box out of which a stick figure emerges, a horse that the stick figure mounts and rides away, another figure with a detached head, a clown, a house, a face that swallows two small figures, and two men shaking hands.

This latter image is the starting point for one of the most surprising transformations of all (figs. 307b–f). The heads of the men begin to expand, while their hands merge with their bodies. The heads become those of birds and continue to fill the screen, as though the camera were zooming in on them. Even when their outlines have disappeared, the "zoom" continues. The eye on which it is centered now grows—except that it is no longer an eye but a pair of bellows that will become the starting point for the next transformation.

What was the motivation for these strings of continuous but unrelated images? We must ultimately conclude that their reason for being was the self-indulgent pleasure they afforded the artist, combined with a visualization of his mental activity. The technique is a graphic equivalent of literary "stream of consciousness" or "free association." One naturally thinks of James Joyce's contemporaneous work and that of the Imagists and Vorticists a bit later. The surprise experienced in observing these unexpected juxtapositions is related to that experienced by players of the Surrealist game of the Exquisite Corpse.[31] As a strand of cinematic narrative, the sequences do not "tell a story," and their order is apparently arbitrary. Of far greater importance is the high degree of formal complexity presented by these moving lines. As they fluctuate between representational images and purely nonobjective compositions, these metamorphic sequences all tend strongly toward abstraction. One often senses that Cohl's main goal was to create movement and change for their own sake as visualizations of his mental images. Even when viewed dispassionately as objects, the frames of his films present intriguing abstract patterns (fig. 308). Projected on the screen, these same lines define moving planes and haptic spatial relationships in an almost sculptural way.

The tendency toward abstraction contributes to the ever-present sense of ambiguity between readings of the screen space as a two-dimensional plane and as a three-dimensional illusionistic space. Cohl often used this ambiguity playfully to confuse the viewer, as when the trompe-l'oeil hole is torn in the "background" in *Fantasmagorie*, or when drawn images of objects or people change to the "real" object (fig. 309). The same thing happens when Cohl's hand enters the picture and destroys, by its scale and obvious three-dimensionality, the illusionistic space of the drawings or cutouts in the

307. *Le Retapeur de cervelles*
(cat. 80), 1911.

308. *Les Joyeux Microbes.*
Enlargement of 35mm strip showing
frames of a transformation sequence.

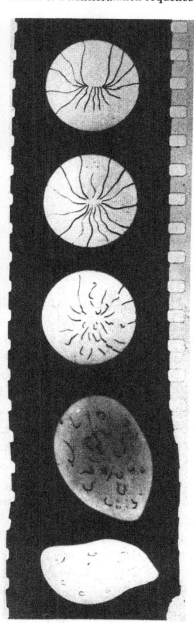

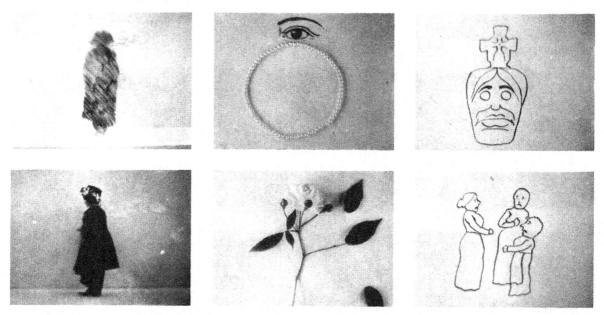

309. *Génération spontanée* (cat. 36), 1909.

same frame. Mixing solid objects with two-dimensional drawings further undermines cinematic illusionism—an effect demonstrated by the little bottles in *Les Joyeux Microbes* and *Le Songe du garçon de café*. Cohl was clearly not at all interested in recreating the perspectival effects of traditional graphic arts, as McCay, Barré, Bray, and most other animators would attempt. His manipulations of cutouts to achieve accurate foreshortening in the "Pieds Nickelés" films and in the Rabier collaborations prove that Cohl was capable of producing such effects if he so desired. But instead he preferred to remind the viewer that he or she was watching a moving drawing on a surface, with an artist hovering just off camera.

The world of plastic, amorphous reality in Cohl's films also extended to all its inhabitants, as exemplified by his treatment of the human figure. The basis of his attitude was demonstrated by the Incoherent "Portrait garanti ressemblant" (Portrait, Resemblance Guaranteed, fig. 310). Mimetic functions of art, it implies, should be reserved for the portrait photographer. The function of the Incoherent artist, by contrast, was to distort and make ugly in order to achieve a jarring or even repulsive effect.

Take, for example, the tableaux in *Les Douze Travaux d'Hercule*, in which the hero's limbs constantly separate from his body and drift away. A comparison with an 1886 drawing by Habert diagnoses Hercules' problem: he was suffering from "The Effects of Incoherence" (fig. 311). The exaggerated stretching of limbs and organs in many of Cohl's drawings also served as gag material for his films.[32] Even the taboo subjects of decapitation and cannibalism were frequently pictured with abandon. The most outrageous example of a scatological subject may be illustrated by what happened to the persistent insurance salesman and his harried mark in *Le Placier est tenace* (The Salesman Is Tenacious, cat. 65). After trying to evade the salesman at home and at work, the client is forced to resort to extraordinary measures, such as attempting to escape by balloon (fig. 312). In desperation he allows himself to be eaten by cannibals. In the animated portion of the film, the unabashed salesman follows his quarry down into the temporary refuge inside the cannibal's stomach—tinted red, of course! The man escapes by diving into the lower portion of the drawing (leading to the intestines). In the negative preserved at Gaumont, we see the cannibal hiding behind a tree to relieve himself. When he returns, the (presumably excreted) client runs from behind the tree with the salesman in hot pursuit. In recent prints made by Gaumont, this sequence has been deleted. One scene in *He Poses for His Portrait* is even more shocking. We see the artist's hallucination as, tormented by Snookums's screaming, he imagines that he eats the baby, engorging him whole, headfirst (fig. 313).

These examples prove that Emile Cohl's previous art was a mine of forms and ideas that exercised a strong influence on his films. But we should avoid the *post hoc, ergo*

310. "Portrait garanti ressemblant," 1884 Incoherents Exhibition.

311. Eugène (?) Habert: "Effets de l'Incohérence," 1886 Incoherents Exhibition.

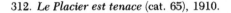

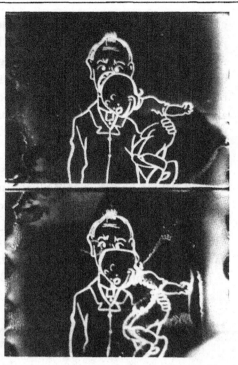

312. *Le Placier est tenace* (cat. 65), 1910.   313. *He Poses for His Portrait* (cat. 153), 1913.

propter hoc reasoning that the form and content of his films were merely determined by his earlier work. Despite these connections, there was little in Cohl's nineteenth-century art—always static—to prepare him or his audience for this exciting, new kinetic dimension that he created from 1908 to 1921.

CONCLUSION: THE "MYSTERIOUS ART"

Cohl developed recurring metaphors for expressing his attitudes toward the cinema and his conception of the filmmaker as an artist, not just as a technician or producer of commodities. Foremost, the viewing devices in his films—microscopes, X-ray machines, footprint decoders, and magic glasses—all inscribe the gaze in idealized visionary apparatuses.

Of these wonderful mechanisms, the most successful was certainly the one in *Le Binettoscope* (cat. 47). "Binettisme" was, even in Cohl's day, an obsolete word for the art of making portrait caricatures, as used, for example, in Nadar's *Binettes contemporaines*. Thus the "binettoscope" was an appropriate name for the magic box invented by the film's clown protagonist (fig. 314). He explains to the audience in pantomime gestures that he will make some faces appear. Instead of drawing, he aims his machine

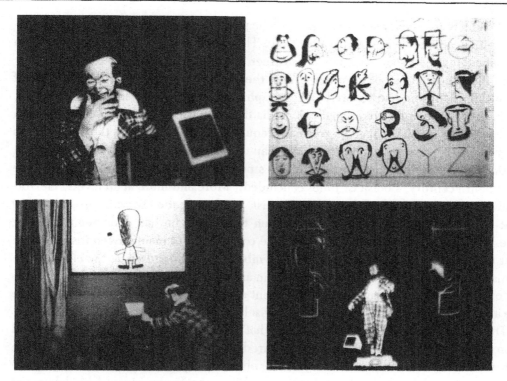

314. *Le Binettoscope* (cat. 47), 1910.

at the screen behind him and turns the crank. There is a parade of constantly changing faces that culminates in the transformation of the letters of the alphabet one by one into twenty-six chattering caricatures. For the finale, the clown returns with the binettoscope under his arm and mounts a pedestal. On both sides, against the black background, huge grotesque animated faces materialize and grimace at him.

One can read the film as an allegory. There is clearly an analogy between the clown with his machine and Cohl with the cinematograph. They both make their devices function as projectors of animated caricatural imagery. There is an interesting progression. At first the images on the screen-within-a-screen are supposed to represent projected films, since they stop moving when the clown stops cranking. With each successive shot, the point of view shifts closer to the screen until we no longer actually see the clown or his projector. In the climactic scene the clown makes it clear that the caricatures have taken on life of their own because when he places the binettoscope at his feet the faces remain animated, larger than life. They even become aggressively hostile toward their creator. By summoning these animated beings into existence, the clown accomplishes with his binettoscope what Robertson claimed to have done with his Fantascope, vivifying fantasmagorical images of nonexistent beings.

The film is an excellent demonstration of the process of self-figuration—a characteristic of much animation as a genre after Cohl. The clown in the film may easily be seen as embodying the two aspects of Cohl's career: artist and animator.

As Pierrot, or in one of his other guises, the clown appeared in a dozen or more of Cohl's films. But he had entered Cohl's graphic-arts iconography long before, when, costumed either in his traditional commedia dell'arte attire or in that of the modern clowns Footit and Chocolat, Pierrot had frequently frolicked among the Incoherents (cf. figs. 55, 56). Artists ranging from Watteau to Picasso used the clown as an emblem of the social position of the artist. In her study of this image in the art of the late nineteenth century, Louisa E. Jones concluded: "More and more at all levels, Pierrot-Clown became an image of the martyred artist, an identification so widespread by 1900 that it was difficult for many observers then to imagine he had ever been anything else."[33] To Lévy and his followers it was the connotation of manic, even insane mirth that made the clown appealing as a group symbol. In *Le Binettoscope*, the clown is the genial impresario who disdains seriousness in art, life—and cinema; he is also the creator of "binettoscopic" imagery, the equivalent of animated cartoons. Combined, these are also the attributes of Cohl, picturing himself as the Incoherent artist of the cinema.

The theme of drawings coming to life that *Le Binettoscope*, *Fantasmagorie*, and many other films explore was perhaps inspired by the filmmaker's meditations on the nature of the animation process. During the phases of drawing, retracing, and photography, the artist has only an intuitive idea of how the final results of his labor will appear. But when the work is finished and the film is projected, the sense of surprise and gratification that results from seeing the drawings move "by themselves" could be expressed by the myth of having endowed a work of art with an independent existence. This mythic aspect is embodied in the literal meaning of the French term for cartoons, *dessins animés*, suggesting that life has been breathed into the drawings. Eventually this highly romantic conception of the artist-animator as paternal and the filmed results as filial would become the central trope of most animation. To express it another way, the narrative archetype is a variation on the story of Pygmalion and Galatea, made applicable to the cinema.

Les Beaux-Arts mystérieux (cat. 63) is an even better demonstration of Cohl's reflexive conception of the cinema. The first seven tableaux are structured alike. Charcoal crayons, a paintbrush, wooden soldiers, pins and thread, cut flowers, an ink pen, and a box of matches enter the frame and make pictures by drawing, sketching, or arranging themselves in formation. Then each composition dissolves into a still photograph for a second or two, then becomes a moving film image, lurching into motion much as Lumière films are said to have been originally projected.

The fourth sequence is a representative one (fig. 315). A spool of thread and a pincushion (made from a toy chick) move across a sheet of paper. The pins then stick themselves into the paper in an apparently random pattern. But when the thread weaves itself around them, it reveals the outline of the Arc de Triomphe. The pins and thread gradually dissolve into a photograph (actually a freeze-frame) of the Arc. The movie footage shows a man walking directly toward the camera lens, maximizing the cinema's capacity to generate the illusion of deep space.

This sequence, and others like it, establish a hierarchy of image-making methods. First we see childish ways of using matches, pins, and other playthings to form primitive likenesses of objects—the Eiffel Tower, the Arc de Triomphe, etc. We are reminded of the childish games that Cohl invented, using matchsticks to form pictures, and the pins and thread in his game "ABC Strings." These crude representations are then magically transformed into the higher degree of indexical signification made possible by photography. Then another mimetic leap takes place as the picture becomes a moving cinematograph image—the ultimate stage of development, for Cohl's age, of pictorial representation. The order of each sequence recapitulates Cohl's own progression in the graphic arts, from the childlike drawings of his youth and Incoherent period to his eventual commitment to cinematography and animation, the "beaux-arts mystérieux."

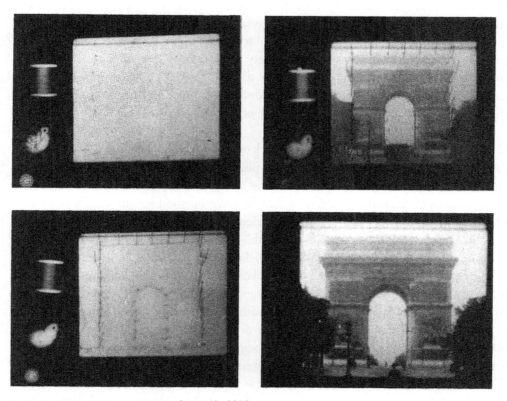

315. *Les Beaux-Arts mystérieux* (cat. 63), 1910.

In the eighth and final tableau, shreds of animated papier-mâché are photographed in backward motion. Slowly they reconstitute themselves into the mask of a clown with an insane laughing face. By now we recognize this image as Cohl's alter ego and the hallmark of the Incoherent artist, rejecting the established world of commercial art (and cinema) with an aesthetic defiance. Again, Jones's comments on Romantic poets may be generalized to describe Cohl:

> Above all grotesque imagery in this period deals with failed idealism, especially that of alienated writers confronted with the power of financiers and courtesans who easily symbolized the excesses of ruthless material appetite. Those poets who are most attracted by pierrots and clowns are those who celebrate the failure of art in modern society, their own noble failure, even sterility, as a kind of inverted success and heroic martyrdom; who attack society's extravagant frivolity as just a gay mask hiding nothingness, emptiness, a spiritual void. In this iconography, the clown's smile may betoken not joy, or even the enforced gaiety of a Romantic melancholy merry man, but the mindless leer of stupidity and appetite, "la bêtise"—real or feigned—with all its animal connotations.[34]

In this film, certainly one of Cohl's most personal and hermetic, we actually observe the unraveling of the clown's mask to reveal the vacuum inside. In his art we see the love of the grotesque and his fear of and attraction to madness as a radical alternative to the boring sameness of middle-class French society. And in his public vilification of the film industry, we do sense some measure of satisfaction derived from contemplating his career as that of the heroic martyr, the alienated artist. For Cohl the mask of the clown quite naturally served as the visual signature of the artist-animator.

THE leitmotif of this study of the life and work of Emile Cohl has been the emphasis on the intertextuality of his work. By necessity, pluralist methods have been utilized in its analysis. The work was there long before the analysis, and it is my hope that Cohl's oeuvre remains in the foreground, now that we have finished scrutinizing it.

Throughout his career in the cinema, which was quite long by early standards—longer than Méliès's, almost as long as Griffith's—Emile Cohl never lost touch with his background in the popular graphic arts. He picked up its threads whenever he recycled gags from his own comic strips or borrowed jokes from his former colleagues. There was also the conception of an artist working independently with the materials available—an attitude that frequently clashed with the industrial aspirations of cinema producers. The history of Cohl's work is not the story of one art form gradually evolving into another, but rather the account of the institution of the atelier being supplanted by the institution of cinema-as-assembly-line. Pragmatically, for Cohl (as it had been for Méliès) it was misplaced faith in the promise of film as an artisanal enterprise that rendered his position impractical. At the same time, it placed him in a marginal position vis-à-vis the mainstream film industry—a position that later would become part of the definition of institutionalized animation, ghettoized by the industry as "short subject" material on feature programs and as fare suitable for children but not for adults.[35] As a caricaturist, Cohl had chosen to view society from its margins. His adoption of the most marginalized branch of cinema, animation, was not a departure for him; it was his characteristic way of doing things.

Our study of Cohl shows that animation is integral to film history (and art history) and cannot be cordoned off for separate analysis. In addition to many specific debts to his graphic-arts background, there is also a pervasive, but intangible, resonance of the spirit and philosophy of the Incoherents in his cinematic work. Occasionally the Incoherent basis of his cinema makes certain passages as opaque as Symbolist poetry, and for some of the same reasons. Like clarity, grace, and rationality, accessibility was not necessarily considered a virtue.

Writing in 1900, Adolphe Brisson, the critic of caricature, postulated four kinds of humorists: the caricaturist proper, the parodist, the satirist, and the fantasist.[36] Cohl would have mingled happily with the latter class. The fantasist "obeys no other rules besides his own caprice. He invents, he combines, he suggests."[37] These are the same attributes for which Cohl will be rightly remembered in both cinema and graphic art.

Although Cohl's aesthetic roots grew from the nineteenth century, there is also a very modern quality about his films that must not be overlooked. His rejection of verisimilitude, of which the cinema was so spectacularly capable, in favor of imaginary scenes sketched with semi-abstract patterns of moving light anticipated the interests and methods of his neighbors in Montmartre and Puteaux, the Cubists. They, too, were moviegoers who would have appreciated the kinetic plastic universe that Cohl created with ink, scissors, and motion-picture camera. Once, around 1912, Picasso allegedly told Daniel-Henry Kahnweiler that he had wondered about the possibilities of using a cinematographic method for representing movement and actually acknowledged the animated cartoon as the source of his inspiration.[38] If Kahnweiler's memory is correct in placing this conversation before World War I, then Picasso was inspired by one of Cohl's films, probably viewed at a favorite haunt of the artist and his friends (such as the poet Max Jacob), the Gaumont Palace at the Place Clichy. We know that Picasso's and Apollinaire's friend Léopold Survage was already at work on his monumental non-objective animated cartoon, *Le Rhythme coloré*, on the eve of the war.

Certain images in Cohl's films anticipate Cubist motifs. In *Le Binettoscope*, to mention one, there is a drawing of the moon with the insane physiognomy that Cohl often gave it (fig. 316). A rift spreads down the face from the top, dividing it into an image that can be read ambiguously as either a single frontal face or as two profile faces with noses pressed together. It is not unlike Picasso's "double" portraits that represent frontal and profile facial views simultaneously.[39]

It would be going too far to suggest that Cohl was inspired by Cubist painting, or vice

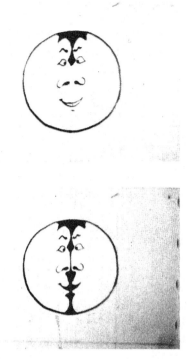

316. *Le Binettoscope* (cat. 47), 1910.

versa. But it is nevertheless clear that he was in tune with the new exploratory attitude toward spatial, temporal, and pictorial problems that dominated the avant-garde art of Paris in the first decades of the twentieth century. We should also not allow the high-brow/lowbrow distinction to obscure the intertextuality of Cubism, which was itself influenced by popular graphic art and certainly by cinema. Although Cohl did not set out to be one, did not associate with them (and in fact occasionally poked fun at them), he could arguably be counted among these artists as, one might say, a modernist in spite of himself.

Attesting to his love for his second profession is the sheer quantity of his film productions and his intense concentration on them, especially considering that in this period there were fortunes to be made elsewhere in the film industry by doing far less demanding work. Obviously he made animated cartoons more for personal gratification than for pecuniary reward, and in so doing he conforms to the personality profile of many great subsequent animators. While one always wishes that more of Cohl's films and those of his colleagues remained, even with the evidence that we have, it is certain that his presence was crucial to the formation of the cartoon genre.

First, there was his tangible influence on the invention and dissemination of animation technology in Europe and in the United States, where his films functioned as models for James Stuart Blackton, Winsor McCay, J. R. Bray, and others. Second, he was primarily responsible for introducing much of the iconography and gag humor of early animation. The theme of drawings coming to life, to mention only the most important, was to become a central trope. Every one of Max and Dave Fleischer's "Out of the Inkwell" cartoons, for example, abolished the demarcation between real and drawn images by having Koko the Clown move freely into the animator's environment (fig. 317). Like the clown in *Fantasmagorie*, Koko was infinitely resilient and suffered no injury from his potentially destructive misadventures. He also lived in an ambiguously defined spatial world, not confined to the plane of the sketch pad but not existing comfortably in the world of three-dimensional beings either. At the end of each film, Koko had to return to the inkwell.

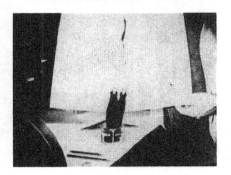

317. Max and Dave Fleischer: *The Awful Fly* ("Out of the Inkwell" series), ca. 1920.

Third, Cohl's refinement of the "hand of the artist" motif, away from theatricality and toward a generic sign of self-figuration, helped to give animation its definition as a distinct genre system. Later his "Newlyweds" series was instrumental in aligning the new genre—named "animated cartoons" for the first time in reference to one of Cohl's films—with comic-strip art and facilitating indirectly the entry of McCay and other comic artists into the industry.

Cohl's influence was also of a less tangible, more far-reaching nature. His dry humor and love of the bizarre ally him spiritually with animators ranging from Max and Dave Fleischer, Otto Messmer, Len Lye, Norman McLaren, Tex Avery, Chuck Jones, Harry Smith, Larry Jordan, and Jordan Belson to a generation of young contemporary independent animators—filmmakers not bound by the formal hard-edge American style of McCay and Disney or by the limitations of the normal Cartesian universe. One modern-day inheritor seems to be Robert Breer, whose animations reincarnate Cohl's sensitivity to pure linear motion for its own sake. *A Man and His Dog Out for Air* (1957) not only revived the free-form possibilities of the retracing method first seen in the "fantoche" films, it also included a scene in a circular frame that irresistibly recalls *Les Joyeux Microbes*. Breer has said of Cohl that he was a significant artist "because the medium itself, in a way, freed him from certain restraints."[40]

Other filmmakers who were also sensitive to the fantasy potential of the medium paid their respects to the first animator. René Clair, who loved the early Gaumont and Pathé films and shared Cohl's sense of the fantastic, included a sequence of animated matches in *Entr'acte* (1924). Even more remarkable is a scene in Jean Vigo and Boris Kaufman's *Zéro de conduite* (1932) in which a villainous inspector enters a classroom full of tumultuous schoolboys. When he looks at a drawing on the teacher's desk (executed while the teacher was doing a handstand), it comes to life and moves through some excellent Cohl-like transformations (fig. 318). Is it a coincidence that in the preceding scene one of the schoolboys had just asked each of his classmates individually to hand over their

318. Jean Vigo and Boris Kaufman: *Zéro de conduite*, 1932.

paste? As he walks up and down the aisles, he repeats Cohl's favorite pun—the one on his own name: "Donne-moi ta colle . . . ta colle . . . colle . . . colle."

We cannot know whether these references in Clair's and Vigo's films were made intentionally or not; but we do know that the old filmmaker, who was still alive and vocal at the time, would have been in complete sympathy with his young successors' exuberant, anarchic, and imaginative definition of the art of cinema.

NOTES

319. Medallion presented to Cohl by the Société d'encouragement
pour l'industrie nationale, 1936.

The following abbreviations are used in the notes:

CCC: Courtet-Cohl Collection
CJ: *Ciné-Journal* (Paris)
Carnet: Cohl manuscripts (see main bibliography)
MPW: *Moving Picture World* (New York)

MS I; II: Cohl manuscripts (see main bibliography)
NL: *La Nouvelle Lune (Paris)*
PCG: *Phono-Ciné Gazette* (Paris)

PREFACE

1. Robertson Davies, *Leaven of Malice*, 178.
2. Jean Renoir, "Parlant français," *Ce Soir*, February 17, 1938, in his *Ecrits, 1926–1971*, 152–153.

CHAPTER ONE

1. Charles Fontane, "Le Plus Ancien Parisien," *L'Intermédiaire des chercheurs et curieux*, December 30, 1937, col. 973. Also Emile Cohl, hand-drawn genealogical chart, CCC.
2. Emile Cohl, MS I. All biographical information up to 1870 derives from this source.
3. Cohl, "Comment c'est formé une collection de timbres-poste."
4. Richard Terdiman, *Discourse/Counter-Discourse*.
5. Pierre et Paul, "Emile Cohl," *Les Hommes d'Aujourd'hui* no. 288.
6. Philippe Roberts-Jones, *De Daumier à Lautrec*, 20. He describes the neighborhood as roughly a lozenge with the Bourse in the center, bounded by the present Métro stations 4-Septembre, Cadet, Sentier, and Palais-Royal.
7. Duranty, "La Caricature et l'imagerie en Europe pendant la guerre de 1870–71," *Gazette des Beaux-Arts*, April 1872, 324.
8. Jean Berleux, *La Caricature politique en France pendant la guerre, le siège et la Commune*; Jacques Lethève, *La Caricature et la presse sous la IIIe République*.
9. The number of newspapers varied inversely with the degree of repressive measures that were exerted, such as "caution money," taxation, and prior censorship. According to Robert J. Goldstein, "The loosening of press controls in 1868 led to an immediate upsurge in the press once more, but a period of strict controls in the 1870s held down further growth" ("Freedom of the Press in Europe, 1815–1914," *Journalism Monographs* no. 80, February 1983, 15).

10. One of these albums, *La Commune par E.C. et F.M.*, has been attributed incorrectly to Cohl by the Bibliothèque Nationale. It is an abridged version of *La Commune, album de 55 portraits*, published by Mordret in 1871. Berleux identified "F.M." as Hippolyte Mailly and "E.C." as Charles Vernier (*La Caricature politique en France*, 132).
11. Anon. [Cohl?], "Emile Cohl," *Le Grand Larousse de XIXe siècle*, 894.
12. Cohl, "Comment c'est formée une collection de timbres-poste."
13. Pierre et Paul, "Emile Cohl."
14. Jerrold Seigel, *Bohemian Paris*, 217.
15. Pierre et Paul, "Emile Cohl."
16. Cohl, "Lettre," in Charles Fontane, *Un Maître de la caricature: André Gill*, iii–viii.
17. Jules Lermina, *Histoire de cent ans*, vol. 3, 358.
18. *Le Temps*, August 12, 1868. Gill was responding to the official announcement published on the same date in *Le Moniteur universel*. For a complete account of the trial, see Valmy-Baysse, *André Gill*, 118–126.
19. Alfred Darcel, "Les Musées, les arts et les artistes pendant la Commune," *Gazette des Beaux-Arts*, January–March, May–June 1872; André Gill, *Vingt Années de Paris*; Stewart Edwards, *The Paris Commune*.
20. *Journal Officiel*, May 17, 1871.
21. Roberts-Jones, *De Daumier à Lautrec*, 134; Lethève, *La Caricature et la presse*, 41; Arsène Alexandre, *L'Art du rire et de la caricature*; Henri Beraldi, "André Gill," in *Les Graveurs du XIXe*

siècle, 134–144; Jean Adhémar, "Gill (André)," in *Inventaire du fonds, français après 1800*, vol. 9, 111–136.

Daumier himself requested a meeting with Gill in Carjat's studio. See Carjat, *Le Journal*, April 27, 1895, cited in Roberts-Jones, *De Daumier à Lautrec*, 154. For the Gill-Daumier relationship, see also Adhémar, *Daumier*, and Heinrich Schwarz, "Daumier, Gill and Nadar," *Gazette des Beaux-Arts*, February 1957, 89–106. For the Pissarro *Portrait of Cézanne* (1874, Von Hirsch Collection, Basel), see Ralph E. Shikes and Paula Harper, *Pissarro: His Life and Work*, figure 124.

22. Terdiman, *Discourse/Counter-Discourse*, 66.

23. Ibid.

24. Valmy-Baysse described Gill at the time of his meeting with Cohl as becoming obsessed with money and desiring to become a millionaire. He saw Gill's career as declining rapidly with *La Lune Rousse* after 1878 and considered Gill in his "second cycle" of life (*André Gill*, 245–246).

25. Michel Legros has heard from relatives that Cohl's pseudonym was chosen because it was "Jewish sounding," which seems strange in the light of later events, also that he wished to emulate the name of a friend, the dandy and journalist Aurélien Scholl. No one in the family, however, has a really convincing theory. I base my pun theory on Cohl's lifelong interest in puns and on the affection for word games by Gill and his friends. Cohl was only a professional name; legally his name remained Courtet.

26. Roberts-Jones, "Le Portrait-charge," in *De Daumier à Lautrec*, 89–108. The term derives from *charger*, to exaggerate by making ridiculous.

27. André Salmon, *Souvenirs sans fin*, 18. See also Emile Goudeau, *Dix Ans de bohème*; Jules Lévy, *Les Hydropathes*; Raymond de Casteras, *Avant le Chat Noir: Les Hydropathes*; Harold B. Segal, *Turn-of-the-Century Cabaret*, 5–9; Achille Astre, "Les Hydropathes," in *Les Spectacles à travers les âges*, 353–355; Charles Rearick, *Pleasures of the Belle Epoque*. The founders among Goudeau's friends were Rollinat, Abram, Lorin and Rives. The first meeting was held on October 11, 1878, and was so successful that larger quarters had to be found.

28. Lévy, *Les Hydropathes*, 8.

29. Pierre Labracherie, *La Vie quotidienne de la bohème littéraire aux XIXe siècle*, chapter 10; Seigel, *Bohemian Paris*, 221–222.

30. Jules Claretie, *L'Indépendance belge*, February 1879, cited in Goudeau, *Dix Ans de bohème*, 209.

31. Félix Galipaux, *Les Souvenirs de Galipaux*, 80.

32. *L'Hydropathe* was not founded by Cohl, as Lethève states in *La Caricature et la presse*, 36.

33. Lambert and Henri Demare were imprisoned. See *Le Carillon*, October 21, 1879; Cohl, *L'Hydropathe*, October 28, 1879.

34. Paul Vivien, "L'Hydropathe Emile Cohl," *L'Hydropathe*, April 5, 1880. Cohl's paintings were probably inspired by Gill's "realist" canvases.

35. Goudeau, *Dix Ans de bohème*, 156–157.

36. Lévy, *Les Hydropathes*, 12.

37. Anatole Jakovsky, *Alphonse Allais, le tueur à gags*; Paul Acker, *Humour et humoristes*. In the 1870s Charles Cros was a poet associated with the Parnassians and the Vivants. He was a regular at the Café de la Nouvelle-Athènes and a friend of Duranty, Degas, and Manet. The latter illustrated Cros's *Le Fleuve* in 1874.

38. Achille Astre, *Les Spectacles à travers les âges*, 355. The original sign is on display at the Musée de Montmartre (Jeanine Warnod, *Le Bateau-Lavoir*, 29). There are conflicting accounts as to which came first, the pun or the sign. My guess is that they were simultaneous. A rabbit similar to that on the sign appears in *La Lune Rousse*, July 1, 1877. A poem by Gill, "Au Lapin Agile," is reproduced in Astre, 355. At this writing, a cabaret known as the Lapin Agile is still in business.

39. Henri de Weindel, "Le Chat-Noir," *L'Illustration*, January 20, 1894, 51–53; William Rubin, "Shadows, Pantomimes and the Art of the 'Fin de Siècle,'" *Magazine of Art* 46, March 1953. For a discussion of Gill's role in the popularization of the Butte Montmartre, see Jeanine Warnod, *Le Bateau-Lavoir, berceau de l'art moderne*.

40. Robert Justin Goldstein, "Approval First, Caricature Second: French Caricaturists, 1852–81," *Print Collector's Newsletter* 19, May–June 1988, 48–50.

41. S. Heymann, *NL*, September 21, 1880.

42. Dr. Asinus, *NL*, November 21, 1880.

43. *NL*, December 19, 1880.

44. Jules Jouy, born 1855, became a popular entertainer at the Chat Noir. He died insane in 1897. He should not be confused with Jules de Jouy, a prominent lawyer and friend of Manet.

45. Cohl, A. Cahen, Edouard Norès, *Plus de têtes chauves! vaudeville echévelé en 1 acte* (Paris: Fantaisies-Parisiennes, June 13, 1881). The *Almanach des Spectacles* gives the date of June 11 as the premier.

46. Sélénio, *NL*, July 3, 1881.

47. *Almanach des Spectacles*, 1881.

48. Cohl, Cahen, and Norès, *Auteur par amour, opérette en 1 acte* (Paris, La Scala, September 9, 1882).

49. Cohl's photograph of Trézenick, Georges Rall, and Henri Gauthier-Villars is reproduced in Caradec, *Feu Willy*.

50. Another hoax was attributed to Cohl in *Les Hommes d'Aujourd'hui* no. 444, February 5, 1897: "M. Arthur Meyer, of the *Gaulois*, and others, accepted very seriously for a few days after the sentencing of Gilles and d'Abadie, Gilles' humorous memoirs which were supposed to have been written in his diary by Gilles and obtained from him. The memoirs were in reality only an invention of Jouy's mind and a calligraphic manuscript of the caricaturist Emile Cohl." On his own copy of this issue, Cohl wrote, rather ambiguously, "Quelle blague!"

51. Sélénio, *NL*, May 29, 1881.

52. Cohl also was advertised as a contributor to *Le Capitan* in 1883, but none of his drawings has been identified in a search of that journal.

53. Félix Galipaux described Bellot's banquets: "At these luncheons they recited verse, sang, and the pianist Ben-Zayoux made a Chaudron piano groan. Actors, men of letters and musicians reunited each month to dine. Bellot was named president, the dinners came to be known as the 'Bon Bock,' and met monthly at the old cabaret Les Vendanges de Bourgogne on rue Jessaint. One was not admitted easily. You had to show a soft hand, that is, be in the letters or arts. Daudet, Monselet, André Gill, Carjat (the poet-photographer) . . . Charles and Antoine Cros, Monprofit, Grenet-Dancourt, Boudouresque de l'Opéra, Georges Lorin, and other singers and composers would come there" (*Les Souvenirs de Galipaux*, 115–116).

54. Philippe Roberts-Jones, "Les Incohérents et leurs expositions," *Gazette des Beaux-Arts*, October 1958, 231–236.

55. Jules Lévy, "L'Incohérence, son origine, son histoire, son avenir," *Le Courrier Français*, March 12, 1885; Lévy, *La Chronique Parisienne*, September 9, 1883.

56. Reproduced in Roberts-Jones, "Les Incohérents et leurs expositions."

57. Lévy, *Catalogue illustré de l'exposition des arts incohérents*, 1884.

58. *NL*, October 15, 1884.

59. Lévy, "L'Incohérence, son origine, son histoire, son avenir."

60. Fontane, *Un Maître de la caricature: André Gill*, vol. 1, 66–67; Gill, *Vingt Années de Paris*, 65.

61. Cohl, "Le Patron," *NL*, October 27, 1881.

62. Jules Vallès, *Le Réveil*, October 23, October 31, 1881, reproduced in Valmy-Baysse, *André Gill*, 294–301. A spirited defense of Gill, led by Jean Richepin, was also launched (see Valmy-Baysse, 300–303). As late as 1926, when he left his calling card after a visit (CCC), Cohl and Richepin were still friends.

63. Cohl, "André Gill à Charenton," *NL*, January 1, 1882.

64. Reproduced in Fontane, *Un Maître de la caricature: André Gill*, vol. 1, 151.

65. *Le Temps*, May 12, 1882; *Le Voltaire*, May 14, 1882; *NL*, May 21, 1882.

66. *Le Temps*, January 12, 1883. Even works held by other creditors were pursued. On January 16, *Le Temps* reported that the banker (and former Hydropathe) Lepelletier had won the right to keep Gill caricatures that had been advanced as collateral on a loan.

67. Jules Claretie, "La Vie à Paris," *Le Temps*, January 19, 1883.

68. Paul Eudel, *L'Hôtel des ventes et la curiosité en 1883*, cited in Fontane, *Un Maître de la caricature: André Gill*, vol. 2, 265–266.

69. *NL*, January 28, 1883; H. Mireur, *Dictionnaire des ventes d'art*, 335. *Le Nouveau-né*, which had been exhibited in the 1881 Salon, sold for 1,510 francs; *Le Joueur de guitare*, 460 francs; *Le Requiem du Rossignol*, 500 francs; *Le Fou*, 600 francs.

70. Alphonse Daudet, Preface to Gill, *Vingt Années de Paris*, i.

71. Jacques Dairel, *La Ville de Paris*, November 4, 1883.

72. Fontane, *Un Maître de la caricature: André Gill*, vol. 1, 162–163.

73. Léon de Lora, *Le Clairon*, December 15, 1883.

74. The capital may have been provided by his father's 1879 estate. Many original Gill drawings, probably unsold remnants, are still preserved in the Courtet-Cohl collection.

75. Cohl, "André Gill et son oeuvre," *NL*, November 30, December 15, 1883.

76. Although signed "And. Gill," the drawing was almost certainly by Cohl.

77. Pierre et Paul, "Emile Cohl."

78. Dr. Christian stated the cause of death as a deformity of the skull (see Fontane, vol. 2, 286–287 for the autopsy). But a modern neuropathologist might suspect a stroke, an injury from Gill's fall in Belgium, a tumor, tubercular meningitis, syphilis, or any number of possible nervous disorders aggravated by Gill's alcoholism. The possibility of lead-based paint poisoning might also be explored. (I am grateful to Marilyn Crafton and Robert Goldstein for their opinions.)

79. Edmond Deschaumes, *La Chronique Parisienne*, May 10, 1885. Reprinted in Fontane, *Un Maître de la caricature: André Gill*, but with errors and omissions.

80. Etienne Carjat, *Le Cri du Peuple*, October 19, 1887.

81. Cohl, "André Gill et son oeuvre."

82. Cohl, "Lettre," in Fontane, *Un Maître de la caricature: André Gill.*
83. Nevertheless, Cohl did continue to submit brain-teasers and poetry under the pseudonym Colibri (hummingbird).
84. Caradec, *Feu Willy,* 57.

CHAPTER TWO

1. L.-G. Mostrailles, *Têtes de pipes.*
2. Ibid., 40–44.
3. Ibid., 181.
4. The other portraits were of Fernand Icres, Georges Lorin, Edmond Haraucourt, Robert Cazé, Francis Enne, Emile Peyrefort, E. Monin, Grenet-Dancour, Georges Rall, Léo Trézenik, Jean Rameau, Carolus Brio, and Henri Beauclair.
5. Oscar Méténier, *Petit Bottin des lettres et des arts.*
6. Elizabeth Anne McCauley, *A.A.E. Disderi and the Carte de Visite Portrait Photograph,* 57–61.
7. Nadar, *Paris-Photographe,* November 30, 1892.
8. André Gill, *Vingt Années de Paris,* 114.
9. Charles Blanc, *Grammaire des arts du dessin,* quoted in McCauley, *A.A.E. Disderi,* 139. Similar views were expressed by John Ruskin.
10. Cohl, "L'Ombre," *Le Courrier Français,* September 17, 1885.
11. *Le Monde Illustré,* April 17, 1886, 247. The ball took place at the Salle Métra, rue Vivienne.
12. Roberts-Jones, "Les Incohérents et leurs expositions."
13. Charles Joliet, *Le Roman incohérent.* Steinlen's illustrations have been assigned number 546 in Cauzat's catalogue raisonné, *Théophile Steinlen.*
14. Jean Adhémar has identified Lautrec's "Les Batignolles, trois ans et demi avant Jésus-Christ."
15. Curty de Saint-Volfor, "Le Louvre incohérent," *La Chronique Parisienne,* October 24, 1888.
16. John Grand-Carteret, *Les Moeurs et la caricature en France.*
17. Ibid., 529–530.
18. Ibid.
19. Lévy, *Catalogue illustré de l'exposition des arts incohérents,* 1893.
20. Cauzat, *Steinlen,* catalogue number 730.
21. Lévy, "Introduction," *Catalogue illustré de l'exposition des arts incohérents,* 1884.
22. Cohl, MS II.
23. See other group portraits in *Le Charivari* through the years 1887–1890.
24. Individual issues are difficult to date because the *livraisons* were often published without dates. They seem to have appeared irregularly and were not always dated when accessioned by the Bibliothèque Nationale.
25. Other portraits were François Coppée (no. 243), Paul Verlaine (244), Daubray (Michel-René Thibault) (276), Paul Bourget (285), and Maurice Rollinat (303).
26. The date of 1891 John Rewald assigns the drawing in *Post-Impressionism,* p. 547, is too early. It was probably done in 1898, based on known dates of other issues.
27. Lionel Prejger collection; reproduced in Goldschmitt and Schimmel, *Unpublished Correspondence of Henri de Toulouse-Lautrec,* plate 45.
28. Pierre et Paul, "Emile Cohl."
29. Jules Lermina, *L'Auberge des Adrets.*
30. Galipaux, *Galipettes; Encore des Galipettes.*
31. Coquelin cadet, *Pirouettes.*
32. MS II, notation for November 1887: "Chez Vanier And. Gill et son oeuvre par Lods et Cohl."
33. *Le Grand Dictionnaire Larousse,* 1890, Second supplement, fascicule 22, p. 894.
34. Jules Oudot, *Chanson fin de siècle.*
35. P. Niche, *Chansons à la blague.*
36. Norman L. Kleebatt, "The Dreyfus Affair: A Visual Record," in Kleebatt (ed.), *The Dreyfus Affair: Art, Truth & Justice,* 4. In this same volume Drumont is described as "a shy, brooding publicist of genius, who became the most outstanding purveyor of anti-Semitism in French history" (Michael Marrus, "Popular Anti-Semitism," in Kleebatt, 50).
37. MS II for 1893–1895.
38. In his younger days Drumont had been a fervent Republican, so it is possible that Cohl had been aware of him even earlier, perhaps through Gill's connections.
39. *La Libre Parole Illustrée,* December 23, 1893. Illustrated in Kleebatt (ed.), *The Dreyfus Affair,* cat. no. 400, p. 53.
40. The extent of Cohl's collaboration is not known, since a complete run of *La Libre Parole Illustrée* is not held at the Bibliothèque Nationale. These are the works I have identified at the B.N. (all signed J. Chanteclair): "Sur le Pothau, Pendant le retour," August 28, 1897; "Méline Pain-Cher," September 4, 1897; "L'Amiral Besnard," Septem-

ber 11, 1897; "Edouard Drumont réglant la question du Panama," September 11, 1897. None of these illustrations is overtly anti-Semitic.

At the major exhibition *The Dreyfus Affair: Art, Truth & Justice* at the Jewish Museum in New York, September 13, 1987–January 15, 1988, the following works by Cohl were shown: Cat. no. 42, "Naquet, Le Défenseur des pauvres youppins," June 1, 1895 (signed J. Chanteclair); Cat. no. 76, "A propos du Judas Dreyfus," November 10, 1894 (J. Chanteclair); Cat. no. 77, "Savonnage infructueux," November 17, 1894 (J. Chanteclair); Cat. no. 78, "Quel Temps de chien . . . !," January 5, 1895 (J. Chanteclair); Cat. no. 400, "Les Qualités de Juif, d'après Gall," December 23, 1893 (Emile Courtet); Cat. no. 402, "Prime Gratuite offerte par *La Libre Parole*," Poster (Emile Courtet). The curators of the exhibition apparently were not aware of the association of these works with Emile Cohl.

41. The bibliography is extensive. On anti-Semitism in general, see the four-volume work by Léon Poliakov, *Histoire de l'antisémitisme*; Michel Winock, *Edouard Drumont et Cⁱᵉ: Antisémitisme et facisme en France*. For Cohl's period, see Stephen Wilson, *Ideology and Experience: Antisemitism in France at the Time of the Dreyfus Affair*; Pierre Sorlin, *"La Croix" et les juifs (1880–1899)*; Alfred Gendrot, *Drumont; "la France juive" et "la Libre parole"*. For the Affair, see Guy Chapman, *The Dreyfus Case: a Reassessment*; Douglas W. Johnson, *France and the Dreyfus Affair*; Marcel Thomas, *L'Affaire sans Dreyfus*.

42. Michael Marrus, "Popular Anti-Semitism," 59.

43. Stephen Wilson, *Ideology and Experience*, 206. I have not been able to determine whether Cohl contributed to the subscription for a monument to Colonel Henry, which forms the basis of Wilson's study. We assume that he was a contributor.

44. Ibid., 208.

45. For a thorough discussion, see Phillip Dennis Cate, "The Paris Cry: Graphic Artists and the Dreyfus Affair," in Kleebatt (ed.), *The Dreyfus Affair*, 62–95.

46. Linda Nochlin, "Degas and the Dreyfus Affair: A Portrait of the Artist as an Anti-Semite," in Kleebatt (ed.), *The Dreyfus Affair*, 108–109. She describes Degas as a voracious reader of *La Libre Parole*.

47. Legros, letter to the author, May 9, 1988, and conversations. There are some discrepancies in both Cohl's diary and the version of the story in *Feu Willy* (58). Caradec writes that the son was recognized by Emile Courtet at birth, and that the divorce did not come until later.

48. Legros has furnished me a copy of the death certificate, which shows that Marie-Louise Servat died at 3:00 p.m., at 99, boulevard Arago, on December 31, 1891. Uncharacteristically, Cohl recorded the death incorrectly in his diary as December 1890, not 1891. My only explanation is that it shows that there was a lapse of memory when he made the entry at a later date. The date was recorded accurately by Caradec. There is some mystery concerning the burial of Germaine Villars. Legros believes that her funeral cards were printed, but not distributed, and that she was buried in Bagneux under her own name in a Servat family plot. Her remains were transferred to Père-Lachaise in Paris in 1898, but along with other deceased family members because of lack of space, not because of any scandal.

49. Bénézit, vol. 3, 163.

50. The turn-of-the-century boom in the children's publishing field was dominated by the publishing house of Offenstadt, which began *Le Petit Illustré* in 1901, and by its nearest rival, Arthème Fayard, who published *Les Belles Images* and *La Jeunesse Illustrée*. See Sadoul, *Ce que lisent vos enfants; la presse enfantine en France, son histoire, son évolution, son influence*; Caradec, *Histoire de la littérature enfantine en France*.

51. Unfortunately I have found no extant issues after 1901, although the notation "Ill. Nat." appears in MS II until 1904, and the magazine continued to be published until 1921.

52. See Roberts-Jones, "La Satire des moeurs," in *De Daumier à Lautrec*, 61–68.

53. The definitive work on the subject is by David Kunzle, *History of the Comic Strip, Volume 1: The Early Comic Strip, 1450–1825*. I follow the four conditions he set as defining the comic strip: a graphic work characterized by (1) a sequence of separate images; (2) a preponderance of image over text; (3) intended for mass-media reproduction; (4) telling a moral or topical story.

54. For example, Grandville, *Les Petites Misères de la vie humaine*, 73.

55. Cohl, "Comment c'est formée une collection de timbres-poste."

56. Colibri [Emile Cohl], *La Clé des jeux d'esprit*.

57. The caricatures were of Georges Clemenceau, Clément Fallières, Général Picquart, King Edouard VII, Guillaume Briand, Henri-Charles Dujardin-Beaumetz, Adolphe Brisson, King Léopold II, Alphonse [Alfonso XIII], Emperor François [Franz] Joseph, François Combes, Théophile Delcassé, Lépine, Caran d'Ache, Willette, Charles Léandre, Dranem, and "un Ami" (advertisement in *Nos Loisirs*, CCC).

CHAPTER THREE

1. Deslandes and Richard, *Histoire comparée du cinéma*, vol. 2, 21.
2. Deslandes, *Le Boulevard du cinéma à l'époque de Georges Méliès*, takes the reader on a walking tour of early cinema Paris exhibition sites.
3. René Brest and André Courtet, "Il y a 20 ans, l'inventeur du dessin animé mourait à l'hôpital," *Les Nouvelles Littéraires*, February 13, 1958. Also, manuscript in Cinémathèque Française collection.
4. F. Ambrière, "A l'aube du cinéma: les souvenirs de Robert Péguy," *L'Image* no. 32, 1932.
5. Théophile Pathé, *Le Cinéma*, 151.
6. Cohl, "Oui, je suis le père du dessin animé," *Paris-Soir*, September 15, 1934. Brest, "Il y a 20 ans," gave the date of 1904.
7. Lo Duca, *Le Dessin animé*, 16.
8. Mitry, *Histoire du cinéma*, vol. 1, 156.
9. Jean-Georges Auriol, "Les Premiers Dessins animés cinématographiques; Emile Cohl," *La Revue du cinéma*, January 1930, 12–19; Sadoul, *Histoire générale du cinéma*, vol. 2, 455; Marie-Thérèse Poncet, *Dessin animé; art mondial*, 169–173.
10. Auriol, "Les Premiers Dessins animés."
11. L.-R. Dauven, "En visite chez M. Emile Cohl qui inventa les dessins animés," *Pour Vous*, August 1933.
12. J.-P. Liasu, "Comment un plagiat permit à Emile Cohl d'inventer chez Gaumont les dessins animés," *Comoedia*, January 24, 1936.
13. René Jeanne, *Cinéma 1900*, 203. Also in Jeanne and Charles Ford, "Emile Cohl et le dessin animé," in *Histoire encyclopédique du cinéma, vol. I. le Cinéma français, 1895–1929*, 133–139.
14. Carnet I.
15. *L'Argus Phono-Cinéma*, July 4, 1908.
16. Arnaud, unpublished account books containing shooting schedules and personal appointments, Deslandes collection.
17. MS II.
18. Auriol, "Les Premiers Dessins animés cinématographiques: Emile Cohl," 12.
19. This does not preclude the existence of such a film; the Gaumont records prior to 1907 are very incomplete.
20. Alice Guy, *Autobiographie d'une pionnière du cinéma*, 77–78. The Gaumont film has been restored by the Archives du Film and was screened at the 1984 Perpignan conference.
21. *La Tomate*, 1903; *Le Soleil*, 1904; *La Revue mondiale*, 1904–1905. See Francis Lacassin, *Louis Feuillade*.
22. Deslandes suggested in a conversation that Arnaud and Cohl were acquainted before the caricaturist came to Gaumont. This may well be true, but I have found no documentation. For a sample poem by Arnaud, see *Le Sourire*, December 21, 1901. It shared the page with one by another unknown, Max Jacob, who within a few years would become the foremost "Cubist" poet.
23. For additional sources and discussion, see Richard Abel, "1907–1914: Before the Canon," in *French Film Theory and Criticism, 1907–1929*; Abel, "Yhcam Discoursing on the Cinema: France, 1912," *Framework* 32/33, 1986, 150–170; Abel, "The Contribution of the French Literary Avant-Garde Poets to Film Theory and Criticism (1907–1924)," *Cinema Journal* 14, 3, Spring 1975, 18–40. For treatments of a slightly later period, see Stuart Liebman, "French Film Theory, 1910–1921," *Quarterly Review of Film Studies* VIII, 1, Winter 1983, 1–24; Abel, "On the Threshold of French Film Theory and Criticism, 1915–1919," *Cinema Journal* XXV, 1, Fall 1985, 12–33. For equivalent German texts, Anton Kaes, *Kino-Debatte, Texte Zum Verhältnis von Literatur und Film, 1909–1929*. For a different approach, a survey of the output of one studio, see Emmanuelle Toulet, "Une année de l'édition cinématographique Pathé: 1909," in Pierre Guibbert (ed.), *Les Premiers Ans du cinéma français*, 133–142.
24. For the Charity Bazaar fire, see José Baldizzone, "L'Incendie du Bazar de la Charité," *Archives* 12, March 1988; Deslandes and Richard, *Histoire comparée du cinéma*, vol. 2, 22–28. For a typical popular contemporaneous account, see "La Catastrophe," *L'Illustré Soleil du Dimanche*, May 16, 1897.
25. "Because of the variety of the spectacle, the extremely moderate price and the minimum intellectual effort that it demands of the public, for an immense popular crowd the cinema has replaced the theater much as, for many, the newspaper has killed the book. For the people, who remain fixed in a childish state, the cinema offers an album of images to flip through and evokes historical facts for them in an eloquent form. It initiates them into elegant and worldly milieux where they would not otherwise penetrate, and shows them the shimmering luminous truth of exotic countrysides that their imagination could never conceive" (*Le Dimanche Illustré*, 1908, quoted in Marcel Lapierre, *Les Cents visages du cinéma*, 80).
26. Mitry, *Histoire du cinéma*, vol. 1, 158.
27. "It suffices to state that every day sees the opening of a new cinema.

"In Paris today there is scarcely a theater, a music hall, or a café-concert which does not have its own cinematograph.

"The fashion is to utilize the unused days and times to give a single show of a few hours to which the public is admitted for a price varying from 25 centimes to two francs.

"We note that newspaper offices, department stores, restaurants, circuses, etc., etc. also have their cinematographs, offered free to their regular clientele.

"Let us not forget the cinematograph-advertisements installed every few steps in the streets and public places. Thus we count more than 100 continually functioning cinemas in Paris, grossing, according to figures checked by the Public Assistance office, up to 100,000 francs a day.

"100,000 francs a day, in other words, a receipt equal to all the principal theaters of Paris" (François Valleiry, "Les Cinématographes," *PCG*, April 1, 1907).

28. Georges-Michel Coissac, *Le Fascinateur*, October 1908. There were even statements entered into legal evidence that testified to the spread of cinema. A lawyer in 1908 began his plea: "The tribunal knows of the truly extraordinary vogue during the past years of cinematographic representations" (Maître Signorino, *Les Cinématographes et les droits d'auteur*, 1).

29. "The cinematograph, the odious, intolerable cinematograph, is in the process of turning into, like an appendicitis, the national malady. . . .

"Born of the traveling carnivals where the crowds jostle, then came the introduction of the projector to the theater, certain second rank music halls having found it advantageous to spice up a malingering program with a few hectometers of film. A famous industrialist added to his furniture gallery a pompous screening room for showing animated scenes. Finally advertisers seized upon this facile and vulgar way of stopping in their tracks three hundred boobies who, with noses in the air, learn of the excellence of Archipel wine and Nicolas pastilles between *The Ride of the Cuirassiers* and *The Private and the Nanny*" ("Cinéma-fureur," *Le Cri de Paris*, quoted in *Le Cinéma*, November 10, 1907).

30. "This reputation [of the cinema] must stick to the young ladies who frequent it as though it were a training ground for their dirty tricks. The fair itself is nothing anymore but merry-go-rounds, crêpes and 'cinema,' 'cinema,' crêpes and merry-go-rounds, along the whole kilometer, from Barbès to Clichy" (Léonce Balitrand, *PCG*, August 15, 1908).

31. *PCG*, April 15, 1907.

32. Georges Prud'homme, "Trop de . . . Pathé," *Paris-Moderne*, August 3, 1908. Thanks to Peter Schofer for his translation.

33. Sée explained how long the cinema had attracted him: "For four or five years since the 'Pathés' and the 'Gab-Kas' have conquered Paris boulevard by boulevard, street by street, building by building; since the little nooks and crannies and luxury night spots (where the luxury is plunged into blackness every five minutes) have been multiplied to infinity; since a man that one might mistake for a concierge in uniform has stood in front of almost every doorway directing you with a benevolent braided arm toward the grilled ticket window, then leading you to your seat through a shadowy path; since we have been transported immediately from the everyday banalities of the street to foreign countries and other people; since those happy days when there was not an afternoon when I did not slide myself into a seat as a furtive spectator in one of those theaters in order to appease my appetite for change, my puerile taste for spectacles, and my sedentary passion" (Edmond Sée, "Cinématographes," *PCG*, March 15, 1908).

34. Gustave Babin, "Les Coulisses du cinématographe," *L'Illustration*, March 28, 1908. He continued: "The marvelous spectacle has left the boulevard basement that sheltered its debut to invade the neighboring music hall which overwhelms it with its luxury and fashion, the theater, the circus, and all the fair exhibits. As soon as the curtain drops on a stage, because of lack of success or because it's the vacation season, the luminous screen is installed and fills up the house, with no cancellations."

35. *Catalogue illustré des Grands Magasins Dufayel*, Paris, 1912. One could find there, between 1896 and 1914, "Parisians, provincials and foreigners who came to admire *The Voyage of President Fallières to the Scandinavian Countries, Ali-Baba, [The] Paris-New York [Auto Race]* and a quantity of other views, comic, documentary, and fairy-tale, that captivate the big and little with their charm from 2:00 to 6:00. The musical accompaniment, the richness of the coloring, the lectures, the soloists and choirs, the scrupulous imitation of sounds, and the humoristic acting in diverse tableaux give to this spectacle, where all is in the best taste, a truly artistic character. Cold buffet presented by Potel & Chabot, five o'clock tea, and instrumental concert" (*Comoedia*, August 4, 1908).

36. See Deslandes, "Le Cinéma forain," in *Histoire comparée du cinéma*, vol. 2, 83–243; Sadoul,

"L'Apogée du cinéma forain," in *Histoire générale du cinéma*, vol. 2, 335–346; Jacques Garnier, "Les Cinémas," in *Forains d'hier et d'aujourd'hui*, 318–338.

37. Quoted in *L'Echo de Paris*, June 28, 1908.

38. Robert C. Allen, *Vaudeville and Film, 1895–1915: A Study in Media Interaction*, 161–182; Allen, "Contra the Chaser Theory," *Wide Angle* no. 3, Spring 1979, 4–11; Charles Musser, "Another Look at the 'Chaser Theory,' " *Studies in Visual Communication* 10, 4, Fall 1984, 24–44; Allen, "Looking at 'Another Look at the "Chaser Theory," ' " ibid., 45–50; Musser, "Reply to Allen," ibid., 51.

39. J. B., *L'Orchestre*, July 12, 1907.

40. Louis Scheider, "Les Théâtres à Paris," *L'Etoile belge*, quoted in *PCG*, August 15, 1908.

41. *PCG*, February 15, 1907.

42. "Cinema already occupies a large place in modern spectacle. Little by little it invaded the stage where they tried to banish it under the pretext that it is not 'artistic.' In spite of some pessimists, its progress has been constant. . . . Cinema is entering—and through the front door—our subventioned theaters" (Jack, "Ciné-Chronique," *Filma*, September 1908).

43. The Omnia originally seated about 300 spectators (see *PCG*, January 1, 1907; *Ciné-Journal*, May 16, 1914). The theater was controlled by Pathé's holding company, Omnia, directed by the lawyer Edmond Benoit-Lévy. (For his biography, see Jeanne, *Cinéma 1900*, 97–105.) Only Edison and Pathé films were shown there in 1908. Premium admissions of three francs were charged. After countless remodelings, the Omnia is still in business at the same location.

44. See *Le Cinéma et l'Echo du Cinéma*, February 14, 1913.

45. *PCG*, December 1, 1907; January 1, 1908; *L'Orchestre*, year of 1908; Deslandes, *Le Boulevard du cinéma à l'époque de Georges Méliès*, 84.

46. Indeed it remained the largest cinema in Europe until the 1950s. Since the vast auditorium was too large for film audiences, it was originally partitioned in the center by a 1300-square-meter wall. The films were rear-projected from a special booth attached to the exterior wall. Its nearly unmanageable size led to operating difficulties. In August 1911 it was purchased by Gaumont and became the Gaumont-Palace until it was demolished in 1972. See Sadoul, *Histoire générale du cinéma*, vol. 2, 401; Mitry, *Histoire du cinéma*, vol. 1, 178; Deslandes, "Victorin-Hippolyte Jasset," *L'Avant-Scène du Cinéma* no. 163, November 1975, supplement no. 85, 241–296. See especially p. 259 for photographs of the Hippodrome/Gaumont-Palace in its glory and its ruins.

47. Leon E. Johns, "The Largest Moving Picture Theater," *The Nickelodeon [Motography]*, April 1909, 94–95; "The Year's Business at Paris Hippodrome," *The Nickelodeon*, July 1909.

48. He complained that films ran continuously without separating intervals and that there was no attempt to coordinate musical accompaniment. In New York, he said, 175 theaters charged ten cents for admission (fifty centimes), and 150 charged five cents (G. B., "Exploitation du ciné à New-York," *PCG*, June 1, 1908). See also Russell Merritt, "Nickelodeon Theaters," in Tino Balio, *The American Film Industry* (1st edition), 59–82; David Bowers, *Nickelodeon Theatres*.

49. G. Dureau, "Du Choix d'un programme," *CJ*, October 19, 1909. He echoed a frequent thought that the Golden Age of the exploiters was over: "The time is no more when animated projections had that charming youthful freshness which seduced effortlessly by the miracle of its age. The good crowds no longer have this innocence on which [exhibitors] used to speculate. Audiences have seen a lot, retained a little, discriminate well and exercise criticism. Even the children are harsh, because theirs is an age without pity and also because they have a livelier sense of reality than was believed.

"[Previously . . .] audiences swallowed anything: the guardian of the peace who turned the gas lamp valve the wrong way, and the arrival of the famous train from the suburbs. It was the Golden Age."

Filma also issued a warning: "The public is more and more numerous and faithful and is becoming, it must be recognized, more and more demanding. Justifiably they complain about the bad quality of the images projected in front of them, their acumen improving itself with practice, they do not hesitate to criticize a puerile scenario, poor projection and especially *jittery pictures*" (December 1908).

50. "Scènes de plein air; Scènes à trucs; Sports—acrobatie; Scènes historiques, politiques et d'actualité; Scènes militaires; Scènes grivoises d'un caractère piquant; Danses et ballets; Scènes dramatiques et réalistes; Féeries et Contes; Scènes diverses" (Pathé Frères, *Films et Cinématographes*).

51. *Kinéma*, March 1909.

52. E. V. Lucas, "The Cinematoscope—A Power," *The Optical Lantern and Cinematograph Journal*, June 1906, 94.

53. R. Binet and G. Hausser, *Sociétés de cinémato-*

graphie; études financiers (their exclamation point).

54. For Pathé, see Deslandes, *Histoire comparée du cinéma*, vol. 2, 99–133, 297–321; Charles Pathé, *Mémoires (souvenirs et conseils d'un parvenu)*; Pathé, *De Pathé Frères à Pathé-Cinéma*. According to Kristin Thompson, Pathé set up its New Jersey plant to make American release prints from its French negatives. Actual production of American films did not begin until 1910. See Kristin Thompson, *Exporting Entertainment: America in the World Film Market, 1907–1934*, 2–10, 18. See also Paul Spehr, *The Movies Begin*, 70–74.

55. Binet and Hausser, *Sociétés de cinématographie*.

56. Lux, founded by Pathé's former engineer Henri-Joseph Joly in 1906, was the first company in France incorporated specifically for the manufacture of films. Binet also listed Le Film d'Art (February 1908), Kino-Plak (1908), Cinéma Gloria (October 1908), Le Lion (September 1908), Compagnie Générale de Cinématographes (already bankrupt), Cinématographes Parlantes, and the Animated Photograph (an English firm whose directors had disappeared in October). Méliès was already a minor producer by this time, releasing about 8,000 meters in 1908, mostly to fulfill quotas for his American commitments.

57. According to an apologist, rentals would correct the condition of "too many small cinemas, too many bad programs, too many films worn to a frazzle" (Francis Mair, *PCG*, July 15, 1907).

58. *L'Argus Phono-Cinéma*, March 29, April 4, 1908.

59. "In the year following the coup d'état of the house of the rooster [Pathé], Gaumont has advanced disproportionately, the number of new clients and the quality of the merchandise sold having permitted an amelioration of quality" (*L'Argus Phono-Cinéma*, September 5, 1908). See also *CJ*, February 27, 1910.

60. Thompson, *Exporting Entertainment*, 2–25. Janet Staiger, "Combination and Litigation: Structures of U.S. Film Distribution, 1891–1917," *Cinema Journal* 23, 2, Winter 1984, 41–72.

61. Jeanne Thomas Allen, "Decay of the MPPC," in Balio, *The American Film Industry*, 119–134.

62. Binet and Hausser had stressed, "One fact is undeniable: the present saturation of the French market. There is local overproduction and lately the different producers have tried to form a trust to limit production."

This "European trust" was aborted by the refusal of Pathé to support it. Charles Pathé, only too happy to see his competition suffer, wrote a Machiavellian letter to Méliès: "The remedy will come from the excessiveness of the illness; the doctor can do nothing more. It is the surgeon who must take matters in hand" (Quoted in *PCG*, December 1, 1908; quoted with editorial changes in Sadoul, *Histoire générale du cinéma*, vol. 2, 481; translated in *MPW*, December 19, 1908).

63. "It is easy to turn the crank, especially when it's an electric motor that does the work. They are not as preoccupied with the more fundamental thing, the creation of the scenario.

"The situations which authors can handle, apart from documentaries, travelogues, sociological studies, etc., are not very numerous.

"So there is a veritable steeplechase to find situations susceptible of making an interesting scenario.

"They fall into clichés. With such limited means, the words plagiarism, copying, even theft, spring to mind" (Gédéo, "Chronique," *Phono-Cinéma Revue*, April 1908).

Dantin, a popular journalist, included an amusing parody of film subjects in an article for *La Liberté*: "It seems that the cinematograph is in a slump. After a very short Golden Age—like all Golden Ages—it has seen its success decline with appalling rapidity.

"The entrepreneurs of spectacles believed the public to be more vulgar than it really is, and thinking to satisfy it served up in their darkened rooms the most idiotic buffoonery, the stupidest melos.

"Read a cinema program and you'll only find titles like *My Mother-in-Law's Wig*, *In Love with His Concierge*, *The Charcoal Man's Fiancée*, *I Lost My Pants*, etc. These grotesque farces all end with a wild chase with wet nurses, amputees, gendarmes, etc. They yield the sheet [the screen] only to express-melos in which the countess marries, loses her child, throws herself in the river, is saved by a bearded Savoyard and rediscovers eighteen years later her daughter whom she recognizes by a laundry mark—all in one minute, four and three-fifths seconds" (October 17, 1908).

64. Jack, "Ciné-Chronique," *Filma*, September 1908, 8.

65. Gédéo, *Phono-Cinéma Revue*, April 1908.

66. *L'Orchestre*, June 18–September 6, 1907. Performances were at 2:30 and 9:00; admissions ranged from 50 centimes to 4 francs.

67. *Le Matin*, quoted in *PCG*, March 1, 1908.

68. Gustave Babin, "Films d'Art," *L'Illustration*, October 31, 1908. The advertising for Gaumont's "Théâtro-Film" reveals that objections to trivial subjects had been effective: "The public, currently so impassioned about this art—so interest-

ing—is beginning to tire a bit from the same rather rapid and jostling scenes.

"Today they are asking for a new effort. They want something better. They are more mature and can understand these little plays. They crave those that not only express ideas with such truth, intensity of expression, and justice, but also, without the security of speech, emit real emotions.

"It is from this desire for a more natural, lifelike and artistic cinema that Théâtro-Film was created" (*CJ*, July 4, 1908).

69. "To furnish the repertoire, it was soon necessary to create plays. A Pleiad of writers and dramaturges for the cinematograph was born. Humorists, poets, and romancers looked for the 'play to do.' Some of them paged through the archives and pulled out some 'three-acters' that had been sleeping in theater managers' dusty boxes. In reality, it is an easy genre. It is hardly necessary to have style. It suffices to group some amusing or tragic ideas around a fast action. While this new dramatic art is easy, it is scarcely remunerating. One writes on spec. A good play is worth forty francs. For a successful play the author can get double. But the demands of the public have increased. The frequent customer is becoming difficult. Competition is keen. In Paris there are right now more than a hundred places where a cinematograph functions every night" (Edmond Claris, "Le Théâtre cinématographique," *La Nouvelle Revue*, February 15, 1909).

70. Similar protection was not granted in the United States until the 1911 Supreme Court decision against Kalem for their film of *Ben Hur*.

71. E. Maugras and M. Guegan, *Le Cinématographe devant le droit*; E. Potu, *La Protection internationale des oeuvres cinématographiques, d'après la convention de Berne, revisée en 1908*; Jean Marchais, *Du cinématographe dans ses rapports avec le droit d'auteur*; André Gaudreault, "La Transgression des lois du copyright aux débuts du cinéma: conséquences pratiques et séquelles théoriques," *Film Exchange* no. 28, 1984, 41–49.

72. Francis Lacassin, "Les Fous Rires de la Belle Epoque," in *Pour une contre-histoire du cinéma*, 73–87.

73. *L'Argus Phono-Cinéma*, October 31, 1908, Deslandes, "Victorin-Hippolyte Jasset," 252–263.

74. Charles Ford and René Jeanne, *Le Cinéma et la presse, 1895–1960*.

75. Béranger's hearings took place in May. Meanwhile, a scandalous trial was in progress involving the arrest of several cabaret owners. The press described in lurid detail one case in particular that included nude "lesbian" scenes (*Le Journal*, July 28, 1908, cited in Patrick Waldberg, *Eros, modern style*). The young Colette created a sensation early in her theatrical career when she bared one of her breasts on stage.

The threat of censorship was a constant concern for producers and exhibitors. See Antoine Delecroz, "La Censure," *Le Cinéma*, December 20, 1907.

76. F. Bolen, "Un Historian oublié, G.-M. Coissac," *Ecran*, October 1975, 4–5.

77. *L'Argus Phono-Cinéma*, October 28, 1908. The film was undoubtedly a hoax and had several precedents: *The Speculator* (R. W. Paul, 1898), *Chagrin d'amour* (Zecca, 1898), and *Burlesque Suicide* (Edison, 1902).

78. "What [Parisian children] clamor for above all are stories of outlaws. Ah! When the cinematograph shows them nocturnal burglars and police dogs exercising their duties, what joy in the theater! But why do all the boys take the side of the victims or the heroic police dogs, while the little girls are in favor of the bandits? . . . When the dogs chase the thieves—an admirable scene—the boys cheer on the dogs, the girls encourage the thieves. This presages terrible troubles in the young households of the year 1920. . . . Decidedly, Parisian boys are good boys, but Parisian girls, exquisite elsewhere, are pretty little scoundrels" (J. Ernest Charles, "Psychologie cinématographique," *Gil-Blas*, March 20, 1908).

79. Maxime Leproust, "Le Théâtre cinématographique," *PCG*, January 1, 1907.

80. "Such is the power of illusion that a photograph projected on a screen can move our emotions as well as reality can. Not only does the cinematograph give a very sufficient and inexpensive reproduction of organized spectacles, it reproduces, and this time under even better conditions, great outdoor spectacles, whether natural, such as landscapes, or artificial, such as a hippopotamus hunt—posed certainly, but posed on the banks of the Upper Nile with the natives and the beasts in the environment in which they evolved" (Rémy de Gourmont, "Cinématographe," *Mercure de France*, September 1907).

81. "The beauty of the theater, the art of the theater, is in its impression of creating its own life every night *for that very night!* . . . . but the nervous anticipation is (I dare say) immobilized, once and for all, by cinematographic scenes. And the nonchalant deposit of actors' voices into a phonograph and their gestures of one single evening, fixed, then raised from the dead every evening, cast upon a sheet. . . . What a shame! What sadness.

And what an accusation!" (Edmond Sée, *PCG*, March 15, 1908).

82. Gédéo, *Phono-Cinéma Revue*, April 1908. This quote would have been appreciated by André Bazin, who argued that early cineastes saw the moving image with a "mummy complex," that is, with the powers to preserve a life-in-death likeness. See his "Ontology of the Photographic Image," in *What is Cinema*, vol. 1, 9–16. The complex also existed with regard to the phonograph. For a good example of the exploitation of the preservative powers of the phono, see Charles Musser and Carol Nelson, *Lyman Howe*, forthcoming.

83. One early description noted that moving-picture scenes "succeed each other in a vertiginous series with one giddy vision after another. In a few minutes, America and Asia surge up and dissipate. One passes by chasms. One floats along immense rivers and the countryside goes by with such speed that the whole audience is taken with the illusion, evoked by a powerful and invisible machine, of feeling really carried away, of being swept along across countries" (Anon., "Les Trucs du cinématographe," *Lectures pour Tous*, June 1908).

84. Claretie, "La Vie à Paris," *Le Temps*, September 10, 1908.

85. "It's a passion; it's crazy! And everyone, young and old, parents and children, are taken by it. The theater, the circus, the revue—superannuated pleasures! Now we have better. With dinner scarcely over, we quickly drop into some darkened room where a beam of electric light strikes a large white screen" (Anon., "Les Trucs du cinématographe").

86. Henri Agel, *Esthétique du cinéma*; Liebman, "French Film Theory, 1910–1921"; David Bordwell, *French Impressionist Cinema: Film Culture, Film Theory, Film Style*.

87. Valleiry, "Les Cinématographes," *PCG*, April 1, 1907. René Doumic, who published an essay in *La Revue des Deux Mondes* in 1913, has usually been credited as the first to proclaim the "Age of Cinema."

88. Babin, "Les Coulisses du cinématographe."

89. Jeanine Warnod, *Le Bateau-Lavoir*.

90. André Salmon, *Souvenirs sans fin; l'air de la Butte*, 22–23; see also his *Souvenirs san fin; deuxième époque*, 88–89. Jacob's passion was genuine. Later he wrote poems about the cinema that experimented with "cinematic" form and content. (See Standish Lawder, *The Cubist Cinema*, note 29, p. 248.)

In 1914 Jacob formed the Society of Friends of Fantomas with Picasso, Apollinaire, and Maurice Raynal. Raynal, who was writing some of the first independent film reviews ever in Apollinaire's magazine, described the club in *Les Soirées de Paris*, July–August 1914. See also Robert Rosenblum, "Picasso and the Typography of Cubism," in *Picasso in Retrospect*, 49–76.

91. Lawder, *The Cubist Cinema*.

92. Henri Bergson, *L'Evolution créatrice*, was published in 1907 and within a year had gone into five editions. For a brief chronological account, see Gilles Deleuze, *Cinéma 1: L'Image-Mouvement*, 9–22, 83–89. As Deleuze notes, Bergson's original formulation was a notion derived from the classical philosophical paradigm of Xeno's Paradox.

93. Michel Georges-Michel, "Henri Bergson nous parle du cinéma," *Le Journal*, February 20, 1914. Bergson continued, "The cinematograph has been able to set painters back on the right track. You know what a revolution in painting was caused by instantaneous photography. At the time of that discovery artists noticed the attitudes of running horses and saw that the way they had been represented was not exact. They rectified that with this result: inspired by the positions caught by surprise on instantaneous photographs, the artists could then only create figures that were usually stiff, lifeless. Mathematical exactitude won, certainly. But the impression of truth was lost. The cinematograph is teaching painters that photography was wrong. In reproducing a movement according to his personal impression, the artist has blended several successive views into just one, giving the illusion of life and therefore of movement. He will find these positions again on the screen."

Bergson noted with pleasure that Auguste Rodin was making sculptural models based on phases of motion, that César Franck was using the cinema to demonstrate the playing of the cello to his students, and he speculated that actors could improve their performance by studying cinematographic recordings. He concluded, "[T]he cinematograph, while amusing the crowds, is seriously helping, and will help, the intellectual, the artist, the historian and even the philosopher."

94. Marianne W. Martin, *Futurist Art and Theory, 1909–1915*; Marjorie Perloff, *The Futurist Moment: Avant-Garde, Avant Guerre, and the Language of Rapture*; R. W. Flint (ed.), *F. W. Marinetti: Selected Writings*; Umbro Apollonio (ed.), *Futurist Manifestos*; Michael Kirby, *Futurist Performance*; Paul Hammond, "Kostrowitzky's Kinema," *Afterimage* no. 10, Autumn 1981, 56–69.

95. Gaston Modot, quoted in Lacassin and Raymond

Bellour, "Du burlesque au surréalisme," in *Pour une contre-histoire du cinéma*, 170–171.

96. Fernande Olivier, *Picasso et ses amis*, 99.

CHAPTER FOUR

1. *Kinematograph and Lantern Weekly*, October 15, 1908.

2. George Kleine, unpublished manuscript, December 17, 1909, Library of Congress, Manuscripts Division, Kleine archives, Box 24.

3. Jasset, for example, was allegedly fired for excessive interest in the female members of the Gaumont staff (Deslandes, "Victorin-Hippolyte Jasset," 249).

4. Henri Fescourt, *La Foi et les montagnes, ou le septième art au passé*, 79.

5. *See*, for example, Ambrière, "A l'aube du cinéma: les souvenirs de Camille de Morlhon," *L'Image* no. 11, 1932, 23–26. This statement may be a reference to the Dreyfus case.

6. Fescourt, *La Foi et les montagnes*, 73.

7. *L'Argus Phono-Cinéma*, August 29, 1908. The Museum of Modern Art print was formerly attributed to Emile Cohl.

8. The scenario, usually attributed to Feuillade, was claimed by Robert Péguy to be his first one: "It was called, I believe, *The Police as Caricature Shows Them, and as They Are*. [Feuillade] had me paid royally—twenty-five francs!" (Ambrière, "A l'aube du cinéma: les souvenirs de Robert Péguy").

9. *L'Argus Phono-Cinéma*, February 15, 1908.

10. Lacassin erroneously attributes the scenario to Feuillade and dates it 1906. It was probably directed by Bosetti.

11. Feuillade, interviewed by Robert Florey, 1921, quoted in Lacassin, "Louis Feuillade," *Pour une contre-histoire du cinéma*, 30.

12. Even Robert Nelson's 1965 avant-garde film *O Dem Watermelons* was based on similar gags. Surrealist poet Robert Desnos wrote: "The generation that coincided with the age of cinema opened its eyes to see whole villages madly pursuing pumpkins and laughed at the gags of the little chimney sweep and the cook's boy" (*Paris-Journal*, April 13, 1923).

13. Victorin Jasset, "Etude sur la mise en scène," *CJ*, October 28, 1911.

14. Benjamin Carré, unpublished autobiographical manuscript.

15. J. Douglas Gomery, *The Coming of Sound to the American Cinema: The Transformation of an Industry*; Harry Geduld, *The Birth of the Talkies*.

16. *PCG*, May 1, 1907.

17. Léon Gaumont, "Comment ai-je été amené m'oc-cuper du film parlant," preface to P. Hemardin-guer, *Le Cinématographe sonore*. See also F. Honoré, "Le Cinématographe parlant," *L'Illustration*, December 31, 1910, 502–503; Anon., "Les Jouets transformés par la science," *Lectures pour Tous*, December 1906, supplement.

18. According to a 1908 Edison survey, summarized by Kristin Thompson (*Exporting Entertainment*, 12), Pathé films constituted 34.2 percent of films screened at selected New York and New Jersey theaters. The closest competitor was Vitagraph, with 15.9 percent.

19. Lacassin, "Le Cinéma selon Léon Gaumont à travers ses lettres à Feuillade," in *Pour une contre-histoire du cinéma*, 55–71.

20. Quoted in *CJ*, October 27, 1908.

21. Lacassin, "Alice Guy," in *Pour une contre-histoire du cinéma*, 19. The film is also known as *Le Coup de vent* and *Le Chapeau*.

22. Carré, autobiographical manuscript, 103.

23. Arnaud Carnet, Deslandes collection.

24. There is no confirmation of a list of "trick films realized in collaboration with Emile Cohl" that Jean Mitry published in "Feuillade," in his *Filmographie universelle*.

25. Katherine S. Kovács, "Georges Méliès and the *Féerie*," *Cinema Journal* 16, 1, Fall 1976, 1–13.

26. *MPW*, August 21, 1909. Other pageants include cat. nos. 21, 35, 46, 68, and 71.

27. This film is known to be Cohl's because notes and a list of the characters appearing in it are found in Carnet I.

28. Gaumont, letter to Feuillade, February 17, 1909, in Lacassin, "Le Cinéma selon Léon Gaumont."

29. Carré, unpublished autobiographical manuscript, 106–107.

30. Gaumont, *Le Petit Parisien*, clipping ca. 1943, Rondel collection, Bibliothèque de l'Arsenal.

31. Dauven, "En visite chez M. Emile Cohl qui inventa les dessins animés."

32. Cohl, "Les Dessins animés," *Echo de Paris*, March 2, 1923.

33. Cohl, "Les Dessins animés et à trucs, causerie faite au Ciné-Club le 12 juin, 1920," *Journal du Ciné-Club*, CCC.

34. Emile Reynaud, French patent no. 194.482, December 1, 1888, quoted in Deslandes, *Histoire comparée du cinéma*, vol. 1, 285.

35. J.-B. de Tronquières, "Dessins animés," *Larousse Mensuel*, August 1925, 861–864.

97. *Journal du Soir*, August 20, 1908.

98. Lacassin, "Les Fous Rires de la Belle Epoque."

99. Salmon, *Souvenirs sans fin: l'air de la Butte*.

36. Entitled *Gamineries* and *Premier cigar*, CCC. Facsimiles are available from the Cinémathèque Québécoise. The little boy in the pictures is André Courtet, which would date the flip books around 1909–1910.

37. Cohl, "Oui, je suis le père du dessin animé."

38. Dauven, "En visite chez Emile Cohl."

39. *PCG*, February 15, April 15, 1907.

40. At this point it might be useful to offer some definitions to which we shall adhere for the remainder of the discussion. *Animation* is the broadest term referring to the technique of photographing by single-frame exposures with the intention of producing a synthetic movement on the screen (although perceptually there is no distinction between animated movement and ordinary movement). The term also refers to the class of all films made by the technique.

When making such a film, the filmmaker must manipulate the subject (objects, drawings, etc.), distinguishing animation from time-lapse or slow-motion cinematography, which condenses or attenuates a natural motion. In creating the synthesized illusion of motion, the degree of change between frames must conform to the limits of the "*phi*-phenomenon." This is a complicated formula that means, put simply, that if the object's position changes too much, the illusion of movement will be lost. (Those interested in a technical discussion may refer to Mitry's *Esthétique et psychologie du cinéma*, vol. 1, 313–416.)

An *animated film* is any one that was made predominantly by using the technique of animation. Sometimes more specialized kinds are distinguished according to the kinds of subjects (puppets, clay, drawings) or the techniques used (cels, cutouts, computer, etc.).

Animated Cartoon, like the French *dessin animé*, usually refers only to films made by the technique of drawing animation, but also has a generic connotation, implying adherence to certain evolved norms of length, characterization, representation of space, etc.

41. Frederick A. Talbot, *Moving Pictures: How They Are Made*, 242.

42. *L'Orchestre*, daily issues, July 1907.

43. *Le Fascinateur*, February 1908.

44. Babin, "Les Coulisses du cinématographe," *L'Illustration*, April 4, 1908. Babin's description of the film was colorful: "All amateurs and habitués of the cinema who know its repertoire have seen those mysterious scenes I mean: a table loaded with food which is consumed, no one knows how, by some invisible being, something like the Spirit of the Ancestors for which Victor Hugo, in his Guernsey gatherings, reserved an empty seat. A bottle pours its own wine into a glass, a knife hurls itself onto a loaf of bread, then slices into a sausage; a wicker basket weaving itself; tools performing their work without the cooperation of any artisan. So many strange marvels that one could see every night for several months. And even tipped off as I was, and as my readers are, I still could not find the last word of the riddle."

45. Ibid.

46. Jon Gartenberg, "Vitagraph Before Griffith: Forging Ahead in the Nickelodeon Era," *Studies in Visual Communication* 10, 4, Fall 1984, 22. The film was screened at the 1984 festival in Perpignan, France. In *Before Mickey* I mistakenly attributed the film to Arnaud and Thiberville because of the *L'Illustration* article, incautiously ignoring the lack of any supporting documentation.

47. Arnaud and Boisyvon, *Le Cinéma pour tous*, 73.

48. "At the same time as these fantasies of the fairy sort, of which Méliès was one of the first and best directors, one also could see films that animated inert objects: A table set for a meal, but the guests gave us the pleasure of not showing up, permitting us to be diverted by the dishes, the napkins, the glasses, the bottles, the bread, and the food which garnished everything and became turbulent actors. The knife and the fork suddenly threw themselves on the chicken, cutting off effortlessly a slice of thigh, taking it to the plate without a dinner guest and there cutting it up. Then without losing time, the knife sliced some bread which, well bred, placed itself to the left of the plate. The napkin left the ring that imprisoned it and unfolded briskly, as the wine bottle all by itself poured a bumper into the glass which was repulsing with horror the attentions of the coffee pot. . . .

"These little scenes were very successful in their day, intriguing then and still strongly intriguing the spectators who, having ascertained the effects, would love to know the causes" (de Tronquières, "Dessins animés").

49. Guy, *Autobiographie d'une pionnière du cinéma*, 66.

50. "Blackton Sketches," *The Phonoscope*, November 1896, cited by Charles Musser, "American Vitagraph: 1897–1901," *Cinema Journal* 22, 3, Spring 1983, 8. The circumstances of Blackton's meeting with Edison have been clarified for the first time by Musser in this article. Blackton sketched Edison from a photograph, not from life. He may have used the "blue pencil trick," preparing his sheet first in blue, which would not register on orthochromatic film, then retracing it in ink or charcoal for the filming. More details on the

lightning sketch act are available in *Before Mickey*, 48–57.

51. *The Enchanted Drawing* was probably photographed in the fall of 1900 (most likely in October) at the Vitagraph "studio" at 116 Nassau Street. Litigation between the Vitagraph partners and Edison had been resolved (for the time being) by an agreement reached in September 1900. Smith and Blackton proceeded to make several short films, including their "Hooligan" series, some views of the Galveston hurricane damage, and some comedies. Edison then copyrighted these latter Vitagraph films, including *The Enchanted Drawing*. Blackton was still performing and, we can guess, intended to use the film as part of his stage act.

52. Close inspection of Blackton's films shows that splicing was often used to refine the timing of the substitutions.

53. Paul Hammond, *Marvelous Méliès*, 134–135; John Frazer, *Artificially Arranged Scenes: The Films of Georges Méliès*, 60. Albert Smith recalled that it was during the filming of a stop-action scene ruined by clouds of steam in the background that the idea of animation arose (*Two Reels and a Crank*, 51). Of course it is possible that Blackton and Smith, and the Europeans, could have discovered the technique independently.

54. *A Visit to The Spiritualist*: "This is acknowledged by exhibitors to be the funniest of all moving magical films. A countryman is seen entering the office of the spiritualist and paying his fee. He is then mesmerized and sees funny things. He drops his handkerchief on the floor and as he reaches for it, it gradually grows larger and larger, dancing up and down, and going through funny antics until before the eye of the spectator it turns into a ghost of enormous proportions. It then vanishes and as the countryman is in the act of sitting in the chair, the ghost suddenly appears and the countryman receives a great fright. He then jumps up and throws off his hat and coat, and they immediately fly back on his body. He repeatedly throws them off and they as often return. The scene finally closes by numerous shots and hobgoblins appearing and disappearing before the eyes of the frightened countryman, who finally leaves the room in great haste. 100 ft" (Edison Manufacturing Company, *Catalogue No. 94 Edison Films*, 40–41, cited in Musser, "American Vitagraph: 1897–1901," 27). The film is included in the American Federation of the Arts 1986 program, *Before Hollywood*.

55. This remake may be the one now in circulation; it may or may not be by Blackton and Smith.

56. Smith and Koury, *Two Reels and a Crank*, 51.

57. Musser, "American Vitagraph: 1897–1901," 39. The following films have been attributed tentatively to Vitagraph by Musser (p. 32): *An Animated Luncheon* (copyrighted by Edison, February 28, 1900); *Uncle Josh in a Spooky Hotel* (March 21, 1900); *Uncle Josh's Nightmare* (March 21, 1900).

58. Gartenberg, "Vitagraph Before Griffith," 7–23. I have relied on his 1905–1907 filmography.

59. Kristin Thompson, *Exporting Entertainment*, 5–6. I am grateful to Thompson, Charles Musser, and Patrick Loughney for their opinions regarding my hypothesis. I am also grateful to Barry Salt, who, in a 1988 conversation, expressed strong reservations about the dating of the Melbourne-Cooper films mentioned. Obviously this is an area for further research.

60. *MPW*, March 16, 1907.

61. "The true single-frame animation technique was applied to a series of drawings by J. Stuart Blackton in 1906 to produce the first true filmed animated motion pictures in *Humorous Phases of Funny Faces*, and it was only after this that single frame animation technique was used in European films. Claims that this happened earlier appear to be bogus" (Barry Salt, *Film Style and Technology: History and Analysis*, 72).

62. Another hypothesis is that Smith did not remember the correct title of his film. It is possible that he was recalling the animated circus toy sequence in *A Midwinter Night's Dream* (1906).

63. *Edison Films*, no. 288, July 1906 (cumulative), 35, for *How Jones Lost His Roll*; 37, for *The Whole Damm Family*. . . . I have followed the catalogue spelling. On the print the title is *"Dam."*

64. *Optical Lantern and Cinematograph Journal*, September 1906, 109.

65. *Views and Films Index* 1, 10, June 30, 1906, cited in Anthony Slide, *Selected Early Film Criticism: 1896–1911*, 51.

66. The animation itself is quite smooth, but the sequence is flawed. The lighting is darker than the rest of the film. Presumably this is because artificial light had to be used (to avoid flicker), while the rest of the film was shot in a mixture of artificial and natural light. Also, the scene is slightly out of focus—the only time this is known to have occurred in Blackton's animated work.

67. An additional 1907 Vitagraph film using animation, *Bobby's Daydream*, has been cited by Russell Merritt in "Dream Visions in Pre-Hollywood Film," 69, but I have not been able to document this film's release.

68. I am grateful to Kristin Thompson for bringing

the latter film to my attention. It was screened at the Pordenone Festival in 1987.

69. *Optical Lantern and Cinematograph Journal*, March 15, 1906, 62.

70. Gartenberg, "Vitagraph Before Griffith," 12.

71. Carlos Fernández Cuenca, *Segundo de Chomón, Maestro de la fantasía y de la técnica (1871–1929)*. I am grateful to Donna D. Clarke for her translation. Juan-Gabriel Tharrats produced a 98-minute documentary film in 1979 entitled *Cinematografo 1900: Homenaje a Segundo de Chomón*. His book *Los 500 films de Segundo de Chomón* appeared as this book was going to press.

72. *MPW*, December 19, December 26, 1908. The film, which survives, was called *Electric Hotel* and was 476 feet in length.

73. Henri Langlois, "Notes sur l'histoire du cinéma," *La Revue du Cinéma*, July 1948, 2–15. Jean Mitry attributes the film to Gaston Velle and dates it 1904. It appears for the first time in the Pathé catalogue for 1906. Carlo Montanaro has pointed out that two quite different versions of *Le Théâtre du Petit Bob* are in circulation, and that there are problems in dating. The version illustrated in *Before Mickey* (p. 22) was taken from the 1907 edition of *Pathé Frères; Films et Cinématographes*, p. 56. The title was given as *Le Théâtre de Bob* (Pathé cat. no. 1356), and the length as 105 meters. It was listed as *Le Théâtre du petit Bob* in *Phono-Ciné-Gazette* on April 1, 1906. The story synopsis indicates that the film began with Bob receiving the gift of a theater with "the latest playthings" from his father. This description corresponds to *El Teatro del pequeño Bob*, the version Montanaro recovered in Argentina, with 16 shots and excellent object animation. The second film is another export version with English titles: *Bob's Electric Theater*. It contains only 8 shots. (It is this version that is illustrated here as fig. 152.) Montanaro attempts to date this version by an ingenious formal comparison between the two prints, and leans toward a pre-1906 release. However, he wisely concludes, "These deductions could go on forever. The ball is now in the court of our colleague scholars" ("The Strange Case of *Le Theatre du Petit Bob*," *Griffithiana* 32–33, September 1988, 278–280).

74. *PCG*, April 15, 1908. The story tells of a man and his wife who are moving to a new home with the aid of a new electric invention. When the switch is thrown, "everything in the place starts to move, and soon the house is entirely dismantled, and we see all the furniture filing out of the house and along the street like living objects" ("Magnetic Removal," *MPW*, June 27, 1908, 672 feet).

75. For a detailed Chomón filmography, see Tharrats, *Los 500 films de Segundo de Chomón*, 55–292.

76. A preliminary list of Booth's films could be gleaned from Denis Gifford's *British Film Catalogue, 1895–1970*.

77. "No. 1818: *Hand of the Artist*: A world-favored 'trick' subject. Life-like portrait sketches produced by the Hand; a coster and his 'Donah' magically come to life, embrace and dance in a cakewalk. Other surprising effects follow in rapid succession, the Hand of the Artist repeatedly producing new wonders. After each subject plays its part, the Hand crumples up the paper and disperses it in the form of confetti" (*Charles Urban Trading Company Catalogue*, 1909). The film was released in the United States on April 6, 1907.

78. *Comedy Cartoons* (April 1907) and *The Haunted Bedroom* (July 1907) capitalized on Blackton's successes.

79. "No. 2060: *The Sorcerer's Scissors*: By the Hand of the Artist. Amusing, amazing and entrancing magic. By reason of its beauty and the grace and fascination of the beings created by the scissors, which come to life and skillfully perform, this film will enchant audiences of every class" (*Charles Urban Trading Company Catalogue*, 1909).

80. *Biograph Bulletin* no. 99, May 23, 1907.

81. *Biograph Bulletin* no. 100, June 8, 1907. Since the film is not known to exist, the use of animation has not yet been confirmed.

82. *Biograph Bulletin* no. 105, August 31, 1907.

83. Anon., "Les Trucs du cinématographe," *Lectures pour tous*, June 1908.

84. Gaumont's claim to priority was probably based on a section of the patent describing the photography of these movements: "To photograph these successive movements which take place on the map, I am supposing that the map is in place horizontally, that a cinematograph is fixed to the ceiling with the lens directed toward the map. Naturally the cinematograph will not pass the film with the usual camera speed, taking only a few images per second in order to permit the displacement by hand magnets which act on the silhouettes cut from soft iron. After the negative has been printed in the usual way to obtain the positives, these are then shown on the projecting cinematograph at a speed suitable for showing the action happening rapidly, without interruption, in such manner that the spectators will have in a projection of short duration the illusion of all the events and movements of several successive hours and even of a whole day."

Gaumont apparently intended to film at a variable camera speed in order to speed up the motions of his "battle." Elsewhere, when he uses the phrase "photographier successivement," he is referring to successive troop movements and not to frame-by-frame exposures. Admittedly, the terminology is suggestive, but Gaumont would have to wait until Cohl made *La Bataille d'Austerlitz* (cat. 30) to see his idea realized using animation.

85. Crafton, *Before Mickey*, 28–33.
86. *Edison Films* no. 288, July 1906 (cumulative), 35.
87. *MPW*, March 16, 1907.
88. *Optical Lantern and Kinematograph Journal*, February 15, 1907, 100; March 15, 1907, 122.
89. Richard de Cordova's comments on the star system ca. 1910 may apply to animation a decade earlier: "What has undoubtedly misled many historians is that this knowledge [of picture personalities] emerged in an explicitly secretive context. The 'truth' of the human labor involved in film was constituted as a secret, one whose discovery would be all the more pleasurable since it would emerge out of ostensible attempts to conceal it" ("The Emergence of the Star System in America," *Wide Angle* 6, 4, 1985, 4–13). See related discussions on the introduction of new technology in Peter Baxter, "On the History and Ideology of Film Lighting," *Screen* 16, 3, Autumn 1975, 83–106; Patrick L. Ogle, "Technological and Aesthetic Influences upon the Development of Deep Focus Cinematography in the United States," *Screen Reader 1*, 1977, 81–108; Peter Wollen, "Cinema and Technology: A Historical Overview," in his *Readings and Writings: Semiotic Counter-Strategies*, 169–177.
90. Jasset, "Etude sur la mise en scène."
91. According to Russell Merritt, "[F]or *A Mid-Winter's Night Dream* . . . Blackton and Smith prepared a press release that exposed the secrets of the special effects photography that animates the teddy bear, monkey, and tabletop toys" ("Dream Visions in Pre-Hollywood Film," in Leyda et al. [eds.], *Before Hollywood*, 69).
92. "Stop Camera Tricks," *Kinematograph and Lantern Weekly*, April 30, 1908.
93. *Kinematograph and Lantern Weekly*, June 11, 1908.
94. L. Gardette, "Some Tricks of the Moving Picture Maker," *The Nickelodeon* 2, 2, 53. See also the anonymous article "Trick Pictures" in the same issue, p. 37.
95. Smith and Koury, *Two Reels and a Crank*, 26.
96. Star-Film cat. nos. 37, 57, 61, and 73.
97. "The artist is presented, with his board, his only appearance. The hand rapidly outlines a human head, into the chalky jaws of which it inserts a cigarette. The chalk head smokes, and finally eats, the cigarette. The head of a woman is drawn, which gradually fills and becomes undoubtedly human. Eyes of feminine longing are turned in the direction of a chalk-outline teapot, which materializes into the real thing, from the spout of which the woman's head drinks with satisfaction. The woman's head resumes its chalky outline, and disappears, feature by feature.

"The hand of the artist cuts out of paper the figure of a clown. This is placed inside a magic ring drawn on the blackboard. The paper clown changes into a real embodied Pierrot, who dances, juggles with hoops, and finally dissolves by a rapid pinwheel movement into a vivacious head.

"Head (life-size) of the Pierrot. Smoke is seen to issue from the mouth, and comical facial expressions are produced. Again the wheel movement and the clown disappears. The head of a man is now drawn in chalk. This gradually assumes life and gesticulates in a marvelous manner. The head is seen to split from the crown to chin, the halves fall apart as if hinged, and from the eyes are drawn numberless yards of fine tape.

"From the inside the two halves of the head are produced champagne and liqueur in bottles, cigars, cigarettes and glasses. The halves of the head are rejoined, life and comic gesticulations again occur, and the hand of the artist wipes the whole from the blackboard, section by section, though muscular action remains even in the last portion left—one eye—which winks at the audience in an impudent manner before being finally wiped out" (*MPW*, June 22, 1907. Other reviews indicate that Booth's sketches were transformed into faces by means of dissolves. See *Optical Lantern and Kinematograph Journal*, April 15, 1907).
98. "These unusually vivid, engrossing and comic pictures are rapidly drawn upon post cards without apparent human agency. The pencil moves mysteriously and a penknife sharpens the point in full view of the audience, no hand controlling either instrument" (*Charles Urban Trading Company Catalogue*, 1909).
99. Léon Poirier, who was secretary at the Gymnase in 1907 and 1908, recalled some film installations and dated them around July 16, 1908: "I had to stay in Paris for 48 hours at the Gymnase to supervise the technicians of Gaumont, the cinematograph king, with his new invention the talking cinematograph which he named the Chronophone, to whom we had rented the theater for the summer season (to the great scandal of Gavault, Bernstein, Bataille and the rest). Orchestra seats at twenty sous. If it hadn't been an oven, it would have been a revolution" (*A la recherche d'autre chose*, 68. See also his *24 Images à la seconde*, 18–32). It is possible that Poirier was mistaken about the date.

100. Louis Scheider, "Les Théâtres à Paris."
101. *L'Argus Phono-Cinéma*, September 19, 1908.
102. Cohl, Carnet I.
103. de Tronquières, "Dessins animés." This source, Cohl's *Larousse Mensuel* essay, forms the basis of this discussion of techniques.
104. "Facts from France," *Kinematograph and Lantern Weekly*, September 17, 1908.
105. *L'Argus Phono-Cinéma*, October 3, 1908. In November the title was changed to *Les Jeux fantastiques*. Originally it was *Phantom Games*, an export of the London-based Wrench Company.
106. *MPW*, February 6, 1909. French title unknown.
107. de Tronquières, "Dessins animés." Also Cuenca, *Segundo de Chomón*, 66.
108. de Tronquières, "Dessins animés."
109. *Kinematograph and Lantern Weekly*, November 12, 1908.
110. L. Gardette, "Teaching History by Motogra-

phy," *The Nickelodeon*, October 4, 1909, 119–120.
111. It was probably inspired by Chomón's *Le Déménagement*.
112. Arnaud carnet.
113. *MPW*, September 3, 1910.
114. *CJ*, June 27, 1909.
115. *Kleine Catalogue of Subjects*, April 27, 1909.
116. *MPW*, February 13, 1909.
117. de Tronquières, "Dessins animés."
118. Ibid.
119. According to Mme. Courtet-Cohl, Cohl occupied much of his spare time folding these origami "cocottes" for the amusement of the grandchildren.
120. de Tronquières, "Dessins animés."
121. E. Kress, *L'Appareil de prise du vues cinématographiques*, 22–35.
122. de Tronquières, "Dessins animés."
123. Cohl, Carnet II.

CHAPTER FIVE

1. MS II.
2. "He [Zecca] was in charge of the supervision of the studios and the weekly programs up until the war. He took care of recruiting directors, decorators and actors. He determined the choice of subjects" (Charles Pathé, *De Pathé Frères à Pathé-Cinéma*, 6). See also Ambrière, "A l'aube du cinéma: les souvenirs de Zecca," *L'Image* no. 13, 1932.
3. Lacassin, "Les Fous Rires de la Belle Epoque." He does not identify Cohl as director of the "Jobard" series.
4. The character names are derived from the Pathé synopsis, courtesy of the Archives du Film.
5. *CJ*, August 19, 1911.
6. Archives du Film collection. I am grateful to Jean Adhémar and Frantz Schmitt for making copies of these documents available.
7. Auriol, "Les Premiers Dessins animés cinématographiques," 15.
8. Compare *Les Allumettes fantaistes* to *Les Allumettes animées*; *Les Extraordinaires exercices de la famille Coeur de Buis* to *Les Frères Boutdebois*; and *Quelle drôle de blanchisserie* to *Le Linge turbulent*.
9. MS II.
10. *MPW*, October 15, 1910.
11. Arnaud, "An Artist's Impressions," *Eclair-Bulletin* no. 36, February 1913.
12. Harlé, "Les Etapes de l'industrie," *La Cinématographie Française*, November 1935; M. L. Schneider, "The Eclair Story," *American Cinematographer*, April 1975; Deslandes, "Victorin-Hip-

polyte Jasset," 249–251; Eileen Bowser, "Eclair in America."
13. Kristin Thompson, *Exporting Entertainment*, 16. Accusations against Pathé were rampant in the French trade press.
14. *MPW*, February 27, 1909.
15. Terry Ramsaye, *A Million and One Nights*, vol. 1, 495. Murdock had also served as president of the American branch of the Kinemacolor corporation (Ramsaye, 568). Robert C. Allen, *Vaudeville and Film, 1895–1915: A Study in Media Interaction*, 254–259; John Dimeglio, *Vaudeville U.S.A.*; Thompson, *Exporting Entertainment*, 20–23.
16. *CJ*, November 8, 1909.
17. *Kinematograph and Lantern Weekly*, quoted in *MPW*, February 12, 1910.
18. *MPW*, May 28, 1910.
19. Henry C. Jenkins's research on early comedy production reveals that there was a decrease in comedy releases in the United States from 1908 to 1910, corresponding to Pathé's loss of dominance, but a sharp rise in 1911 and 1912. This data provides background not only for Eclair's entry into comedy production but for Sennett's Keystone, which commenced in September 1912. (Henry C. Jenkins, "Film Comedy before Mack Sennett," forthcoming.) See also Tom Gunning, "The Cinema of Attractions: Early Film, Its Spectator and the Avant-Garde," *Wide Angle* 8, 3/4, 1986, 63–70.
20. *CJ*, February 25, 1911; Bowser, "Eclair in America."
21. The first production was *Hands Across the Ocean/*

Les Main qui se joignent par dessus l'océan, re-
leased simultaneously in Paris and New York in
November 1911. The subject, appropriately, was
Franco-American cooperation during the Ameri-
can Revolution. *CJ*, November 4, 1911; Paul
Spehr, *The Movies Begin*, 74–76.

22. *MPW*, January 20, 1912.
23. *MPW*, January 27, 1912.
24. See Richard Koszarski, *Universal Pictures*, for
the early history of the studio. For a detailed description of Eclair's American alliances during this
period, see Thompson, 23–27. According to Bowser, there is some question about how closely associated Eclair was with Universal.
25. Carré, autobiographical manuscript, 135.
26. *MPW*, November 30, 1912.
27. Irving Browning, "Francis Doublier, Cameraman Fifty Years Ago," *American Cinematographer*, October 1944, 332. Only film stock licensed
by the MPPC (the Trust) was legal, and the only
company so licensed was Eastman, in Rochester,
N.Y. I am grateful to Edward Doublier, Francis
Doublier's son, for other biographical information. Doublier's Lumière camera is the one on
display at the International Museum of Photography, George Eastman House, Rochester, New
York.
28. Cohl, "Sur les dessins animés."
29. For McManus's biography, see Martin Sheridan,
Comics and Their Creators, 42–48.
30. John Canemaker, *Winsor McCay: His Life and
Art*.
31. Kalton C. Lahue, *World of Laughter, the Motion
Picture Comedy Short*, 45; Steven Higgins, "Mutt
and Jeff Meet the Horsleys," in Eileen Bowser
(ed.), *The Slapstick Symposium*, 37–48.
32. *MPW*, February 15, 1913.
33. *MPW*, February 22, 1913.
34. *Moving Picture News*, quoted in *Eclair Bulletin*
no. 39, April 1913.
35. *MPW*, quoted in *Eclair Bulletin* no. 39, April
1913.
36. *Eclair Bulletin* no. 49, August 1913.
37. *MPW*, September 6, 1913.
38. *MPW*, November 15, 1913.
39. *MPW*, November 8, 1913.
40. Cohl carried with him a letter from the mayor of
Fort Lee introducing him "to whom it may concern" as an upstanding member of the community
(CCC).
41. *MPW*, April 4, 1914.
42. The Fort Lee site was never used by Eclair as a
shooting studio again. The move west had been
planned before the fire and may have been related
to Cohl's return to France. Universal acquired the
labs and studios, which it leased to William Fox.

For some interesting photographs of the "ruins,"
see Irving Browning, "A Crumbled Movie Empire," *American Cinematographer*, August 1945.
There are also excellent views in Theodore Huff
and Mark Borgatta's amateur film, *Ghost Town:
The Story of Fort Lee*, shot in the 1930s (Wisconsin Center for Film and Theater Research).

43. *MPW*, September 5, September 26, 1914.
44. *MPW*, April 11, April 24, 1908. Some foreign
films were being detained in the New York customs house.
45. *MPW*, December 19, 1908.
46. de Tronquières, "Dessins animés."
47. *MPW*, March 27, 1909.
48. *MPW*, July 31, 1909.
49. *MPW*, September 18, 1909.
50. *MPW*, December 18, 1909.
51. "Trick Pictures," *The Nickelodeon*, August 1909,
37–38.
52. Gardette, "Teaching History by Motography."
53. Colin N. Bennett, *The Handbook of Kinematography*, 94.
54. The first to stress the possible close relationship
between Blackton and McCay was Michael Patrick Hearn, "The Animated Art of Winsor
McCay," *American Artist*, May 1975.
55. New York *Dramatic Mirror* 62, 1600, August 21,
1909, 20, quoted in Slide, *Selected Early Film
Criticism: 1896–1911*, 77.
56. Montgomery Phister, "People of the Stage," Cin-
cinnati *Commercial*, November 28, 1909.
57. "Moving Pictures that Move," New York *Telegraph*, April 12, 1911.
58. *CJ*, June 3, 1911.
59. Cohl, "Sur les dessins animés."
60. *The Story of a Mosquito* was released by Univer-
sal-Jewel in 1916 as *Winsor McCay and His Jersey
Skeeters*.
61. New York *Telegraph*, August 13, 1912.
62. *Hotel Honeymoon* (Solax, July 12, 1912) contained a brief animated sequence directed by
Henri Menessier that showed the moon smiling
down on two lovers (Lacassin, "Alice Guy," 19).
63. See George Pratt, "Early Stage and Screen: a
Two-Way Street," *Cinema Journal* 14, 2, Winter
1974–1975, 16–19.
64. Arnaud and Boisyvon, *Le Cinéma pour tous*. For
another eyewitness account, see Claude Bragdon,
"Mickey Mouse and What He Means," *Scribner's*, July 1934, 40–43.
65. I am indebted to André Martin's pioneering work
in *Barré L'Introuvable*.
66. Cohl, "Sur les dessins animés."
67. The New York Public Library has complete press
books and other material on file for *Cartoons in a
Seminary, in the Barbershop, in the Country, in*

a Hotel, in the Kitchen, in the Laundry, in the Parlor and *Cartoons on Tour.*

68. Dauven, "En visite chez M. Emile Cohl." In fact, Barré's cartoons were the second American ones to appear in France, after Cohl's "Newlyweds."

69. John Canemaker, "Profile of a Living Legend: J. R. Bray," *Filmmaker's Newsletter*, January 1975, 28–31. I am grateful to Harvey Deneroff for sharing his unpublished interview with Bray.

70. In his interview with Canemaker, Bray himself contradicts his date of 1908 when he states, "McCay had made two cartoons, I think, before I did, and he had good animation." This would place Bray's first film after the 1912 *Story of a Mosquito.*

71. U.S. Patent 1,107,193 *et seq.*. For further legal details, see David Callahan, "Cel Animation: Mass Production and Marginalization in the Animated Film Industry," *Film History* 2, 3, 1988, 223–228; Richard Koszarski (ed.), "Bray-Hurd: The Key Animation Patents," *Film History* 2, 3, 1988, 229–266.

72. *CJ*, February 1, 1915. For background, see Richard Abel, *French Cinema: The First Wave, 1915–1919*, 13–14; Thompson, 196.

73. *CJ*, March 18, 1916.

74. *Le Film*, April 22, August 12, 1916.

75. *CJ*, *Le Film*, July 15, 1916.

76. *Le Film*, July 15, 1916.

77. Louis Delluc [?], "Des Dessins animés," *Le Film*, May 20, 1916.

78. Two of Rabier's books were actually published by the ancient Pellerin firm: *Attrapeur . . . attrapeur et demi* (1902) and *Drôl's de bêtes, drôl's de gens* (1906).

79. *Bonhomme de neige; conte féerique en 20 tableaux lumineux* (Paris: Vieu, 1910); *Château de loufoques, comédie burlesque en trois actes* (Paris: Stock, 1911).

80. *Les Maîtres humoristes: Benjamin Rabier.*

81. Rabier correspondence, CCC, 60 letters and related documents.

82. Rabier to Cohl, July 23, 1916.

83. Rabier to Cohl, July 31, 1916.

84. Rabier to Cohl, ca. September 26, 1916.

85. Rabier to Cohl, ca. October 3, 1916.

86. René Navarre to Cohl, October 15, 1916.

87. *CJ*, October 28, 1916.

88. *Le Film*, November 25, 1916.

89. Rabier, *Flambeau, chien de guerre* (Paris: Tallandier, no date).

90. Navarre to Cohl, November 7, 1916.

91. Rabier to Cohl, November 12, 1916.

92. Rabier to Cohl, November 13, 1916.

93. Rabier to Cohl, November 27, 1916.

94. Mme. Navarre did, in fact, die on December 23, 1916.

95. Rabier to Cohl, January 8, 1917.

96. Rabier to Cohl, January 15, 1917.

97. Rabier to Cohl, January 17, 1917.

98. Navarre to Cohl, February 7, 1917.

99. Danvers, *Le Film*, May 28, 1917.

100. Rabier to Cohl, October 10, 1917.

101. J.-B. de T, "Emile Cohl," *Annuaire générale de la cinématographie française* 1917–1918.

102. Several of Rabier's 1920s Pathé-Baby (9.5 mm) format films are in the Archives du Film. For more on Rabier's career, see Maurice Hamel, "Benjamin Rabier," in *ABC artistique et littéraire*, July 1920.

103. Courtet-Cohl Collection.

104. In *Coeur de Rana*, a later Rabier film (Archives du Film), a squirrel grinds up a mouse, then eats him.

105. Danvers, *Le Film*, February 5, 1917.

106. Danvers, *Le Film*, April 2, 1917.

107. Danvers, *Le Film*, March 12, 1917.

108. Twelve of the seventeen films described in *Le Film*, July 3, 1917, were made in America.

109. Nordisk was the last European firm to close its American office in November 1916. According to *Le Film*, November 18, 1916, "Presently there are no European films regularly released in America."

110. Alphonse Boudard, "Pour un boulevard des Pieds-Nickelés", Francis Lacassin, "De Forton à Pélos," in Forton, *La Bande des Pieds-Nickelés*; Sadoul, *Ce que lisent vos enfants*; Caradec, *Histoire de la littérature enfantine en France.*

111. Sadoul, ibid., 8.

112. Pierre Boileau, Preface to Forton, *Les Pieds Nickelés s'en vont en guerre* (Paris: Azur, 1966). Forton continued the strip until his death in 1934, at which time it was continued posthumously by other artists.

113. Despite published statements that the original negatives exist at the Cinémathèque Française, the staff was not able to confirm their existence for me. Most of the Eclair material in the collection was destroyed in World War II.

114. Cohl was simulating a trick that appeared earlier in *Slippery Jim*, a Pathé film preserved by the Museum of Modern Art.

115. Rabier to Cohl, January 8, 1917.

116. After Louis Delluc became editor of *Le Film* in June 1917, there was a sharp decrease in the amount of space allotted to reviews of animated films, and short films in general. This is one reason why there is so little trade-press description of the "Pieds Nickelés" series.

117. *Le Film*, August 13, 1917.
118. His service was delayed because Cohl did not have a work permit. Of course, as a French citizen he did not *need* a work permit, but the bureaucracy of the American army was not prepared to deal with enlisting foreigners.
119. *CJ*, April 9, 1921.
120. Harlé, "Les Etapes de l'industrie."
121. Mitry, *Histoire du cinéma*, vol. 2, 136–140; Abel, *French Cinema*, 11–18.
122. Léon Gaumont, interview originally published in *The Bioscope*, 1918, clipping file, Bibliothèque de l'Arsenal.
123. *CJ*, April 19, 1919.
124. Jungstedt, *Kapten Grogg och hans Vänner*. I am grateful to Caroline Bruzelius for translating this book for me, and to Jungstedt for his communications.
125. The following are the Paris release dates for the Bergdahl films: *Kapten Groggs underbara resa/Le miraculeux voyage de Capitaine Grogg* (June 1, 1919), *Kapten Grogg i ballong/Le voyage de Capitaine Grog en ballon* (March 1, 1919); *När Kapten Grogg skulle porträtterat/Le capitaine Grog y veut faire son portrait* (October 11, 1919); *Kapten Grogg vid Nordpolen/Le capitaine Grog au Pôle Nord* (April 19, 1919); *Kapten Grogg och fru/Le capitaine Grog et sa femme* (December 6, 1919); *Kapten Grogg bland vilda djur/Le capitaine Groog [sic] chez les fauves* (August 9, 1919).

CHAPTER SIX

1. Bert Green, "The Making of Animated Cartoons," *Motion Picture Magazine*, May 1919, 51–52. Another translation appeared in *Ciné pour Tous*, May 8, 1920.
2. Georges Dureau, Preface to Cohl, "Les Dessins animés," *CJ*, May 17, 1919.
3. Cohl, "Les Dessins animés," *CJ*, May 17, 1919.
4. Cohl maintained that he was not the proverbial "Grand pélican blanc/ qui se dévor les flancs/pour nourir ses enfants" (the great white pelican that devours its flanks to feed its offspring).
5. Meeting noted in MS II.
6. Michel de Ghelderode, "Ciné-clubs et Avant-garde," in Francis Bolen (ed.), *Histoire authentique, anecdotique, folklorique et critique du cinéma belge depuis ses lointaines origines*, 83.
7. Cohl, "Les Dessins animés et à trucs; causerie faite au Ciné-Club le 12 juin 1920," *Le Journal du Ciné-Club*.
8. V.G.D., *Ciné-Tribune*, June 1920.
9. Cohl, "Sur les dessins animés," *Ciné-Tribune*, July 15, 1920.
10. Cohl, *CinéMagazine*, January 28, 1921.
11. Arnaud and Boisyvon, *Le Cinéma pour tous*, 72–85.
12. Arnaud's quotations are almost verbatim from "Sur les dessins animés," but he adds more passages. This suggests that he was quoting from a longer (perhaps unedited) version of the manuscript.
13. Anon., "Emile Cohl," *Mon Ciné*, February 22, 1922.
14. Anon., "La Santé d'Emile Cohl," *CJ*, March 4, 1922.
15. MS II. Publi-Ciné continued to operate until 1945.
16. Musée Galliera, *Exposition de l'art dans le cinéma français* (ex. cat.), 1924. Much of the material exhibited found its way into the collection of the Cinémathèque Française, where a small case was devoted to Emile Cohl. Richard Abel discusses the significance of the "major coup" of the Galliera exhibition in *French Cinema*, 254–256. Jean Epstein gave a lecture on June 17, 1924, that touched on animation, presumably mentioning Cohl's exhibits.
17. de Tronquières, "Dessins animés."
18. Georges-Michel Coissac, *Histoire du cinématographe*, 410.
19. Fontane, *Un Maître de la caricature: André Gill*.
20. MS II.
21. Auriol, "Les Premiers Dessin animés cinématographiques: Emile Cohl." Auriol used the qualifier "cinematographic" to distinguish Cohl's work from that of Reynaud.
22. Ibid., 19.
23. Cohl, "Comment c'est formée une collection de timbres-poste."
24. O'Galop's original drawing was submitted to the Michelin brothers around 1898. It showed a rotund man lifting a glass and toasting, "Nunc est bibendum!" (Now is the time to drink.) At the Paris-Amsterdam race the driver Théry was the first to nickname André Michelin "Bibendum," and the name was thereafter attached to the man who resembled a pile of tires designed by O'Galop ("The Bib Story," Lake Success, New York: Michelin).
25. Cohl may have drawn the background.
26. Bruno Edera, "Evolution synoptique des origines et des pionniers du film d'animation en Europe," Annecy Festival notes, 1971; Maillet, "Les Pionniers français de l'animation," *L'Ecran*, January 1973, 20–28.

27. O'Galop, "Comment fait-on un dessin animé," *Cinéma-Magazine*, February 1921. A photograph of O'Galop at his animation table appeared in the March issue.

28. Maillet, *Le Dessin animé français*. In an interview with André Martin in 1966, Lortac stated that he and Cohl had worked together at Eclair and added that Cohl's support was "purely technical." (I am grateful to Maillet for Martin's transcription.)

29. Maillet, *Le Dessin animé français*; Marcel Lapierre, *Les Cent Visages du cinéma*, 314.

30. *Le Canard en . . . ciné*, typewritten prospectus with a strip of film attached, Bibliothèque Nationale.

31. Lortac's novel *L'Aventure commencera ce soir* won a prize in 1942 and in 1965 was made into the movie *Un Soir, par hasard*.

32. Auriol, "Les Premiers Dessins animés cinématographiques: Emile Cohl," cited animator Max Pinchon.

33. Cohl, quoted in Auriol, ibid., 18.

34. Cohl, quoted in Arnaud and Boisyvon, *Le Cinéma pour tous*, 85.

35. Maillet, *Le Dessin animé français*.

36. Gus Bofa, "Du Dessin animé," *Les Cahiers du Mois* 16–17, 1925, 53.

37. Marcel Brion, "Félix le Chat, ou la poésie créatrice," *Le Rouge et le Noir*, July 1928.

38. Maurice Bessy, "Dessins animés: Koko, Mickey, Félix et Co.," *CinéMagazine*, February 1930, 28–30.

39. Jean Morienval, quoted in Anon., "Europe's Highbrows Hail 'Mickey Mouse,'" *The Literary Digest* 110, 6, August 8, 1931, 19.

40. Gregory A. Waller, "Mickey, Walt and Film Criticism from *Steamboat Willie* to *Bambi*," in Gerald Peary and Danny Peary (eds.), *The American Animated Cartoon*, 50.

41. Newspaper clipping, CCC.

42. Dauven, "En visite chez M. Emile Cohl qui inventa les dessins animés."

43. Cohl, "Oui, je suis le père du dessin animé," *Paris-Soir*, September 15, 1934.

44. The drawing by Cohl in the picture (labeled "the ancestor") was obviously made for the occasion, but it has been reproduced as a still from *Fantasmagorie*. Indelli recalled that Cohl would stop by for coffee, but that was the limit of his collaboration. For a photograph of the animator with Méliès and Cohl and a brief biography, see Maillet, "Mimma Indelli," in *Le Dessin animé français*.

45. J.-P. Liasu, "Si Walt Disney est le père de Mickey, un français, Emile Cohl, n'est-il pas son grand-père?" *Comoedia*, January 6, 1936.

46. Liasu, "A 80 ans, Emile Cohl qui inventa les dessins animés touche cents francs par mois et ne peut même pas se payer le cinéma," *Comoedia*, January 10, 1936.

47. Liasu, "Comment un plagiat permit à Emile Cohl d'inventer chez Gaumont les dessins animés," *Comoedia*, January 24, 1936.

48. Jean Rollot, "Les Deux Clients du petit café de Saint-Mandé," *L'Intransigeant*, January 25, 1938.

49. One highly speculative guess as to the identity of Cohl's rich "dark woman" would be Colette. However, there is no evidence that she ever communicated with him; she certainly never mentioned his films while she was reviewing for *Le Film* or for *Filma*. See *Colette at the Movies* (Alain and Odette Virmaux, eds.). It is unlikely that Cohl would have publicized his distant, though still for him, rather unpleasant relationship with Colette and Willy.

50. Liasu, "Le 30ᵉ Anniversaire du dessin animé," *Comoedia*, November 6, 1936.

51. Pierre Bourgeon, letter to Cohl, August 6, 1936, CCC.

52. Gaumont had been named to the society in 1929 in recognition of his work on the Chronophone.

53. M. Lacoin, "Allocution du Président," *Bulletin de la Société d'Encouragement pour l'Industrie Nationale*, March-April 1937, 101. In passing, Lacoin made the interesting remark that Cohl's films had been projected recently at various clubs like the Cercle du Cinéma. I am grateful to A. Haigron for his search of the society's old records.

54. Rollot, "Les Deux Clients du petit café de Saint-Mandé."

55. Roland Bouvard, "Emile Cohl," *L'Epoque*, January 22, 1938.

56. Robert André, "Emile Cohl," *Le Figaro*, October 11, 1937.

57. Marcel Lapierre, *Paris-Soir*, April 28, 1937.

58. André, "Emile Cohl." *L'Intransigeant* (January 25, 1938) confirmed that "his children loved him very much. They themselves have two children and their situation . . ." (their ellipsis).

59. André, "La Grande Misère d'Emile Cohl," *Le Figaro*, October 31, 1937.

60. Fontane, "Le Plus Ancien Parisien," *L'Intermédiaire des Chercheurs et Curieux*, December 30, 1937, col. 973.

61. A.-P. Richard, "Emile Cohl," *La Cinématographie Française*, December 31, 1937.

62. *Excelsior*, January 22, 1938.

63. Norpois, *L'Epoque*, January 14, 1938.

64. Norpois, *L'Epoque*, January 22, 1938.

65. See also *Bref*, January 30, 1938; *Le Figaro*, January 22; *Candide*, January 27; *Journal des Débats*,

January 23; *Comoedia*, January 22; *La Liberté*, January 22.

66. Liasu, "Emile Cohl," *Le Figaro*, January 22, 1938.

67. René Jeanne, "Emile Cohl," *L'Illustration*, February 5, 1938, 161.

68. *L'Express*, May 2, 1972, quoted in Madeleine Malthête-Méliès, *Méliès, l'enchanteur*, 440.

69. Marcel Lapierre, *Les Cent Visages du cinéma*; Lo Duca, *Le Dessin Animé*; René Jeanne and Charles Ford, *Histoire encyclopédique du cinéma*.

70. Jean Adhémar, *L'Inventaire du fonds français après 1800*, vol. 5, 68. Bénézit, *Dictionnaire des peintres, sculpteurs, dessinateurs et graveurs*, 1949 edition, vol. 2, 567–568.

71. Marie-Thérèse Poncet, *Dessin animé, art mondial*, 169–173.

CHAPTER SEVEN

1. Francis Lacassin, "Bande dessinée et langage cinématographique," *Cinéma 71*, September 1971, and in *Pour un neuvième art: La bande dessinée*. Translated by David Kunzle, "The Comic Strip and Film Language," *Film Quarterly*, Fall 1972, 11–19. Thanks to David Cast for his ideas on these articles and the whole subject.

2. Pierre Couperie, *A History of the Comic Strip*, 9.

3. John Fell, *Film and the Narrative Tradition*, 89. See also Fell, "Cellulose Nitrate Roots: Popular Entertainments and the Birth of Film Narrative," in Leyda, et. al (eds.), *Before Hollywood*, 40.

4. Maurice Horn, *Seventy-Five Years of the Comics*, 13–14.

5. Mitry, "Comic Strips," *Histoire du cinéma*, vol. 2, 20–22.

6. Kunzle, "Supplementary Note," essay appended to Lacassin, "The Comic Strip and Film Language," 19–23; Kunzle, *History of the Comic Strip; Volume I: The Early Comic Strip, 1450–1825*.

7. Horn, *Seventy-Five Years of the Comics*, 13.

8. Lacassin, "The Comic Strip and Film Language," 11.

9. Kunzle, "Supplementary Note."

10. Fell, *Film and the Narrative Tradition*, 89. See also Fell, "Motive, Mischief and Melodrama: the State of Film Narrative in 1907," in Fell (ed.), *Film Before Griffith*, 281–282.

11. Fell describes a hypothetical "cinematic" strip that would apply neatly to "On Fire": "Some successive drawings encapsulated action as it progressed within an unchanging perspective, maintaining one camera angle as it were. To continue the story, other drawings either shifted perspective on the same scene or moved to quite different locations. Thus in movie parlance, shots might be as many as nine, but more often numbered five or six.

"Picture to picture, the likenesses of comic pages to movie continuity are inescapabale. The panel-to-panel 'cuts' in the comic strip characteristically maintain screen positions, match action, and direct visual attention with sophistication often well in advance of their film contemporaries" ("Cellulose Nitrate Roots," 40).

12. Barry Salt, *Film Style and Technology: History and Analysis*, 124.

13. Tom Gunning, "The Non-Continuous Style of Early Film (1900–1906)," in Roger Holman (ed.), *Cinema 1900–1906*, vol. 1, 219–229.

14. "[H]istorians have usually treated this change [in cutting] as an untroubled evolution—with editing freeing Porter, Griffith, and their followers to explore the 'grammar' of film. What I am suggesting here is that cutting was not entirely a liberation; it posed tremendous problems of how to maintain a clear narrative as the central interest of the film, while juxtaposing disparate times and spaces. The continuity rules that filmmakers devised were not natural outgrowths of cutting, but means of taming and unifying it" (Kristin Thompson, in Bordwell, Staiger, and Thompson, *The Classical Hollywood Cinema*, 162).

15. David Bordwell, *Narration in the Fiction Film*, provides a survey and analysis of the problems of film narration.

16. Among the reactions, the artist Kober says in his self-portrait, in rough translation, "I'd give a page of my life for it—or a page of *Le Rire*." *Une Dame vraiment bien* was released by Gaumont in August 1908.

17. André Gaudreault, "Detours in Film Narrative: the Development of Cross-Cutting," *Cinema Journal* 19, 1, Fall 1979, 39–59.

18. Fell, *Film and the Narrative Tradition*, 89.

19. Horn, *Seventy-Five Years of the Comics*.

20. Lacassin, "The Comic Strip and Film Language."

21. Tom Gunning, "The Non-Continuous Style of Early Film (1900–1906)," in Roger Holman (ed.), *Cinema 1900–1906*, vol. 1, 221.

22. Fell, "Cellulose Nitrate Roots," 40.

23. "Before and after 1907, the values expressed in cinema are primarily those of the middle-class: what Harry Braverman calls the old middle class for the pre-1907 period and the new middle class in the post-1907 period" (Charles Musser, "The Nickelodeon Era Begins: Establishing the Frame-

work for Hollywood's Mode of Representation," *Framework* 22/23, Autumn 1983, 10–11).

24. Pierre Fresnault-Deruelle, *La Bande Dessinée: L'univers et les techniques de quelques "comics" d'expression française*.

25. Anon., *Scientific American*, December 22, 1877. It was precisely this "illusion of real presence" that Bazin identified as the "myth of total cinema." "In their imaginations they saw the cinema as a total and complete representation of reality; they saw in a trice the reconstruction of a perfect illusion of the outside world in sound, color and relief" ("The Myth of Total Cinema," *What is Cinema?*, 17–22).

26. *La Caricature*, January 3, 1880.

27. Robida, *Le Vingtième Siècle; la vie électrique*; Boleslas Matuszewski, *La Photographie animée* and *Une Nouvelle Source de l'histoire; création d'un dépôt de cinématographie historique*.

28. Gordon Hendricks, *Eadweard Muybridge; the Father of the Motion Picture*; W. J. Homer, "Eakins, Muybridge and the Motion Picture Process," *Art Quarterly*, Summer 1963; Beaumont Newhall, "Muybridge and the First Motion Picture," *Image*, January 1956.

29. *La Nature*, December 14, 1878. See also Aaron Scharf, "Marey and Chronophotography," *Artforum*, September 1976, 62–70; A. R. Michaelis, "E. J. Marey: Physiologist and the First Cinematographer," *British Journal of Photography*, December 2, 1955. Especially interesting are Nadar's comments on Marey in *Quand j'étais photographe*, 246–263.

30. Scharf, *Art and Photography*; Van Deren Coke, *The Painter and the Photograph*.

31. In his *Pages d'histoire, album de Figaro*, 1901, nos. 15 and 16, were events "seen by the cinematograph." For biography and portraits, see "L'Esprit de Caran d'Ache," *Lectures pour Tous*, January 1909, 681–684.

32. Edouard Destaines, "Un Humoriste," *La Vie Militaire*, May 3, 1884.

33. Henri Flamans, "Le Kinétoscope," *Le Magasin Pittoresque*, August 1, 1894, 247. He stated that the first Kinetoscope belonged to "M. Georgiade." This was obviously George Georgiades, who, with another former Edison assistant, George Trajedes, entered into an agreement with R. W. Paul in London to manufacture unlicensed Kinetoscopes. Edison was powerless to stop this and other European infringements (Hendricks, *The Kinetoscope*, 115–116).

34. Deslandes, *Histoire comparée du cinéma*, vol. 1, 215–240; Veda Semarne, *Industry and Invention: The Lumière Cinématograph and the Origins of Film, 1895–1904*.

35. G. Colomb, "A travers la science," *L'Illustré Soleil du Dimanche*, March 29, 1896.

36. Emile Lutz, *Le Courrier Français*, April 18, 1896. The Théâtrophone was a telephone system that brought "live" performances to subscribers. See Perron, "Le Théâtrophone," *Le Magasin Pittoresque*, June 15, 1893, 183–184.

37. Sadoul, *Histoire générale du cinéma* vol. 1, 303–304; Deslandes, *Le Boulevard du cinéma à l'époque de Georges Méliès* (includes a filmography of Pirou in an appendix).

38. Joseph-Renaud, *Le Cinématographe du mariage* was an 1897 novel that documents another facet of early projection by mimicking the spiel of the "barker" who introduced and commented on each subject screened.

39. A viewer who disliked being photographed sued unsuccessfully in 1905. See Deslandes, "Une Grave Décision," *Histoire comparée du cinéma* vol. 1, 256.

40. Erwin Panofsky, "Style and Medium in the Motion Pictures," 18. For American equivalents of these films, see John Hagen, "Erotic Tendencies in Film, 1900–1906," in Roger Holman (comp.), *Cinema 1900–1906*, 231–237.

41. Avelot may have been inspired by numerous previous cartoons premised on the mistaking of the film image for reality. He may also have known Edison's 1902 film *Uncle Josh at the Moving Picture Show*.

42. *Le Courrier Français*, January 2, 1898.

43. Francisque Sarcey, quoted in Deslandes, *Histoire comparée du cinéma*, vol. 1, 27.

44. *Le Rire*, June 29, 1901.

45. The images in Villon's strip also resemble Edison's *Serpentine Dance—Annabelle*.

46. Another way in which one might have been made aware of this visual peculiarity would have been when films were projected (as they often must have been) with the framing out of proper adjustment, so the frame line would have appeared on the screen.

47. In the United States Winsor McCay's strip "Little Sammy Sneeze" might have been inspired by the famous set of pictures called "Fred Ott's Sneeze," which had been published in *Harper's*. (See *Before Mickey*, 94–97.)

48. "The [French foreground] form of staging could show no less of the actors than nearly their full height, from just above the ankles to just above the head" (Salt, *Film Style and Technology*, 106).

49. Jean Adhémar, "Les Journaux amusants et les premiers peintres cubistes," *L'Oeil* 4, 1955.

50. Pierre Cabanne, *Dialogues with Marcel Duchamp*, 34.

51. See Edward Branigan, *Point of View in the Cin-*

ema: A Theory of Narration and Subjectivity in Classical Film, for a survey of the numerous conventions that have developed for representing screen space and subjectivity.

52. Jasset, "Etude sur la mise en scène."
53. Sadoul, *Histoire générale du cinéma,* vol. 1, 296–298. Sadoul asked Lumière about his sources, but the old filmmaker did not recall any.
54. The same may be said for Porter's adaptation of

Hearst's cartoon "Terrible Teddy, the Grizzly King" into a 1901 film of the same name. See Charles Musser, "The Early Cinema of Edwin S. Porter," *Cinema Journal* 19, 1, Fall 1979, 6–8.

55. Guy, *Autobiographie d'une pionnère du cinéma,* 79.
56. Méliès contributed caricatures to the anti-Boulanger paper *La Griffe.* Two are reproduced in Malthête-Méliès, *Méliès, l'enchanteur.*

CHAPTER EIGHT

1. This simplified schema is borrowed from H. R. Rookmaaker, *Gauguin and 19th Century Art Theory,* 70.
2. Camille Mauclair, *Servitude et grandeur littéraire,* quoted in Rookmaaker, ibid., 106.
3. Joliet, "Avertissement," *Le Roman incohérent.*
4. For more on Robertson, see Olive Cook, *Movement in Two Dimensions,* and Charles Musser, "Toward a History of Screen Practice," *Quarterly Review of Film Studies* 9, 1, Winter 1984, 65.
5. It is interesting that the bourgeois stereotype in the comic strip carried over into modern painting, as in Juan Gris's *L'Homme au café.*
6. Inexplicably, most American prints have been copied "flipped," with the left-right direction reversed. My frame enlargements conform to the original version.
7. The best-known "star-women" are those in Méliès's *Trip to the Moon* (1902), but pre-1910 cinema abounds with similar personifications.
8. In *A Trip to the Moon,* the moon was used specifically as a parodistic foil to the scientists who fired a rocket ship at it. Their progressive "modern" science is mocked by the irrational and unexpected occurrences they encounter on the lunar soil.
9. The same "impossible" space exists in *Le Voyage à travers l'impossible,* by Méliès, 1904, except that the "astronauts" are on the sun.
10. See Aaron Sheon, "The Discovery of Graffiti," *Art Journal,* Fall 1976, 16–22.
11. Cohl, "Oui, je suis le père du dessin animé."
12. *MPW,* March 23, 1909.
13. Ernest Maindron, *Marionnettes et guignols;* Jacques Chesnais, *Histoire générale des marionnettes;* Judith Wechsler, "The Literary Marionettes," in *A Human Comedy: Physiognomy and Caricature in 19th Century Paris,* 56–63.
14. de Weindel, "Le Chat-Noir."
15. Scenario reproduced in Chesnais, *Histoire générale des marionnettes,* 174.
16. Ibid., 113.
17. Cohl, "Oui, je suis le père du dessin animé."
18. Robida, *Le Vingtième Siècle; la vie électrique.*
19. One article appeared on a page beside Cohl's

drawing in *Nos Loisirs* ("Nouveaux Microbes," April 18, 1909) explaining how "a professor of the bacteriology laboratory of Yale University" had counted 586,000 microbes living on dollar bills. We see the same inscription of science onto popular culture and then onto film in Biograph's *Love Microbes* in 1907. Charles Musser has shown that the journalist Ella Wheeler Wilcox was responsible for vulgarizing the notion that "love is composed of microbes, good and bad, 'benign' and 'pernicious' " ("The Nickelodeon Era Begins," 5).

20. Jean Comandon, "Le Cinématographie des infiniment petits," *Lectures pour Tous,* January 1910.
21. Dr. de L.B., "La Chirugie nouvelle," *L'Illustration,* June 10, 1899.
22. Dr. Doyen, *Le Micrococcus néoformans et les néoplasmes.*
23. Dr. Doyen, "Mes Films chirurgicaux," *Le Journal,* January 2, 1914; Deslandes, *Jasset,* 250–251.
24. Gaumont, *Les Nouveautés cinématographiques,* 1910.
25. Roberts-Jones, "L'Actualité artistique et la caricature ou la satire des arts," in *De Daumier à Lautrec,* 109–130.
26. Lévy, "L'Incohérence, son origin, son histoire, son avenir."
27. *Catalogue de l'exposition des arts incohérents* 1886, 17–18.
28. This was apparently a favorite joke, for Cohl used several variants in other caricatures.
29. Robert L. Herbert, *Neo-Impressionism,* 23–25.
30. *Le Film,* April 15, 1916.
31. In the game of the Exquisite Corpse, each player draws part of a human body on a folded sheet of paper, then passes it on to the next player. No one can see the completed image until the paper is unfolded at the end of the game to reveal the composite drawing.
32. Compare, for example, the deformities of "Ah Quel Nez" with *L'Avenir dévoilé par les lignes des pieds* and *Le Songe de garçon de café.*
33. Louisa E. Jones, *Sad Clowns and Pale Pierrots; Literature and the Popular Comic Arts in Nineteenth-Century France,* 121.

34. Ibid.
35. Kristin Thompson, "Implications of the Cel Animation Technique," in de Lauretis and Heath, *The Cinematic Apparatus*, 106–118.
36. Adolphe Brisson, *Nos Humoristes*, v–vi.
37. Ibid.
38. D.-H. Kahnweiler, quoted in Lawder, *The Cubist Cinema*, 21.
39. Compare to Picasso's "Baigneuse," 1908–1909, reproduced in John Golding, *Cubism*, plate 4b.
40. Lucy Fischer, "Talking with Robert Breer," *University Film Study Center Newsletter*, October 1976, 5–7. I discussed this interpretation with the filmmaker in 1975, but he did not recall any influence of Emile Cohl on *A Man and His Dog Out for Air*.

CATALOGUE OF FILMS

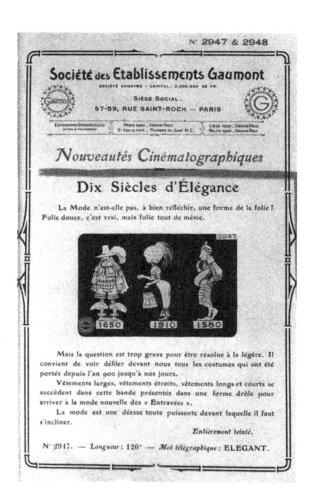

320. Page from Gaumont's catalogue, "Nouveautés
Cinématographiques."

INTRODUCTION

The catalogue raisonné is a familiar scholarly tool in music and art-historical research, but its application to film history may warrant a brief explanation because, as far as I know, this is the first such attempt.

The method is to assemble all the available information about each film into an analytical list arranged, usually, in chronological order. The purpose is twofold: to record all the known works, suspected works, and mistaken attributions that constitute the total oeuvre of the artist; and to aid historians, collectors, and connoisseurs in identifying previously unknown works.

The value of such a catalogue may be questioned in the case of a modern director whose career is well documented in production credits, company records, and other readily accessible sources. The standard "filmography" is adequate. But for early filmmakers—those of Cohl's era—such records seldom exist. Matters of authorship, dating, and whether the work still survives are of as much concern to the film scholar or collector as they are to the print specialist who is cataloguing or identifying a rare and valuable graphic work.

One result of such a catalogue is to remove the identifiable works from the vast pool of anonymous films. Archivists can apply the data to unidentified films in their collections. Historians can concentrate their attention on other filmmakers. Critics and theorists can base their judgments on examples bearing accurate dates and attributions. Museums, cinémathèques, and distributors will be guided in arranging retrospective screenings and programs.

TYPES OF INFORMATION CATALOGUED

Title. The title of the film is given in the language of the original production. If a print of the film is known to exist, the title is marked by an asterisk. If a title is a tentative attribution, pending more information, it is identified as such. I have included all titles proposed by others and by myself for which no corroborative information has been found, but which cannot definitely be disproved. Variant titles are given whenever necessary.

Production company.

Production company's catalogue number. When known, it can be invaluable for identifying fragmentary prints. The original laboratories often printed the number on the intertitles specifically for the purpose of marking the film in case the main title was lost. These numbers were invariable, regardless of the country to which the film was exported. The numbers accompanied the catalogue descriptions of the films as well. Usually—but not always—the sequential order of these numbers indicates the order in which the films were released.

Length. These figures are not reliable because they were normally inflated to make the film more attractive to potential buyers. The figures herein are derived from company catalogues, trade-periodical listings, and from the Courtet-Cohl filmography (see below). They can be used only as a rough guide when identifying an unknown film. European lengths are metric; American and British are in feet. The indication "split reel" means that the film was mounted on a 1,000-foot reel with another film, so the length could be anywhere from 200 to 800 feet. All lengths apply to 35mm stock.

Release date. Due to European marketing methods, this date is not always easily determined. A preview screening was arranged for buyers and renters, orders were taken, and prints were made up for delivery about three weeks later. The advertisement of the film in trade papers, such as *Ciné-Journal*, probably anticipated by about a month the actual appearance of the film on French screens. For Gaumont films, the date is that on which the film was advertised in its catalogue, *Les Nouveautés cinématographiques* (available now only from private collectors). This date is followed by confirming dates of trade press advertising. For later films, I have followed the dates in the Courtet-Cohl filmography, except when they are demonstrably incorrect. The difficulty was compounded by the World War I, which delayed releases and disrupted trade-press documentation. However, for those films released in the United States, the release dates are definite and were documented in all the major trade papers.

Production date. This is the date that Cohl wrote on various manuscripts. With only rare exceptions it is possible to verify these notations.

Foreign release. If a film was released in Britain or the United States, its release title, date, and length are given. The same is the case for American films released in France. This is the first time this information appears anywhere. It is especially important for the 1913–1914 "Newlyweds" series, the titles of which have been previously unknown in France.

Attributions. This catalogue includes all references to Cohl's films made by the authors who have discussed his work in detail. The most important source was the filmography compiled by his grandson, *Pierre Courtet-Cohl*. It is an unpublished six-page list of titles and dates amalgamating several fragmentary lists left by Cohl. Cohl himself seems to have based his lists partially on his collection of *company catalogues and press clippings* (most of which have now been dispersed to the Cinémathèque Française and the Archives du Film) and partially on his memory. Therefore it varies from highly reliable to very inaccurate. I have added corroborative evidence to this list whenever possible.

In the early days of filmmaking it was not uncommon for several directors to work on a single film. The films listed by Cohl undoubtedly included all those to which he contributed—even if his assistance was only in the form of a scenario or small portion of the shooting. Unfortunately, there is usually no way to distinguish a production made almost entirely by Cohl from one in whose production he was a minor factor, and the reader must bear this in mind. Cohl was an animation-and-

trick-photography specialist, so the live-action framing sequences that frequently accompany his films should almost always be assumed to have been filmed by another studio technician. Whenever a collaborator has been identified, I have indicated that fact in the notes.

Location of extant prints. The archives that hold prints of the films in the catalogue have been listed. It is certain that more prints of Cohl's films exist in other archives and—especially—in private collections. The existence of this list, with its descriptions and international release titles, should aid in the identification of more prints. It should be understood that a project such as this is in a constant state of revision, as new prints are found and attributions are challenged.

A few prints are available for sale and rental by commercial distributors, and these have been noted.

Genre. This refers either to the description of the film in the trade press under the standard rubrics ("comique," "scène à trucs," etc.) or, in the case of animated films, the type of animation if it is known ("objects," "cutouts," etc.).

Description/Documentation. I have reproduced as many descriptions as possible from period sources, such as trade publications and catalogues. The original Pathé scenarios generously provided by Frantz Schmitt of the Archives du Film have been included. These are important documents for archivists, collectors, historians, and critic-theorists of early cinema, especially if the film is now lost. If no source appears in parentheses, the description is from my own viewing notes.

Order of arrangement. I have chosen to list the films in the order in which they were released because that is the only objectively verifiable method. If the films could be listed in the order of their production or completion, then the list might be arranged somewhat differently. There are two exceptions: films delayed by the war and those without verifiable release dates have been listed according to their notation in the Cohl documents or on the Courtet-Cohl list.

SUMMARY OF ABBREVIATIONS

* = Print exists

Archives du Film = Centre National de la Cinématographie; Service des Archives du Film, Bois d'Arcy

Attrib = Previous attributions

Auriol = J.-G. Auriol, "Les Premières Desssins animés cinématographiques," *La Revue du Cinéma*, January, 1930, 12–19

BFI = National Film Archive, The British Film Institute, London

CC-number = Pierre Courtet-Cohl, "Liste des films d'Emile Cohl," unpublished manuscript. The numbers refer to the position of individual films on the list.

Ciné Française = Cinémathèque Française, Paris

Ciné G-A = Cinémathèque Gaumont-Actualités, Joinville-le-Pont

Ciné Québécoise = Cinémathèque Québécoise, Montréal

DC = Donald Crafton

Eastman House = International Museum of Photography; The George Eastman House, Rochester

Edera = Bruno Edera, "Evocation synoptique des origines et des pionniers du film d'animation en Europe, 1888–1928," Festival d'Annecy, 1973 (mimeographed)

H d'A = "Rapport présenté par M. Henry d'Allemagne au nom du Comité des Constructions et des Beaux-Arts sur M. Emile Cohl . . . ," Bulletin de la Société pour l'En-couragement de l'Industrie Française, May 1937

KW = The Kinematograph and Lantern Weekly (London)

L'Argus = L'Argus Phono-Cinéma (Paris)

LD = Lo Duca, Le Dessin animé: histoire, esthétique, technique (Paris: Prisma, 1948)

MOMA = Film Collection of the Museum of Modern Art, New York

MPW = Moving Picture World (New York)

MS II, Carnets I, II, III = Cohl manuscripts (see main bibliography)

PCG = Phono-Ciné Gazette (Paris)

Poncet = Marie Thérèse Poncet, Dessin animé, art mondial (Paris: Le Cercle du livre, 1956)

Prod = Production data

Sadoul = Georges Sadoul, Dictionary of Film Makers, trans., edited, and updated by Peter Morris (Berkeley: University of California Press, 1972)

TC = Sharon Russell, Trickfilm (ex. cat.), Film Center of the School of the Art Institute of Chicago, 1975, 11.

SCENARIOS

S - 1. *Le Mouton enragé*
Gaumont (116m); Release: 20 Jun 08 (*L'Argus*, 4 Jul 08); Prod: "mai: 1er scénario Gaumont . . . Mouton enragé" (MS II), 25 Fr paid, 1 May 08 (Carnet I, II); Attrib: CC-1, LD as Apr 08, TC; Genre: comedy.
Note: Directed by Etienne Arnaud. Noted in Arnaud's carnet (Coll. Deslandes): "Le Mouton enragé (?)" (18 Jan 08).
Cf. related drawing by Moloch in text.

S - 2. *Le Violoniste* (or *L'Agent et le violon, Violon et l'agent*)
Gaumont; Release: 29 Jun 08 (CC—unverified); Prod: 25 Fr paid 7 May 08 (Carnet I, II); Attrib: CC-2; Genre: Drama.

S - 3. *Le Prince azur*
Gaumont; Release: 17 Aug 08 (CC—unverified); Prod: 25 Fr paid 15 Jun 08 (Carnet I, II); Attrib: CC-4; Genre: Féerie.

S - 4. *La Force de l'enfant*
Lux (150m); Release: Jul 08 (CC; *L'Argus*, 19 Sep 08); Prod: 7 Jul 08 (Carnet II, MS II); Attrib: CC-10, LD as Mar 08, TC; Genre: Drama.
Note: Appeared on program of Cinéma-Palace (Boulevard Bonne-Nouvelle), 18 Sep 08.

S - 5. *Le Veau*
Gaumont; Release: none; Prod: 25 Fr paid 7 Jul 08 (Carnet I); Attrib: CC-11; Genre: Comedy.
Note: "Arnaud" entered by title in Carnet I.

S - 6. *L'Automate*
Gaumont; Release: 14 Sep 08 (CC); Prod: 25 Fr paid 14 Aug 08 (Carnet I, II); Attrib: CC-17; Genre: Comedy.

S - 7. *Le Coffre-Fort*
Lux; Release: unknown; Prod: 14 Aug 08 (Carnet II, MS II), CC-12; Genre: Drama.

S - 8. *Le Miracle des roses*
Gaumont (114m); Release: 12 Oct 08 (*CJ*, 10 Oct 08); Prod: 25 Fr paid 15 Jun 08 (Carnet I, II); Attrib: CC-5, H d'A, LD, TC; Genre: Féerie.

Note: Directed by Etienne Arnaud. Noted in Arnaud's carnet: "Les Roses" (16 Apr 08).

S - 9. *L'Hôtel du silence**

Gaumont (cat. 2062, 226m); Release: 12 Oct 08 (*L'Argus*, 20 Oct 08; *PCG*, 1 Nov 08); Prod: 25 Fr paid 27 Jul 08 (Carnet I, II, MSII); USA: *The Automatic Hotel* (7 Nov 08, 757 ft.); GB: *Silent Hotel* (8 Oct 08, 745 ft.); Attrib: CC-15, H d'A, LD, TC; Prints: Ciné Française, Ciné G-A (destroyed); Genre: Trick.

A guest checks into a modern hotel where all the manual labor is done by electricity and magic. In his room, meals appear and disappear automatically. He tries to sleep in an alarm-bed that ejects him. After other mishaps he attempts to leave but is stopped by the electric door until he pays his bill and leaves a tip.

S - 10. *La Sequestrée*

Gaumont; Release: 9 Nov 08 (CC—unverified); Prod: 25 Fr paid 20 Jun 08 (Carnet I, II, MS II); Attrib: CC-9; Genre: Drama.

S - 11. *La Monnaie de 1.000 Fr*

Gaumont; Release: 9 Nov 08 (*CJ*, 12 Nov 08; *L'Argus*, 7 Nov 08); Prod: 25 Fr paid 23 Jun 08 (Carnet I, II); Attrib: CC-6; Genre: Comedy.

S - 12. *Blanche comme neige*

Gaumont; Release: 9 Nov 08 (CC—unverified); Prod: 25 Fr paid 20 Jun 08 (Carnet I, II, MS II); Attrib: CC-7; Genre: Féerie.

S - 13. *La Vengeance de Riri*

Gaumont; Release: 9 Nov 08 (CC—unverified); Prod: 25 Fr paid 20 Jun 08 (Carnet I, II, MS II); Attrib: CC-8; Genre: Comedy.

S - 14. *Le Journal animé* (or *Mon Journal*)

Gaumont (cat. 2106, 78m); Release: 7 Dec 08 (*CJ*, 10 Dec 08); Prod: 25 Fr paid 20 Jul 08 (Carnet I, MS II); USA: *Current News Items* (2 Jan 09, 254 ft.); GB: *Animated Newspaper* (3 Dec 08, 238 ft.); Attrib: CC-14, H d'A, Auriol, LD, Sadoul, Edera, TC; Genre: Trick.

"This subject portrays very vividly the impression perceived by an earnest newspaper reader from the items he is reading, and embodies an innovation in the production of moving picture films. The reader of the paper is viewed from the back, and as he peruses the various articles, the impressions he receives are reproduced in moving pictures presented in miniature form covering the space of the paper he is reading" (Kleine cat.).

Note: Although usually attributed to Cohl, the payment of 25 Fr shows he was responsible for the scenario only. The trick described is probably Arnaud's "hole in the wall" shot.

A drawing "Le Vent" at the Cinémathèque Française (repro. Auriol) is not from this film, as claimed.

S - 15. *Si nous buvions un coup*

Gaumont (95m); Release: 26 Apr 09 (*CJ*, 23 Apr 09); Prod: 25 Fr paid 16 Jul 08 (Carnet I, II, MSII); Attrib: CC-13, LD, TC; Genre: Comedy.

1908 FILMS

1. *Fantasmagorie**

Gaumont (cat. 2032, 36m); Release: 17 Aug 08 (*CJ*, 25 Aug 08; *Filma*, Jul 08; *PCG*, 1 Sep 08; *L'Argus*, 25 Aug 08); Prod: 250 Fr paid 23 May 08 (Carnet I, MS II); USA: *Metamorphosis* (date unknown); GB: *Black and White* (30 Jul 08, 120 ft.); Attrib: CC-3, Auriol, H d'A, LD, Poncet, Sadoul, Edera, TC; Prints: Ciné Française, Eastman House, MOMA, Ciné Québécoise, Commercial Distribution; Genre: Animated Drawings.

"Scène tirée de dessins humoristiques et du plus drôle effet" (Gaumont cat.).

"On a black background, tiny grotesque figures in white outline go through a series of movements which cannot fail to win a laugh from all kinds of audiences. An amusing scene shows three figures; one is dancing in a frame representing the proscenium of a theatre, another is seated watching, when the third enters. She is a female with a huge hat, which she refuses to remove, whereupon the man behind pulls out the feathers one by one and at last tears off the hat altogether" (*KW*, 30 Jul 08).

Note: Shot analysis in text.

2. *Le Cauchemar du fantoche*

Gaumont (cat. 2087, 80m); Release: 14 Sep 08 (*L'Argus*, 19 Sep 08; *PCG*, 15 Oct 08); Prod: 250 Fr paid 27 Jul 08 (Carnet I, II, MS II); USA: *The Pup-

pet's Nightmare (16 Oct 08, 267 ft.); GB: *Living Blackboard* (17 Sep 08, 262 ft.); Attrib: CC-16, Auriol, LD, Poncet, Sadoul, Edera, TC; Genre: Animated Drawings.

"A Series of clever, wonderful and novel Animated Drawings by our Black and White artist" (*KW*, 17 Sep 08).

Note: Appeared on program of Cinéma-Palace, 18 Sep 08.

The drawings at the Cinémathèque Française that are claimed to be from this film are not the originals.

3. Tentative. *Le Château de cartes*

Gaumont (93m); Release: L'Argus, 3 Oct 08; USA: *A House of Cards* (7 Nov 08, 310 ft.); Attrib: TC; Genre: Féerie/Trick.

"A beautifully hand colored magic film of excellent quality and detail. His Satanic majesty makes his appearance time and time again in a most congenial manner, and to the perplexity of the principal characters participating in the presentation" (Kleine cat.).

Note: There is no documentation supporting this attribution.

4. Tentative. *La Vie à rebours*

Gaumont (133m); Release: *CJ*, 10 Oct 08; *PCG*, 1 Nov 08; USA: *The World Upset* (18 May 09); GB: *The World Turned Upside Down* (1 Apr 09, 287 ft.); Attrib: H d'A, LD, Sadoul, TC; Genre: Trick.

Humorous effects result by means of backward-motion photography. Smoke goes into a man's pipe; cars drive in reverse, etc.

Note: There is no documentation supporting this attribution.

5. *Un Drame chez les fantoches**

Gaumont (cat. 2007, 72m); Release: 9 Nov 08 (*CJ*, 12 Nov 08); Prod: 250 Fr paid 24 Aug 08 (Carnet I, II, MS II; USA: *A Love Affair in Toyland* (21 Nov 08, 240 ft.); GB: *Mystical Love-Making* (29 Oct 08, 233 ft.); Attrib: CC-18, Auriol, H d'A, LD, Poncet, Sadoul, Edera, TC; Prints: Ciné Française, Ciné G-A, MOMA, BFI, Eastman House, Commercial Distribution; Genre: Animated Drawings.

"*Black and White* and *Living Blackboard* testify to the extraordinary success of this kind of film subject, and our artist has again produced a series of clever, wonderful and novel animated drawings

which make a story both amusing and entertaining" (*KW*, 29 Oct 08).

"A chalkline series of grotesque caricatures in the land of puppets. A fickle maiden gets herself into numerous embarrassing complications with her host of admirers, but the artist with lightning rapidity overcomes all obstacles and brings the maiden out victorious" (Kleine cat.).

"A unique and exceptionally attractive Gaumont film. It cannot be described, but a game common many years ago known as 'geometry at play' comes nearest to it. It is funny and in such an unexpected and unique way that it wins rounds of applause wherever it is shown" (*MPW*, 21 Nov 08).

Note: The drawings at the Cinémathèque Française that are claimed to be from this film are not the originals.

6. *Les Allumettes animées*

Gaumont (cat. 2125, 77m); Release: 16 Nov 08 (*CJ*, 19 Nov 08); Prod: 250 Fr paid 16 Sep 08 (Carnet I); 2 Sep 08 (Carnet II); Aug 08 (MS II); USA: *Animated Matches* (5 Dec 08, 257 ft.); GB: *Animated Matches* (12 Nov 08, 250 ft.); Attrib: CC-19, H d'A, LD, Sadoul, Edera, TC; Genre: Animated Objects.

"No matches—buying a box—explosion and fright—entering his room—attempt to light his pipe—room blown up—animated matches—his pipe lighted at last." . . . "Whenever an attempt is made to light up, an explosion occurs. . . . A box of matches which behave in a most eccentric manner" (*KW*, 12 Nov 08).

"A series of magic productions with a box of matches. Well rendered and highly entertaining throughout" (*MPW*, 5 Dec 08).

". . . a box of matches on the screen; it opens and a match jumps out and stands up by itself; another follows and stands by the first, and a third places itself across the others, forming a letter H. Little by little an entire word is thus formed, or sometimes a geometrical figure" (L. Gardette, "Teaching History by Motography" *The Nickelodeon* [*Motography*], 4 Oct 09, 119).

7. *Le Cerceau magique**

Gaumont (cat. 2023, 103m); Release: 23 Nov 08 (*CJ*, 26 Nov 08; *Filma*, Dec 08); Prod: 250 Fr paid 28 Sep 08 (Carnet I); 24 Sep 08 (Carnet II); GB: *Magic Hoop* (19 Nov 08, 330 ft.); Attrib: CC-20, H

D'A, LD, Edera, TC; Prints: Ciné Française (incomplete version printed from "stuck" negative), Ciné G-A; Genre: Trick/Animated Drawings and Objects.

A girl meets a man in a park. He repairs her broken hoop and shows her how to do magic tricks with it. When she hangs it on the wall of her room, animated drawings and objects appear in it.

8. *N.I. ni, c'est fini*

Gaumont (14m); Release: 23 Nov 09 (*CJ*, 26 Nov 08); Prod: 25 Fr paid 10 Nov 08 (Carnet I, II); Attrib: CC-24, H d'A, LD, Edera, TC; Genre: Trick.

Note: Title equivalent to "That's all, folks," suggesting that the film was probably a closing trailer.

9. *Les Frères Boutdebois**

Gaumont (cat. 2117, 90m); Release: 14 Dec 08 (*CJ*, 17 Dec 08); Prod: 250 Fr paid 22 Oct 08 (Carnet I, MS II); 17 Oct 08 (Carnet II); USA: *Acrobatic Toys* (2 Jan 09, 294 ft.); GB: *Brothers Wood* (3 Dec 08, 296 ft.); Prints: MOMA, Ciné G-A (destroyed); Genre: Animated Objects (puppets).

"Prodigieux tours de force de deux petits bons-hommes de bois qui laissent loin dernière eux les marionnettes les plus perfectionées" (Gaumont cat.).

["Two wooden chaps' prodigious feats far surpass those of the most perfect marionettes."]

"Showing the doings of a couple of Acrobatic Wooden Dolls, whose performances are nothing short of marvellous" (*KW*, 3 Dec 08).

10. *Le Petit Soldat qui devient dieu*

Gaumont (110m); Release: 21 Dec 08 (*CJ*, 24 Dec 08); Prod: 250 Fr paid 27 Oct 09 (Carnet I, MS II); 10 Oct 08 (Carnet II); Attrib: CC-21, H d'A, LD, Edera, TC; Genre: Féerie, possibly with animated puppets.

"[T]he dolls come to life and dance and perform acrobatic feats" (*KW*, 17 Dec 08).

1909 FILMS

11. *Les Transfigurations*

Gaumont (123m); Release: 4 Jan 09 (*CJ*, 7 Jan 09); Prod: 250 Fr paid 30 Oct 08 (Carnet I, MS II); Attrib: CC-23, H d'A, LD, Poncet, Sadoul, Edera, TC as "Transfiguration"; Genre: Trick/Animated Drawings (?).

12. *Soyons donc sportifs**

Gaumont (cat. 2156, 124m); Release: 11 Jan 09 (CC—unverified); Prod: 250 Fr paid 17 Nov 08 (Carnet I, II, MS II); USA: *A Sportive Puppet* (9 Feb 09, 403 ft.); Attrib: CC-25, H d'A, LD, Edera, TC; Prints: Ciné G-A; Genre: Animated Objects (puppets).

"This subject portrays in a vivid manner the operations of a puppet in his efforts to see the sights. Many very entertaining and novel productions of magic" (Kleine cat.).

"A poor attempt on the part of Messrs. Gaumont. The audience did not seem to appreciate the amount of time and the tedious work required to produce such a trick film; to everyone it was too much of a wooden toy affair" (*MPW*, 13 Feb 09).

"The Gaumonts are to be commended for producing a film so entertaining" (*MPW*, 20 Feb 09).

13. *La Valise diplomatique** (or *Bourse*)

Gaumont (cat. 2164, 190m); Release: 11 Jan 09 (*CJ*, 14 Jan 09); Prod: 5 Dec 08 (Carnet I, II); USA: *The Ambassador's Despatch [sic] Case* (6 Feb 09, 624 ft.); Attrib: CC-26, H d'A, LD, TC; Print: Ciné G-A (partially destroyed); Genre: Comedy with trick photography.

". . . shows vividly how a bit of information in the hands of an over-zealous reporter caused a flurry in the financial world" (Kleine cat.).

Note: The Cinémathèque Gaumont-Actualités has confused its print with *Moderne école*.

Carnet I shows that Cohl was responsible for only ten meters of this film (probably the trick photography). The film is noted "pour Arnaud." He was paid 50 francs for his share of the work. According to Arnaud's carnet, he directed this film between 20 Nov and 1 Dec 08.

Based on a story in *Lectures pour Tous*, August 1908, 933–939.

14. *Les Beaux-Arts de Jocko**

Gaumont (cat. 2177, 100m); Release: 1 Feb 09 (*CJ*, 4 Feb 09); Prod: 250 Fr paid 23 Dec 08 (Carnet I, II, MS II); USA: *The Automatic Monkey* (27 Apr 09, 324 ft.); GB: *Jacko [sic] the Artist* (28 Jan 09,

297 ft.); Attrib: CC-28, H d'A, LD, TC; Print: Ciné Française, Ciné G-A (destroyed); Genre: Animated Objects (puppet) and Drawings.

"Jacko [sic], the clever monkey, is able to paint as well with his hind legs and tail as with his hands. He models in clay, plays the violin, mouth organ and accordion and is a marvel with toy bricks" (KW, 28 Jan 09).

"[W]e find Jocko, a full size automatic monkey, taking a hand at the fine arts. He demonstrates his ability with the brush and palette—wins laurels as a sculptor, tries architecture and proves an apt scholar of music" (Kleine cat.).

"The actions of the beast are amusing and the film gets many a laugh before closing" (MPW, 1 May 09).

Note: The drawings at the Cinémathèque Française that are claimed to be from this film are not the originals.

15. La Lampe qui file

Gaumont (cat. 2190, 100m); Release: 15 Feb 09 (CJ, 11 Feb 09); Prod: 250 Fr paid 6 Jan 09 (Carnet I, II, MS II); USA: The Smoking Lamp (13 Mar 09, 324 ft.); Attrib: CC-29, H d'A, LD, Poncet, Sadoul, Edera; Genre: Trick/Animated Drawings.

"The principal character is a man of habits who is returning from a night's carousal. Without divesting himself of his apparel, he goes to sleep on his bed and soon gives a most vivid demonstration of 'S-N-A-K-E-S.' The smoke from the lamp forms a frame for the visions portrayed. Nothing vulgar or offensive, and of excellent quality" (Kleine cat.).

Note: The drawings at the Cinémathèque Française that are claimed to be from this film are not the originals.

16. Japon de fantaisie

Gaumont (cat. 2203, 102m); Release: 15 Feb 09 (CJ, 11 Feb 09); Prod: 250 Fr paid 13 Jan 09 (Carnet I, II, MS II); USA: Japanese Magic (23 Mar 09, 326 ft.); GB: A Japanese Fantasy (25 Feb 09, 330 ft.); Attrib: CC-30, H d'A, LD, TC; Genre: Trick/Animated Objects (puppets).

"[A] clever series of illusions in which a Japanese lantern, several dolls, chickens, mice and grasshoppers play a very prominent part" (Kleine cat.).

"We overheard considerable guessing among the audience at Keith's Bijou Dream as to how the clever transformations were accomplished. Gau-

mont's man is up to all the tricks of the camera" (MPW, 27 Mar 09).

17. L'Omelette fantastique

Gaumont (cat. 2202, 119m); Release: 22 Feb 09 (CJ, 18 Feb 09); Prod: 250 Fr paid 19 Dec 09 (Carnet I, II, MS II); USA: Magic Eggs (21 Apr 09, 384 ft.); Attrib: CC-27, H d'A, LD, TC; Genre: Trick/Animated Objects; colored.

"An exceptionally clever series of optical illusions in which a basket of eggs and the chef take prominent parts. The chef gets a few ideas on the mysteries of the culinary art and is stupefied by a veritable storm of eggs" (Kleine cat.).

Note: Appeared on Hippodrome program 27 Feb–5 Mar 09.

Noted in Arnaud carnet: "Les oeufs Cohl" (3 Dec 08) and "Scène à Cohl—les oeufs" (9 Dec 08).

18. L'Agent de poche*

Gaumont (cat. 2213, 204m); Release: 27 Feb 09 (CJ, 25 Feb 09); Prod: Jan 09 (Carnet I, MS II); USA: Pocket Policeman (23 Mar 09, 674 ft.); Attrib: CC-31, H d'A, LD, TC; Print: Ciné G-A, although they have confused it with L'Agent a le bras long (Gaumont cat. 2344); Genre: Trick.

"Numerous demonstrations of the adaptability of a pocket edition officer. In time of need the citizen takes from his pocket a neatly rolled parcel; this is unrolled and the uniformed officer ready for service is at hand" (Kleine cat.).

19. Le Docteur Carnaval

Gaumont (74m); Release: 29 Mar 09 (CJ, 19 Mar 09); Prod: Mar 09 (Carnet I, MS II); Attrib: CC-35, H d'A, LD, TC; Genre: Féerie; colored.

Note: Mitry attributes this film to Louis Feuillade (Filmographie universelle, vol. 2, 203).

20. Les Grincheux

Gaumont (105m); Release: 5 May 09 (CJ, 27 May 09; Kinéma, Mar 09); Prod: Feb 09 (Carnet I, MS II); Attrib: CC-34, H d'A, LD; Genre: Trick.

Note: Appeared on Hippodrome program 10 Apr–16 Apr 09.

21. L'evantail animé*

Gaumont (cat. 2257, 86m); Release: 19 Apr 09 (CJ, 10 Apr 09); Prod: Mar 09 (Carnet I, MS II); USA: Historical Fan (12 Jun 09, 278 ft.); GB: Magic

Fan (15 Apr 09, 270 ft.); Attrib: CC-36, H d'A, LD; Print: Ciné G-A; Genre: Féerie; colored.

"A delightfully pleasing and beautifully hand-colored series of panoramic views, giving the history of the fan. A large ostrich feather fan opens and closes alternately, showing each time a different scene and the various styles of fans in use throughout ages and by many peoples. Scenes illustrated are: Adam and Eve—The Egyptians—The Greeks—Romans—16th Century—Modern Use. Highly interesting throughout" (Kleine cat.).

"[I]ts chief objection is that few will understand the meaning of the panoramic pictures shown. Adam and Eve appear to be understood by everyone, but the Egyptians, the Greeks, the Romans, the sixteenth century and modern use are all alike and somewhat obscure, and a larger proportion will never know what the pictures mean. A legend explaining each one would have made the series much more satisfactory. The technical quality and the coloring are alike beyond criticism" (*MPW*, 19 Jun 09).

22. *Les Joyeux Microbes**

Gaumont (cat. 2261, 102m); Release: 19 Apr 09 (*CJ*, 10 Apr 09); Prod: Feb 09 (Carnet I, MS II); GB: *The Merry Microbes* (*KW*, 15 Apr 09, 273 ft.); Attrib: CC-32, H d'A, LD, Poncet, Sadoul, Edera, TC; Prints: Archives du Film, Ciné Française, MOMA, Ciné G-A, Commercial Distribution; Genre: Animated Drawings and Objects.

Note: Shot analysis in text.

23. *Clair de lune espagnol**

Gaumont (cat. 2278, 98m); Release: 3 May 09 (*CJ*, 29 Apr 09); Prod: Apr 09 (Carnet I, MS II); USA: *The Man in the Moon* (17 Jul 09, 317 ft.); GB: *The Moon-Struck Matador* (29 Apr 09, 282 ft.); Attrib: CC-37, H d'A, LD, TC; Print: Kleine coll., Library of Congress (FLA 1643); Genre: Féerie with Animated Drawings; colored.

"A magic film from the Gaumont studios which illustrates a battle in the moon, and a good deal more of supposed occurrences among the heavenly bodies. It is pleasing and well photographed. The man who prepares the plays for the Gaumonts, or the one who selects them, perhaps, seems afflicted with a perpetual liver difficulty and selects generally only those more or less lugubriously inclined. Perhaps this was sneaked in without his knowing it.

If that is the case more sneaking should be done. It is a welcome change" (*MPW*, 31 Jul 09).

Note: Film made in collaboration with Arnaud. Cohl's Carnet I notes: "1/2 Arnaud"; and Arnaud's carnet notes work on "Clair de Lune Español" 26–27 Feb 09.

24. *Les Locataires d'à coté**

Gaumont (cat. 2217, 90m); Release: 3 May 09 (*CJ*, 29 Apr 09); Prod: Apr 09 (Carnet I, MS II); GB: *Next Door Neighbors* (29 Apr 09, 276 ft.); Attrib: CC-38, H d'A, LD, Sadoul, TC; Print: Ciné G-A as "Les Locataires d'en face" (print in poor condition); Genre: Animated Drawings and Objects.

Two adjoining rooms are divided by a vertical black strip representing the common wall. A young couple on the left half of the screen are engaged in amorous conversation. Hearing them, an old couple on the right side peep through a hole in the wall at them. The young man hears them and understands what they are up to. Magically, he creates an explosion. The young couple then undergo a series of transformations, to the amazement of the onlooking old couple. They bring in a neighbor to see what is happening, but all he sees through the hole is a large rolling eye looking back at him, and he concludes that his neighbors have been drinking. The young magician then makes the old couple on the right disappear, leaving only a fading spiral design (superimposition).

25. *La Bous Bous Mie**

Gaumont (cat. 2290, 148m); Release: *CJ*, 6 May 09; Attrib: Ciné G-A as "le bous bous mi"; Prints: Ciné G-A, MOMA; Genre: Comedy.

While their masters are away for the evening, the servants have a wild party. Everyone starts to dance the infectious Bous Bous Mie, including the police and the masters when they return.

Note: Cohl did not include this film in his filmography, perhaps indicating that the attribution is incorrect or that he wrote only the scenario.

26. *Moderne Ecole**

Gaumont (cat. 2271, 165m); Release: 7 Jun 09 (*CJ*, 29 May 09); Prod: Mar 09 (Carnet I, MS II); Attrib: CC-33, H d'A, LD, TC; Print: Ciné G-A (fragment); Genre: Trick.

As the pages of a book turn, Washington, Shakespeare, Peter the Great, Napoleon, Dante, Bolivar, Cervantes, and Goethe walk up the "page," salute, then exit.

Note: The Cinémathèque Gaumont-Actualités has its print confused with *La Valise diplomatique*. The film was made in collaboration with Arnaud. According to the Arnaud carnet, it was shot on 12 and 16 Feb 09. Cohl's carnet has the notation "1/2 Arnaud." Since there are notes relating to the extant scenes, it is likely that the fragment at the Ciné G-A is the portion of the film completed by Cohl.

27. *Le Linge turbulent**

Gaumont (cat. 2309, 69m); Release: 7 Jun 09 (*CJ*, 29 May 09); Prod: May 09 (Carnet I, MS II); Attrib: CC-40, H d'A, LD, TC; Print: Ciné G-A; Genre: Animated Objects.

Note: Made in collaboration with Arnaud, who noted in his carnet: "Le linge américain" (26 Sep 08).

28. *Monsieur Clown chez les lilliputiens**

Gaumont (cat. 2324; 90m); Release: 21 Jun 09 (*CJ*, 11 Jun 09); Prod: May 09 (Carnet I, MS II); Attrib: CC-42, H d'A, LD, TC; Print: Ciné G-A; Genre: Animated Objects (puppets).

The scene is a circus ring with an audience of animated puppets. A bear performs the "Indian rope trick." M. Clown and an elephant enter and perform on a balancing chair. After numerous other routines, all the animals return for a curtain call.

28. *Les Couronnes**

Gaumont (cat. 2327, 138m); Release: 28 Jun 09 (*CJ*, 27 Jun 09); Prod: Apr 09 (Carnet I, MS II); USA: *Laurels* (21 Aug 09, 447 ft.); Prints: Ciné G-A, MOMA, Genre: Féerie; colored.

"Framed in a wreath of roses we see a little Greek dancer, who sways and postures before an epicurean party of ancients, followed by a laurel wreath and encircling a scene showing school children of 1830 receiving their marks of diligence at a distribution of rewards; then the wreath of bay tendered by the Roman Senators to Caesar on the culmination of his career; now a beggar receives a loaf called a "crown" from a charitable passerby; Christ is shown crowned with thorns by the rabble; following the divine drama we see the old comedian's wreath presented to him at a performance. The next view shows the Emperor Charlemagne crowning his son Lewis. The film closes with the wreath of orange blossoms encircling a bridal party" (Kleine cat.).

"A Gaumont illustrating different varieties of laurels, such as the schoolboy laurels, the sovereigns' crowns and the reward of the winner in ancient times, the real laurel wreath. The pictures are delicately tinted, and while they admit of no particular strength in acting, being records of the crowning of different classes of people with varying laurels, the series is entertaining and leaves a pleasant impression. The pictures are technically good and the idea of framing each one in a laurel wreath adds to the effect" (*MPW*, 21 Aug 09).

30. *La Bataille d'Austerlitz*

Gaumont (90m); Release: 28 Jun 09 (*CJ*, 27 Jun 09); Prod: May 09 (Carnet I, MS II); USA: *The Battle of Austerlitz* (ca. Aug 09); Attrib: CC-42, LD as "Film schématique de la bataille d'Austerlitz"; Genre: Animated Maps.

"La maison Gaumont a essayé de reproduire schématiquement sur une carte le mouvement et l'ensemble de cette bataille grandiose" (*CJ*, 27 Jun 09).

["The Gaumont company attempted to reproduce schematically on a map the movements and general effect of this grandiose battle."]

"As an educational picture, the value of this film is unquestioned; as a popular subject for this country, there may be some question as to the interest the public would take in it" (L. Gardette, "Teaching History by Motography," *The Nickelodeon* [*Motography*], 4 Oct 09, 120).

31. *Porcelaines tendres**

Gaumont (cat. 2374, 76m); Release: 2 Aug 09 (*CJ*, 26 Jul 09); Prod: May 09 (Carnet I, MS II); USA: *Sèvres Porcelain* (25 Aug 09, 194 ft.); Attrib: CC-43, LD, TC; Print: Ciné G-A; Genre: Féerie; colored.

"Several unique specimens of highly ornamented porcelain are shown in series. In each case, the varying pieces of ware are in reality formed of living people. After a short time has been allowed for admiration of each article, it disintegrates into the individual models, who pose in various figures and dances. In the following pictures are seen a powderbox, a clock, candle sticks, a loving cup and a vase, all of wonderfully ornate design, beautifully colored" (Kleine cat.).

"[W]hen the pieces disintegrate into the original models who pose in various dances and drills the surprise of the audience is marked" (*MPW*, 11 Sep 09).

32. *Les Chaussures matrimoniales**
Gaumont (cat. 2362, 127m); Release: 2 Aug 09 (*CJ*, 26 Aug 09); Prod: Jun 09 (Carnet I, MS II); Attrib: CC-47, LD, TC; Print: Ciné G-A, Archives du Film; Genre: Animated Objects.
A bedroom comedy is performed by newlyweds' shoes.

33. Tentative. *L'Ecole du soldat*
Gaumont (151m); Release: *CJ*, 2 Aug 09; Attrib: LD, TC; Genre: Comedy.
Note: There is no documentation supporting this attribution.

34. *L'Armée d'Agénor*
Gaumont (151m); Release: 9 Aug 09 (CC—unverified); Prod: Jun 09 (Carnet I, MS II); Attrib: CC-45; Genre: Comedy.

35. *Les Chapeaux des belles dames**
Gaumont (cat. 2386, 110m); Release: 23 Aug 09 (*CJ*, 16 Aug 09); Prod: Jun 09 (Carnet I, MS II); Attrib: CC-44, LD; Print: Ciné G-A; Genre: Féerie.

36. *Génération spontanée**
Gaumont (cat. 2383, 103m); Release: 23 Aug 09 (*CJ*, 16 Aug 09); Prod: Jun 09 (Carnet I, MS II); USA: *Magic Cartoons* (1 Sep 09, 340 ft.); Attrib: CC-46 as "Les Générations comiques," LD, Poncet, TC; Print: Ciné G-A; Genre: Animated Drawings.
"An old and learned doctor discovers the secret of spontaneous generation and makes a microscopic germ which in its growth gives birth to the following people who dissolve into one another with startling mystery: A girl, after passing through numerous forms, becomes a ferocious doorkeeper. He in turn evolves into a sheriff's officer, who changes to a fisherman of great weight, whose evolution forms a collector and a policeman, who in turn dissolve into a series of designs" (Kleine cat.).
"[P]ictures like this are for amusement only, and are perfectly adapted to their purpose. The Gaumont studios have sent out a number of excellent pictures of this character, of which the one shown this week is not the least" (*MPW*, 18 Sep 09).

37. Tentative. *Les Châteaux de la Loire*
Gaumont (147m); Release: *CJ*, 23 Aug 09; Attrib: H d'A, LD, TC; Genre: Travelogue.
Note: According to his Carnet I, Cohl was traveling in July and therefore may have assisted on this film. However, there is no further documentation.

38. *La Lune dans son tablier*
Gaumont (cat. 2400, 130m); Release: 30 Aug 09 (*CJ*, 23 Aug 09); Prod: Jul 09 (Carnet I, MS II); USA: *Moon for Your Love* (20 Nov 09, 424 ft.); Attrib: CC-48, LD, TC; Genre: Féerie; colored (12m only).
"The story is enacted amid scenes of the Middle Ages and the costuming and settings are appropriate and most pleasing. A poor young student loves a fair girl who tells him that she will only love him if he brings her the moon out of the sky and puts it in her apron. Nothing daunted, the gallant scholar is about to sell his school books in order to get money to secure the services of an enchantress who will be able to get the moon for him. He consults a good fairy, who leads him to the witch's cave where they undertake his mission and flit through the skies on their broomsticks. They capture the moon and bring it back with them to earth. Our hero takes the moon to his sweetheart and she accepts it with his love, which terminates happily in the advent of a beautiful baby boy" (Kleine cat.).

39. *Don Quichotte*
Gaumont (cat. 2430, 209m); Release: 13 Sep 09 (*CJ*, 6 Sep 09); Prod: Jul 09 (Carnet I, MS II); USA: *Don Quixote* (2 Nov 09, 721 ft.); Attrib: CC-49, LD, Sadoul as 1908, TC; Genre: Animated Objects (puppets); colored.
"Histoire chevalresque de Don Quichotte et de Sancho Pança" (Gaumont cat.).
Note: A long résumé of the tableaux of the story, based on the Cervantes novel, appears in *MPW*, 2 Nov 09.

40. *Un Chirugien distrait*
Gaumont (93m); Release: 11 Oct 09 (*CJ*, 4 Oct 09); Prod: 26 Jul 09 (Carnet I, MS II); Attrib: CC-51, LD, TC; Genre: Comedy.

41. *Le Miroir magique**

Gaumont (cat. 2454, 85m); Release: *CJ*, 11 Oct 09; USA: *Telltale Reflections*; Attrib: Ciné G-A; Print: Ciné G-A as "Miroir hypnotique"; Genre: Trick.

"Showing a weird invention called a hypnotic mirror in action. Placed before anyone, the polished surface reflects the actual thoughts within their minds. Its uses in the courtroom, the home and the schoolhouse are cleverly shown. When the mechanism tells a wife the truth about her husband, something commences" (Kleine cat.).

"[T]his is a whimsical idea, and it received applause for its whimsicality. Of course, being a Gaumont it is an excellent photograph" (*MPW*, 20 Nov 09).

Note: Cohl did not include this film in his filmography.

Mitry attributes the film to Feuillade (*Filmographie universelle*, vol. 2, 203); however, because it utilizes the "hole in the wall" trick throughout, it is most likely the work of Arnaud, perhaps from a Cohl scenario.

42. Tentative. *Le Ratelier**

Gaumont (cat. 2450, 108m); Release: *CJ*, 19 Oct 09; USA: *A Set of Teeth* (16 Nov 09, 354 ft.); Attrib: TC; Prints: Commercial Distribution; Genre: Comedy.

Grandma's dentist gives her a pair of false teeth that chase everyone, including the police.

Note: The original attribution, made by a private American collector, is unsupported by any documentation. The tricks in the film are done by wires; there is no animation.

43. *Un Coup de Jarnac*

Gaumont (105m); Release: 1 Nov 09 (*CJ*, 24 Oct 09); Prod: Jul 09 (Carnet I, MS II); USA: *Jarnac's Treacherous Blow* (31 May 10, 340 ft.); Attrib: CC-50, LD; Genre: Drama.

"The acting is good, and the staging accurately reproduced court and other scenes in the time of Henry II" (*MPW*, 11 Jun 10).

Note: This film was adapted from the play *Un Coup de Jarnac*, presented at the Folies-Dramatiques in 1907. It portrays a historical event. On 10 July 1544 Vivonne de la Chataignerie and Guy Chabot de Jarnac fought a duel. When his oppo-

nent's back was turned, Jarnac struck him across the legs. Vivonne refused medical aid, preferring death to a crippled life.

44. *Les Lunettes féeriques**

Gaumont (cat. 2460, 122m); Release: 8 Nov 09 (*CJ*, 1 Nov 09); Prod: Aug 09 (Carnet I, MS II); USA: *X-Ray Glasses* (4 Dec 09, 410 ft.); Attrib: CC-52, Auriol, LD, Poncet, Sadoul, TC; Print: Ciné G-A; Genre: Animated Drawings and Objects.

"Grandfather gets a pair of magic spectacles, which he claims to possess the miraculous power of showing the tastes and inclinations of the person who puts them on. There are present at the time a large family gathering—a father, mother, sons and daughters, and grandchildren—and each member of the party in turn puts on the spectacles. Then we see on the curtain all that is passing in the mind of the wearer clearly portrayed in each eye, just as if we were looking through opera glasses" (Kleine cat.).

"A series of interesting pictures showing numerous magical changes, in geometrical forms and otherwise, all worked out in the admirable manner for which Gaumont's films of this character are famous. Some of the magic films produced by this one will not detract from the reputation of the producer" (*MPW*, 18 Dec 09).

45. *Affaires de coeur**

Gaumont (cat. 2506, 113m); Release: 6 Dec 09 (CC—unverified); Prod: Oct 09 (MS II); Attrib: CC-53, H d'A, LD, TC; Print: Ciné G-A; Genre: Animated Drawings.

"The particularly puzzling and odd step-by-step effect exhibited by the film of the 'Affair of Hearts' [sic] order, in which purely mechanical arrangement and re-arrangement of geometrical areas of black and white follow up each other in a sort of kaleidoscopic sequence, are also produced by means of the vertical camera, combined with infinite pains on the part of the artist operator. By the same means also automatic writing, drawing, etc., of all sorts is produced, the camera being stopped after each picture or two for a few more short strokes to be added or taken away" (Colin N. Bennett, *The Handbook of Kinematography* [London: Kinematograph Weekly, 1911], 94).

1910 FILMS

46. *Cadres fleuris**

Gaumont (cat. 2589, 110m); Release: 17 Jan 10 (*CJ*, 10 Jan 10); Prod: Nov 09 (MS II); USA: *Floral Studies* (24 May 10, 240 ft.); Attrib: CC-54, H d'A, LD, TC; Print: Ciné G-A; Genre: "Fantaisie" (*CJ*); Colored.

"Good photography" (*MPW*, 4 Jun 10).

A series of floral arrangements revolve before the camera. Most of the interest derives from the hand coloring.

47. *Le Binettoscope* (or *Le Binetoscope*)

Gaumont (cat. 2568, 113m); Release: 17 Jan 10 (*CJ*, 10 Jan 10); Prod: Nov 09 (MS II); USA: *The Comedy-Graph* (19 Feb 10, 338 ft.); Attrib: CC-55, Auriol, H d'A, LD, Poncet, Sadoul, TC; Prints: Ciné Française, Ciné Québécoise, Eastman House; Genre: Animated Drawings.

Note: Analysis in text.

48. *Les Chaînes*

Gaumont (116m); Release: 14 Feb 10 (*CJ*, 6 Feb 10); Prod: Jan 10 (MS II); Attrib: CC-58, LD; Genre: Féerie.

Note: Mitry attributes this film to Feuillade (*Filmographie universelle*, vol. 2, 204).

49. *Rêves enfantins**

Gaumont (cat. 2621, 108m); Release: 28 Feb 10 (*CJ*, 20 Feb 10); Prod: Dec 09 (MS II); Attrib: CC-56, LD, TC; Print: Ciné G-A; Genre: Animated Objects, Drawings, Cutouts.

Mother and Father tuck their son in to sleep with his toy dog. The dog cuts out some paper figures which undergo transformations.

50. *En route**

Gaumont (126m); Release: 7 Mar 10 (*CJ*, 27 Feb 10); Prod: Jan 10 (MS II); Attrib: CC-57, H d'A, LD, Poncet, TC; Print: BFI as "Early Cartoon" (fragment); Genre: Animated Cutouts.

A cave man watches the motion of animals and has visions of modern methods of transportation.

51. *Singeries humaines*

Gaumont (113m); Release: 14 Mar 10 (*CJ*, 6 Mar 10); Prod: Jan 10 (MS II); USA: *The Jolly Whirl* (16

Jul 10, 312 ft.); Attrib: CC-59, H d'A, LD, TC; Genre: Trick.

"Several young men are enjoying an especially happy hour at lunch in a café when one announces that he is possessed of mediumistic powers. His companions challenge him to display his ability in affecting inanimate objects. This serves to introduce a series of remarkable exhibits in which he thoroughly mixes chairs, tables, carts and people. The situations follow one another very rapidly and keep the onlooker in a first class state of suspense" (Kleine cat.).

52. *Le Champion du jeu à la mode**

Gaumont (cat. 2681, 93m); Release: *CJ*, 13 Mar 10; Prod: Feb 10 (MS II); USA: *Solving the Puzzle* (26 Apr 10, 305 ft.); Attrib: CC-61, LD; Print: Ciné G-A; Genre: Animated Objects.

"Bande comique à trucs du nouveau et célèbre jeu américain, le puzzle" (*CJ* 13 Mar 10).

["Comic trick film about the celebrated new American game, the jigsaw puzzle."]

"The film presents a drawing room meeting of enthusiastic puzzle workers. One gentleman has new ways of solving his puzzle. He puts a handkerchief over the game and immediately the puzzle is made. Under the handkerchief, we see how, piece by piece, it is put into a finished picture. His success makes him an object of envy, however, and the gentleman meets with considerable trouble before the party is over" (Kleine cat.).

"The picture is of the light sort, but it is of considerable interest because it is so well done" (*MPW*, 7 May 10).

53. *Le Songe du garçon de café* (or *Le Rêve du garçon de café*)

Gaumont (cat. 2689, 113m); Release: 11 Apr 10 (*CJ*, 9 Apr 10); Prod: Feb 10 (MS II); USA: *The Hasher's Delirium* (21 May 10, 368 ft.); Attrib: CC-60, Auriol, H d'A, LD, Poncet; Prints: Ciné G-A, Commercial Distribution; Genre: Animated Drawings, Cutouts; tinted (44m).

"Four customers are having a peaceful game of cards in a quiet cafe. The atmosphere being heavy, the waiter falls asleep and has a beautiful dream in which two angels come and play to him on violins with such charm that he is transported to the seventh heaven. The dream changes and we see him going through many amusing and fantastic scenes. Finally, customers, annoyed by his snores, wake him by pouring seltzer over him" (Kleine cat.).

54. *Le Petit Chantecler**

Gaumont (cat. 2699, 154m); Release: 11 Apr 10 (*CJ*, 9 Apr 10); Prod: Feb 10 (MS II); Attrib: CC-63, H d'A, LD, Sadoul, TC; Print: Ciné G-A; Genre: Animated Objects (puppets).

Dolls act out scenes based on Le Bargy and Rostand's *Chantecler*.

55. *Les Douze Travaux d'Hercule**

Gaumont (cat. 2720, 164m); Release: 11 Apr 10 (*CJ*, 14 May 10); Prod: Mar 10 (MS II); USA: *Hercules and the Big Stick* (21 Jun 10, 505 ft.); Attrib: CC-64, H d'A, LD, Poncet, TC; Print: Ciné G-A; Ciné Française; Genre: Animated cutouts.

A comic cutout figure of Hercules—plump and middle-aged—acts out the twelve mythological adventures (the lion of Nemea, deer of Menale, etc.). Finally he bribes Cereberus with sausages and carries off Queen Hippolyte.

Note: Mitry attributes the film to Feuillade (*Filmographie universelle*, vol. 2, 204).

56. *Le Mobilier fidèle**

Gaumont (cat. 2716, 132m); Release: 2 May 10 (*CJ*, 20 Apr 10); Prod: Mar 10 (MS II); Attrib: CC-62, H d'A, LD, TC, Print: Ciné G-A; Genre: Animated Objects.

A woman is modeling a dress for her husband when they notice that movers are pulling up before their house. When the movers attempt to take a chair, it folds its legs around one of them. A rug and a screen move out the door by themselves. When a mover sits on a piano stool, it spins around rapidly. In another apartment the landlord is seen demanding rent from a man polishing a Thonet rocking chair. The movers enter and take his furniture too. All the furniture is now out in the street. Back in the original room the walls and floors are bare. But the furniture reenters, and everything assumes its original position. The man returns, sees it, and falls down in gratitude.

Note: The film currently in distribution as *Le Mobilier fidèle* is actually *Le Garde-meuble automatique* (*Automatic Moving Company*, dir. Roméo Bossetti, Pathé-Comica, 1912).

57. Tentative. *Le Journal folichon*

Gaumont (134m); Release: *CJ*, 28 May 10; Attrib: TC; Genre: Comedy.

Note: There is no documentation supporting this attribution.

58. *Le Peintre néo-impressionniste**

Gaumont (cat. 2761, 143m); Release: 10 Jun 10 (*CJ*, 11 Jun 10); Prod: Apr 10 (MS II); Attrib: CC-66, H d'A, LD, Poncet, TC; Prints: Ciné G-A, MOMA, Ciné Québécoise, Commercial Distribution; Genre: Animated Cutouts; tinted (93m).

Note: Analysis in text.

59. Tentative. *Judgement du bouffon*

Gaumont (128m); Release: *CJ*, 11 Jun 10; Attrib: LD; Genre: Comedy (?).

Note: There is no documentation supporting this attribution.

60. *Le Tout Petit Faust**

Gaumont (cat. 2768, 125m); Release: 18 Jun 10 (*CJ*, 18 Jun 10); Prod: Apr 10 (MS II); USA: *The Beautiful Margaret* (26 Jul 10, 410 ft.); Attrib: CC-65, H d'A, LD, Sadoul, TC; Prints: Ciné G-A, Ciné Québécoise, MOMA; Genre: Animated Objects (puppets).

"All showmen and most audiences are familiar with the story. This makes the burlesque possible, for without a common knowledge of the original drama a portion of the comedy would be lost. The various parts are played by puppets in the hands of clever and careful operators" (Kleine cat.).

61. *Les Quatre Petits Tailleurs**

Gaumont (cat. 2789, 140m); Release: 8 Jul 10 (*CJ*, 9 Jul 10); Prod: May 10 (MS II); USA: *The Four Little Tailors* (23 Aug 10, 506 ft.); Attrib: CC-67, H d'A, LD, TC; Print: Ciné G-A; Genre: Animated Objects.

"A humorous skit depicting the efforts of four tailors to win the hand of the master's daughter when he promises to give her to the one most prolific in his business. The love story gives a touch of life to some good trick photography. One sews without a thread, the second sews without a needle and the third sews the wings of a fly. The fourth merely does well what a tailor should do and gets the girl, putting the seal of approval upon the man who does his work well" (Kleine cat.).

62. L'Enfance de l'art

Gaumont (105m); Release: 15 Jul 10 (CJ, 16 Jul 10); Prod: May 10 (MS II); Attrib: CC-68, H d'A, LD, Poncet, Sadoul, TC; Genre: Trick; tinted.

63. Les Beaux-Arts mystérieux*

Gaumont (cat. 2822, 113m); Release: 5 Aug 10 (CJ, 6 Aug 10); Prod: Jun 10 (MS II); Attrib: CC-69, H d'A, LD, Poncet, TC; Prints: Ciné G-A, Ciné Française; Genre: Trick/Animated Objects; tinted.

Note: Analysis in text.

64. Monsieur Stop

Gaumont (120m); Release: 5 Aug 10 (CC—unverified); Prod: Jun 10 (MS II); Attrib: CC-70, Auriol, TC; Genre: Trick.

Note: May possibly be the film with American title The Times are out of Joint (24 Sep 10).

65. Le Placier est tenace*

Gaumont (cat. 2865, 155m); Release: 9 Sep 10 (CJ, 10 Sep 10); Prod: Jul 10 (MS II); Attrib: CC-71, LD, Poncet, TC as "Placière tenace"; Print: Ciné G-A; Genre: Comedy/Animated Cutouts; tinted (70m).

A tenacious insurance salesman pursues his client through unbelievable adventures that include chasing him out of his own house, from his bank, in a balloon, and, finally, into the stomach of a cannibal.

66. Toto devient anarchiste

Gaumont (100m); Release: 9 Sep 10 (CC—unverified); Prod: Jul 10 (MS II); Attrib: CC-72; Genre: Comedy.

67. Histoire de chapeaux*

Gaumont (cat. 2899, 120m); Release: 26 Sep 10 (CJ, 24 Sep 10); Prod: Jul 10 (MS II); Attrib: CC-73, LD, Poncet; Prints: Ciné G-A, BFI as "Headdresses of Different Periods"; Genre: Animated Cutouts.

68. La Télécouture sans fil

Gaumont (120m); Release: 26 Sep 10 (CC—unverified); Prod: unknown; Attrib: CC-74.

69. Rien n'est impossible à l'homme*

Gaumont (cat. 2916, 146m); Release: 14 Oct 10 (CJ, 8 Oct 10); Prod: Aug 10 (MS II); Attrib: CC-75, Auriol, Poncet, Sadoul, TC; Print: Ciné G-A; Genre: Animated Cutouts.

A series of tableaux illustrating the marvels of modern science.

Note: Print at the Cinémathèque Gaumont-Actualités is temporarily lost.

70. Dix siècles d'élégance

Gaumont (cat. 2947, 126m); Release: 31 Oct 10 (CJ, 29 Oct 10); Prod: Sep 10 (MS II); Attrib: CC-76; Genre: Animated Cutouts; tinted.

"La Mode n'est-elle, à bien réfléchir, une forme de la folie? Folie douce, c'est vrai, mais folie tout de même. Mais la question est trop grave pour être résolue à la légère. Il convient de voir défiler devant nous tous les costumes qui ont été portés depuis l'an 900 jusqu'à nos jours. Vêtements larges, vêtements étroits, vêtements longs et courts se succèdent dans cette bande présentés dans une forme drôle pour arriver à la mode nouvelle des 'Entravées.' La mode est une déesse toute puissante devant laquelle il faut s'incliner" (Gaumont cat.).

["When you think about it, isn't fashion a kind of madness? A mild madness, but madness nonetheless. But the question is too serious to be answered lightly. It is helpful to see displayed before us all the outfits worn from the year 900 until now. Large and small clothes, long and short clothes follow one another in this film, which presents them humorously in order to arrive at the newest style, the 'hobble-skirt.' Fashion is a powerful goddess before whom all must bow."]

71. Monsieur de Crac* (or Le Baron de Crac)

Gaumont (cat. 2970, 100m); Release: 31 Oct 10 (CJ, 29 Oct 20); Prod: Sep 10 (MS II); USA: The Wonderful Adventures of Herr Munchausen (5 Mar 12); Attrib: CC-77, Auriol, Poncet; Prints: Ciné G-A, BFI; Genre: Animated Cutouts.

Baron de Crac (the French name for Munchausen) is seen in eight tableaux representing some of his famous adventures.

72. Bonsoirs russes

Gaumont (120m); Release: 31 Oct 10 (CC—unverified); Attrib: CC-80; Genre: Trick (?).

74. *Le Grand Machin et le petit chose*
Gaumont (84m); Release: 31 Oct 10 (*CJ*, 3 Dec 10); Prod: Sep 10 (MS II); Attrib: CC-78, Poncet; Genre: unknown.

75. *Les Chefs-d'oeuvres de Bébé**
Gaumont; Release (?): 21 Oct 10 (CC—unverified); Attrib: CC-81, Poncet; Print: Archives du Film; Genre: unknown.
Note: Probably began in collaboration with Feuillade for his "Bébé" series. See still in text.

76. *La Musicomanie**
Gaumont (cat. 3235, 107m); Release: 22 Nov 10

1911 FILMS

78. Tentative. *L'Automate acrobatique*
Pathé (cat. 4081); Release: ca. Feb 11; Attrib: TC; Genre: Trick (?).
"Est-ce un acrobate? Est-ce un mannequin? Telle est la question qui se pose devant cette curieuse attraction, agréablement présentée par un gracieux impresario" (Scenario).
["Is it an acrobat? Is it a model? That is the question posed by this curious attraction, presented agreeably by a gracious impresario."]
Note: There are no documents supporting this attribution.

79. Tentative. *La Chambre ensorcelée*
Pathé (cat. 4154, 135m); Release: *CJ*, 25 Mar 11; Attrib: Sadoul, TC; Genre: Trick.
"Un voyageur, descendant dans un 'Family House,' y est assailli par des faits mystérieux. Un mauvais génie semble le poursuivre et le harceler de ses méchants desseins. Les vêtements qu'il quitte se trouvent immédiatement remplacés sur lui par d'autres vêtements dissemblables. Enfin, les objets qu'il veut saisir se dérobent sous sa main et la chambre se vide peu à peu de tout ce qu'elle contient. Le voyageur, isolé entre quatre murs nus, après d'hallucinantes obsessions, quitte affolé cette maison inhospitalière et ensorcelée" (Scenario).
["A traveler stopping at a Bed and Breakfast is assailed by mysterious happenings. A poltergeist seems to follow and pester him with its mischievous schemes. The clothing he removes is replaced immediately by different clothes. Finally the ob-

jects he grasps undress themselves in his hands, and the room empties itself piece by piece of all its contents. The traveler, alone inside four bare walls with his obsessive hallucinations, leaves the unfriendly haunted house in terror."]
Note: There are no documents supporting this attribution.

(*CJ*, 24 Dec 10); Prod: Oct 10 (MS II); Attrib: CC-82; Prints: Ciné G-A, Ciné Québécoise; Genre: Animated Cutouts.
Note: Last Gaumont film.

77. Tentative. *Santippe* (?)
Note: On the occasion of the celebration of the thirtieth anniversary of the cartoon organized by Lo Duca and Bourgeon, a Cohl film called *Santippe* ("110 metres de 1910") was projected. This film has not been identified. See J. P. Liasu, "Le 30e Anniversaire du dessin animé," *Comoedia*, 6 Nov 36.

80. *Le Retapeur de cervelles**
Pathé (cat. 4156, 130m); Release: *CJ*, 1 Apr 11; Prod: Dec 10 (MS II); Attrib: CC-83, LD, Poncet, TC; Prints: Ciné Française, Eastman House, BFI as "Brains Repaired"; Genre: Animated Drawings.
"Isidore Palmer étant tombé dans un gâtisme inquiétant, son épouse le conduit chez le célèbre docteur Trépanoff. Celui-ci après avoir examiné son cerveau à l'aide d'un instrument très perfectionné, nommé céphaloscope, découvre la petit bête qui le travaille, et n'hésite pas à la lui extirper. Tandis qu'il opère, nous voyons défiler les élucubrations fantaisistes et extravagantes créés par le cerveau malade et torturé du pauvre Isidore. L'enchaînement de ses idées folles amène sur l'écran les silhouettes les plus cocasses et les plus inattendues. Enfin l'opération est terminée et Isidore, tout à fait guéri, remercie avec effusion l'habile Esculape" (Scenario).
["Isidore Palmer, having lapsed into alarming idiocy, is taken by his wife to the celebrated Dr. Trepanoff. After examining his brain with a recently perfected instrument called the cephaloscope, the doctor discovers the little beast that is working on him and proceeds to extirpate it. While he is oper-

ating, we see file before us the fantastic and extravagant elucubrations created by the sick, tormented brain of poor Isidore. His mad thoughts bring to the screen a chain of the oddest and most unexpected silhouettes. Finally the operation is over, and Isidore, completely cured, effusively thanks this talented Esculapian."]

81. *Les Aventures extraordinaires d'un bout de papier*

Pathé (115m); Release: *CJ*, 22 Apr 11; Prod: Dec 10 (MS II); Attrib: CC-84, Auriol, Poncet; Genre: Animated Objects.

Note: This was probably the first film completed for Pathé.

82. *Le Musée des grotesques*

Pathé (cat. 4226, 90m); Release: *CJ*, 6 May 11; Prod: Jan 11 (MS II); Attrib: CC-85, Poncet, TC; Genre: Animated Drawing.

"Ce film nous offre, par les déformations successives d'un tracé, une amusante série de silhouettes humoristiques, dignes du crayon d'un maître" (Scenario).

["The successive alterations of a line, this film offers us an amusing series of humorous silhouettes, worthy of a master's pen."]

83. *Le Cheveu délateur*

Pathé (cat. 4248, 115m); Release: *CJ*, 20 May 11; Attrib: DC; Genre: Animated Drawings.

"M. Martinet, en bon père de famille soucieux de l'avenir de sa fille Aline, qu'il marie, s'adresse à la science d'un mage très distingué, pour apprendre de lui l'avenir de son gendre. Le mage, après l'examen minutieux d'un cheveu du fiancé, découvre à son client un horizon gros de nuages; A peine marié, l'homme auquel le père imprudent a confié le bonheur de sa fille, fuit à l'étranger avec sa dot et, après une vie d'aventures, achève en prison une carrière orageuse. . . . Le gibet est sa dernière étape. Ces révélations alarmantes ont pour résultat de faire chasser sur l'heure le malheureux prétendant qui ne comprend rien à sa disgrâce, tandis que l'habile Lédor s'empresse de prendre sa place auprès de la charmante Aline" (Scenario).

["Mr. Martinet, as a good father, is anxious about the future of his daughter Aline, whom he is giving in marriage. He avails himself of the science of a distinguished magician to learn about the fu-

ture of his son-in-law. The magician, after minutely examining one of the fiancé's hairs, reveals to his client a horizon full of clouds. Scarcely married, the man to whom the father has imprudently entrusted the happiness of his daughter will flee the country with the dowry and, after a life of misadventure, will finish his stormy career in prison—with the gibbet the final step. Within the hour, these alarming revelations result in chasing away of the unfortunate suitor, who does not comprehend the reason for his disgrace. Meanwhile, the cunning Lédor (the magician) eagerly takes his place next to the charming Aline."]

Note: Although not recorded by Cohl in his filmography, the frames deposited at the Bibliothèque Nationale, as well as the description of the animation sequence, clearly identify this as one of his works.

84. *Les Bestioles artistes*

Pathé (cat. 9026, 83m); Release: ca. May 11—unverified; Prod: Feb 11 (MS II); Attrib: CC-86; Genre: Trick/Animated Objects.

"L'araignée, brodeuse experte, exécute une dentelle de fort bon goût; le colimaçon, n'est pas un maître cubiste, mais il ne s'en révèle pas moins paysagiste délicat. C'est en suite le tour de la souris, digne émule du maître Rodin, et enfin le Rabier de ce petit monde, le criquet, nous campe un coq altier" (Scenario).

["The spider, expert at embroidery, executes an exquisitely tasteful lace. The snail isn't a Cubist master, but he proves himself to be a no less delicate landscapist. And so on for the mouse, a worthy emulator of master Rodin, until finally the Rabier of this little world, the cricket, gives us a haughty rooster for us."]

85. Tentative. *C'est roulant*

Pathé (cat. 4317, 90m); Release: *CJ*, 24 Jun 11; Attrib: TC; Genre: Comedy.

"Des agents, poursuivant une bande de malfaiteurs, ont la mauvaise inspiration de se cacher, pour les surprendre, dans des tonneaux vides. Les bandits, en les découvrant dans cette singulière retraite, ne laissent pas échapper l'occasion qui s'offre à eux de se débarrasser de leurs ennemis en les lançant dans une course vertigineuse. Les malheureux agents, plus morts que vifs, exécutent une extraordinaire randonnée, dévalant les pentes, bousculant les autos, escaladant les maisons. . . . Ils viennent échouer finalement dans le port, où ils parviennent enfin à quitter le logis cher au philosophe Diogène" (Scenario).

["While chasing a gang of crooks, the police have the dubious inspiration of hiding themselves inside some empty casks to surprise the criminals. The bandits discover this singular hiding place and take advantage of this opportunity to shake off their enemies by launching them on a vertiginous chase. The unfortunate policemen, more dead than alive, careen down slopes, jostle autos, and roll up on houses. They run aground in the port, where they are finally able to leave the dwelling place dear to the philosopher Diogenes."]

Note: There are no documents supporting this attribution.

86. *Jobard est demandé en mariage*

Pathé (cat. 4377, 112m); Release: ca. Jul 11—unverified; Prod: Mar 11 (MS II); Attrib: CC-88; Genre: Comedy.

"Jobard, à son réveil, reçoit une déclaration ardente, sous forme d'une missive ainsi conçue: 'Monsieur, je vous ai vu! Vous êtes beau!! Je désire me marier avec vous!! Rendezvous à trois heures au café du Mystère. . . . J'y serai. . . .' Jobard pousse le cri de victoire de César: 'Veni, vidi, vici' et, tout frétillant, arrive au rendez-vous où il, s'attire diverses algarades pour avoir cru reconnaître, en d'honnêtes bourgeoises, celle qui'il cherche. Enfin, il fait connaissance avec son adoratrice; C'est la caissière de l'établissement, grosse femme mafflue et couperosée, qui jette sa coupe sur le pauvre Jobard et le conduit, en moins d'un mois, vers les douceurs de l'Hyménée!" (Scenario).

["Jobard awakens to receive an ardent declaration in the form of a missive composed thusly: 'Monsieur, I have seen you! You are handsome!! I want to marry you!! Meet me at three o'clock at the Café du Mystère . . . I'll be there. . . .' Jobard shouts Caesar's victory cry: 'Veni, vidi, vici.' He arrives at the rendezvous all aflutter and incurs various insults for having thought to recognize in some respectable bourgeois ladies the one he is searching for. Finally he meets his admirer, the cashier of the café, a fat, chubby-cheeked, blotched woman who makes a pass at poor Jobard and leads him, in less than a month, to the joys of wedlock."]

Note: Lucien Cazalis starred in all the "Jobard" films.

87. *Jobard ne peut pas rire*

Pathé (cat. 4401, 130m); Release: *CJ*, 5 Aug 11; Prod: Apr 11 (MS II); Attrib: CC-89; Genre: Comedy.

"Jobard ne peut pas rire. Il essaie vainement de faire naître un sourire sur son visage. Chez lui, le muscle du rire ne fonctionne pas. . . . Désolé, il recourt à son médecin, qui, après avoir appliqué des méthodes héroïques, se déclare également impuissant. La nouvelle d'un héritage qui vient de lui échoir ne parvient pas davantage à le dérider. Mais en se rendant chez le notaire, la vue d'une femme en jupe culotte réussit à accomplir le miracle. . . . Jobard rit à gorge déployée. Il se tord et se tire-bouchonne. Même la nouvelle que son oncle ne lui laisse en héritage que des dettes ne parvient pas à éteindre ce rire inextinguible" (Scenario).

["Jobard can't laugh. He tries in vain to crack a smile. His laughing muscle isn't functioning. He goes, depressed, to his doctor, who, after applying heroic methods, declares himself equally powerless. The news of an inheritance that has come to him can't even cheer him up. But while going to the notary, the sight of a lady in culottes succeeds in accomplishing a miracle—Jobard laughs at the top of his voice. He convulses and twists. Even the news that his uncle has left him only an inheritance of debts cannot dampen his inextinguishable laughter."]

88. *Jobard a tué sa belle-mère*

Pathé (cat. 4426, 150m); Release: *CJ*, 12 Aug 11; Prod: Apr 11 (MS II); Attrib: CC-90; Genre: Comedy.

"Jobard déteste cordialement sa belle-mère et entretient vis-à-vis d'elle la paix armée. . . . Après une querelle à propos d'un rond de cuir, que belle-maman veut se faire payer par son gendre, Jobard s'amuse à la terroriser en jouant au fantôme. Belle-maman s'évanouit et Jobard, croyant l'avoir tuée, hésite entre la crainte et la joie. Néanmoins, ses mauvais sentiments désarment devant la mort, et il va acheter une belle couronne et commander la voiture des Pompes funèbres pour enterrer dignement son bourreau. De Charybde en Scylla, Jobard, qui est distrait, change successivement sa couronne contre un pneu, une couronne de pain, et enfin contre un rond de cuir. A son retour, belle-maman, qui est revenue de son évanouissement oublie son ressentiment à la vue de l'objet convoité qu'elle croit devoir à une délicate intention de son malheureux gendre" (Scenario).

["Jobard heartily detests his mother-in-law and maintains an armed peace with her. After a quarrel about her wanting him to pay for an air-cushion, Jobard has some fun scaring her by playing ghost. She faints, and Jobard, thinking he has killed her, is torn between fear and joy. Nevertheless, her death disarms his bad feelings and he goes to buy a floral wreath and make arrangements to bury his tormentor fittingly. From Charybdis to Scylla, Jobard, who is beside himself, exchanges his wreath for a tire, a ring of bread, and finally an air-cushion. Upon his return, his mother-in-law has recovered from her swoon and forgets her resentment when she sees this coveted object and takes it as a friendly gesture from her unfortunate son-in-law."]

89. *Jobard, garçon de recettes*

Pathé (cat. 4444, 124m); Release: ca. Aug 11—unverified; Prod: Apr 11 (MS II); Attrib: CC-91; Genre: Comedy.

"Jobard agréé comme garçon de recettes, est chargé du recouvrement d'une créance à Bourézy-le-Crâne. Le directeur de la banque cosmopolitaine, où il est employé, ne lui a pas caché les dangers du métier. Aussi n'est-ce pas sans une certaine appréhension que le nouveau garçon de recettes débarque dans la localité sous-dite. Mais quel n'est pas son étonnement de voir son arrivée saluée par la municipalité qui l'acclame et l'accompagne musique en tête. . . . C'est que Bourézy-le-Crâne attend M. le Préfet pour l'inauguration d'une bande de la promenade, a pris l'élégant Jobard pour le représentation de l'Autorité. . . . Lorsqu'il s'aperçoit de sa méprise, le pauvre Jobard passe un mauvais quart d'heure et ce n'est que grâce au refuge que lui offrent de providentiel water-closet, qu'il échappe au lynchage de la foule furieuse" (Scenario).

["Jobard is working as a bank messenger and is asked to recover a debt in Bourézy-le-Crâne. The director of the city bank where Jobard is employed has not concealed the risks of the profession. So it is not without some apprehension that the new errand boy leaves for Bourézy-le-Crâne. Imagine his surprise when he is welcomed by a brass band upon his arrival. It seems that the town was waiting for the prefect to dedicate a park and mistook the elegant Jobard for him. When they learn of their error, poor Jobard has a bad quarter-hour, and it was only thanks to the refuge offered by a providential WC that he was able to escape lynching by the angry mob."]

90. *Jobard, amoureux timide*

Pathé (cat. 4473, 91m); Release: ca. Aug 11—unverified; Prod: Apr 11 (MS II); Attrib: CC-92; Genre: Comedy.

"Jobard, amoureux paralysé par une insurmontable timidité, se laisse disputer le coeur de la jeune fille qu'il aime par de nombreux adorateurs plus entreprenante. . . . Cependant, le rôle de soupirant n'est pas sans danger, et notre héros, provoqué en duel par un rival, lavera l'injure dans le sang. . . . Le malheureux duelliste tremble comme une feuille, lorsqu'un billet de sa Dulcinée lui arrive sur le terrain et lui apprend qu'il est aimé. . . . Animé d'un courage sans égal, Jobard bondit sur son adversaire comme un lion et . . . le met en fuite! L'amoureux, triomphant, épousera sa bien-aimée" (Scenario).

["Jobard the lover is paralyzed by insurmountable shyness and finds himself contending with numerous bolder admirers for the heart of the girl he loves. However, the role of wooer is not without danger, and our hero is provoked to a duel by a rival, and Jobard must bathe the injury in blood. The unfortunate duelist is on the field of honor trembling like a leaf when a note from his Dulcinea arrives informing him that she loves him. Animated by courage without equal, Jobard pounces on his adversary like a lion—and makes him flee! The triumphant lover will marry his sweetheart."]

91. Tentative. *Les Melons baladeurs*

Pathé (cat. 4475, 125m); Release: *CJ*, 2 Sep 11; Attrib: Sadoul, TC; Genre: Comedy.

"De braves paysans conduisent leur baudet, portant péniblement un lourd chargement de pastèques, lorsque, dans une rue en pente, la voiture vient à basculer et verse les melons dans la descente. Nos paysans ont beau courir, les melons courent plus vite qu'eux, et ce n'est qu'après une poursuite inénarrable et désopilante jusque dans les égouts, que les braves gens rentrent enfin en possession de leur bien" (Scenario).

["Some sturdy peasants are leading their donkey, pitifully overloaded with watermelons, when the cart upsets on a steep street, dumping the melons down the slope. Our peasants have a good chase, but the melons go faster than they do, and it is only after an incredible sidesplitting pursuit as far as the sewers that our good folks finally recover their goods."]

Note: There are no documents supporting this attribution. However, the resemblance to Gaumont's 1908 *La Course aux potirons* suggests that the idea could have been Cohl's.

92. *Jobard, portefaix par amour*
Pathé (cat. 4489, 97m); Release: ca. Sep 11—unverified; Prod: Apr 11 (MS II); Attrib: CC-93; Genre: Comedy.

"Jobard, qui s'est épris d'une charmante voyageuse, le harcèle de ses déclarations, et se fait portefaix pour la suivre. Succombant sous son fardeau inusité, Jobard tombe aux pieds de sa bien-animée, lorsqu'un mari peu commode intervient, enferme dans une malle le pauvre amoureux et le jette . . . pardessus bord! Jobard, miraculeusement sauvé, échappe à la fureur de terrible Othello" (Scenario).

["Jobard is smitten by a charming fellow traveler and harasses her with his declarations. He becomes a porter to follow her. Succumbing to this unaccustomed burden, he falls at the feet of his sweetheart. Meanwhile, an obliging husband intervenes, shuts the unfortunate suitor in a trunk and throws it overboard! Jobard is miraculously saved and escapes the wrath of this terrible Othello."]

93. *Jobard change de bonne*
Pathé (cat. 4496, 118m); Release: ca. Sep 11—unverified; Prod: May 11 (MS II); Attrib: CC-94; Genre: Comedy.

"Jobard, maître de maison inflexible, change sa vieille bonne, qui buvait, contre une jeune et accorte servante, dont les beaux yeux ont vite raison de sa sévérité. Jobard, amoureux de sa bonne, descend aux pires concessions, et accomplit les plus grosses besognes, tandis qu'en son absence, la jeune beauté reçoit tout un escadron. Jobard, ayant emprunté son uniforme à un cuirassier, après avoir mystifié et confondu l'essaim joyeux, rétablit l'ordre chez lui" (Scenario).

["Jobard is a stern master of his house and replaces his old tippling maid with one who is young

and sprightly and whose beautiful eyes quickly overcome his severity. Jobard is in love with her, so he makes concessions and does her heaviest work for her. During his absence the young beauty receives a visit from an entire squadron. Jobard, having borrowed the uniform of a cavalryman, mystifies and confuses the happy throng before restoring order in his home."]

94. *Jobard ne peut pas voir les femmes travailler*
Pathé (cat. 4530, 199m); Release: ca. Sep 11—unverified; Prod: May 11 (MS II); Attrib: CC-95; Genre: Comedy.

"Jobard, ému par le prolétariat féminin, essaye d'adoucir leurs peines. . . . Sa charité l'entraîne à se faire tour à tour chiffonnier, blanchisseur, marchand des quatre-saisons etc. . . . Mais ces diverses professions ne lui portent pas bonheur, et ce n'est qu'après une multitude de péripéties qu'il rentre chez lui. Mais rentré au foyer conjugal, les théories de Jobard changent de face. . . . Et notre prosélyte, transformé en Sybarite, s'allonge paresseusement dans un fauteuil tandis que sa femme travaille pour lui comme une mercenaire" (Scenario).

["Jobard, moved by the plight of the female members of the proletariat, tries to reduce their labor. His charity leads him to become a rag collector, a launderer, spice seller, etc. But these various professions do not bring him happiness, and after several turns of fortune he goes home. But when he is back in the conjugal foyer, Jobard's theories do an about-face. Our proselyte becomes a Sybarite and lounges lazily on a couch, while his wife works for him like a slave."]

95. *Jobard, fiancé par interim*
Pathé (cat. 4577, 100m); Release: ca. Sep 11—unverified; Attrib: DC; Genre: Comedy.

"Cet amusant sketch nous montre Jobard, chauffeur du vicomte Gaston Darcy, chargé de la délicate mission de remplacer son maître auprès d'une jeune et charmante jeune fille qu'on veut présenter à celui-ci comme fiancée. Gaston, qui a une sainte horreur du mariage, a trouvé ce subterfuge audacieux, grâce auquel, Jobard s'étant conduit comme un mufle et comme un malappris, le célibataire endurci se voit banni à jamais de la famille où l'on prétendait le faire entrer. . . . Mais à la vue de la fiancée qui lui était destinée, Gaston, saisi de remords, et peut-être de regrets, fait sentir au pauvre Jobard tout le poids de son injuste colère" (Scenario).

["This amusing sketch shows us Jobard, chauffeur for Viscount Gaston Darcy, charged with the delicate mission of filling his master's place when a charming young girl is being presented to the viscount as his fiancée. Gaston has a holy horror of marriage and has contrived this audacious subterfuge by which Jobard, behaving like an ill-bred cad, is to get the hardened bachelor banished forever from the fiancée's family. But seeing the woman for whom he had been destined, Gaston is seized with remorse, and maybe some regret, and makes poor Jobard feel the weight of his unjust anger."]

Note: This film is not included in Cohl's filmography.

96. *Jobard chauffeur*

Pathé; Release (?): ca. Sep 11; Attrib: CC-96; Genre: Comedy.

Note: Probably an alternate title for *Jobard, fiancé par interim*.

97. *Les Fantaisies d'Agénor Maltracé*

Pathé (cat. 4318, 110m); Release: *CJ*, 7 Oct 11; Prod: Mar 11 (MS II); Attrib: CC-87, Auriol, Poncet; Genre: Animated Drawings.

"Agénor Maltracé, tout frais éclos, fait dans le monde une entrée sensationnelle. Son histoire, en silhouettes comiques, se déroule dans ce film. . . . Après une jeunesse mouvementée, notre héros de papier, à la vue des femmes en jupe-culotte, est saisi du desir de convoler en justes noces. Il jette

son dévolu sur une élégante beauté, à laquelle il adresse une ardente déclaration, lorsque son ennemi le plus acharné se dresse devant lui et le confond. . . . Agénor, désespéré, se voue au célibat" (Scenario).

["Agénor Maltracé, newly hatched, makes a sensational entry into the world. This film tells his story in comic silhouettes. After a lively youth, our paper hero sees some women in culottes and is seized by a desire to marry. He fixes his choice on an elegant beauty and addresses an ardent declaration to her, while his most implacable enemy rises up to silence him. Disheartened Agénor takes a vow of celibacy."]

98. *La Revanche des esprits*

Pathé (100m); Release: *CJ*, 25 Nov 11; Prod: Jul 11 (MS II); Attrib: CC-97, Auriol, Poncet: Genre: Trick/Animated Drawings.

"Pour être resté incredule aux manifestations spirites des forces inconnus qu'évoquent sa femme et sa fille, Monsieur ne tarde pas à devenir la victime des esprits frappeurs, et casseurs de vaiselle" (*Bulletin hebdomadaire Pathé Frères* no. 42, 1911).

["In order to remain skeptical about some manifestations of spirit forces that his wife and daughter conjured up, Monsieur is anxious to become the victim of table-knocking and plate-breaking ghosts."]

Note: This film starred Cazalis. It was Cohl's last film for Pathé.

99. *La Boîte diabolique*

Eclipse (113m); Release: *CJ*, 23 Dec 11; Prod: Nov 11 (MS II); Attrib: CC-98, Poncet, TC; Genre: Trick.

1912 FILMS

100. *Les Exploits de feu Follet*

Eclipse (101m); Release: *CJ*, 13 Jan 12; Prod: Nov 11 (MS II); Attrib: CC-99, Poncet; Genre: Comedy/Animated Drawings (?).

101. *Les Jouets animés*

Eclipse (113m); Release: *CJ*, 10 Feb 12; Prod: Dec 11 (MS II); Attrib: CC-100, TC; Genre: Animated Objects.

102. *Les Allumettes fantaisistes*

Eclipse (102m); Release: *CJ*, 9 Mar 12; Prod: Jan

12 (MS II); Attrib: CC-101 as "Allumettes magiques"; TC as "Allumettes fantastiques"; Genre: Animated Objects.

103. Tentative. *Pêle-mêle cinématographique*

Eclipse (125m); Release: *CJ*, 30 Mar 12; Attrib: TC; Genre: "comédie d'actualités" (*CJ*).

Note: There are no documents supporting this attribution.

104. *Les Extraordinaires Exercices de la famille Coeur de Buis*

Eclipse (104m); Release: *CJ*, 13 Apr 12; Prod: Feb 12 (MS II); Attrib: CC-102, TC; Genre: Animated Objects.

Note: The length of 403m given for this film in *Le Courrier cinématographique* (20 Apr 12) was probably a typographical error.

105. *Campbell Soups*
Eclair (100m); Release: Apr 12 (CC—unverified); Prod: Mar 12 (MS II); Attrib: CC-103, Poncet; Genre: Advertising (or Comedy?).

106. *Les Métamorphoses comiques*
Eclipse (103m); Release: *CJ*, 1 Jun 12; Prod: Apr 12 (MS II); Attrib: CC-104, Poncet; Genre: Animated Drawings (?).

107. *Dans la Vallée d'Ossau*
Eclipse (100m); Release: 2 Jul 12; Prod: May 12 (MS II); Attrib: CC-105; Genre: Travelogue.

108. *Quelle Drôle de blanchisserie*
Eclipse (110m); Release: unknown; Prod: Jun 12 (MS II); Attrib: CC-106; Genre: Animated Objects.

109. *Une Poule mouillée se sèche*
Eclipse (200m); Release: unknown; Prod: Jun 12 (MS II); Attrib: CC-107; Genre: Comedy.

110. *Poulot n'est pas sage*
Eclipse (200m); Release: unknown; Prod: Jun 12 (MS II); Attrib: CC-108; Genre: Comedy.

111. *Ramoneur malgré lui*
Eclipse (200m); Release: unknown; Prod: Jun 12 (MS II); Attrib: CC-108; Genre: Comedy.

112. *Le Marié a mal aux dents*
Eclipse (?) (200m); Release: unknown; Prod: unknown; Attrib: CC-110; Genre: Comedy.

1913 FILMS

120. [*La Guerre de Turquie*]
Animated Weekly (25m); Jan 13; Attrib: CC-121, Poncet.

121. [*Castro à New-York*]
Animated Weekly (15m); Jan 13; Attrib: CC-123, Poncet.

113. *Le 1er Jour de vacances de Poulot*
Eclipse (200m); Release: unknown; Attrib: CC-111; Genre: Comedy.

114. *Exposition de jeunes gens à marier*
Eclipse (109m); Release: *CJ*, 10 Aug 12; Attrib: CC-112, Poncet; Genre: Trick.

115. *Réclames*
Eclair (20m); Release: ca. Aug 12 (CC—unverified); Attrib: CC-113; Genre: Advertising/Animated Drawings (?).

116.. *Le Prince de Galles et Fallières*
Eclair-Journal (5m); Release: ca. Aug 12 (CC—unverified); Attrib: CC-114, Poncet; Genre: Animated Drawing (?).

117. *Fruits et légumes vivants*
Lux (89m); Release: ca. Sep 12 (CC—unverified); Prod: Jun 12 (MS II); USA: *Wonderful Fruits* (7 Feb 13, 315 ft.); Attrib: CC-116, Auriol; Genre: Animated Objects.
"A clever trick film which will amuse and please your audience" (*MPW*, 7 Feb 13).

118. *La Marseillaise*
Eclair (99m); Release: ca. Sep 12 (CC—unverified); Attrib: CC-115, Poncet; Genre: Animated Drawings (?).

119. [*Moulaï Hafid et Alphonse*]
Animated Weekly (13m); Sep 12; Attrib: CC-117, Poncet.
Note: Bracketed title indicates that the original English title is unknown.
"Animated Weekly" refers to Universal's newsreel. The lengths and dates are from the CC filmography and cannot be verified.

122. [*Rockfeller*] [*sic*]
Animated Weekly (15m); Jan 13; Attrib: CC-25, Poncet.

123. [*L'Assurance*]
Animated Weekly (17m); Jan 13; Attrib: CC-126, Poncet.

364 ■ C A T A L O G U E

124. [*Le Charbon*]
Animated Weekly (20m); Feb 13; Attrib: CC-128, Poncet.

125. [*Le Subway*]
Animated Weekly (22m); Feb 13; Attrib: CC-129, Poncet.

126. [*Le Graft*]
Animated Weekly (18m); Feb 13; Attrib: CC-130, Poncet.

127. [*Le deux présidents*]
Animated Weekly (20m); Mar 13; Attrib: CC-131, Poncet.

128. [*Wilson et le balai*]
Animated Weekly (20m); Mar 13; Attrib: CC-133, Poncet.

129. [*Les Policewomen*]
Animated Weekly (15m); Mar 13; Attrib: CC-134, Poncet.

130. [*Wilson et les chapeaux*]
Animated Weekly (20m); Mar 13; Attrib: CC-135, Poncet.

131. [*Gaynor et les restaurants de nuit*]
Animated Weekly (25m); Mar 13; Attrib: CC-137, Poncet.
Note: William Jay Gaynor, the mayor of New York, died in October 1913.

132. [*Universal marques*]
Mar 13; Attrib: CC-138, Poncet.
Note: Apparently refers to a pretitle trademark for the Universal "Animated Weekly" series.

133. *When He Wants a Dog, He Wants a Dog* (Newlyweds, no. 1)
Eclair-NY (split reel); Release: 16 Mar 13; Prod: Dec 12 (MS II); France: *Zozor veut un chien* (*CJ*, 4 Oct 13, *Film-Revue*, 29 Aug 13, 125m); Attrib: CC-119 as "Le Chien," Poncet; Genre: Animated Drawings and Cutouts.
"Snookums decides suddenly that he must have the dog, and he proceeds to let out an awful string of those terrible wows when doggie rides away in the automobile of his owner. Papa Newlywed does

his best to buy the dog, but without success. Finally he decides to become a bold, bad burglar and goes in the night to take forcible possession of the pet, but the result is most interesting as well as funny because Papa Newlywed gets decidedly the worst of the encounter. He returns home in a barrel to find Snookums sleeping peacefully and his wife cautioning him not to make any noise" (*MPW*, 8 Mar 13).
"[A] unique little comedy which has been very cleverly worked out, evidently with pasteboard designs and figures. The peculiar manner of its progression and the whimsical play of the different designs which eventually resolve themselves into the figures of two men, a woman, a baby and a dog, will no doubt prove most entertaining and laughter-provoking" (*MPW*, ibid.).
"Dès ses premiers pas, en effet, Zozor est parti pour la popularité, c'est à dire pour la gloire, et son amusante silhouette est déjà plus connue des foules que celles de nos ministres. Il est impossible de voir apparaître à l'écran ces dessins animés sans donner libre cours à la plus franche hilarité. Les interprètes de ces abracadabrantes fantaisies ne sont pas des artistes que se seraient appliqués à imiter des bonshommes en carton. Ce sont ces bonshommes eux-mêmes qui entrent en action pour la plus grande joie de nos yeux" (*Film-Revue*, 29 Aug 13).
["From his first steps, Snookums is headed straight for popularity, even glory, and the crowds already know his silhouette as well as those of our politicians. It is impossible to see these animated cartoons appear on the screen without giving free rein to hilarity. The performers in these magical fantasies are not actors trying to imitate characters drawn on paper. They are the characters themselves that spring joyously into action before our eyes."]
Note: All films in "The Newlyweds" series were based on drawings by George McManus.

134. *Business Must Not Interfere* (Newlyweds, no. 2)
Eclair-NY (split reel); Release: 23 Mar 13; Prod: Jan 13 (MS II); France: *Bébé d'abord, les affaires après* (*CJ*, 18 Oct 13—deliverable 31 Oct 13, 107m); Attrib: CC-120 as "Le Tambour," Poncet; Genre: Animated Drawings and Cutouts.

"This time the trouble is with Snookums and the telephone, and his father has a real struggle to satisfy him. Snookums has a drum and father wants to telephone, but since Snookums believes in having a good time, and having a good time with him at least at that present minute, means getting all the noise possible out of his drum, father has his troubles in trying to use the 'phone. The way father rushes around to try and figure out how he is going to keep baby pleased and still be able to use the 'phone gives ample opportunity for many, many laughs" (*MPW*, 15 Mar 13).

Note: Scenario published in *Film-Revue* 12 Sep 13, pp. 12–13.

Alternate title, *Their Only Child*, appears in *Eclair Bulletin* no. 39, Apr 13.

135. [*Wilson et les tarifs*]
Animated Weekly (18m); Apr 13; Attrib: CC-140, Poncet.

136. [*Le Brigand de la Californie*]
Animated Weekly (25m); Apr 13; Attrib: CC-142, Poncet.

137. *He Wants What He Wants When He Wants It* (Newlyweds, no. 3)
Eclair-NY (split reel); Release: 6 Apr 13; Prod: Jan 13 (MS II); France: *Zozor est entêté* (*CJ*, 15 Nov 13; *Film-Revue* 17 Oct 13—deliverable 28 Nov 13, 121m); Attrib: CC-122 as "L'Eau"; Genre: Animated Drawings and Cutouts.

"When Snookums discovered this break in the pipe and the splashing water, he thought it was great fun to sit there and let the water spray over his nice clean clothes. His mother promptly got him out of the mess and summoned a plumber, but he almost lifted the roof with his explosive 'wows.' After a few strenuous hours, 'Da-da' came to the rescue, and going to the pipe, which our friend Mr. Plumber had just repaired, Papa Newlywed got busy with a hammer and a spike and reopened the pipe so that Snookums might enjoy himself in the nice little lake. Snookums was shortly shouting 'Da-da' and all seemed well, until the neighbors on the floor below came up to complain about the water which was damaging their apartment" (*MPW*, 29 Mar 13).

Note: Scenario published in *Film-Revue*, 17 Oct 13.

138. *Poor Little Chap He Was Only Dreaming* (Newlyweds, no. 4)
Eclair-NY (split reel); Release: 20 Apr 13; Prod: Feb 13 (MS II); France: *La Rêve de Zozor* (*CJ*, 6 Sep 13; *Film-Revue*, 1 Aug 13, 100m or 94m); Attrib: CC-127 as "Le Lait"; Genre: Animated Drawings and Cutouts.

"Funny is hardly a strong enough word—Snookums when seen in the animated cartoon form of the *Eclair* series is positively a 'scream.' It is doubtful if there has ever been presented on any screen anywhere a series of subjects which have become so wonderfully successful in such a short time as the great *Eclair* cartoon pictures of the homely little 'Snookums' and his parents, 'The Newlyweds.' This fourth in this great series is a hit from beginning to end. The action is so snappy and the drawings are so cleverly manipulated that you cannot help but be worked up to an enthusiasm which makes you roar with laughter. When the poor little chap started to cry, Da-da thought it was because there was no milk in the house, and so he started on a run to the nearest store. Here he aroused the proprietor, who had been sleeping peacefully, and purchased a bottle of milk for a dollar. But in running back to the house Da-da slipped on some ice and landed on one ear. Incidentally, the bottle of milk was broken. Back went Da-da on the run, and again he got the storekeeper out of bed. This time the previous milk cost two dollars for the bottle, but Da-da 'should worry' when it was going to make 'Snookums' happy. So he raced home and climbed cautiously up the steps, which were covered with ice. Into the house he crept quietly, so as not to disturb the precious darling. But it was dark in the house and Da-da's only match soon burned out—the very next step, and he went headlong over a chair, breaking the second bottle of milk. He was making a few remarks on the subject in no gentle tone, when 'Snookums' mother appeared and cautioned him against making such a disturbance, since Snookums was sleeping so peacefully. You'll get many laughs out of this because the animated cartoons are a thousand times funnier than any human beings could possibly be" (*Eclair Bulletin* no. 39, Apr 13).

"Le mot 'cocasse' est insuffisant pour qualifier les dessins animés de ce film ultra-fantaisiste qui apparaissent à l'écran. C'est un long éclat de rire de la première jusqu'à la dernière image, et nous croyons qu'il est difficile d'apporter plus de joyeuse humeur dans une conception cinématographique de ce genre" (*Film-Revue*, 1 Aug 13).

["The word 'funny' is insufficient to describe the animated cartoons appearing on the screen in this ultrafantastic film. It's a continual peal of laughter from the first image to the last, and we think it would be difficult to come up with any more joyous humor than this, in this kind of cinematographic conception."]

139. [*Les deux suffragettes*]
Animated Weekly (20m); May 13; Attrib: CC-144, Poncet.

140. [*Marques W.T. et M.W.*]
Animated Weekly (?) (40m); May 13; Attrib: CC-145, Poncet.

141. [*Le Moustique*]
Animated Weekly (30m); May 13; Attrib: CC-146, Poncet.

142. *Bewitched Matches**
Eclair-NY (split reel); Release: 4 May 13; Prod: Jan 13 (MS II); France: *Les Allumettes ensorcelées* (*CJ*, 24 Jan 14, 156m); Attrib: CC-124; Prints; Dist: Em Gee Film Library; Genre: Animated Objects.
"An old witch causes Schmoker's matches to form all sorts of curious and entertaining things, including a windmill, skeleton, etc." (*MPW*, 10 May 13).
"One of [the matches] even walks a tight rope and stands on his head on it" (*MPW*, 17 May 13).

143. *He Loves to Watch the Flight of Time* (Newlyweds, no. 5)
Eclair-NY (split reel); Release: 18 May 13; Prod: Mar 13 (MS II); France: *Zozor et le Taxi* (*CJ*, 3 Jan 14, 165m); Attrib: CC-132 at "L'Auto"; Genre: Animated Drawings and Cutouts.
"And here comes our friend Snookums with more screamingly funny antics. Watching the dial on a taxi cab is like a fall on slippery pavement. It is funny only when the other fellow suffers. But Dada Newlywed is a game little father and when he saw how much it tickled Snookums to see the numbers flash—well, he just wouldn't let that little darling howl so he and that beautiful wife just rode around all afternoon with the precious one. Once

or twice they thought they would quit, but Snookums set up a howl, and so back they climbed for another little ride. Finally Dada had a thought, and so he told Mr. Chauffeur to drive into the country. And what do you think? When they were out about five miles, Snookums, that little bunch of sweetness, went to sleep. And was Dada going to take chances on his waking up again—not on your life! He might want to see those numbers flash some more—and so Papa plunked down forty odd simoleans for their 'joy ride' and he carried Snookums back to his little trundle bed. Here is another scream from start to finish and it is sure to be another of the great Newlyweds series of animated cartoons, which have proved to be the laughing hit of the year. Be sure you get this one" (*Eclair Bulletin*, May 13).

144. [*Le Poker*, no. 2]
Eclair-NY (160m); Release: unknown; Attrib: CC-136, Poncet.
Note: It is unknown to which film this French title refers.

145. [*Les Cubistes*]
Animated Weekly (20m); Jun 13; Attrib: CC-148, Poncet.

146. [*L'Oncle Sam et son complet*]
Animated Weekly (20m); Jun 13; Attrib: CC-149, Poncet.

147. [*Le Polo Bateau*]
Animated Weekly (15m); Jun 13; Attrib: CC-150, Poncet.

148. *He Ruins His Family's Reputation* (Newlyweds, no. 6)
Eclair-NY (split reel); Release: 1 Jun 13; Prod: Nov 12 (MS II); France: *Zozor ruine la reputation de sa famille* (*CJ*, 29 Nov 13, 225m); Attrib: CC-118 as "Le Poker," Poncet; Genre: Animated Drawings and Cutouts.
"And now our funny little friend Snookums has started real trouble for his poor Dada. A few of the neighbors and Dada were having a nice quiet little game when the door-bell rang and when Snookums' beautiful mother went to the door, she found the minister. Well, the gang made a hurried effort to hide the things, and the chips, cards, etc. were

stuffed under the couch, before the Reverend Sir was admitted. Dada and his friends then tried to keep the minister's attention concentrated on other things, and planned to get rid of him before he suspected anything. But poor little Snookums was rather inquisitive about this hurried hiding of these nice little chips and so he secured the minister's hat and proceeded to dig out the chips from under the couch and to fill the hat with them. When the minister decided to go, to the great relief of everyone, the big scandal finally came out. When he lifted his high hat to place it on his head, there was shower of white, red and blue chips that told their story" (*MPW*, 1 Jun 13).

149. *He Slept Well* (Newlyweds, no. 7)

Eclair-NY (split reel); Release: 15 Jun 13; Prod: Apr 13 (MS II); France: *Zozor dort bien* (*CJ*, 18 Apr 14; *L'Echo du Film*, 1 May 14; *Le Film*, 17 Apr 14, 141m, 158m, or 160m); Attrib: CC-141 as "La Mascarade"; Genre: Animated Drawings and Cutouts.

"This time Dada has made arrangements to go to a fancy dress ball, and he has secured a wonderful costume. He is dressed as 'chanticleer.' The 'precious one' thought the costume very fine before they started, but he was left alone with the maid, who was given strict instructions to 'phone if she should need them. Well, just as they were having a wonderful time at the ball, one of the servants called Dada to one side, and told him that the maid had phoned that Snookums was crying. Without waiting for any further word, Dada ran out of the hall and down the street like mad to see what ailed his darling. On the way he caused a colored gentleman to faint, when he saw such a big chicken and had an altercation with a large bull dog, but he reached home finally, somewhat the worse for wear. When he rushed in Snookums was sleeping as peaceful as could be" (*MPW*, 15 Jun 13).

150. *He Was Not Ill, Only Unhappy* (Newlyweds, no. 8)

Eclair-NY (split reel); Release: 29 Jun 13; Prod: May 13 (MS II); France: *Zozor et l'épingle de nourrice* (*CJ*, 4 Apr 14; *Le Film*, 3 Apr 14—deliverable 17 Apr 14, 138m or 185m); Attrib: CC-143, Poncet; Genre: Animated Drawings and Cutouts.

"Poor little dear! This time our Snookums is in real trouble. No, he was not ill, but—believe me—

he was unhappy. And the household and all the neighbors had their share of trouble until the poor little fellow found a real friend in his dear mother's mama. She found the cause of all this trouble, and it was no small cause. After Snookums had caused his Dada and his mama to do everything but send in a fire alarm, Grandmother Newlywed found a great big safety pin—and it was sticking poor little Snookie where he could feel it, and feel it good. No wonder he yelled" (*MPW*, 29 Jun 13).

151. [*Wilson Row Row*]

Animated Weekly (20m); Jul 13; Attrib: CC-154, Poncet.

152. *It is Hard to Please Him, but It Is Worth It* (Newlyweds, no. 9)

Eclair-NY (split reel); Release: 13 Jul 13; Prod: May 13 (MS II); Attrib: CC-147 as "Les Ballons rouges," Poncet; Genre: Animated Drawings and Cutouts.

"Da! Da! What does little Snookums want now? Nice man is coming down the street with big, bright balloons. Mother must get him one. Now home for nursie to see it. Poor fat nursie must add another accomplishment for Snookums' benefit. She puffs and pants, and puffs and pants some more to keep the balloon blown up for Baby dear. 'Pshaw! It's busted,' says nursie, at which Snookums bursts forth with the preliminary 'Wow' which his mother knows as the overture to his vocal entertainment. She is not in a musical mood so she telephones Dada and tells him to come right home with some toy balloons for Precious. Dada comes home and he and mother and nursie are well nigh exhausted keeping the balloons blown up for baby dear, when it occurs to Dada to let the old bicycle pump do the work. But little sugar-plum is no longer interested: he drops off into the sleep of innocence at mother's feet, and his devoted subjects sigh with relief as he is carried off to bed" (*MPW*, 13 Jul 13).

153. *He Poses for His Portrait* (Newlyweds, no. 10)*

Eclair-NY (split reel); Release: 27 Jul 13; Prod: Jun 13 (MS II); France: *Le Portrait de Zozor* (*CJ*, 25 Jul 14, 102m); Attrib: CC-151 as "Le Peintre", Poncet; Print: MOMA; Genre: Animated Drawings and Cutouts.

"So then we shall have a portrait of boo'ful Snookums. Muvver says he's like Dada. Dada says he's like Muvver. Both agree he's the prettiest baby ever and should have a portrait painted. A famous painter is engaged. He is happy to paint their darling, but—'Come, kitty, kitty, kitty.' Snookums doesn't want a picture; he wants to pull its 'ittle tail. Snookums cries. They are distracted. A wild hunt for the elusive kitten takes place. The famous painter scrambles around under beds and bureaus and finally gets Snookums the kitten, but Snookums gets his goat. A battle royal between the most wonderful baby and its latest prize, and again a kitten hunt is in order. Another moment and the doting parents find themselves and their Snookums politely dismissed; next moment the painter collapses in the arms of sympathetic friends and relates the indignities Snookums would heap on his exalted head" (*Eclair Bulletin*, 27 Jul 13).

154. [*Thaw et Lasso*]
Animated Weekly (15m); Aug 13; Attrib: CC-156, Poncet.

155. [*Bryant et les discours*]
Animated Weekly (16m); Aug 13; Attrib: CC-157, Poncet.

156. *Clara and Her Mysterious Toys*
Eclair-NY (split reel); Release: 10 Aug 13; Prod: Jul 13 (MS - II); France: *Les Jouets de Clara* (*CJ*, 14 Feb 14, 98m); Attrib: CC-152 as "Les Joujoux de Clara", Poncet; Genre: Animated Objects.
"Little Clara Horton, the 'Eclair Kid,' is shown at the rainy day pastime of cutting paper up into bits. Tiring of this, Clara throws a handful into the air. The pieces automatically gather toward a common center, and marshal themselves about into a toy aeroplane which takes flight as easily as though controlled at the helm. As this fades more bits thrown up by the child form a box of colors that weave themselves into many pretty designs which culminate in the words, 'you're welcome.' It is still raining, so another handful transposes itself into a Japanese doll, which grows under your eyes limb by limb. Mme. Butterfly, as Clara calls the doll, grows smaller and smaller until she disappears to a dot which suddenly assumes the form of a paper square. As you look, a gorgeous butterfly appears on this and flutters its wings gracefully. The scene fades back into the first picture of little Clara, but she is now surrounded by the very toys you have seen instead of the paper bits. She daintily throws 'a million of kisses' to you in farewell" (*MPW*, 10 Aug 13).

157. [*Thaw et l'araignée*]
Animated Weekly (20m); Sep 13; Attrib: CC-158, Poncet.

158. [*Diana marques*]
Animated Weekly (?) (100m); Sep 13; Attrib: CC-160, Poncet.

159. *A Vegetarian's Dream*
Eclair-NY (split reel); Release: 7 Sep 13; Prod: Aug 13 (MS II); Attrib: CC-153 as "Les Légumes"; Genre: Animated Objects.
"In order to give some genuine laughs to audiences the world over, a high-salaried artist labored patiently with the pen and scissors for *a whole month* to evolve nearly 80,000 drawings which were required to produce this unique reel. . . . Mr. Slim, let us suppose, goes to sleep after an overhearty meal of his favorite vegetables, and dreams the surprising antics which are here reproduced. Turnips, beets, beans, squashes, their aunts, uncles, and cousins, sprout and grow before your eyes, melting one into the other. Every now and then a surprising incident takes place, as when the lemons play leapfrog, and an intellectual leek photographs two stage-struck froggies with a moving picture camera. Some well-behaved lemons suddenly turn into little pigs. A trussed chicken dances tantalizingly through the picture, followed by two onions. Miss Pink Onion is deserted by young Mr. Red Onion. She dejectedly leans over a glass and weeps. It fills up quickly, and the young lady falls in and drowns just as her lover returns. On seeing her fate, Mr. Red Onion sobbingly drowns himself also. This very unusual trick subject will certainly be one of the real hits of the year" (*Eclair Bulletin*, Aug 13).

160. *He Loves to Be Amused* (Newlywed, no. 11)
Eclair-NY (split reel); Release: 19 Oct 13; Prod: Aug 13 (MS II); Attrib: CC-155 as "Le Chapeau," Poncet; Genre: Animated Drawings and Cutouts.
" 'Da, Da! [*sic*]' Papa Newlywed and his lovely wife looked up apprehensively. That sound had a

strangely familiar strain to it. Could it be true? Yes. Their own precious Snookums was on the warpath again. 'Da, da!' They were seated on the shore watching somebody's bow-wow fetch the sticks thrown into the water. Snookums pulled tails too hard. 'Da, da!' Snookums joyously threw papa Newlywed's hat into the nice, wet water. Bow-wow's mean owner would not let him fetch the hat, so poor papa had to go in and get it himself. Then Snookums threw it back again and papa got another ducking. Then papa 'panked 'is 'ittle precious. Wa-a-a-a-a-a-ah-h-h-h-h! My but he did howl! Mama Newlywed terribly upset and they brought him a great, big, beautiful doll. When his lungs gave out, Snookums peeped at the doll. It winked at him. Enough! Snookums was his father's son and took it to his heart. So home went the Newlywed family. Papa Newlywed slinking behind so no one should see his nice new clothes all wet and muddy. And Snookums, he was now so cute and good that his gratified parents placed a regal crown upon his mischievous little head" (*Eclair Bulletin*, 56, Oct 13).

161. *Unforeseen Metamorphosis*
Eclair-NY (split reel); Release: 16 Nov 13; Prod: Sep 12 (MS II); Attrib: CC-159 as "Les Métamorphoses malheureuses"; Genre: Animated Drawings.

"Without a doubt the cleverest film of drawings ever made. From one dazzling and mystifying transformation to another these drawings jump. A dog becomes a man. A beautiful flower is evolved from George Washington's portrait. There are many little humorous touches interspersed in this reel and the quick exchanges from the ridiculous to the sublime are bound to keep audiences in a continual roar. Again, very many beautiful scenes of New York's waterfront and view [*sic*] of interest throughout the country are flashed, only to resolve

themselves into some astonishing shape or form. From the flash of a gun we see a canoe floating peacefully down the water and this disappears to be replaced by a single line, which forms itself into a beautiful prism and then gives way to something equally startling" (*MPW*, 8 Nov 13).

"[A] highly original and entertaining series of movable drawings, introducing animals, street parades, fruits and the like. One of the best series of this kind we have seen" (*MPW*, 15 Nov 13).

162. [*Exposition de caricatures*]
Eclair-NY; Release: unknown; Attrib: CC-162, Poncet; Genre: Animated Drawings (?).
Note: May refer to an unreleased American film.

163. *He Likes Things Upside Down* (Newlyweds, no. 12)
Eclair-NY (split reel); Release: 14 Dec 13; Prod: Oct 13 (MS II); Attrib: CC-161 as "Il aime tout à l'envers," Poncet; Genre: Animated Drawings and Cutouts.

"Snookums is being amused by the neighbor's kid next door who gracefully stands on his head for minutes at a time. When he refuses to keep this position permanently, Snookums raises a holler. The Newlyweds are highly indignant at the neighbor's child for refusing to keep his head-standing position for the edification of Snookums. Newlywed stands on his head until he is black in the face, but is unable to maintain this position all the time. Poor Newlywed is at his wit's end, but suddenly a happy thought strikes him. His little Snookums shall have things upside down. He retires and gracefully redonning his trousers in the reverse, sticks his hands through the bottom of his trousers and waves them as feet, for the enjoyment of Snookums and the kid at last has things upside down" (*MPW*, 14 Dec 13).

1914 FILMS

164. *He Doesn't Care to Be Photographed* (Newlyweds, no. 13)
Eclair-NY (split reel); Release: 25 Jan 14; Prod: Nov 13 (MS II); Attrib: CC-163 as "Il ne veut pas être photographié," Poncet; Genre: Animated Drawings and Cutouts.

"Newlywed buys a camera and attempts to photograph the kid. He tries to pose him but his dar-

ling refuses to stand for it. He chases him into the bedroom. Baby crawls under the bed, papa follows him, but it is too dark to take a picture there. Chased by Newlywed the kid runs under the table and from there around and in back of the piano. Newlywed, assuming a graceful attitude, attempts to photograph him from the top of the piano and comes near to breaking his neck. He gets him at last with a startling rear view and snaps the button. He is about to take another but Baby sets up a howl and it is all off" (*Eclair Bulletin* no. 59, Jan 14).

165. [*Pickmeup est un sportman*]
Eclair-NY (split reel); Release: unknown; Prod: Dec 14 (MS II); Attrib: CC-164, Poncet.
Note: May refer to an unreleased film.

166. [*La Baignoire*]
Eclair-NY (split reel); Release: unknown; Prod: Jan 14 (MS II); Attrib: CC-165, Poncet.
Note: May refer to an unreleased film.

167. [*Il aime le bruit*]
Eclair-NY (split reel); Release: unknown; Prod: Jan 14 (MS II); Attrib: CC-166, Poncet.
Note: May refer to an unreleased film in "The Newlyweds" series.

168. [*Il joue avec Dodo*]
Eclair-NY (split reel); Release: unknown; Prod: Mar 14 (MS II); Attrib: CC-168.
Note: May refer to an unreleased film in "The Newlyweds" series. This was Cohl's last American film.

169. *L'Enlèvement de Déjanire Goldebois*
Eclair (115m); Release: 12 Feb 17; Prod: May 14 (MS II); Attrib: CC-169; Genre: Animated Objects (puppets).
". . . avec des poupées et quelques jouets " (*Le Film*, 12 Feb 17).

Note: The release of this film was delayed because of the war. It was Cohl's first after returning to Epinay.

170. *L'Avenir dévoilé par les lignes des pieds**
Eclair (170m); Release: *CJ*, 3 Mar 17; *Le Film*, 12 Mar 17; Attrib: CC-170, Poncet; Print: Archives du Film (one minute missing); Genre: Animated Drawings.
"L'Union [Eclair], non plus, ne s'est pas foulée! car elle ne présente qu'un film . . . dont les dessins animés ingénieux. Bon petit film qui aurait pu être accompagné d'un ou deux autres. Rationner les programmes tout comme les plats au restaurant, est-ce de la bonne politique commerciale? Je ne le crois pas" (Guillaume Danvers, *Le Film*, 12 Mar 17).
["Union-Eclair is taking things easy since they're only presenting one film—of ingenious animated cartoons. A good little film that should have been accompanied by one or two others. To ration programs like courses in a restaurant—is it good commercial politics? I think not."]
Note: The release of this film was delayed because of the war.
Description in text.

171. *Le Ouistiti de Toto*
Eclair (94m); Release: unknown; Prod: Jul 14 (MS II); Attrib: CC-171; Genre: Trick.
Note: Cohl received payment of 940 Fr (i.e., ten Fr/meter) in Jan 15, but it is unlikely the film was ever released (Carnet III).

1915 FILMS

172. *Le Voisin trop gourmand*
Eclair (114m); Release: unknown; Prod: Jan 15 (MS II) (Carnet III); Attrib: CC-173, Poncet; Genre: Animated Drawings (?).
Note: May never have been released. Cohl was paid 684 Fr for the film on Jan 15 (Carnet III).

173. *La Trompette anti-neurasthénique*
Eclair (150m); Release: unknown; Prod: Jan or May 15; Attrib: CC-175, Poncet.
Note: "Livré Jan 15, 684 Fr" (Carnet III), but listed as May 15 in MS II.

174. *Bande sociale*
Eclair (80m); Release: unknown; Prod: Jan 15 (MS II as "Bande Boissière"); Attrib: CC-172, Poncet.

175. *Ce qu'ils mangent*
Eclair-Journal (12m); Feb 15; Attrib: CC-174, Poncet.
Note: The Eclair-Journal films were made for inclusion in Eclair's newsreel. The lengths and dates cannot be verified.

176. *Fantaisies truquées*
Eclair (100m); Release: unknown; Prod: Jul 15 (MS II); Attrib: CC-177.

177. *La Blanchisserie américaine*
Eclair (120m); Release: unknown; Prod: Aug 15 (MS II); Attrib: CC-178.

178. *Fruits et légumes animés*
Eclair (120m); Release: unknown; Prod: Sep 15 (MS II); Attrib: CC-179.

179. *Les Braves Petits Soldats de plomb*
Eclair (140m); Release: unknown; Prod: Oct 15 (MS II); Attrib: CC-180.

180. *Carte de la Serbie*
Eclair-Journal (10m); Oct 15; Attrib: CC-181, Poncet.

181. *Taisez-vous, méfiez-vous*
Eclair-Journal (10m); Nov 15; Attrib: CC-183, Poncet.

182. *Une Drame sur une planche à chaussures*
Eclair (122m); Release: *CJ*, 13 Jan 17; *Le Film*, 26 Mar 17; Prod: Dec 15 (MS II); Attrib: CC-184; Genre: Animated Objects.
"Un comique à trucs très amusant . . . où je ne vois M. André Séchan que quelque mètres. Quand lui fera-t-on tourner un bon film digne de ses succès passés?" (Danvers, *Le Film*, 26 Mar 17).
["An amusing trick comedy in which I saw André Séchan for only a few meters. When will they make a film for him worthy of his past success?"]
Note: The release of this film was delayed because of the war.

183. *Bonne année*
Eclair-Journal (10m); Dec 15; Attrib: CC-185, Poncet.

1916 FILMS

184. *Hôtel des Anglais et Ruhl, Nice*
Eclair-Journal (40m); Jan 16; Attrib: CC-186.
Note: Advertising or travel film shot during Cohl's stay in Nice 14 Dec 15–15 Jan 16.

185. *La Main mystérieuse*
Eclair (102m); Release: *CJ*, 19 Feb 16; Prod: Jan–Feb 16 (MS II); Attrib: CC-187; Genre: Trick.
Note: Partially filmed in Nice.

186. *Le Terrible Bout de papier*
Eclair (105m); Release: *CJ*, 11 Mar 16; Prod: Nov 15 (MS II); Attrib: CC-182, Poncet; Genre: Animated Objects.

187. *Les Exploits de Farfadet*
Eclair (104m); Release: *CJ*, 1 Apr 16; Prod: Feb 16 (MS II); Attrib: CC-188, Poncet; Genre: Animated Drawings (?).

188. *Les Tableaux futuristes et incohérents*
Eclair (125m); Release: *CJ*, 8 Apr 16; Prod: Mar 16 (MS II); Attrib: CC-189, Poncet; Genre: Animated Drawings and Cutouts.

"L'ironie des titres et sous-titres n'est pas comprise" (*Le Film*, 15 Apr 16).
["The irony of the titles and subtitles is not understood."]

189. *Pulchérie et ses meubles*
Eclair (161m); Release: *CJ*, 6 May 16; Prod: Apr 16 (MS II); Attrib: CC-190; Genre: Animated Objects.

190. *Les Evasions de Bob Walter*
Eclair (276 or 280m); Release: *CJ*, 20 May 16; *Le Film*, 27 May 16; Prod: May 16 (MS II); Attrib: CC-191; Genre: Trick (?).
Note: Mlle. Bob Walter was a turn-of-the-century music hall performer.

191. *Mariage par suggestion*
Eclair (270 or 275m); Release: *CJ*, 1 Jul 16; *Le Film*, 8 Jul 16; Prod: May 16 (MS II); Attrib: CC-192; Genre: Comedy/Trick.

192. *Les Victuailles de Gretchen se révoltent*
Eclair (120m); Release: *CJ*, 24 Mar 17; *Le Film*,

2 Apr 17; Prod: Jul 16 (MS II); Attrib: CC-193; Genre: Animated Cutouts.

"[N]ous font espérer d'autres films plus conséquents" (*Le Film*, 2 Apr 17).

["We hope for other, more consequential, films."]

Note: The release of this film was delayed because of the war.

193. *Figures de cire et têtes de bois*
Eclair (100m); Release: *CJ*, 12 Aug 16; *Le Film*, 26 Aug 16; Prod: Aug 16 (MS II); Attrib: CC-194; Genre: Animated Objects.

Note: The film included some animated "cocottes en papier" (*Le Film*).

194. *Ses Ancêtres*
Eclair (110m); Release: *CJ*, 9 Sep 16; *Le Film*,
16 Sep 16; Prod: Jun 15 (MS II); Attrib: CC-176, Poncet; Genre: Animated Drawings and Cutouts.

Note: "Livré Jan 15" (Carnet III); release probably delayed because of the war.

195. *Carte de Picardie*
Eclair-Journal (10m); Sep 16; Attrib: CC-195, Poncet.

196. *Croquemitaine et Rosalie*
Eclair (110m); Release: *CJ*, 21 Oct 16; *Le Film*, 29 Sep 16; Prod: Sep 16 (MS II); Attrib: CC-196, Poncet.

197. *Bonne année*
Eclair-Journal (6m); Dec 16; Attrib: CC-200.

1917 FILMS

198. *Jeux de Cartes*
Eclair (125m); Release: *CJ*, 27 Jan 17; *Le Film*, 5 Feb 17; Prod: Oct 16 (MS II); Attrib: CC-197; Genre: Animated Objects (?).

". . . d'une photo plus qu'une insuffissant. J'ai raison de croire que les copies . . . ne sont pas des copies définitives, mais des copies d'enchantillonage" (Danvers, *Le Film*, 5 Feb 17).

[". . . more than insufficient photography. I have reason to believe that the copies . . . are not release prints, but answer prints."]

199. *La Journée de Flambeau* (or *Flambeau, chien perdu*)
Navarre/AGC; Release: none; Prod: Nov 16 (MS II); Attrib: CC-198; Genre: Animated Drawings and Cutouts; based on drawings by Benjamin Rabier.

This film was never completed; although Rabier completed a film with this title in 1919, it is unlikely that it contained any of Cohl's original footage.

200. *Flambeau au pays des surprises* (or *Flambeau aux lignes*)
Navarre/AGC; Release: none; Prod: Dec 16 (MS II); Attrib: CC-199, Poncet; Genre: Animated Drawings and Cutouts; based on drawings by Rabier.

This film was never completed.

201. *Le Père tranquille et le garnement*
Producer unknown; Release: unknown; Attrib: CC-206 as "Apr 17."

202. *Les Aventures de Clémentine*
Navarre/AGC (170m); Release: *CJ*, 21 May 17; *Le Film*, 28 May 17; Attrib: CC-204, Poncet; Genre: Animated Drawings and Cutouts; based on drawings by Rabier.

". . . nous donnent les débuts à l'écran du dessinateur Benjamin Rabier. Clémentine est une mère canne qui protège ses canetons contre les dangers qui les menacent. Gros succès pour les dessins animés de Benjamin Rabier qui sont des plus amusant et qui ont fort bien commencé la série de notre spirituel caricaturiste" (Danvers, *Le Film*, 28 May 17).

["[The film] shows us the screen debut of the illustrator Benjamin Rabier. Clementine is a mother duck protecting her ducklings from menacing dangers. Great success for Benjamin Rabier, our witty caricaturist, and a good start for his series of animated cartoons, which are the funniest."]

203. *Les Aventures des Pieds-Nickelés* (no. 1)
Eclair (125m); Release: *CJ*, 2 Jun 17; *Le Film*, 11 Jun 17; Prod: Dec 16 (MS II); Attrib: CC-201, Poncet; Genre: Animated Drawings and Cutouts.

"Depuis dix ans le journal *L'Epatant* publie les aventures des Pieds Nickelés. 1.000.000 de lecteurs voudront voir à l'écran les trois amis: Croquignol, Ribouldingue, et Filochard" (*CJ*, 2 Jun 17).

["The paper *L'Epatant* has published the adventures of the Pieds Nickelés for ten years. A million readers want to see their three friends Croquignol, Ribouldingue, and Filochard on the screen."]

Note: An unidentified fragment from one film in this series is at the Archives du Film.

All films in the "Pieds Nickelés" series were based on the drawings of Louis Forton.

204. Tentative. *Les Cartes animées*
AGC (110m); Release: *Le Film*, 4 May 17; Attrib: DC; Genre: Animated Maps.

". . . l'avance franco-brittanique sur le front occidental nous font, par un ingénieux et original procédé, assister à la synthèse graphique de la retraite allemande, de l'avance brittanique en Artois et de l'avance française de Soissons à Reims" (*Le Film*, 4 May 17).

["[The film shows] the Franco-British advance on the western front and demonstrates, by means of an ingenious and original process, a graphic synthesis of the German retreat, the British advance in Artois, and the French advance from Soissons to Reims."]

Note: It is likely that Cohl sold this film to AGC but cannot be proven.

205. *Les Fiançailles de Flambeau**
Navarre/AGC (145m); Release: *CJ*, 23 Jun 17; Prod: Jan 17 (MS II); Attrib: CC-203, Poncet; Print: Ciné Française; Genre: Animated Drawings and Cutouts; based on drawings by Rabier.

Note: Discussed in text.

206. *Les Aventures des Pieds Nickelés* (no. 2)
Eclair (120m); Release: *CJ*, 1 Jul 17; *Le Film*, 21 Jul 17; Prod: Feb 17 (MS II); Attrib: CC-202, Poncet; Genre: Animated Drawings and Cutouts.

"Amusants dessins animés un peu court" (*Le Film*, 21 Jul 17).

207. *Les deux armées*
Eclair-Journal (10m); Sep 17; Attrib: CC-205, Poncet.

208. *Verdun*
Eclair-Journal (15m); Sep 17; Attrib: CC-207, Poncet.

209. *Ypres*
Eclair-Journal (8m); Oct 17; Attrib: CC-209, Poncet.

210. *Canal Dieppe-Paris*
Eclair-Journal (10m); Nov 17; Attrib: CC-210, Poncet.

211. *Emprunt (transformation)*
Eclair-Journal (11m); Nov 17; Attrib: CC-211, Poncet.

212. *Emprunt (paysan)*
Eclair-Journal (12m); Nov 17; Attrib: CC-211, Poncet.

213. *Les Aventures des Pieds Nickelés* (no. 3)
Eclair (ca. 120m); Release: *Le Film*, 26 Nov 17; Prod: Oct 16 (MS II); Attrib: CC-208, Poncet.

214. *Le Pain rationné*
Eclair-Journal (10m); Nov 17; Attrib: CC-216, Poncet.

215. *Etude Zeppelin (le ballon)*
Eclair-Journal (30m); Dec 17; Attrib: CC-213, Poncet.

216. *Emprunt (le mur)*
Eclair-Journal (10m); Dec 17; Attrib: CC-217, Poncet.

217. *Etude Zeppelin (la nacelle)*
Eclair-Journal (28m); Dec 17; Attrib: CC-214, Poncet.

218. *Etude Zeppelin (la passerelle)*
Eclair-Journal (30m); Dec 17; Attrib: CC—219, Poncet.

219. *Canon de Côtes*
Eclair-Journal (20m); Dec 17; Attrib: CC-219, Poncet.

220. *Bonne Année*
Eclair-Journal (10m); Dec 17; Attrib: CC-221, Poncet.

1918–1920 Films

221. *Les Aventures des Pieds Nickelés, ou Filochard se distingue* (no. 4)*

Eclair (125m); Release: *CJ*, 19 Jan 18; *Le Film*, 28 Jan 18; Prod: Dec 17 (MS II); Attrib: CC-218, Poncet; Print: Archives du Film (incomplete); Genre: Animated Drawings and Cutouts.

222. *Le Gotha*

Eclair-Journal (20m); Jan 18; Attrib: CC-220, Poncet.

223. *Les Mines* (or *Comment les Boches posent leurs mines*)

Eclair-Journal (20m); Jan 18; Attrib: CC-222, Poncet.

224. *Mine et Contre-mine*

Eclair-Journal (?); Feb 18; Attrib: CC-224, Poncet.

225. *Etude schématique d'un haut fourneau*

Eclair-Journal (20m); Feb 18; Attrib: CC-225, Poncet.

226. *Un Habit d'Arlequin* (*L'Autriche*)

Eclair-Journal (20m); Feb 18; Attrib: CC-226, Poncet.

227. *La Transfusion du sang*

Eclair-Journal (20m); Mar 18; Attrib: CC-227, Poncet.

228. *Les Aventures des Pieds Nickelés* (no. 5)

Eclair (125m); Release: *CJ*, 16 Mar 18; *Le Film*, 2 Apr 18; Prod: Feb 18 (MS II); Attrib: CC-223; Genre: Animated Drawings and Cutouts.

229. *Les Usines Renault*

Eclair-Journal (?); Attrib: CC-228, Poncet.

Note: This and the following Eclair-Journal films can be dated only between mid-1918 and May 1920.

230. *Paris sous les bombes*, CC-229.

231. *Un Quartier de Paris*, CC-230.

232. *Paris s'agrandit*, CC-231.

233. *Emprunt* (*la machine*), CC-232.

234. *Emprunt* (*les trois usines, port, etc.*), CC-233.

235. *Un Wagon déchargé*, CC-234.

236. *Auto-Avion-Sous-marine*, CC-235.

237. *Dérivation de la Seine*, CC-236.

238. *Un Compteur à Gaz*, CC-237.

1921–1923 Films

239. *La Maison du fantoche*

AGC (195m); Release: Apr 21 (AGC cat.); Prod: May 20 (MS II as "! cherche un logement"); Attrib: CC-238, Poncet; Genre: Animated Drawings (?).

240. *Pages d'Histoire*

Aigle Film/Editions d'Art Français (200m); Release: unknown; Prod: unknown; Attrib: DC; Genre: Historical (?).

This film, known only by an advertisement (fig. 203), was intended for release on May 5, 1921, the centenary of the death of Napoleon. The scenario was prepared by C. Charley, and the film was to be made by Cohl. It was probably never released.

241. Advertising Films

Between 1921 and 1923, Cohl collaborated on advertising films for Lortac's company, Publi-Ciné. The following are the known titles of these short productions (followed by their number in the CC filmography).

La Kabyline (239); *Kino chocolat* (240); *Néol cirage* (241); *Les Malles de France* (242); *Le Trombonne* (245); *Voulez-vous du Charbon?* (253); *Les Cigarettes St. Michel* (254); *Pastilles pour la toux* (256); *La T.S.F. Paris à New-York* (257); *Le Maroc*; *Les Hommes nouveaux* (258); *Soda Romano* (259); *Tour du monde en 80 minutes* (260); *Que d'eau! Que d'eau!* (262); *Empress cirage* (263); *Béatrix*

Vals (264); *Machines Dubied* (265); *Vitalis Lemonade, Oasis* (266); *Vitalis Lemonade, Café* (267); *Soirée italienne, Fonolyprix* (268); *Machines Dubied, Bonheur* (269); *Machines Dubied (l'Epave)* (270); *Machines Dubied, le Travail c'est la liberté* (271); *Bal masqué italien* (272); *La Sardine* (273); *Cigarettes Macédones, Découverte* (274); *Fils, ou Conscrit* (275); *Cigarettes St. Michel, Cannibales* (276); *Biscuits Delta, Myam-myam* (277); *Biscuits Delta, Nuit terrible* (278); *Chaussures Aurora, terrible* (279); *Vermouth Jacobins* (280); *Talmone, Toto naufragé* (281); *Talmone, un succès* (282); *Talmone, phénomène* (283); *Talmone, le sphinx* (284); *Talmone, un bon truc* (285); *Eau d'Ambre, Egyptienne* (286); *Eau d'Ambre, Secret de Vénus* (287);

Talmone, Femme précieuse (288); *Talmone, le harem* (289); *Talmone, mari gourmand* (290); *Voitures d'enfants* (291); *Mr. Campinchi* (292); *T.S.F.* (293); *Café le Chat Noir* (294); *Café Sanka* (295); *Le Coril, en Chine* (296); *Bernot, Muguet* (297); *Hôtel S.I.T.E.A.* (298); *Hôtel Cure* (299).

242. Educational/Scientific Projects
These films were planned but probably never completed:
L'Oeil (246); *Pages d'Histoire*, no. 2 (248); *L'Oreille*, or *Comment nous entendons* (250); *De Quoi sont-ils fait?* (251); *Statistiques des Régions libérés* (252; may have been released by Publi-Ciné); *La France renaît* (261); *Les Dents* (300).

INCORRECT ATTRIBUTIONS

The following films have been attributed to Cohl but can be proven to be incorrect. For further explanation, see text.

La Course aux potirons (The Pumpkin Race), Bosetti-Feuillade, Gaumont, 1908.

Le Ski, Arnaud, Gaumont, 1908.

La Vie à l'envers, Fromage de tête et tête de fromage, Consultation aux rayons X, Nettoyage par le vide; all Gaumont, ca. 1908; incorrectly identified as collaborations between Cohl and Feuillade.

Les Agents tels que nous les representons, Feuillade-Péguy, Gaumont, 1908.

Poudre de vitesse, Bosetti, Pathé-Comica, 1911.

Le Garde-meuble automatique (Automatic Moving Company), Bosetti, Pathé-Comica, 1912.

Professor Bonehead Is Shipwrecked, Harry S. Palmer, Gaumont-American, ca. 1916.

BIBLIOGRAPHY

321. Emile Cohl, ca. 1895

SELECTED BIBLIOGRAPHY

ORDER OF ARRANGEMENT

UNPUBLISHED SOURCES

Arnaud, Etienne. Gaumont Carnet, Coll. Jacques Deslandes.
Brest, René and André Courtet. MS Notes on Cohl's life. Cinémathèque Française.
Carré, Benjamin. *Autobiography*.
Cohl, Emile. Numerous letters, Manuscripts, Notes, Carnets, Drawings and assorted Documents, Coll. Mme. André Courtet-Cohl.

Kleine, George. Manuscripts. Manuscripts Division, Library of Congress.
Lortac. Interviewed by André Martin, 1966. Transcription Coll. Raymond Maillet.
Rabier, Benjamin. Corr. with Emile Cohl, 1916–1917. Coll. Courtet-Cohl.

EMILE COHL AS AUTHOR

Cohl, Emile. "André Gill et son oeuvre." *La Nouvelle Lune*, November 30, December 15, 1883.
———. "André Gill" (Inaugural speech for a bust of Gill). *Le Jour*, April 30, 1895.
———. *Auteur par amour, opérette en 1 acte* (Paris: La Scala, September 9, 1882). Paris: Bathlot, 1883.
———. "Les Dessins animés; quel est le père de ce genre fameux?" *Ciné-Journal*, May 17, 1919.
———. "Les Dessins animés." *L'Echo de Paris*, March 2, 1923.
———. "Les Dessins animés et à trucs, causerie faite au Ciné-Club le 12 juin, 1920." *Le Journal du Ciné-Club*, n. d.
———. Letter. In Fontane, *Un Maître de la caricature: André Gill*. Paris: Editions d'Ibis, 1927.
———. Letter. In Mostrailles, *Têtes de pipes*. Paris: Vanier, 1885.

———. "Oui, je suis le père du dessin animé." *Paris-Soir*, September 15, 1934.
———. *Plus de têtes chauves! vaudeville échevelé en l acte* (Paris: Fantaisies Parisiennes, June 13, 1881). Paris: Tresses, 1882.
———. "Sur les dessins animés." *Ciné-Tribune*, July 15, 1920.
Colibri (pseudonym). *La Clé des Jeux d'esprit*. Paris: Dubrueil, 1887.
Tronquières, J.-B. de (pseudonym). "Dessins animés." *Larousse Mensuel*, August 1925, 861–864.
———. "Emile Cohl." *Annuaire général de la cinématographie française et étrangère*. Paris: Eds. du Ciné-Journal, 1917–1918, 115.
Véga (pseudonym), and Armand Lods. *André Gill*. Paris: Vanier, 1887.

EMILE COHL AS ILLUSTRATOR

Catalogues illustrés de l'expositions des arts incohérents. Paris: 1884, 1886, 1889, and 1893.
Coquelin cadet. *Pirouettes*. Paris: Lévy, 1888.
Galipaux, Félix. *Encore des Galipettes*. Paris: Marpon et Flammarion, 1889.
———. *Galipettes*. Paris: Lévy, 1887.
Lermina, Jules. *L'Auberge des adrets*. Paris: A l'en-

seigne de l'auberge des adrets chez Mousseau, 1887.
Mostrailles, L.-G. *Têtes de pipes*. Paris: Eds. Vanier, 1885.
Oudot, Jules. *Chansons fin de siècle*. Paris: Ferreyrol, 1891.

EMILE COHL AS SUBJECT

Anon. "L'Art dans le cinéma français." *Le Petit Journal*, May 23, 1924.
———. "Emile Cohl." *Dictionnaire des lettres françaises; le dix-neuvième siècle*. Paris: Fayard, 1971, 256.
———. *Dictionnaire des peintres français*. Paris: Seghers, 1961.
———. *Filme Cultura* (Brazil). November–December 1970, 58.
———. *Mon Ciné*. February 22, 1922.
———. National Film Theatre (London), program notes. n. d.
———. *La Revue encyclopédique*, vol. 5. 1895, 126.
———. "Nos dessinateurs." *Le Courrier Français*, September 13, 1885.
———. "La Santé d'Emile Cohl." *Ciné-Journal*, March 4, 1922.
Adhémar, Jean. *Inventaire du fonds français après 1800*, vol. 5. Paris: Bibliothèque Nationale, 1949, 68.
Allemaigne, Henry d'. "Emile Cohl." *Bulletin de la Société d'encouragement pour l'industrie nationale*, March–April 1937, 113–116; reprinted as "Le Travail d'Emile Cohl." *La Cinématographie française*, December 31, 1937, 1–3.
André, Robert. "La Grande Misère d'Emile Cohl." *Le Figaro*, October 11, 1937.
———. "Emile Cohl." *Le Figaro*, October 31, 1937.
Auriol, Jean-Georges. "Les Premieres Dessins animés cinématographiques: Emile Cohl." *La Revue du cinéma*, January 1930, 12–19.
Bénézit, Emmanuel. "Emile Cohl." *Dictionnaire des peintres, sculpteurs, dessinateurs et graveurs*, vol. 2. Paris: Grund, 1949 (rev. ed.), 567–568.
Bourgeon, Pierre. "Le Trentième Anniversaire de l'invention des dessins animés." *La Cinématographie Française*, September 26, 1936.
Bouvard, Roland. "Emile Cohl." *L'Epoque*, January 22, 1938.
Boussinot, Roger. "Emile Cohl." *L'Encyclopédie du cinéma*. Paris: Bordas, 1967, 356–366.
Brest, René. "Il y a 20 ans l'inventeur du dessin animé mourait à l'hôpital." *Les Nouvelles Littéraires*, February 13, 1958.
Brivot, A. "Emile Cohl." *Humour-Magazine* (Paris), October 1952.
Chabloz, Jean-Pierre. "Emile Cohl, père du dessin animé." *Le Tribune de Genève*, April 20, 1947.
Coissac, Georges-Michel. *Histoire du cinématographe*. Paris: Cinéopse, 1925, 411.
Courtet-Cohl, Pierre. "Les Beaux-Arts mystérieux; portrait d'Emile Cohl" (program notes). Annecy: Festival du cinéma d'animation, 1971.

———. "Emile Cohl, mon grand-père." *Animatographe* no. 2, May–June 1987.
Coutisson, J.-P. "Nouvelles précisions sur une invention française" (mimeograph). Paris: Agence d'Information Cinégraphique, January 4, 1938.
Dauven, L.-R. "En visite chez M. Emile Cohl qui inventa les dessins animés." *Pour Vous*, August 1933.
Fontane, Charles. "Le Plus Ancien Parisien." *L'Intermédiaire des chercheurs et curieux*, December 30, 1937, col. 973.
———. *Un Maître de la caricature: André Gill*. Paris: Editions d'Ibis, 1927.
Gardette, L. "Teaching History by Motography." *The Nickelodeon*, October 4, 1909, 119–120.
Gaumont, Léon. Interview with Robert André, *Le Petit Parisien*, August 11, 1943.
Jeanne, René. *Cinéma 1900*. Paris: Flammarion, 1965, 202–212.
———. "Le Dessin animé, cette invention française signée Emile Cohl a cinquante ans." *Le Tribune de Genève*, May 2, 1958.
———. "Emile Cohl." *L'Illustration*, February 5, 1938, 161.
Jeanne, René, and Charles Ford. "Emile Cohl et le dessin animé." *Histoire encyclopédique du cinéma Vol. 1: le cinéma français, 1895–1929*. Paris: Laffont, 1947, 133–139.
Lapierre, Marcel. *Les Cent Visages du cinéma*. Paris: Grasset, 1948, 65–67.
———. "Trois Hommes ont inventé les dessins animés." *Paris-Soir*, April 28, 1937.
Larousse. *Grand Dictionnaire du XIXe siècle*. 1890, 2e supplément.
Le Maire, Eugène. "L'Industrie du dessin animé." *Bulletin de la Société d'encouragement pour l'industrie nationale*, March–April 1937, 151–175.
Lethève, Jacques. *La Caricature et la presse sous la IIIe République*. Paris: Colin, 1961, 36, 150.
Lévy, Jules. "Emile Cohl." *Le Chat Noir*, May 4, 1895.
Liasu, Jean-Pierre. "A 80 ans, Emile Cohl qui inventa les dessins animés touche cents francs par mois et ne peut même pas se payer le cinéma." *Comoedia*, January 10, 1936.
———. "Comment un plagiat permit à Emile Cohl d'inventer chez Gaumont les dessins animés." *Comoedia*, January 24, 1936.
———. "Si Walt Disney est le père de Mickey, un français, Emile Cohl, n'est-il pas son grand-père?" *Comoedia*, January 6, 1936.
Lo Duca, Giuseppe. "De Cohl à Winsor McKay [sic]." *Le Dessin animé: histoire, esthétique, technique*. Paris: Prisma, 1948, 15–24.

Lorin, Georges. "L'Hydropathe Emile Cohl." *L'Hydropathe*, April 5, 1880.

Lortac. "Emile Cohl, créateur des dessins animés" (ex. cat). Paris: Salon des Humoristes de Paris, 1939, 65–67.

Maillet, Raymond. "Le Cauchemar du fantoche." *Une Ecole de Paris* (ex. cat). Annecy: VIIIe Journées Internationales du cinéma d'animation, 1971.

———. "Les Pionniers français de l'animation." *Ecran 73*, January 1973, 20–28.

Martin, André. "Le Dessin animé revient à ses origines." *Arts*, August 20, 1958.

Norpois. "Emile Cohl." *L'Epoque*, January 14, 1938.

———. *L'Epoque*, January 22, 1938.

O'Galop. "Comment fait-on un dessin animé?" *Cinéma-Magazine*, February 1921, 4–10.

Paolella, Roberto. "Emile Cohl." *Filmlexicon degli autori e delle opere*, vol. 1. Rome: Ed. di Bianco e Nero, 1958, col. 1369–1371.

Park, William, and Pascal Vimenet. "Emile Cohl: esquisses." *Animatographe* no. 2, May–June 1987.

Passek, Jean-Loup. "Emile Cohl." *La Grande Encyclopédie*, vol. 5. Paris: Larousse, 1972, 3025.

Pathé, Théophile. *Le Cinéma*. Paris: Corrêa, 1942, 151.

Pierre et Paul. "Emile Cohl." *Les Hommes d'Aujourd'hui* no. 288, 1886.

Poncet, Marie-Thérèse. *Dessin animé, art mondial*. Paris: Le Cercle du livre, 1956, 169–173.

———. "Naissance du dessin animé et sa place dans le monde actuel." *Films et Documents*, February 1953, 961–963.

Richard, A.-P. "Emile Cohl." *La Cinématographie Française*, December 31, 1937, 1.

Rollot, Jean. "Les Deux Clients du petit café de Saint-Mandé." *L'Intransigeant*, January 25, 1938.

Russell, Sharon. "Emil [sic] Cohl." *Trickfilm* (ex. cat). Chicago: Film Center of the School of the Art Institute of Chicago, 1975.

Thieme-Becker. "Emile Cohl." *Allgemeines Lexikon der Bildenden Künstler*. Leipzig: 1912.

Vivien, Paul. "Emile Cohl." *L'Hydropathe*, April 5, 1880.

Milieu

Acker, Paul. *Humour et humoristes*. Paris: Empis, 1899.

Anon. "Ceux qui font rire Paris." *Lectures pour Tous*, February 1907, 380–389.

Apollonio, Umbro (ed.). *Futurist Manifestos*. London: Thames and Hudson, 1972.

Arbour, Roméo. *Les Revues littéraires éphémères paraissant à Paris entre 1900 et 1914*. Paris: Corti, n.d.

Baty, Gaston. *Trois p'tits tours et puis s'en vont*. Paris: Lieutier, 1947.

Bayard, Jean-Emile. *Le Quartier Latin*. Paris: Jouve, 1924.

Bergman, Pär. *"Modernolatria" et "Simultaneità"; recherches sur deux tendances dans l'avant-garde littéraire en Italie et en France à la veille de la première guerre mondiale*. Stockholm: Svenska Bokförlaget, 1962.

Billy, André. *L'Epoque contemporaine, 1905–1930*. Paris: Tallandier, 1956.

———. *L'Epoque 1900, 1885–1905*. Paris: Tallandier, 1951.

———. *Max Jacob*. Paris: Seghers, 1947.

Boussel, Patrice. *L'Affaire Dreyfus et la presse*. Paris: Colin, 1960.

Caradec, François. *Feu Willy*. Paris: J. J. Pauvert, 1984.

———. *Alphonse Allais*. [cited as in preparation, 1984].

Casteras, Raymond de. *Avant le Chat Noir; les Hydropathes, 1878–1880*. Paris: Messein, 1945.

Champsaur, Félicien. *Entrée de clowns*. Paris: Jules Lévy, 1886.

Chesnais, Jacques. *Histoire générale des marionnettes*. Paris: Bordas, 1947.

Clark, T. J. *The Painting of Modern Life: Paris in the Art of Manet and His Followers*. New York: Knopf, 1985.

Cornell, Kenneth. *The Symbolist Movement*. New Haven: Yale University Press, 1951.

Cros, Charles. *Oeuvres complètes* (L. Forestier and Pascal Pia, eds.). Paris: 1964.

Decaudin, Michel. *La Crise de valeurs Symbolistes; 20 ans de poésie française, 1895–1914*. Toulouse: Privat, 1960.

Donnay, Maurice. *Autour du Chat Noir*. Paris: Grasset, 1926.

———. *J'ai veçu 1900*. Paris: Fayard, 1950.

Dorman, Geneviève. *Colette: A Passion for Life*. New York: Abbeville Press, 1984.

Flint, R. W. (ed.). *F. W. Marinetti: Selected Writings*. New York: Farrar, Straus & Giroux, 1971.

Galipaux, Félix. *Les Souvenirs de Galipaux*. Paris: Plon, 1937.

Gendrot, Alfred (Jean Drault, pseud.). *Drumont: La France Juive et La Libre Parole*. Paris: Société française d'éditions littéraires et techniques, 1935.

Goudeau, Emile. *Dix ans de Bohème*. Paris: Librairie illustrée, 1888.

Grand-Carteret, John. *L'Affaire Dreyfus et l'image*. Paris: Flammarion, 1898.

Grillo, R. D. *Ideologies and Institutions in Urban*

France: The Representation of Immigrants. New York: Cambridge University Press, 1985.

Herbert, Robert L. *Neo-Impressionism* (ex. cat.). New York: Solomon R. Guggenheim Museum; Princeton, N.J.: Van Nostrand, 1968.

Jeanne, Paul. *Les Théâtres d'ombres à Montmartre de 1887 à 1923.* Paris: Les Presses Modernes, 1937.

Jeanne, René, and Charles Ford. *Paris vu par le cinéma.* Paris: Hachette, 1969.

Jakovsky, Anatole. *Alphonse Allais, le tueur à gags.* Paris: Les Quatre Jeudies, 1955.

Joliet, Charles. *Le Roman incohérent.* Paris: Lévy, 1887.

Jones, Louisa E. *Sad Clowns and Pale Pierrots; Literature and the Popular Comic Arts in Nineteenth-Century France.* Lexington, Kentucky: French Forum, 1984.

Joseph-Renaud, Jean. *Le Cinématographe du mariage.* Paris: Flammarion, 1897.

Kirby, Michael. *Futurist Performance.* New York: E. P. Dutton, 1971.

Kleebatt, Norman. L. (ed.). *The Dreyfus Affair: Art, Truth & Justice.* Berkeley: University of California Press, 1987.

Kunzle, David. "Popular Arts of the First World War." *Art Bulletin,* December 1973, 646–647.

Labracherie, Pierre. *La Vie quotidienne de la bohème littéraire aux XIXe siècle.* Paris: Hachette, 1967.

Laglaize, Jean-Baptiste. *Pantins et marionnettes.* Paris: Marpon, 1884.

Lehman, A. G. *The Symbolist Aesthetic in France, 1885–1895.* Oxford: Blackwell, 1950.

Lévy, Jules. *Les Hydropathes, prose et vers.* Paris: Delpeuch, 1928.

Lintilhac, E. *Histoire générale du théâtre en France,* 5 vols. Paris, 1904–1910.

Maindron, Ernest. *Marionnettes et guignols.* Paris: Juven, 1900.

Martin, Marianne W. *Futurist Art and Theory, 1909–1915.* Oxford: Clarendon Press, 1968.

Méténier, Oscar. *Petit Bottin des lettres et des arts.* Paris: 1886.

Meyer, Arthur. *Ce que mes yeux ont vu.* Paris: Plon, 1911.

Monnier, Marc. *Faust; tragédie de Marionnettes.* Geneva: Richard, 1871.

Mourey, Gabriel. *Fêtes foraines de Paris.* Paris: Renouard, 1906.

Perloff, Marjorie. *The Futurist Moment: Avant-Garde, Avant Guerre, and the Language of Rapture.* Chicago: University of Chicago Press, 1986.

Poliakov, Léon. *Histoire de l'antisémitisme. Vol. 4: L'Europe suicidaire, 1870–1933.* Paris: Calmann-Lévy, 1977.

Prédal, René. *La Société française (1914–1945) à travers le cinéma.* Paris: Colin, 1972.

Raynal, Maurice. "Montmartre au temps du 'Bateau-Lavoir.' " *Médecine de France* no. 35, 1952, 26.

Rearick, Charles. *Pleasures of the Belle Epoque: Entertainment and Festivity in Turn-of-the-Century France.* New Haven: Yale University Press, 1985.

Rookmaaker, H. R. *Gauguin and 19th Century Art Theory.* Amsterdam: Swets and Zeitlinger, 1972.

Salmon, André. *Souvenirs sans fin: deuxième époque (1908–1920).* Paris: Gallimard, 1956.

———. *Souvenirs sans fin: l'air de la Butte.* Paris: Eds. de la Nouvelle France, 1945.

Sarrazin, Jehan. *Souvenirs de Montmartre et du Quartier Latin.* Paris: Sarrazin, 1895.

Seigel, Jerrold E. *Bohemian Paris: Culture, Politics, and the Boundaries of Bourgeois Life, 1830–1930.* New York: Viking, 1986.

Shikes, Ralph E., and Paula Harper. *Pissarro: His Life and Work.* New York: Horizon Press, 1980.

Sorlin, Pierre. *"La Croix" et les juifs (1880–1899).* Paris: Grasset, 1967.

Souvestre, Pierre, and Marcel Allain. "Les Cabarets montmartrois." *Comoedia illustré,* May 1909, 157.

Terdiman, Richard. *Discourse/Counter-Discourse: The Theory and Practice of Symbolic Resistance in Nineteenth-Century France.* Ithaca, N.Y.: Cornell University Press, 1985.

Thornton, R.K.R. *The Decadent Dilemma.* London: Edward Arnold, 1983.

Vély, Adrien. "Le Cinématographe." *Le Sourire,* February 8, 1908.

Vitoux, Georges. *Le Théâtre de l'avenir, aménagement général, mise en scène, trucs, machinerie, etc.* Paris: Schleicher, 1903.

Waldberg, Patrick. *Eros, modern style.* Paris: J.-J. Paubert, 1964.

Warnod, André. *Drôle d'époque, souvenirs.* Paris: Fayard, 1960.

———. *Fils de Montmartre.* Paris: Fayard, 1955.

———. *Les Peintres mes amis.* Paris: Eds. de l'art, 1965.

Warnod, Jeanine. *Le Bateau-Lavoir: berceau de l'art moderne* (ex. cat.). Paris: Musée Jacquemart-André, 1975.

Weindel, Henri de. "Le Chat-Noir." *L'Illustration,* January 20, 1894, 51–53.

Wilson, Stephen. *Ideology and Experience: Antisemitism in France at the Time of the Dreyfus Affair.* Rutherford, N.J.: Fairleigh Dickinson University Press, 1982.

Winock, Michel. *Edouard Drumont et Cie: Antisémitisme et facisme en France.* Paris: Eds. du Seuil, 1982.

Winter, Marian Hanna. *Le Théâtre du merveilleux.* Paris: Perrin, 1962.

Yaki, Paul (pseud. André Rougé). *Montmartre, terre des artistes.* Paris: Girard, 1947.

CARICATURE AND COMIC STRIPS

Adhémar, Jean. "Cinq siècles de bandes dessinées." *Les Lettres Françaises*, June 7, 1966, 6.
———. "Les Journaux amusants et les premiers peintres cubistes." *L'Oeil*, vol. 4, 1955.

Alexandre, Arsène. *L'Art du rire et de la caricature*. Paris: Librairies-imprimeries réunies [1892].

Anon. *La Galerie comique du dix-neuvième siècle, caricaturistes contemporain*. Paris: Strauss, 1896.
———. *Le Dessin d'humour du XVᵉ siècle à nos jours* (ex. cat). Paris: Bibliothèque Nationale, 1971.

Ashbee, C. R. *Caricature*. London: Chapman and Hall, 1928.

Auriol, Georges, and Jacques Dyssord. *Steinlen et la rue*. Saint-Lazare: Rey, 1930.

Bayard, Jean-Emile. *L'Illustration et les illlustrateurs*. Paris: Delagrave, 1898.

Becker, Stephen. *Comic Art in America*. New York: Simon and Schuster, 1959.

Beraldi, Henri. "André Gill." *Les Graveurs du XIXᵉ siècle*, vol. 7, 1888, 134–144.

Berleux, Jean. *La Caricature politique en France pendant la guerre, le siège et la Commune*. Paris: Labitte, Paul et Cⁱᵉ, 1890.

Blanchard, Gérard. *La Bande dessinée; histoire des histoires en images*. Verviers: Marabout Université, 1969.

Boudard, Alphonse. "Pour un boulevard des Pieds-Nickelés." In Louis Forton, *La Bande des Pieds Nickelés*. Paris: Azur, 1965.

Brisson, Adolphe. *Nos Humoristes*. Paris: Société d'édition artistique, 1900.

Canemaker, John. *Winsor McCay: His Life and Art*. New York: Abbeville Press, 1987.

Caradec, François. *Christophe*. Paris: Pierre Horay, 1981.
———. *Histoire de la littérature enfantine en France*. Paris: Albin Michel, 1977.

Carco, Francis. *Les Humoristes*. Paris: Ollendorf, 1921 (2nd ed.)

Cauzat, Ernest de. *L'Oeuvre gravé et lithographié de Steinlen*. Paris: Société de propagation des livres d'art, 1913.

Champfleury, [Jules]. *Histoire de l'imagerie populaire*. Paris: Librairie de la Société des gens de lettres, 1869.
———. *Histoire de la Caricature sous la République, l'Empire et la Restauration*. Paris: Dentu, 1874.

Couperie, Pierre. *Bande dessinée et figuration narrative* (ex. cat). Paris: Musée des Arts décoratifs, 1967.

Couperie, Pierre and Maurice Horn, et. al. *A History of the Comic Strip*. New York: Crown, 1968.

Courmont, E. *La Photogravure; histoire et technique*. Paris, 1947.

Darcel, A. "Les Musées, les arts et les artistes pendant le siège de Paris." *Gazette des Beaux-Arts*, October, November 1871.
———. "Les Musées, les arts et les artistes pendant la Commune." *Gazette des Beaux-Arts*, January–March, May–June 1872.

Delteil, Loys, and N. A. Hazard. *Catalogue raisonné de l'oeuvre de Honoré Daumier*. Paris: Hazard, 1904.

Dorfman, Ariel, and Armand Mattelart. *How to Read Donald Duck: Imperialist Ideology in the Disney Comic* (trans. David Kunzle). New York: International General, 1975.

Dumont, Jean-Marie. *La Vie et l'oeuvre de Jean-Charles Pellerin*. Epinal: Pellerin, 1956.

Duranty. "La Caricature et l'imagerie en Europe pendant la guerre de 1870–71: La Caricature en France," *Gazette des Beaux-Arts*, April 1872, 322–343.

Edwards, H. "The Caricatures of Claude Monet," *Bulletin of the Art Institute of Chicago*, September–October 1943, 71–72.

Eco, Umberto. *Apocallitici e integrati*. Milan: Bompiani, 1964.

Fontane, Charles. *Un Maître de la caricature: André Gill*. Paris: Eds. d'Ibis, 1927.

Fresnault-Deruelle, Pierre. *La Bande dessinée: L'univers et les techniques de quelques "comics" d'expression française*. Paris: Hachette, 1972.

Fromrich, Yane and D. Rouart. *Grandville* (ex. cat). Nancy: Musée des Beaux-Arts, 1953.

Garcin, Laure. *J.-J. Grandville*. Paris: Losfeld, 1970.

Gaultier, Paul. *Le Rire et la caricature*. Paris: Hachette, 1906.

Gauthier, Patrice. "Nadal, l'ironique imagier." *Giff-Wiff*, December 1965, 23–27.

Geipel, John. *The Cartoon; a Short History of Graphic Art and Satire*. South Brunswick, N.J.: Barnes, 1972.

Georgel, Pierre. "Monet, Bruyas, Vacquerie et le Panthéon Nadar." *Gazette des Beaux-Arts*, December 1968, 331–334.

Gianeri, Enrico ("Gec"). *Storia della caricatura*. Milan, 1959.

Gill, André. *Vingt années de Paris*. Paris: Marpon et Flammarion, 1883.

Goldberg, Reuben. "Comics, New Style and Old." *Saturday Evening Post*, December 15, 1928, 12–13.

Goldstein, Robert J. "Approval First, Caricature Second: French Caricaturists, 1852–81." *Print Collector's Newsletter* 19, May–June 1988, 48–50.
———. "Freedom of the Press in Europe, 1815–

1914." *Journalism Monographs* no. 80, February 1983, 15.

Gombrich, Ernst H. and E. Kris. *Caricature*. Harmondsworth: Penguin, 1940.

Grand-Carteret, John. *Les Moeurs et la caricature en France*. Paris: Librairie illustrée, 1888.

Gubern, Roman. *El Lenguage de los comics*. Barcelona: Ed. Peninsula, 1972.

Hofman, Werner. *Caricature from Leonardo to Picasso*. New York: Crown, 1957.

Horn, Maurice. *Seventy-Five Years of the Comics* (ex. cat). New York: New York Cultural Center, 1971.

Howe, Andrew. "Comic Strip Technique." *Printer's Ink*, September 12, 1935, 13.

Joakimidis, Demetre. "Un Héritage de Töpffer." *Construire* (Geneva), February 10, 1968.

Kempkes, Wolfgang. *Bibliographie der Internationalen Literatur über Comics*. Munich: Verlag Dokumentation; New York: Bowker, 1971.

Kunzle, David. "The Comic Strip." *Art News Annual* 36, 1970, 133–145.

————. "Supplementary Note" (essay appended to) Francis Lacassin, "Comic Strip and Film Language." *Film Quarterly*, Fall 1972, 19–23.

————. *History of the Comic Strip; Vol. 1. The Early Comic Strip, 1450–1825*. Berkeley: University of California Press, 1973.

Lacassin, Francis. "Histoire de la littérature populaire." *Magazine Littéraire*, July–August 1967, 10–15.

————. "Notes sur les apparitions de Félix le Chat dans les bandes dessinées." *Giff-Wiff*, September 1965, 5.

————. "Bande Dessinée et langage cinématographique." *Pour un neuvième art: la bande dessinée*. Paris: Union Générale, 1971.

Lethève, Jacques. *La Caricature et la pressse sous la IIIᵉ République*. Paris: Colin, 1961.

————. *Impressionnistes et symbolistes devant la presse*. Paris: Colin, 1959.

————. *Théophile-Alexandre Steinlen* (ex. cat). Paris: Bibliothèque Nationale, 1953.

Luquet, G. H. *Le Dessin enfantin*. Paris: Alcan, 1927.

Lévy, Jules. "L'Incohérence, son origine, son histoire, son avenir." *Le Courrier Français*, March 12, 1885.

Mantz, Paul. "La Caricature moderne." *Gazette des Beaux-Arts* no. 37, 1888, 286–312.

Mespoulet, Marguerite. *Creators of Wonderland*. New York: Arrow, 1937.

Michiels, Alfred. *Le Monde du Comique et du rire*. Paris: Lévy, 1886.

Mireur, H. *Dictionnaire des ventes d'art*. Paris: Vincenti, 1911.

Mistler, Jean. *Epinal et l'imagerie populaire*. Paris: Hachette, 1961.

Morin, Louis. *Le Dessin humoristique*. Paris: Laurens, 1913.

O'Sullivan, Judith. *The Art of the Comic Strip* (ex. cat). College Park: University of Maryland Department of Art, 1971.

Ragon, Michel. *Les Maîtres du dessin satirique en France de 1830 à nos jours*. Paris: Horay, 1972.

————. *Le Dessin d'humour*. Paris: Fayard, 1960.

Refort, Lucien. *La Caricature littéraire*. Paris: Armand Colin, 1932.

Roberts-Jones, Philippe. *De Daumier à Lautrec*. Paris: Les Beaux-Arts, 1960.

————. *La Caricature du Second Empire à la Belle époque 1850–1900*. Paris: Club Français du Livre, 1963.

————. "Les 'Incohérents' et leur expositions, 1882–1888." *Gazette des Beaux-Arts*, October 1958, 231–236.

————. *La Presse satirique illustrée entre 1860 et 1890*. Paris: Institut Français de Presse, 1956.

Robida, Albert. *Le Vingtième siècle; la vie électrique*. Paris: Librairie illustrée, 1892.

Roger-Marx, Claude. "The Humorists: Willette, Steinlen, Léandre, Véber." In *Graphic Art: The 19th Century*. New York: McGraw-Hill, 1962.

Sadoul, Georges. *Ce que lisent vos enfants; la presse enfantine en France, son histoire, son évolution, son influence*. Paris: Bureau d'éditions, 1938.

Schapiro, Meyer. "Courbet and Popular Imagery." *Journal of the Warburg and Courtauld Institutes* no. 4, 1940–1941, 164–191.

Sheon, Aaron. "The Discovery of Graffiti." *Art Journal*, Fall 1976, 16–22.

Sheridan, Martin. *Comics and Their Creators*. Boston; Hale, 1942.

Schwarz, Heinrich. "Daumier, Gill and Nadar." *Gazette des Beaux-Arts*, February 1957, 89–106.

Valmy-Baysse, Jean. *Le Roman d'un caricaturiste: André Gill*. Paris: Editions Marcel Seheur, n.d.

Waugh, Coulton. *The Comics*. New York: Macmillan, 1947.

Wechsler, Judith. *A Human Comedy: Physiognomy and Caricature in 19th Century Paris*. Chicago: University of Chicago Press, 1982.

Welke, Manfred. *Die Sprache der Comics*. Frankfurt a.M.: 1958.

White, D. M. *The Comic Strip in America: a Bibliography*. Boston: Communications Research Center, 1961.

Zimmermann, H. D. (ed.). "*Comic Strips*," *Colloquium zur Theorie der Bildergeschichte*. Berlin: Akademie der Künste, Gebr. Mann Verlag, 1970.

SPECTACLE BEFORE 1900

Alber et Hégé. *Le Grand Manuel de projection*. Paris: Mazo, 1897.

Astre, Achille. *Les Spectacles à travers les âges*. Paris: Cygne, 1931.

Babst, Germaine. *Essai sur l'histoire des panoramas et des dioramas*. Paris: Marpon, 1892.

Beaudu, Edouard et al. *Histoire du music-hall*. Paris: Eds. de Paris, 1954.

Bessy, Maurice. "Une nuit à Lyon, Monsieur Louis . . ." *La Revue du Cinéma*, September 1948, 49–53.

Breton, J.-L. *La Chronophotographie, la photographie animée, analyse et synthèse du mouvement*. Paris: Bernard, 1898.

Brunel, Georges. *La Photographie et la projection du mouvement*. Paris, 1897.

Civry, René. "Les Cinquante Ans du Musée Grévin." *L'Image* 1, 14, 1932, 25–28.

Coissac, G.-M. "Le Cinématographe." *Le Petit Français Illustré*, May 23, 1896, 193–194.

———. *La Théorie et la practique des projections*. Paris: n.d.

Colomb, Georges ("Christophe"). "A travers la science." *L'Illustré Soleil du Dimanche*, March 29, 1896.

Cook, Olive. *Movement in Two Dimensions*. London: Hutchinson, 1963.

Demenÿ, Georges. *Les Origines du Cinématographe*. Paris: 1909.

Deslandes, Jacques. *Histoire comparée du cinéma Vol. 1: 1826–1896*. Paris: Casterman, 1966

Flamans, Henri. "Le Kinétoscope d'Edison." *Le Magasin Pittoresque*, August 1, 1894.

François-Frank, Charles. *L'Oeuvre de E.-J. Marey*. Paris: 1905.

Garnier, Jacques. "Les Cinémas." In *Forains d'hier et d'aujourd'hui*. Orléans: Garnier, 1968.

Girard, G. "Précurseurs du cinéma: Marionnettes et lanternes magiques." *La Revue du Cinéma* 10, 1930.

Grand-Carteret, John. "Ombres Chinoises." *L'Illustration*, August 27, 1887.

Hendricks, Gordon. *The Edison Motion Picture Myth*. Berkeley: University of California Press, 1961.

———. *The Kinetoscope, America's First Successful Motion Picture Exhibitor*. New York: Beginnings of the American Film, 1966.

Homer, W. I., and John Talbot. "Eakins, Muybridge and the Motion Picture Process." *Art Quarterly*, Summer 1963, 194–216.

Hopwood, Henry V. *Living Pictures*. London: Optician and Photographic Trades Review, 1899.

Huret, Jules. *La Catastrophe du Bazar de la charité; 4 mai, 1897*. Paris: Juven, 1897.

Jenkins, Charles Francis. *Animated Pictures*. Washington: McQueen, 1898.

McCauley, Elizabeth Anne. *A.A.E. Disderi and the Carte de Visite Portrait Photograph*. New Haven: Yale University Press, 1985.

Marek, Kurt W. ("C. W. Ceram"). *Archaeology of the Cinema* (trans. R. Winston). New York: Harcourt, Brace and World, 1965.

Mareschal, G. "Le Théâtrophone." *La Nature*, June 25, 1892, 55–58.

Marey, Etienne-Jules. *La Machine animale; locomotion terrestre et aérienne*. Paris: Alcan, 1886 (4th ed.).

———. *Le Mouvement*. Paris: Masson, 1894.

Matuszewski, Boleslas. *Une Nouvelle Source de l'histoire; Création d'un dépôt de cinématographie historique*. Paris: 1898.

———. *La Photographie animée*. Paris, 1898.

Musser, Charles. "Toward a History of Screen Practice." *Quarterly Review of Film Studies* 9, 1, Winter 1984, 59–69.

Nadar. *Quand j'étais photographe*. Paris: Flammarion, 1900.

Niver, Kemp. *The First Twenty Years*. Los Angeles: Locare Research Group, 1968.

North, Joseph H. *The Early Development of the Motion Picture, 1887–1909* (Ph.D. dissertation). Ithaca, N.Y.: Cornell University, 1950.

Noverre, Maurice. *Emile Reynaud, sa vie, ses travaux*. Brest: Noverre, 1926.

Orna, Bernard. "Cartoons Before Film." *Films and Filming*, December 1954, 12.

Perron. "Le Théâtrophone." *Le Magasin Pittoresque*, June 15, 1892, 183–184.

Popper, F. *Naisance de l'Art cinétique; l'image du mouvement dans les arts plastiques depuis 1860*. Paris: 1967.

Quigley, Martin. *Magic Shadows*. New York: 1960.

Reynaud, Emile. "Note sur le Praxinoscope." *Les Mondes*, 1879, 229–230.

Reynaud, Paul. *Les Maîtres du cinéma; Pantomimes lumineuses; E. Reynaud, peintre du films*. Paris: Cinémathèque Française, 1945.

Rubin, William. "Shadows, Pantomimes and the Art of the 'Fin de Siècle.'" *Magazine of Art*, March 1953.

Scharf, Aaron. "Marey and Chronophotography." *Artforum*, September 1967, 62–70.

Segel, Harold B. *Turn-of-the-Century Cabaret*. New York: Columbia University Press, 1987.

Souriau, Paul. *Esthétique du mouvement*. Paris: Alcan, 1889.

Tissandier, Gaston. "Le Praxinoscope." *La Nature*, February 1, 1879.

———. "Le Praxinoscope à projection." *La Nature*, November 4, 1882.

———. "Le Théâtre optique de M. Reynaud." *La Nature*, July 23, 1892, 127–128.

CINEMA HISTORY RELEVANT TO COHL'S PERIOD

Abel, Richard. "The Contribution of the French Literary Avant-Garde to Film Theory and Criticism (1907–1924)." *Cinema Journal* 14, 3, Spring 1975, 18–40.

———. *French Cinema: The First Wave, 1915–1929.* Princeton: Princeton University Press, 1984.

———. *French Film Theory and Criticism: A History/Anthology, 1907–1939* vol. 1: 1907–1929. Princeton, N.J.: Princeton University Press, 1988.

———. "On the Threshold of French Film Theory and Criticism, 1915–1919." *Cinema Journal* 25, 1, Fall 1985, 12–33.

———. "Yhcam Discoursing on the Cinema: France, 1912." *Framework* 32/33, 1986, 150–170.

Agel, Henri. *Le Cinéma.* Tournai: Casterman, 1954.

Allen, Robert C. "Contra the Chaser Theory," *Wide Angle* no. 3, Spring 1979, 4–11.

———. "Looking at 'Another Look at the "Chaser Theory," ' " *Studies in Visual Communication* 10, 4, Fall 1984, 45–50

———. "Motion Picture Exhibition in Manhattan, 1906–1912." *Cinema Journal* 18, 2, Spring 1979, 2–15.

———. Review of *The Big V: A History of the Vitagraph Company. Cinema Journal* 16, 2, Spring 1977, 81–82.

———. Review of *Spellbound in Darkness. Cinema Journal* 15, 1, Fall 1975, 68–71.

———. *Vaudeville and Film, 1895–1915: A Study in Media Interaction* (Ph.D. dissertation). Iowa City: University of Iowa, 1977.

Almanach du cinéma pour 1922. Paris: CinéMagazine-Edition, 1922.

Altenloh, E. *Zur Soziologie des Kino.* Jena: Schriften zur Soziologie der Kultur, 1914.

Altomara, Rita E. *Hollywood on the Palisades: A Filmography of Silent Features Made in Fort Lee, New Jersey, 1903–1927.* New York: Garland, 1983.

Ambrière, Francis. "A l'aube du cinéma: la carrière de Léonce Perret." *L'Image* 1, 23, 1932, 27–30.

———. "Les Souvenirs de Ferdinand Zecca." *L'Image* 1, 13, 1932, 27–30.

———. "Les Souvenirs de Camille de Morlhon." *L'Image* 1, 11, 1932, 23–26.

———. "Les Souvenirs de Georges Méliès." *L'Image* 1, 19, 1932, 11–15.

———. "Les Souvenirs de Georges Monca." *L'Image* 1, 9, 1932, 12–15.

———. "Les Souvenirs de Prince Rigadin." *L'Image* 1, 17, 1932.

———. "Les Souvenirs de Robert Péguy." *L'Image* 1, 36, 1932.

———. "Louis Feuillade." *L'Image* 1, 27, 1932, 26–30.

Annuaire du commerce et de l'industrie photographiques et cinématographiques. Paris: Mendel, 1911.

Annuaire général et international de la cinématographie. Paris: Plon, 1907.

Anon. "Cinema and Theaters in Paris." *Nation*, August 13, 1914.

———. "En 1907 Charles Jourjon fondait l'Eclair." *La Cinématographie Française*, November 1935, 45–46.

———. "Europe's Highbrows Hail 'Mickey Mouse.' " *The Literary Digest*, August 8, 1931, 19.

———. "Les Jouets transformés par la science." *Lectures pour Tous*, December 1906.

———. "Les Trucs du cinématographe." *Lectures pour Tous*, June 1908, 749–755.

———. "Tricks in Motion Pictures." *Literary Digest*, March 21, 1914, 615–616.

———. "Year's Business at Paris Hippodrome." *The Nickelodeon (Motography)*, July 1909.

Arnaud, Etienne and Boisyvon. *Le Cinéma pour tous.* Paris: Garnier, 1922.

Babin, Gustave. "Les Coulisses du cinématographe." *L'Illustration*, March 28, April 4, 1908.

———. "Films d'Art." *L'Illustration*, October 31, 1908.

Baldizzone, José. "L'Incendie du Bazar de la Charité." *Archives* 12, March 1988.

Banet-Rivet, P. "La représentation du mouvement et de la vie." *Revue des Deux Mondes*, August 1, 1908, 590–621.

Baroncelli, Jacques de. *Le Film et l'art; pantomime, musique, cinema.* Paris: Lumina, 1915.

Baxter, Peter. "On the History and Ideology of Film Lighting." *Screen* 16, 3, Autumn 1975, 83–106.

Ben Aicha, S. *Charles Pathé* (monograph). Paris: IDHEC Archives, n.d.

Bennett, Colin N. "Trick Kinematography." In *The Handbook of Kinematography.* London: Kinematograph Weekly, 1911.

Turpin, G. "Leçon d'Emile Reynaud." *L'Ecran 73* no. 11, 1973.

Vitoux, Georges. *La Photographie du mouvement, chronophotographie, kinétoscope, cinématographe.* Paris: Chamuel, 1896.

Beylie, Claude. "Léon Gaumont: un royaume pour une marguerite." In "Les Pionniers du cinéma français, 1895–1910." *L'Avant-Scène du Cinéma* no. 334, November 1984, 47–50.

Binet, R., and G. Hausser. *Sociétés de cinématographie, études financières.* Paris: Eds. de la "France économique et financière," 1908.

Blackton, James Stuart. Preface to Henry Alberts Phillips, *The Photodrama.* New York: Stanhope-Dodge, 1914.

Bolen, F. "Un Historien oublié (G.-M. Coissac)." *Ecran*, October 1976, 4–5.

Borde, Raymond (ed.). Special issue devoted to the problems of the Cinémathèque Française. *Le Cahiers de la Cinémathèque* no. 22, 1977.

Bordwell, David. *French Impressionist Cinema: Film Culture, Film Theory, and Film Style* (Ph.D. dissertation). Iowa City: University of Iowa, 1974.

Bordwell, David, Janet Staiger, and Kristin Thompson. *The Classical Hollywood Cinema: Film Style and Mode of Production.* London, New York: Routledge and Kegan Paul, Columbia University Press, 1985.

Bottomore, Stephen. "Dreyfus and Documentary." *Sight and Sound* 53, 4, Autumn 1984, 290–293.

Boutillon, Edmond. "Du Cinéma forain à l'exploitation regulière." *La Cinématographie Française*, November 1935, 55–59.

Bowers, Q. David. *Nickelodeon Theatres and Their Music.* New York: Vestal Press, 1986.

Bowser, Eileen. "Eclair in America." Lecture presented to FIAF, Paris, 1988.

———. "Griffith's Film Career Before *The Adventures of Dolly*." In Fell (ed.). *Film Before Griffith.* Berkeley: University of California Press, 1983, 367–373.

——— (ed.). *The Slapstick Symposium.* Brussels: FIAF, 1988.

Brewster, Ben. "A Scene at the 'Movies.' " *Screen* 23, 2, July–August 1982, 4–15.

Browning, Irving. "A Crumbled Movie Empire." *American Cinematographer*, August 1945, 161–163 + .

Burch, Noël. "Porter, or Ambivalence." *Screen* 19, 4, Winter 1978–1979, 91–105.

Canudo, Ricciotto. "Ecrit par Canudo 1907–1922." *Revue du Cinéma*, May 1948.

———. *L'Usine aux images.* Paris: Editions Chiron, 1927.

Charensol, Georges. *Panorama du Cinéma.* Paris: Editions Kra, 1930, 1947.

——— et al. *Le Cinéma.* Paris: Larousse, 1966.

Charles, J. Ernest. "Psychologie du Cinématographe." *Gil-Blas*, March 20, 1908; reprinted in *L'Argus Phono-Cinéma*, March 29, 1908.

Claris, Edmond. "Le Théâtre cinématographique." *La Nouvelle Revue*, February 15, 1909, 544–551.

Coissac, Georges-Michel. *Les Coulisses du cinéma.* Paris: Eds. Pittoresques, 1929.

———. *Histoire du cinématographe des ses origines jusqu'à nos jours.* Paris: Eds. du Cinéopse, 1925.

Collins, F. A. *The Cameraman: His Adventures in Many Fields.* New York: 1916.

Comandon, Jean, and P. de Fonbrune. "Le Laboratoire de Cinématographe de l'Institut Pasteur." *L'Illustration*, February 15 and 22, 1941.

Comin, Jacopo. "Ricciotto Canudo." *Bianco e Nero* 1, 1, 1937.

Conant, Michael. *Antitrust in the Motion Picture Industry.* Berkeley: University of California Press, 1960.

Cordova, Richard de. "The Emergence of the Star System in America." *Wide Angle* 6, 4, 1985, 4–13.

Coustet, Ernest. *Traité pratique de cinématographe*, vol. 1. Paris: Mendel, 1913; vol. 2. Paris: Mendel, 1915.

Crafton, Donald. *Marcel Duchamp's "Anémic Cinéma"* (M.A. thesis). New Haven: Yale University, 1974.

Croy, Homer. *How Motion Pictures are Made.* New York: Harper and Bros. 1918.

Delcol, Guy. *Essai de Bibliographie belge du cinéma, 1896–1966.* Brussels: Cinémathèque royale de Belgique, 1968.

Deleuze, Gilles. *Cinéma 1: L'Image-Mouvement.* Paris: Editions de Minuit, 1983.

Delluc, Louis. *Cinéma et Cⁱᵉ; confidences d'un spectateur.* Paris: Grasset, 1919.

Deslandes, Jacques. *Le Boulevard du cinéma à l'époque de Georges Méliès.* Paris: Eds. du Cerf, 1963.

———. "Victorin Hippolyte Jasset." *L'Avant-Scène du Cinéma* 163, November 1975, Anthologie supplement no. 85, 241–296.

Deslandes, Jacques, and Jacques Richard. *Histoire comparée du cinéma* Vol. 2: 1897–1906. Paris: Casterman, 1968.

Diamant-Berger, Henri. *Le Cinéma.* Paris: La Renaissance du livre, 1919.

Dodge, Henry C. "The Movies of War-time Paris." *Photoplay*, June 1916.

Doumic, René. "L'Age du cinéma." *Revue des Deux Mondes*, August 15, 1913.

Doyen, Dr. [Eugène]. "Le Cinématographe et l'enseignement de la chirurgie." *Bulletin phonographique et cinématographique*, November 15, December 1 and 15, 1899.

———. "Mes Films chirugicaux." *Le Journal*, January 2, 1914.

Drinkwater, John. *The Life and Adventures of Carl Laemmle.* New York: Putnam, 1931.

Dupuis, Charles. *La Cinématographie.* Paris: Cahors, 1913.

Epstein, Jean. *Bonjour Cinéma!* Paris: Eds. de la Sirène, 1921.

Esnault, Philippe. *Chronologie du cinéma mondiale.* Paris: Les Grands Films Classiques, 1963.

Faure, Elie. "De la cinéplastique." *L'Arbre d'Eden.* Paris: Eds. Cres, 1922.

Fell, John L. (ed.). *Film Before Griffith.* Berkeley: University of California Press, 1983.

Fescourt, Henri. *Le Cinéma de ses origines à nos jours.* Paris: Eds. du Cygne, 1932.

———. *La Foi et les montagnes, ou le septième art au passé.* Paris: Montel, 1959.

Feuillade, Louis, and André Heuzé. *Tous papas; comédie-vaudeville en 1 acte.* Paris: Joubert, 1909.

Forch, C. *Der Kinematograph und das sich bewegende Bild.* Vienna: 1913.

Ford, Charles. "Ladislas Starevitch." *Films in Review,* April 1958, 190–192;pl.

———. *Max Linder.* Paris: Seghers, 1966.

———. "The First Female Producer" (Alice Guy). *Films in Review,* March 1964, 141–145.

Ford, Charles, and René Jeanne. *Le Cinéma et la presse, 1895–1960.* Paris: Colin, 1961.

Fourniols. *Les Derniers Perfectionnements du cinématographe.* Paris: 1912.

Frazer, John T. *Artificially Arranged Scenes: The Films of Georges Méliès.* Boston: G. K. Hall, 1979.

Gance, Abel. "Un Sixième Art." *Ciné-Journal,* March 9, 1912.

Gartenberg, Jon. "Camera Movement in Edison and Biograph Films, 1900–1906." *Cinema Journal* 19, 2, Spring 1980, 1–16.

———. "Vitagraph Before Griffith: Forging Ahead in the Nickelodeon Era." *Studies in Visual Communication* 10, 4, Fall 1984, 22.

Gaudreault, André (ed.). *Cinema 1900–1906: An Analytical Study,* vol. 2. Brussels: FIAF, 1982.

———. "Detours in Film Narrative: The Development of Cross-Cutting." (English adaptation by Martin Sopocy and Charles Musser.) *Cinema Journal* 19, 1, Fall 1979, 39–59.

———. "Système du récit filmique." *Mannheimer Analytika* 7, 1987, 267–278.

———. "Temporality and Narrativity in Early Cinema." In Fell (ed.). *Film Before Griffith.* Berkeley: University of California Press, 311–329.

———. "La Transgression des lois du copyright aux débuts du cinéma: conséquences pratiques et séquelles théoriques." *Film Exchange* no. 28, 1984, 41–49.

Gaumont, Léon. "Comment ai-je été amené à m'occuper du film parlant." Preface to P. Hemardin-guer, *Le Cinématographe sonore.* Paris: Eyrolles, 1934.

———. Interview in *The Bioscope,* reprinted in trans. *La Cinématographie Française,* February 15, 1919.

———. Interview with Robert André. *Le Petit Parisien,* August 11, 1943.

———. "Quelques souvenirs sur Mme. Alice Guy-Blaché, la première femme metteur en scène." *La Technique Cinématographique,* February 1955, 151.

———. "Response à l'enquête de la *Technique Cinématographique* sur le cinéma dans 40 ans et sur ses débuts." *La Technique Cinématographique,* December 1934, 330.

Gaumont (Company). *Notice sur les Etablissements Gaumont.* Paris: Gaumont, 1923.

———. *Notice sur les Etablissements Gaumont.* Paris: Gaumont, June 1924.

———. *Notice rétrospective sur les Etablissements Gaumont, 1895–1929.* Paris: Gauthiers-Villars, 1935.

Geduld, Harry. *The Birth of the Talkies.* Bloomington: Indiana University Press, 1975.

Georges-Michel, Michel. "Henri Bergson nous parle du cinéma." *Le Journal,* February 20, 1914.

Germain, José. "Quand le cinéma naissait à Vincennes." *L'Image* 1, 37, 13–15.

Ghelderode, Michel de. "Ciné-clubs et Avant-garde." In Francis Bolen. *Histoire authentique, anecdotique, folklorique et critique du cinéma belge depuis des plus lointaines origines.* Brussels: Memo & Codec, 1978.

Gifford, Denis. *The British Film Catalogue, 1895–1970.* London: Newton Abbot, David and Charles, 1973.

Gomery, J. Douglas. *The Coming of Sound to the American Cinema: The Transformation of an Industry* (Ph.D. dissertation). Madison: University of Wisconsin, 1975.

Gourmont, Rémy de. "Cinématographe." *Mercure de France,* September 1, 1907, 124–127.

Grau, Robert. *The Theater of Science.* New York: Broadway Publishing Company, 1914.

Grimoin-Sanson, Raoul. *Le Film de ma vie.* Paris: Henry-Parville, 1926.

Guibbert, Pierre (ed.). *Les Premiers Ans du cinéma français.* Perpignan: Institute Jean Vigo, 1985.

Gunning, Tom. "Le Style non-continu du cinéma des premiers temps." *Les Cahiers de la Cinéma-thèque* 29, Winter 1979, 24–34. English version as "The Non-Continuous Style of Early Film (1900–1906)." In Roger Holman (ed.). *Cinema 1900–1906: An Analytical Study.* Brussels: FIAF, 1982, 219–229.

———. "The Cinema of Attractions: Early Film, Its

Spectator and the Avant-Garde." *Wide Angle* 8, 3/4, 1986, 63–70.

Guy, Alice. *Autobiographie d'une pionnière du cinéma.* Paris: Denoël, 1975.

Hamman, Joë. *Du Far-West à Montmartre.* Paris: Les Editeurs Français Réunis, 1962.

Hammond, Paul. "Kostrowitzky's Kinema." *Afterimage* no. 10, Autumn 1981, 56–69.

———. *Marvelous Méliès.* New York: St. Martin's Press, 1975.

Hansen, Miriam. "Early Silent Cinema: Whose Public Sphere?" *New German Critique* no. 29, Spring–Summer 1983, 147–184.

Harlé, P.-A. "Les Etapes de l'industrie." *La Cinématographie Française,* November 1935, 27–32.

Hemardinguer, P. *Le Cinématographe sonore.* Paris: Eyrolles, 1934.

Hepworth, Cecil. *Came the Dawn.* London: 1951.

Holman, Roger (ed.). *Cinema 1900–1906: An Analytical Study,* vol. 1. Brussels: FIAF, 1982

Honoré, F. "Le Cinématographe parlant." *L'Illustration,* December 31, 1910, 502–503.

Hugon, P. D. *Hints to Newsfilm Cameramen.* Jersey City: 1915.

Hugues, Philippe d', and Dominique Muller. *Gaumont: 90 années de cinéma.* Paris: Ramsay/La Cinémathèque Française, 1986.

Jasset, Victorin. "Etude sur la mise en cinématographie." *Ciné-Journal,* October 21 and 28, 1911, November 4, 11, and 25, 1911.

Jeanne, René. *Cinéma 1900.* Paris: Flammarion, 1965.

Johns, Leon E. "The Largest Moving Picture Theater." *The Nickelodeon,* April 1909, 94–95.

Johnson, G. L. *Photographic Optics, including the Kinematograph.* London: Johnson Handbooks on Optics, 1909.

Jourjon, Charles (obit.). *La Technique Cinématographique,* October 1934, 243.

Kaes, Anton (ed.). *Kino-Debatte, Texte Zum Verhältnis von Literatur und Film, 1909–1929.* Tübingen: Niemeyer, 1978.

Kiehl, Jean. *Les Ennemies du théâtre; essai sur les rapports du théâtre avec le cinéma et la littérature, 1914–1939.* Paris: 1951.

Koszarski, Richard. *Universal Pictures* (ex. cat). New York: Museum of Modern Art, 1977–1978.

Kovács, Katherine S. "Georges Méliès and the Féerie." *Cinema Journal,* Fall 1976, 1–13.

Kress, E. *L'Appareil de prise de vues cinématographiques.* Paris: Comptoir d'édition de "Cinéma Revue" [1912].

———. *Historique du cinématographe.* Paris: Comptoir d'édition de "Cinéma-Revue," 1912.

———. *Trucs et illusions, applications de l'optique et de la mécanique au cinématographe.* Paris: Comptoir d'édition de "Cinéma-Revue," 1912.

L. B. [Dr. de]. "La Chirurgie nouvelle." *L'Illustration,* June 10, 1899, 367.

Lacassin, Francis. *Louis Feuillade.* Paris: Seghers, 1964.

———. *Pour une contre-histoire du cinéma.* Paris: Union générale d'éditions (10 X 18), 1972.

Langlois, Henri. "Ferdinand Zecca." *La Cinématographie Française,* November 1935, 37.

Lapierre, Marcel (ed.). *Anthologie du cinéma.* Paris: La Nouvelle Edition, 1946.

———. *Les Cent Visages du cinéma.* Paris: Grasset, 1948.

———. *Le Cinéma et la paix.* Paris: Valois, 1932.

Lawder, Standish D. *The Cubist Cinema.* New York: New York University Press, 1975.

Lebrun, Dominique. *Paris-Hollywood: les français dans le cinéma américain.* Paris: Fernand Hazen, 1987.

Leclerc, J. *Le Cinéma, témoin de son temps.* Paris: Nouvelle Éditions Debresse, 1970.

Leprohon, Pierre. *Histoire du cinéma.* Paris: 1961.

Leroy, Paul. *Au Seuil du Paradis des images avec Louis Lumière.* Rouen: Maugard, 1939.

Leyda, Jay, and Charles Musser (eds.). *Before Hollywood: Turn-of-the-Century Film from American Archives* (ex. cat.). New York: American Federation of Arts, 1986.

Liebman, Stuart. "French Film Theory, 1910–1921." *Quarterly Review of Film Studies* 8, 1, Winter 1983, 1–24.

Liesegang, F. P. *Handbuch der praktischen Kinematographie.* Düsseldorf: 1908.

Lo Duca, [Guiseppe]. *Histoire du cinéma, 1895–1958.* Paris: Presses Universitaires, 1958.

———. *Louis Lumière, inventeur.* Paris: Prisma, 1948.

Lo Duca, [Guiseppe], and Maurice Bessy. *Georges Méliès, mage.* Paris: Prisma, 1945.

Löbel, Leopold. *La Technique cinématographique, projection, fabrication des films.* Paris: Dunod et Pinat, 1912.

Lomas, H. M. *Picture Play Photography.* London: 1914.

Mair, F. "Les Etablissements Pathé." *Phono-Ciné-Gazette,* May 15, 1905.

Malthête-Méliès, Madeleine. *Méliès, l'enchanteur.* Paris: Hachette, 1973.

Manz, Hans P. *Internationale Filmbibliographie.* Zurich: 1963.

Massiot, G. *Les Projections scientifiques et amusantes.* Paris: Gauthiers-Villars, 1907.

Maugras, E., and M. Guegan. *Le Cinématographe devant le droit.* Paris: Giard et Brière, 1908.

Maurin, L. *Notes pratiques du cinématographiste.* Paris: Comptoir d'édition de "Cinéma-Revue," 1913.

Mayne, Judith. "Immigrants and Spectators." *Wide Angle* 5, 2, 1982, 32–41.

Méliès, Georges. "Les Vues cinématographiques," *L'Annuaire général et international de la photographie*. Paris: Plon, 1907.

Merritt, Russell L. *The Impact of D. W. Griffith's Motion Pictures from 1908 to 1914 on Contemporary American Culture* (Ph.D. dissertation). Cambridge: Harvard University, 1970.

———. "Dream Visions in Pre-Hollywood Film." In Jay Leyda and Charles Musser (eds.). *Before Hollywood: Turn-of-the-Century Film from American Archives* (ex. cat.). New York: American Federation of Arts, 69–72.

Mesguich, Félix. *Tours de manivelle; souvenirs d'un chasseur d'images*. Paris: Grasset, 1933.

Mitry, Jean. "De Quelques Problèmes d'histoire et d'esthétique du cinéma." *Les Cahiers de la Cinémathèque*, Summer–Fall 1973, 112–141.

———. *Esthétique et psychologie du cinéma*, vol. 1. Paris: Eds. Universitaires, 1963; vol. 2. Paris: Eds. Universitaires, 1965.

———. *Filmographie universelle*, 13 vols. Paris: IDHEC, 1963–1968.

———. *Histoire du cinéma: art et industrie*, vol. 1: 1895–1914. vol. 2: 1915–1925. Paris: Eds. Universitaires, 1968–1969.

———. "Max Linder." *Anthologie du cinéma* 16, June 1966.

Morin, Edgar. *Le Cinéma, ou l'homme imaginaire*. Paris: Eds. de Minuit, 1956.

Moulinier, Pierre. *Catalogue des périodiques français et étrangers consacrés aux cinéma au département des periodiques de la Bibliothèque Nationale*. Paris: IDHEC, 1969.

Musser, Charles. "American Vitagraph: 1897–1901." *Cinema Journal* 22, 3, Spring 1983, 4–46.

———. "Another Look at the 'Chaser Theory.'" *Studies in Visual Communication* 10, 4, November 1984, 24–44.

———. "The Early Cinema of Edwin S. Porter," *Cinema Journal* 19, 1, Fall 1979, 6–8.

———. "The Nickelodeon Era Begins: Establishing Hollywood's Mode of Representation." *Framework* no. 22–23, Autumn 1983, 4–11.

Musser, Charles and Carol Nelson. *High-Class Moving Pictures: Lyman H. Howe and the Traveling Exhibition*. Princeton: Princeton University Press, forthcoming.

Niver, Kemp (ed.). *Biograph Bulletins, 1896–1908*. Los Angeles: Locare Research Group, 1971.

———. *Early Motion Pictures: The Paper Print Collection in the Library of Congress*. Washington D.C.: Library of Congress, 1985.

———. *Motion Pictures from the Library of Congress Paper Print Collection, 1894–1912*. Berkeley: Locare Research, 1967.

Ogle, Patrick L. "Technological and Aesthetic Influences Upon the Development of Deep Focus Cinematography in the United States," *Screen Reader* 1, 1977, 81–108.

Pathé, Charles. "De Pathé Frères à Pathé Cinéma." *Premier Plan* no. 55, June 1970.

———. *Souvenirs et Conseils d'un parvenu*. Nice: 1926.

Pathé Frères. *Cinématographes; appareils et accessoires* (cat.). Paris: April 1905.

———. *Films et cinématographes Pathé* (cat.). Paris: 1907.

Pathé, Théophile. *Le Cinéma*. Paris: Corrêa, 1942.

Paul, R. W. *Animated Photograph Films*. London: 1906–1907.

Perrot, Victor. *Une Grande Première historique: Cinématographe de MM. Lumière Frères*. Paris: Firmin-Didot, 1943.

Poirier, Léon. *A la recherche d'autre chose*. Bruges: Desclée de Brouwer, 1968.

———. *24 Images à la second*. Paris: Mame, 1953.

Poulain, Edouard. *Contre le cinéma, école du vice et crime, pour le cinéma école d'education, moralisation et vulgarisation*. Besançon: Imprimérie de l'est, 1917.

Pratt, George. "Early Stage and Screen: a Two-Way Street." *Cinema Journal*, Winter 1974–1975, 16–19.

———. *Spellbound in Darkness*. Rochester: private, 1966; Greenwich: New York Graphic Society, 1974.

Ramsaye, Terry. *A Million and One Nights*. New York: Simon and Schuster, 1926.

Raynal, Maurice. "Chronique cinématographique." *Soirées de Paris*, irregular appearances, 1913–1914.

Renoir, Jean. *Ecrits, 1926–1971*. Paris: Pierre Belfond, 1974.

Rhode, Eric. *A History of the Cinema*. New York: Hill and Wang, 1967.

Robin, Pierre. "Petite Histoire d'une grande maison." *Pathé Magazine* no. 16, 1957.

Rosen, J. *Le Cinématographe; son passé, son avenir et ses applications*. Paris: Société d'éditions techniques [1911].

S. D. "Cinema and Theaters in Paris." *The Nation*, August 13, 1914, 201.

Sadoul, Georges. "Entretien avec Louis Lumière." *Cahiers du Cinéma*, October 1964.

———. *Histoire générale du cinéma*, 5 vols. Paris: Denoël, 1973 (rev. ed.).

Salt, Barry. *Film Style and Technology: History and Analysis*. London: Starword, 1983.

Schmitt, Frantz. "Le Parisien et les débuts du ciné-matographe, 1895–1914." In *Le Parisien chez lui aux XIXᵉ siècle, 1814–1914* (ex. cat.). Paris: Archives Nationales, 1977, 152–161.

Schneider, M. L. "The Eclair Story." *American Cinematographer*, April 1975.

Semarne, Veda. *Industry and Invention: The Lumière Cinematograph and the Origins of Film, 1895–1904* (Ph.D. dissertation). New Haven: Yale University Press, 1987.

Signorino (Maître). *Les Cinématographes et les droits d'auteur, plaidoirie de Maître Signorino pour les hériters de Charles Gounod, Jules Barbier et Michel Carré*. Paris: Plon, 1908.

Slide, Anthony. *The Big V: A History of the Vitagraph Company*. Metuchen, N.J.: Scarecrow, 1976.

———. *Early American Cinema*. Cranbury, N.J.: A. S. Barnes, 1970.

——— (ed.). *Selected Early Film Criticism: 1896–1911*. Metuchen, N.J.: Scarecrow Press, 1982.

Smith, Albert E. and Phil Koury. *Two Reels and a Crank*. Garden City, N.Y.: Doubleday, 1952.

Spears, Jack. "Edwin S. Porter." *Films in Review*, June–July 1970, 327–354.

Spehr, Paul C. *The Movies Begin; Making Movies in New Jersey, 1887–1920*. Newark, N.J.: The Newark Museum/Morgan and Morgan, 1977.

Steer, Valentia. *The Romance of the Cinema*. London: Pearson, 1913.

———. *Secrets of the Cinema*. London: Pearson, 1920.

Stirling, W. *The Gaumont Speaking Cinematograph Films*. London: 1914.

Talbot, Frederick A. *Moving Pictures: How They Are Made*. Philadelphia: Lippincott, 1912.

Tariol, Marcel. *Louis Delluc*. Paris: Seghers, 1965.

Tharrats, Juan Gabriel. *Los 500 Films de Segundo de Chomón*. Zaragoza: Prensa Universitarias de Zaragoza, 1988.

Thompson, Kristin. *Exporting Entertainment: America in the World Film Market, 1907–1934*. London: British Film Institute, 1985.

Toulet, Emmanuelle. *Le Spectacle cinématographique à Paris de 1895 à 1914* (thesis). Paris: Ecole des Chartres, 1982.

Tranchant, L. *La Cinématographie pour tous*. Paris: Comptoir d'éditions de "Cinéma-Revue," 1913.

Trimbach, Pierre. *Quand on tournait la manivelle il y a 60 ans, ou les mémoires d'un opérateur de la Belle Epoque*. Paris: Eds. CEFAC, 1970.

Turpain, Albert. *Le Cinématographe, histoire de son invention, son développement, son avenir*. Paris: Association française pour l'avancement de la science, 1918.

United States Copyright Office, Library of Congress. *Catalogue of Copyright Entries, Cumulative Series: Motion Pictures, 1912–1939*. Washington D.C.: Library of Congress, 1951.

Urban, Charles. *The Cinematograph in Science*. London: Urban Trading Co., 1909.

Urban Trading Company. *Urbanora: The World's Educator (Catalogue of Scientific and Educational Subjects)*. London: 1908, 1909.

———. *General Catalogue of Classified Subjects*. London: 1909.

Usai, Paolo Cherchi (ed.). *Vitagraph Co. of America: Il cinema prima di Hollywood*. Pordenone: Ed. Studio Tesi, 1987.

Vardac, Nicholas A. *Stage to Screen*. Cambridge: Harvard University Press, 1949.

Verdone, Mario. "Ginna e Corra; cinema e letteratura del futurismo." *Bianco e Nero* no. 10/12, 1967.

Vincent, Carl et al. *Bibliografia generale del cinema*. Rome: Ateneo, 1953.

Virmaux, Alain and Odette Virmaux. *Colette at the Movies* (Sarah W. R. Smith, tr.). New York: Frederick Unger, 1980.

Vogelsang, Judith. "The *New York Times* Notices Movies, 1896–1915." *Cinema Journal* 10, 2, Spring 1971, 45–50.

Walls, Howard L. *Motion Pictures 1894–1912, Identified from the U.S. Copyright Office Records*. Washington D.C.: Library of Congress, 1953.

Selected Film Periodicals

L'Action Foraine (Lyon), 1907–1911.

Almanach des Spectacles (Paris), (annual since 1874).

Amateur Photographer and Photographic News (London), 1885–1918.

Annuaire général de la Photographie (Paris), 1892–1908.

L'Argus du Cinéma (Paris), 1917.

L'Argus Phono-Cinéma (Paris), 1907–1908.

Biograph Bulletins (reprinted: Los Angeles, Locare Research Group, 1971).

The Bioscope (London), 1908–1932.

Le Boulevardier (Paris), 1879–1884, 1891–1925.

Bulletin Ciné-Critique (Paris), 1916.

Bulletin Hebdomadaire Pathé Frères (Paris/Vincennes), 1911–1912.

Bulletin Trimestriel de liason de l'ASIFA (Association Internationale du Film d'Animation) (Paris), 1961—.

La Chronique des Expositions (Paris), 1908–1933.

Ciné-Graphic (Paris), 1918–1920.

Ciné-Journal (Paris), 1908–1914, 1915–1923, 1923–1934.

Ciné-Tribune (Paris), 1920—.
Le Cinéma (Paris), 1907, 1912–1914.
Cinema News and Property Gazette (London), 1912–1970.
Cinéma-Revue (Paris), 1911.
CinéMagazine (Paris), ca. 1920–1925.
Le Cinématographe (Nice), 1912.
Cinematograph Exhibitor's Mail (London), 1913–1914.
La Cinématographie Française (Paris), 1918—.
Cinéopse (Paris), 1919–1939.
Comoedia Illustré (Paris), 1908–1914, 1919–1921.
La Coulisse (Paris), 1872–1937.
Le Courrier Cinématographique (Paris), 1911–1937.
Le Courrier Musical, Théâtral, Cinématographique (Paris), 1899–1913, 1916–1935.
Le Crapouillot (Paris), 1915–1919.
Le Cri du Cinéma (Vincennes), 1915.
L'Echo des Cinémas (Paris), 1912.
L'Echo du Cinéma (Paris), 1912.
L'Echo du Film (Paris), 1912.
Echo du Film (Paris), 1914.
Eclair Bulletin (New York), 1912–1914.
L'Ecran (Paris), 1916—.
Le Fascinateur (Paris), 1903–1914, 1920–1938.
Il Film (Naples), 1911—.
Le Film (Paris), 1914–1920 (?).
The Film House Record (London), 1910–1912.
The Film Index (New York), ca. 1909–1910.
Film-Revue (Paris), 1912–1914, 1935–1938.
Filma (Paris), 1908, 1917.
L'Industriel Forain (Paris), 1887–1935 (?).
L'Intermédiaire Forain (Avignon), 1909—.
Inventions et les Industries Nouvelles (Paris), 1900.
Les Inventions Illustrées (Paris), 1899–1920.
Kinematograph (Düsseldorf), 1913–1915.
Kinéma (Paris), 1908–1909.
The Kinematograph and Lantern Weekly (London), 1907—.
The Kinematograph Monthly Film Record (London), 1912–1922.

Kleine Catalogue of Subjects (Chicago), 1909—.
Le Marchand Forain (Paris), 1909–1934.
Motion Picture Classic (Chicago), 1915–1934.
Motion Picture Daily (New York), 1916–1931.
Motion Picture Herald (New York), 1907–1933.
Motion Picture News (New York), 1909–1930.
Motion Picture Story Magazine (Brooklyn, then Chicago), 1911—.
Montjoie! (Paris), 1913–1914.
Motography (formerly *Nickelodeon*), (Chicago), 1909—.
Movie Pictorial (Chicago), 1913–1916.
Moving Picture News (New York), 1908–1913.
Moving Picture World (New York), 1907–1933.
El Mundo Cinematografico (Madrid?), 1912—.
Les Nouveautés Cinématographiques (Paris), 1905—.
The Optical Lantern and Kinematograph Journal (London), 1904–1907.
L'Orchestre, 1859–1911.
Pathé-Journal (Paris/Vincennes), 1912–1926.
Phono–Ciné Gazette (Paris), 1905–1910.
Photo-Cinéma-Revue (Paris), 1908.
Photoplay Magazine (Chicago), 1911–1922.
The Pictures (London), 1911–1912.
La Revue du Cinéma (Paris), 1928—.
Revue Internationale de Filmologie (Paris), 1948–1962.
Revue Scientific et Technique de l'Industrie Cinématographique et des Industries qui s'y Rattachent (Paris), 1912–1914.
La Rivista Fono-Cinematografica (Madrid?), ca. 1908–1909.
La Scène et l'Ecran (Paris), 1914.
Scenen (Stockholm), 1914.
Les Soirées de Paris (Paris), 1912–1914.
Le Tout-Cinéma; Annuaire général Illustré du Monde Cinématographique (Paris), 1923–1954.
Variety (New York), 1905—.
La Vie Théâtrale (Paris), 1894–1900, 1906–1909 (?).
Views and Films Index (New York), ca. 1908.

ANIMATED FILMS

Special Number devoted to Animation. *A.F.I. Report* (Washington), Summer 1974.
———. *Ecran 73* no. 11, 1973.
———. *Film Comment*, January–February 1975.
Alberti, Walter. *Il Cinema di animazione, 1832–1956.* Turin: Ed. Radio Italiana, 1957.
———. "Cinema di animazione." *Quaderni del Cineforum* (Genoa), [1960].
Amengual, B. "Le Cinéma d'animation, expression privilégée du surréalisme à l'écran." *Etudes Cinématographiques* no. 40–42, 1965.

Anon. "Gaumont Kartoons Are Popular." *MPW*, July 15, 1916.
———. "La Technique du dessin animé trent ans après son invention." *La Nature*, October 1, 1938, 201–210.
Auriol, Jean-Georges. "Les Dessins animés avant le cinéma: Emile Reynaud." *La Revue du Cinéma*, December 1929.
Bennett, Colin. "Animated Cartoons." *The New Photographer*, February 14, 1927.
Bendazzi, Gianalberto. *Due volte l'Oceano: Vita di*

Quirino Cristiani pioniere del cinema d'animazi-one. Florence: La Casa Usher, 1983.

————. *Le Film d'animation du dessin animé à l'image de synthèse.* Grenoble: La Pensée sau-vage/JICA, 1985.

Berryman, C. K. *Development of the Cartoon.* Columbia, Mo.: 1926.

Bertieri, G. "Ub Iwerks; un maestro da riscoprire." *Almanacco Comics* (Rome), 1968.

Bessy, Maurice M. "Dessins animés: Koko, Mickey, Félix and Co." *CinéMagazine*, February 1930, 28–30.

Bofa, Gus. "Du Dessin animé." *Les Cahiers du Mois* 16–17, 1925, 50–56.

Borde, Raymond. "Notes sur l'histoire du dessin animé." *Positif*, July–August 1963, 15–23.

Bragdon, Claude. "Mickey Mouse and What He Means." *Scribner's*, July 1934, 40–43.

Brion, Marcel. "Félix le Chat ou la poésie créatrice." *Le Rouge et le Noir*, July 1928.

Callahan, David. "Cel Animation: Mass Production and Marginalization in the Animated Film Industry." *Film History* 2, 3, 1988, 223–228.

Canemaker, John. "Profile of a Living Legend: J. R. Bray." *Filmmakers Newsletter*, January 1975, 28–31.

————. *Remembering Winsor McCay.* Motion Picture Film, produced 1977.

————. *Winsor McCay: His Life and Art.* New York: Abbeville Press, 1987.

Chevallier, Denys. *J'aime le dessin animé.* Paris: Denoël, 1962.

Collin, P. "L'Evolution dramatique du dessin animé" (unpublished paper). Paris: Archives of IDHEC, 1952–1953.

Cosandey, Roland. *Langages et imaginaire dans le cinéma suisse d'animation.* Geneva: Groupement suisse du film d'animation, 1988.

Crafton, Donald. *Before Mickey: The Animated Film, 1898–1928.* Cambridge, Mass.: MIT Press, 1982.

————. "J. Stuart Blackton's Animated Films." In Charles Solomon (ed.). *The Art of the Animated Image.* Los Angeles: The American Film Institute, 1987, 13–26.

Croy, Homer. *How Motion Pictures Are Made.* New York: Harper and Bros., 1918, 308–327.

Cuenca, Fernàndez-Carlos. *El Mundo del dibujo animado.* San Sebastian: 1962.

————. *Segundo de Chomón, maestro de la fantasía y de la técnica (1871–1929).* Madrid: Editora Nacional, 1972.

Edera, Bruno et al. *Evocation synoptique des origines et des pionniers du film d'animation en Europe* (mimeograph). Annecy: Festival, 1971.

————. "Les Pionniers européens de l'animation." *Ecran 73* 11, 1973, 12–19.

Feild, Robert D. *The Art of Walt Disney.* London: Collins, 1944.

Gardette, L. "Some Tricks of the Moving Picture Maker." *The Nickelodeon*, August 1909, 53–56.

Gianeri, Enrico. *Storia del cartone animato.* Milan: Omnia, 1960.

Gifford, Denis. *British Animated Films, 1895–1985. A Filmography.* Jefferson, N.C.: McFarland, 1987.

Gómez-Mesa, L. *Los Films de dibujos animados.* Madrid: 1929.

Gould, Stephen Jay. "A Biological Homage to Mickey Mouse." In *The Panda's Thumb.* New York: Norton, 1980, 95–107.

Gregory, Carl L. (ed.). *A Condensed Course in Motion Picture Photography.* New York: Institute of Photography, 1920.

Hawthorne, J. "Walt Disney, inventeur de Mickey Mouse." *Revue du Cinéma* 25, 1931.

Hoffer, Thomas W. *Animation: A Reference Guide.* Westport, Conn.: Greenwood Press, 1981.

————. "From Comic Strips to Animation; Some Perspective on Winsor McCay." *Journal of the University Film Association*, Spring 1976, 23–32.

Koszarski, Richard (ed.) "Bray-Hurd: The Key Animation Patents." *Film History* 2, 3, 1988, 229–266.

Jungstedt, Torsten. *Kapten Grogg och hans Vänner.* Stockholm: Sveriges Radios Forlag/Svenska Filminstitute, 1973.

Langlois, Henri. "Notes sur l'histoire du cinéma." *Revue du Cinéma*, July 1948, 2–15.

Laura, E. G. "Filmografia ragionata di Walt Disney." *Bianco e Nero* 7–9, 1967.

Le Maire, Eugène. "L'Industrie du dessin animé." *Bulletin de la Société pour l'encouragement pour l'Industrie Nationale*, March–April 1937, 151–175.

Lescarboura, Austin C. "Cartoons that Move and Sculpture that Lives." In *Behind the Motion Picture Screen.* London: 1920.

Lescarboura, Santos-Angel. *Cine y dibujos animados.* Caracas: Editorial universitaria, 1949.

Lo Duca, [Guiseppe]. "Du Dessin animé à la plastique animée." *La Nature*, May 1939, 314–319.

————. *Le Dessin animé; histoire, esthétique, technique.* Paris: Prisma, 1948.

————. "L'Industrie du dessin animé." *Génie Civil*, October 31, 1936.

Lutz, Edwin G. *Animated Cartoons, How They are Made, Their Origin and Development.* New York: Scribner's Sons, 1920.

McCrory, John. "Animated Cartoons." *MPW*, March 26, 1927, 322+.

————. *How to Draw for the Movies; or, The Process of Cartoon Animation.* Kansas City: Features Publishing, 1918.

Maillet, Raymond. "Les Pionniers français de l'animation." *Ecran 73* 11, 1973.

————. *Le dessin animé français.* Lyon: Institut Lumière, 1983.

————. *Le dessin animé français: 100 ans de création* (ex. cat.). Paris: Musée-galerie de la Seita, 1985.

Maltin, Leonard. *The Disney Films.* New York: 1973.

————. *Of Mice and Magic: A History of American Animated Cartoons.* New York: McGraw-Hill, 1980.

Manvell, Roger. *The Animated Film.* London: Sylvan Press, 1954.

Margadonna, E. M. "Felix, Mickey, Oswald and Co." *Il Convegno* 3–4, 1930.

Martin, André. *Arbre généalogique de l'origine et l'âge d'or du dessin animé américain de 1906 à 1941* (wall chart). Montréal: Cinémathèque Canadienne, 1967.

————. *Barré l'introuvable.* Ottawa: Festival International du cinéma d'animation, 1976.

————. "De Michel Ange à Walt Disney, coup d'oeil aux origines." *Cinéma chez soi,* 25–26, 1959.

————. *Exposition mondiale du cinéma d'animation* (ex. cat.). Montréal: Cinémathèque Canadienne, 1967.

Montanaro, Carlo. "The Strange Case of *Le Théâtre du Petit Bob,*" *Griffithiana* 32–33, September 1988, 278–280.

Peary, Gerald, and Danny Peary (eds.). *The American Animated Cartoon: A Critical Anthology.* New York: E. P. Dutton, 1980.

Pilling, Jayne (ed.). *Starewicz: 1882–1965.* Edinburgh: Edinburgh International Film Festival, 1983.

Poncet, Marie-Thérèse. *L'Esthétique du dessin animé.* Paris: Nizet, 1952.

————. *Etude comparative des illustrations du moyen âge et des dessins animés.* Paris: Nizet, 1952.

————. *Dessin animé, art mondial.* Paris: Le Cercle du livre, 1956.

————. *Walt Disney, 1901–1966.* Paris: Anthologie du Cinéma, 1967.

Rondolino, Gianni. *Storia del cinema d'animazione.* Turin: Einaudi, 1974.

Sadoul, Georges. "Sur le 'huitième art.' " *Cahiers du Cinéma,* June 1962, 8–13.

Second, J. "Film pur et dessins animés." *Revue Internationale de Filmologie,* July–August 1947.

Seeber, Guido. *Der Trickfilm in Seinen Grundsätzlichen Möglichkeiten.* Berlin: Filmtechnik, 1927.

Smith, David R. "Ub Iwerks, 1901–1971." *Filmworld* 14, 1972.

Stephenson, Ralph. *Animation in the Cinema.* London: Zwemmer and Barnes, 1967.

Thieson, Earl. "The History of the Animated Cartoon." *Journal of the Society of Motion Picture Engineers,* September 1933, 242.

White, Kenneth. "Animated Cartoons." *The Hound and Horn,* October/December 1931.

Wilson, H. "McCay before Disney." *Time,* January 10, 1938, 4.

RELATIONSHIPS BETWEEN FILM AND GRAPHIC ART

Benayoun, Robert. "Comics et cinéma." *La Méthode* (Cannes), February 1963.

Caen, Michel. "Comic-strip et celluloid." *Les Lettres Françaises,* July 1968.

Fell, John L. *Film and the Narrative Tradition.* Norman: University of Oklahoma Press, 1974.

Gauthier, Guy. "Les Bandes dessinées." *Image et Son* 20, 1968.

Gombrich, E. H. "Moment and Movement in Art." *The Warburg and Courtauld Institutes Journal,* vol. 27, 1964, 293–306.

Guillemot, C. "Gag cinématographique et dessin humoristique" (unpublished paper). Paris: Archives of IDHEC, 1954–1955.

Kunzle, David. "Supplementary Note" (essay appended to Lacassin, "The Comic Strip and Film Language"). *Film Quarterly,* Fall 1972, 19–23.

Lacassin, Francis. "Bande dessinée et langage cinématographique." *Cinéma 71,* September 1971, and in *Pour un neuvième art: la bande dessinée.* Paris: Union générale, 1971. (Trans. David Kunzle as "The Comic Strip and Film Language." *Film Quarterly,* Fall 1972, 11–19).

Noxon, Gerald. "Cinema and Cubism." *Journal of the Society of Cinematologists* 2, 1962, 23–33.

————. "Pictorial Origins of Cinema Narrative; Chinese Scroll Paintings." *Journal of the Society of Cinematologists* 3, 1963.

————. "Pictorial Origins of Cinema Narrative; Paleolithic Wall Paintings of Lascaux." *Journal of the Society of Cinematologists* 4, 1964.

————. "Pictorial Origins of Cinema Narrative; The Bayeux Tapestry." *Cinema Journal* 7, 1967–1968.

Sadoul, Georges. "Le Cinéma et les bandes dessinées." *Les Lettres Françaises,* July 6, 1966.

Scharf, Aaron. "Painting, Photography and the Image of Movement." *Burlington Magazine,* May 1962, 186–195.

Vitoux, Frédéric. *Cartes postales.* Paris: Gallimard, 1973.

MISCELLANEOUS

Bergson, Henri. *Evolution créatrice*. Paris: Alcan, 1907.

―――. *Creative Evolution* (trans. Arthur Mitchell). Westport, Conn.: Greenwood Press, 1975.

Bordwell, David. *Narration in the Fiction Film*. Madison: University of Wisconsin Press, 1985.

Branigan, Edward. *Point of View in the Cinema: A Theory of Narration and Subjectivity in Classical Film*. New York: Mouton, 1984.

Davies, Robertson. *Leaven of Malice*. New York: Charles Scribner's, 1955.

Langlois, Georges Patrick, and Glenn Myrent. *Henri Langlois: Premier citoyen du cinéma*. Paris: Denoël, 1986.

Lauretis, Teresa de, and Stephen Heath (eds.). *The Cinematic Apparatus*. New York: St. Martin's Press, 1980.

Roud, Richard. *A Passion for Films: Henri Langlois and the Cinémathèque Française*. New York: Viking Press, 1983.

Wollen, Peter. "Cinema and Technology." In *Readings and Writings: Semiotic Counter-strategies*. London: Verso, 1982, 169–177.

INDEX ■ 401

IPPC. See International Producing and Projecting Company
Ibels, Henri-Gabriel, 63
Icres, Fernand, 23, 318n.4
Illustration, L', 65, 68, 94, 126, 233
Illustré National, L', 82, 205, 285
Illustré Soleil du Dimanche, L', 65, 239
Imagerie d'Epinal. See Epinal
Imagist movement, 298
Impressionist movement, 66, 295
Incoherent movement, 29–34, 47–51, 257–58, 272–73, 291–94, 307
Indelli, Léontina (Mimma), 211, 335n.44
International Producing and Projecting Company (IPPC), 158
Intrépide, L', 192
Itala-Film, 159

Jacob, Max, 112, 307, 320n.22, 325n.90
Jasset, Victorin, 109, 116, 137, 158, 251, 326n.3
Je Sais Tout, 98
Jeanne, René, 93, 216
Jenkins, Henry C., 331n.19
Jeunesse Amusant, La, 65
Jewish Museum, 319n.40
Job (Jacques Onfray de Bréville), 62
Jobard series, 153
Joliet, Charles, 48, 258, 265
Joly, Henri-Joseph, 323n.56
Jones, Chuck, 310
Jones, Louisa E., 304, 306
Jordan, Larry, 310
Joseph-Renaud, Jean, 239
Jourjon, Charles, 157, 158, 159, 161, 168, 169, 179, 195
Journal Amusant, Le, 6, 9, 10, 44
Journée de Flambeau, La, 185
Jouy, Jules, 24, 62, 316n.44, 317n.50
Joyeux Microbes, Les, 154, 173, 177–78, 213, 285–90, 300, 310
Judge, 174, 178, 222
Jungstedt, Torsten, 197

Kahn, Gustave, 23
Kahnweiler, Daniel-Henry, 307
"Kapten Grogg," 197
Kaufman, Boris, 310
Kayser, Gabriel, 102
Keaton, Buster, 255
Keith, B. F., 158, 171
Kennedy, Joseph P., 159
Kinetoscope. See Edison Kinetoscope
Kleine, George B., 107, 115, 118, 170
Kober, 227, 336n.16
Kock, Paul-Charles de, 4
Koko the Clown, 208, 309
Kunzle, David, 222
Kupka, Franz, 249

Lacassin, Francis, 217, 218, 230
Lacépède, Etienne de, 158
Laemmle, Carl, 158, 160
Lafitte, Paul, 98
Laforgue, Jules, 23, 54, 291

Langlois (caricaturist), 30
Lantz, Walter, 179
Lapierre, Marcel, 214
Lapin Agile, 24, 113, 316n.38
Larousse Mensuel, 202
Larry, Gaston, 159
Lautréamont, Isadore Ducasse, 267
Lautrec. See Toulouse-Lautrec, Henri de
Léandre, Charles, 86, 203, 319n.57
Lectures pour Tous, 65, 105, 137
Léger, Fernand, 111, 245, 298
Legros, Michel, 64, 316n.25, 318n.85, 319n.48
Léka, Pierre de, 180
Lemaire, 91, 205
Lemaître, Frédérick, 8
Lemot, A. See Uzès
Léopold II, 319n.57
Lépine, 319n.57
Leproust, Maxime, 110
Lermina, Jules, 57
Leroy, Doctor Raoul, 216
Lévy, Jules, 20, 30, 31, 34, fig. 37; 41, 50, 51, 56, 257, 272, fig. 270, 273, 291, 304
Liasu, Jean-Pierre, 211
Libre Parole Illustrée, La, 60, 62, 177, 318n.40
Life, 174, 222
Lightning Sketches, 125, 132
Liljeqvist, M. R., 197
Linder, Max, 109, 153, 251, 255
Lion, Le, 159
Little Moritz, 153
Little Nemo, 172
"Little Nemo in Slumberland," 275
"Little Sammy Sneeze," 172
Little Stanley, 138
Locataires d'à côté, Les, 148
Lods, Armand, 59, 203
Lo Duca, Giuseppe, 92, 210, 212, fig. 210
Loir, Luigi, 23
Lorin, Georges (Cabriol), 9, 11, 20, 23, 52, 316n.27, 317n.53
Lortac (Robert Collard), 202, 206, fig. 207, 335nn.28, 31
Loughney, Patrick, 328n.59
Luce, Maximilien, 54
Lumière, Louis and Auguste Lumière, 111, 161, 213, 216, 238
Lumière cinematographs, 100, 101, 239, 241, 242, 244
Lune, La, 9, 25
Lune Rousse, La, 10, 20, 272
Lutèce, 28
Lux company, 93, 156, 159, 323n.56
Lye, Len, 310

McCay, Winsor, 162–63, 172–75, 200, 204, 223, 230, 275, 309
McLaren, Norman, 142, 310
MacMahon, Marie Edme Patrice Maurice de, 10, 20, 25
McManus, George, 162, fig. 177, 163–64, 175, 183, 193
Mac Orlan, Pierre, 113
Magasin Pittoresque, Le, 65, 238
Maire, Henri, 161
Maison du fantoche, La, 195, 201

CPSIA information can be obtained at www.ICGtesting.com
Printed in the USA
BVOW07s1310040815

411696BV00006B/60/P